THE
GENERALS

RELATED BOOKS BY J.L. GRANATSTEIN

Bloody Victory: Canadians and the D-Day Campaign 1944 (with D. Morton)

Broken Promises: A History of Conscription in Canada (with J.M. Hitsman)

Canada's War: The Politics of the Mackenzie King Government, 1939–45

Canadian-American Relations in Wartime (With R. Cuff)

The Dictionary of Canadian Military History (with D.J. Bercuson)

Mackenzie King: His Life and World

Marching to Armageddon: Canadians and the Great War, 1914–1919 (with D. Morton)

Mutual Hostages: Canadians and Japanese during the Second World War (with P. Roy, M. Iino, and H. Takamura)

A Nation Forged in Fire: Canadians and the Second World War, 1939–1945 (with D. Morton)

The Ottawa Men: The Civil Service Mandarins, 1935–57

Peacekeeping: International Challenge and Canadian Response (with D. Cox and A. Taylor)

Shadows of War, Faces of Peace: Canada's Peacekeepers (with D. Lavender)

War and Peacekeeping: From South Africa to the Gulf — Canada's Limited Wars (with D.J. Bercuson)

THE GENERALS

THE CANADIAN ARMY'S SENIOR COMMANDERS IN THE SECOND WORLD WAR

J.L.GRANATSTEIN

First published in 1993 by
Stoddart Publishing Co. Limited
34 Lesmill Road
Toronto, Canada
M3B 2T6
(416) 445-3333

Canadian Cataloguing in Publication Data

Granatstein, J.L., 1939-
The generals

Includes bibliographical references and index.
ISBN 0-7737-2730-2

1. Generals - Canada - Biography. 2. World War,
1939-1945 - Canada. 3. Canada - History, Military
- 20th century.* 4. Royal Military College of
Canada - History - 20th century. I. Title.
U54.C3G73   1993 355.3'31'09271   C93-093733-3

Jacket design: Brant Cowie/ArtPlus Limited
Printed and bound in the United States of America

Stoddart Publishing gratefully acknowledges the support of the Canada Council, the Ontario Ministry of Culture, Tourism, and Recreation, Ontario Arts Council, and Ontario Publishing Centre in the development of writing and publishing in Canada.

In memory of
Rod Byers and Barry Hunt
and for
Don Schurman, J. Murray Beck,
and Ezio Cappodocia

CONTENTS

ABBREVIATIONS FOUND IN THE TEXT

Armd	Armoured
Bde	Brigade
BGS	Brigade General Staff
Cdn	Canadian
CE	Chief Engineer
CGS	Chief of the General Staff
CIGS	Chief of the Imperial General Staff
C-in-C	Commander-in-Chief
CJWSC	Canadian Junior War Staff Course
CMHQ	Canadian Military Headquarters
CO	Commanding Officer
CofS	Chief of Staff
Comd	Commander
CCRA	Commander Corps Royal Artillery
CRA	Commander Royal Artillery
DA&QMG	Deputy Adjutant and Quartermaster-General
Div	Division
DND	Department of National Defence
DOC	District Officer Commanding
DSO	Distinguished Service Order
DVA	Department of Veterans Affairs
GOC	General Officer Commanding
GOC-in-C	General Officer Commanding-in-Chief
GSO	General Staff Officer
HQ	Headquarters
IDC	Imperial Defence College

MC	Military Cross
MD	Military District
MM	Military Medal
MSC	Militia Staff Course
NCO	Non-Commissioned Officer
NDHQ	National Defence Headquarters
NPAM	Non-Permanent Active Militia
NRMA	National Resources Mobilization Act
PF	Permanent Force
RMC	Royal Military College
TEWT	Tactical Exercise Without Troops
2 i/c	second in command
VC	Victoria Cross

PREFACE

NOW ALMOST FIFTY YEARS BEHIND US, Canada's Second World War experience is fading into a past as distant as the Conquest or Confederation for most of the population. What little postwar generations know of the war comes from textbooks that focus more on the evacuation of Japanese Canadians from the West Coast or the struggles of women to keep wartime jobs in the peace than on the national military-industrial effort that mobilized and armed a million men and women in a great crusade to win a just war. Television programs such as "The Valour and the Horror" provide large dollops of misinformation, sometimes twisting the efforts and sacrifices of those who fought the war to suit the producers' post-Vietnam War sensibilities. No wonder the surviving veterans, their numbers dwindling year by year, feel outraged that their country has forgotten them and, worse still, scorned their sacrifices.

This book may make some veterans angry, too, though not, I trust, for the same reasons. It is an attempt to look at the Canadian army's war from a unique perspective. Although it is a "top down" history, it is not an examination of generals and their great campaigns. Operations naturally enter into this story, but it is not operational history. Nor does Canada's role in making Allied political or battlefield strategy figure in — we had none. Instead, this collective biography of the Canadian army's general officers tries to answer some different questions from those hitherto posed about Canada's war. Who were our generals and where did they come from? What institutions shaped them and what was their standard of military professionalism? Why did they rise? Why did some succeed and some fail? This book also focuses heavily on the role of personality, on army politics, on dealings with politicians and bureaucrats, and on our soldiers' relations with our allies, most notably the British. There were sixty-eight officers who held the rank of major-general or higher during the Second World War (a list appears as Appendix A), a group too large to allow treatment of them all. Instead, I have tried to look at this cadre on a collective basis in the first chapter, where I also talk about the military institutions that shaped them all. The next seven chapters look at key individuals, most notably Generals A.G.L. McNaughton, Harry Crerar, and Guy Simonds, the three dominant figures of the war, as well as representative types, including the Great War generation, staff officers, and militia successes. Chapter 9 tries to explain why there were so few French-Canadian general officers. The final chapter draws some conclusions about these men, the Canadian military experience, and the history of Canadian arms.

There are some great men in these pages, as well as some sadly flawed characters. That is what we might expect. The generals jostled for position and power and perquisites, helped their friends, and cursed their enemies, exactly as people in any profession do. None, however foolish, forgot that he was fighting a war and that his decisions, whether made at National Defence Headquarters in Ottawa, at a training camp in Nova Scotia, at Canadian Military Headquarters in Britain, or in action in Hong Kong, Italy, France, Belgium, the Netherlands, and Germany, directly affected the lives and might cause the deaths of Canadian soldiers. The generals frequently made the wrong decisions, sometimes because politicians pressured them, occasionally because they fooled themselves, and frequently because the German or Japanese enemy was better equipped and better trained than they expected. But they did their best with what they had, and, at the beginning of the war and for some years after, they had very little, as Canada scrambled to make up for its long neglect of the armed forces. Just as effective tanks could not be produced overnight, so able generals could not be conjured up out of nothing. The ill-equipped and ill-trained Permanent Force of 1939, with its 450 regular officers, and the even weaker Non-Permanent Active Militia, with its scarcely trained five thousand amateur officers, could not produce much in September 1939. It took time — and casualties — before the situation could be corrected, before young, able, vigorous officers could emerge. Canada was fortunate that the war situation allowed that time, or our death toll would have been far higher.

And yet, well before the end of war, the First Canadian Army of two corps, with three infantry and two armoured divisions plus two armoured brigades, was as well led, as well equipped, and at least as effective as any Allied force of comparable size anywhere. There was a great national achievement there, one all Canadians ought to know and one too few do. The war against Hitler's Germany had to be fought and it had to be won, and Canada played a substantial part in that great cause. This book is a small contribution in recording that story.

No historian ever works alone, but on this project I received help from a number of colleagues and friends. What struck me from the beginning was how generous this country's best military historians were in offering assistance to someone they might have seen as an enemy infiltrator. Bill McAndrew, Terry Copp, Steve Harris, Serge Bernier, Reg Roy, Jack Hyatt, and LCol John English, distinguished scholars all, offered good advice, freely shared their research materials, and saved me from falling into many ambushes. I owe them a great deal and not least my thanks. Bill McAndrew and Terry Copp also read the whole manuscript in draft to my great benefit, while Steve Harris, Desmond Morton, Fernand Ouellet, and Serge Bernier commented on specific chapters. Paul Dickson, who recently completed his PhD dissertation on General Harry Crerar, must have been nervous about my galloping onto his turf, yet he read my Crerar chapter and helped me, as I tried to assist him, by sharing research. A number of participants in the events of which I write, as well as family members of the generals I cover here, read specific chapters. I am most grateful to Joseph Pope, Major Harry Pope, G/C Victor Stuart, MGen M.P. Bogert, and LGen Henri Tellier, and absolve them of blame for the results.

During my research, I received special assistance from Tim Dube, Paul Marsden, and Barbara Wilson at the National Archives of Canada and from Jacqueline McIvor at the Royal Military College. The Imperial War Museum, the Liddell Hart Centre for Military Archives at King's College, London, the United States Army Military History Institute, the George C. Marshall Library, the Royal Military College Archives, the University of Victoria Archives, the Queen's University Archives, the Directorate of History, National Defence Headquarters, and other repositories in Canada, the United States, and Britain all assisted greatly. The Montgomery Collections Committee of the Imperial War Museum and Viscount Montgomery allowed me to make use of Field Marshal Montgomery's papers; the trustees of the Liddell Hart Centre for Military Archives permitted my use of their collections. Dozens of retired officers let me badger them with questions about their experiences, and many, as well as the families of general officers, gave me full access to their papers (see selected list of primary sources). This book could not have been written without their interest and generous cooperation. A number of research assistants helped greatly, most notably Penny Bryden and Dean Oliver, as well as Paul Notley, Daniel Robinson, Ernesto Ialongo, and Sally Thomas. The usual suspects among my friends provided assurance, reassurance, leads, and advice. I am particularly grateful to John Saywell, Bob Bothwell, David Bercuson, and Norman Hillmer, the latter three of whom read all or most of the manuscript. Norman and Ann Hillmer, Bill Kaplan and Susan Krever, and Bill Young looked after me well on my repeated research forays to Ottawa. The Blue Jays helped mightily at home by providing a winning distraction.

The research and writing of this book were accomplished while I held a Killam Senior Fellowship and a Social Sciences and Humanities Research Council of Canada research grant, and I am more than pleased to acknowledge this generous assistance that allowed the work to proceed without interruption. The Department of History at York University graciously accommodated itself to my absence. Yet again, Rosemary Shipton's able editing saved me (and my readers) from the worst excesses of my prose style and prevented innumerable errors.

This book is dedicated to the memory of Rod Byers and Barry Hunt, cadets with me at the Royal Military College who became fine scholars, one at York and the other at RMC. It is also dedicated to three of our best teachers at RMC, Don Schurman, J. Murray Beck, and Ezio Cappodocia, who tried to pound some history and political science — and other things — into our heads. I have never forgotten Schurman telling me quite bluntly and quite rightly, at our first meeting, "you are not backward in being forward." Writing this book has also helped me to come to terms with my time at Le Collège Militaire Royal and at RMC. I now understand more clearly than before how and why this was the formative experience of my life, for good and ill. The dawn may be delayed, but it comes at last.

Finally, Elaine and Carole assisted in so many ways. This book is for them, and always for Michael, too.

THE
GENERALS

CHAPTER 1

INTRODUCTION: THE OLD ARMY

THE GERMAN GENERAL STAFF, the story goes, used to divide army officers into four categories: the clever and lazy, the clever and hard-working, the stupid and lazy, and the stupid and hard-working. The best generals, the Germans found, came from the clever and lazy; the best staff officers emerged from the clever and hard-working; the stupid and lazy could be useful as regimental officers; but the stupid and hard-working were a menace, to be disposed of as soon as possible.[1] For his part, Winston Churchill once lectured the Chief of the Imperial General Staff, General Sir John Dill, on the need to find employment for an officer much disliked in the British army: "Remember, it isn't only the good boys who help to win wars; it is the sneaks and the stinkers as well."[2]

The German General Staff and Churchill were both correct, of course, and one might reasonably assume that the clever, the lazy, the stupid, and the hard-working, as well as the sneaks and stinkers, existed in the higher ranks of the Canadian army in the Second World War. What did not seem to be found was charisma. With the possible exceptions of Generals A.G.L. McNaughton, Bert Hoffmeister, and F.F. Worthington, most of Canada's senior officers were pallid, colourless figures. Perhaps this was because Canadian generals in the main felt they had to act and look the part, with their role models invariably being British. The Canadian novelist Edward Meade described the dapper, strutting officer exuding efficiency and command: "He carried a cane which he swung with an air of great assurance and determination, in the manner of English officers, and wore a short, cropped, bristling moustache which gave his rather florid face a look of ferocity."[3] That mock-British style sat uneasily on Canadians, and it likely produced only a negative effect on men in the ranks. For his part, Lieutenant-General Guy Simonds chose to ape General Bernard Montgomery by wearing a black beret, though neither Simonds nor any others seem to have been brave enough to wear Monty's khaki sweater, scarf, and corduroy trousers.

According to Farley Mowat, whose book *My Father's Son* is one of the best accounts of Canadians at war, Canadian senior officers tended to act like businessmen more than anything else. "He would be at home as vice president of any big business," Mowat wrote to his parents of his new brigade commander, unnamed but undoubtedly Brigadier J. Desmond B. Smith. "He has lots of 'push' and 'drive' and is determined to get to the top." Even the Germans, according to Mowat, at the time the 1st Canadian Infantry Brigade's Intelligence Officer in northern Italy, sensed the "business" cast of the Canadian high command. "We have been told that in order to become a general in the Canadian Army you have first to be a stockbroker," he quoted from one prisoner of war's interrogation in his Weekly Intelligence Summary on 1 February 1945. "In Germany we choose our generals on the basis of merit." That, Mowat added drily, "will demonstrate how deluded the German soldiers are by Herr Goebbels' propaganda machine."[4] More seriously, the interwar propaganda machine had also affected Allied generalship in the Second World War. British writer Noel Annan observed that the pacifism and disgust with war bred by the slaughter in the trenches from 1914 to 1918 guaranteed that British commanders like Montgomery were slow and cautious. Soldiers brought up on the story of their fathers and uncles at Ypres and Passchendaele and disillusioned by the way the German Wehrmacht had swept them aside in France in May and June 1940 had to be persuaded that their side had overwhelming superiority in numbers and weapons and that their general's plan was foolproof before they would attack.[5] Montgomery showed himself to the troops and amassed men and machines in massive numbers before taking the offensive. His victories from El Alamein onwards, however ponderously they were achieved, were genuine nonetheless, and his careful but unimaginative professionalism set the pattern for British and Canadian generalship.

The few realists among the Allied troops understood that war was about killing. Terence O'Brien in his now-forgotten *Out of the Blue: A Pilot with the Chindits* asked, "What's so damnable about a General whose battle plan produces casualties? As well criticise a butcher for a bloody apron or a gardener for muddy hands — these are concomitants of the job."[6] Canada had its share of cautious generals, those like McNaughton who, even if he despised Montgomery, similarly calculated the cost in lives and wanted to employ maximum firepower to minimize the human price. But it also had its Simondses, imaginative and hard-driving commanders who held that if the objective was not seized today, the cost in casualties would be higher when it had to be attacked a week later. That approach was very much in the minority in the First Canadian Army, however, where generals followed the pattern set by their first commander, General McNaughton.

THE CENTRAL SHAPING EVENT of the Canadian army in the Second World War was the Great War of 1914–18, just as the central institution was the Canadian Corps that had won so proud a name for itself in the trenches. The First World War had forced Canada into the world, and if the struggle began with the dominion rallying to the mother country in a surge of imperial patriotism, before it ended the war created enormous nationalistic pride in English Canada. The war had obliged the people to mobilize and arm themselves, and it had changed domestic politics dramatically through the conscription crisis of 1917 and the Union Government. For those who fought, the Canadian corps of four divisions was the focus of their lives. After rough introductions to battle, the corps by Easter 1917 was a fiercesome instrument of war, well trained, well equipped, and well led, and the taking of Vimy Ridge was both a great military achievement and a supreme and defining moment of Canadian nationalism. The corps' role in the remaining year-and-a-half of war, led for most of that time by Lieutenant-General Sir Arthur Currie, was icing on the cake, and the victories of the "Hundred Days" from the attack on 8 August 1918 to the triumphant entry into Mons on 11 November demonstrated that Canadian soldiers and Canadian generals were the peers of those in any country. The nation and Canadian arms had come of age in the horror of France and Flanders.

In the First World War, Canadian general officers who fought with and helped earn the corps its great reputation were overwhelmingly Canadian-born and Ontario-raised, Protestant, English-speaking, married, and of urban residence at the outbreak of war. At least half had attended university or the Royal Military College, and almost half (42 percent) suffered wounds in action. As A.M.J. Hyatt concluded, "It seems likely that the group of Canadians who served as generals in the First World War was richer, better-educated, more urban, and slightly older than the average Canadian male. Also, the heavy concentration from Ontario and the tiny minority from Eastern Canada . . . demonstrates that the principles used to select a federal cabinet did not apply when it came to selecting generals. Being French-speaking, apparently, was not a particular advantage."[7]

The Second World War was not very different. Of the sixty-eight officers who held ranks of major-general or higher, fifty-three were Canadian-born, while eleven were born in Britain and three in British colonies or to fathers on imperial service; R.O. Alexander, for example, was born in Ceylon, and George Kitching in China.[8] Once again, Protestants were the overwhelming majority among those with a declared denomination, and Anglicans numbered twenty-nine of the fifty Protestants. There was one self-described "freethinker," Major-General Lionel Page. Only seven were Roman Catholic, a group that included five of the six French-Canadian generals; the Protestant francophone was Major-General P.-E. Leclerc, the only French-Canadian to command a division.[9] The generals were almost all of urban origin, only two growing up on farms,[10] and they were also, much as in the Great War, likely to have come from a substantially better-off segment of the population: at least twenty-six attended private schools, with twelve of those spending some time at Toronto's Upper Canada College. Twenty-one had university degrees, most in engineering, law, or medicine, and twenty-one were ex-cadets of the Royal Military College. All of the 1939–45 generals of appropriate age had seen service in the Great War, fifty-eight in all, and forty-one had been decorated for valour, with medals ranging from the Victoria Cross (Major-General George Pearkes) to the Distinguished Service Order, the Military Cross, and the Military Medal.

Just as in that earlier war, most generals were older than might have been expected. Five had been born in the 1870s and were well into their sixties during the Second World War; thirty were born in the 1880s; twenty-three in the 1890s; eight in the first decade of this century; and two (Major-Generals D.C. Spry and George Kitching) in the second. But there were two major differences between the generals of the wars. First, in the Great War, fewer than half of Hyatt's cadre had been regular soldiers. In the Second World War, thirty-nine of the sixty-eight generals emerged from the Permanent Force. The interwar PF, tiny and ill-equipped as it was, had produced more than its share of the country's senior commanders. Second, generals in the 1939–45 war tended to escape the casualty lists, none being killed in action. Only one was wounded in action, Major-General Rod Keller in the bombing of his troops by the United States Army Air Force in August 1944. One (Major-General H.L. Salmon) died in an air accident, one (Major-General C.S.L. Hertzberg) succumbed to smallpox in India, two (Major-Generals Lionel Page and H.H. Matthews) died during the war of illness in Canada, and one (Major-General A.E. Nash) died of injuries sustained in a car accident.

Statistically, if not by weight of influence, the largest number of the generals were infantrymen, twenty-two being "poor bloody infantry" who somehow had survived the Great War's trench combat with their skins and spirits intact. The artillery (eleven) and other arms, most notably engineers, had high representation as well (seventeen in all) and a goodly share of the influence and power, and there were sprinklings of generals from the cavalry, Signals, the Ordnance, and the Service Corps.[11] Despite the often repeated suggestion that McNaughton, Chief of the General Staff from 1929 to 1935 and the first commander overseas after 1939, favoured gunners and engineers, the route to generals' rank, though not necessarily to the key positions, still seemed to lie through the infantry.

All the Second World War generals for whom information could be found were married. The largest number, almost a third, came from Ontario, but there was a more even geographical representation than in the Great War, with Quebec providing some 20 percent of general officers (though over half of those were English-speaking) and the Maritimes, the West, and British Columbia producing roughly 10 percent each. Such distribution is, however, only an approximation; sons of soldiers, like Major-Generals Chris Vokes and Harry Foster, or of Mounties, like Major-General C.F. Constantine, moved with their parents from posting to posting and had no province of origin. Others, like Lieutenant-General Guy Simonds, came with their families from England and, while raised in British Columbia, went away to school to Ontario.[12]

The typical Canadian general of the Second World War was born in the 1880s in Canada, likely in Ontario, to Anglican and English-speaking parents and was in his fifties when war began. He had seen service in the Great War, usually in the infantry, and had been decorated for bravery. After 1919 he remained with the Permanent Force or the militia and, by 1939, was quite senior in rank, usually a colonel or brigadier. Our general saw no action in the 1939 war, however, and retired during or immediately after the war. Most of the sixty-eight general officers of the second war fit this pattern.[13]

Who, then, commanded the troops that did the fighting? The typical battlefield general, one who led troops in action in the Second World War, had not seen Great War service. He was in his mid thirties at the beginning of the war, with some ten-to-fifteen years' service, likely born in Ontario to English-speaking parents who were certainly Protestants. He was a Permanent Force soldier, again likely from the infantry or artillery, who may well have attended the Royal Military College and the British Army Staff College. At the beginning of the war our archetype had been only a lieutenant or more likely a captain or major, and he rose with extraordinary speed as the army expanded. At the end of the war or within a few years of the peace he may well have decided to leave the service to follow civilian pursuits.

All these officers, typical or not, were patriotic in ways that now seem difficult to comprehend. There were many Canadian nationalists among them — after all, most of them had served in the Canadian Corps when English-Canadian nationalism, as Charles Stacey and Pierre Berton have said, had truly been born on Vimy Ridge. But they were also Canadian-born Britishers almost without exception, fiercely loyal to the crown and the empire, convinced that British ways of organizing for and waging war were best, and they believed that Canada's maltreatment of its regular and militia forces through the interwar interregnum was a terrible shame. Their patriotism, their desire to be ready when their King called them, kept them in khaki. Certainly little else could have made them remain in the army, for the pay, conditions of service, and the state of weaponry and training were simply pathetic. The Permanent Force of the interwar years numbered a derisory 4169 all ranks on 31 March 1939, with only 446 officers,[14] and many of those officers were too old for active service or were in ill-health. That this tiny cadre could produce fighting, technical, and staff officers as competent as Generals H.D.G. Crerar, Guy Simonds, Charles Foulkes, Chris Vokes, J.C. Murchie, E.L.M. Burns, Kenneth Stuart, J.H.

MacQueen, Maurice Pope, and D.C. Spry was a miracle of biblical proportions. The Non-Permanent Active Militia, the country's one-night-a-week soldiers, officially numbered approximately 51,400 all told, with 6373 officers, on 31 March 1939;[15] its actual strength was much less, probably as much as 50 percent less. Most of the militia officers were untrained beyond the intricacies of parade-square drill and what little could be learned in annual summer camps, yet this group produced a number of senior officers of distinction. Major-Generals Bruce Matthews, Bert Hoffmeister, Holly Keefler, Harry Letson, C.S.L. Hertzberg, A.E. Walford, and C.P. Fenwick, a now-forgotten Medical Corps officer, and Lieutenant-General Price Montague all emerged from the militia in an equally miraculous fashion.

The word "miracle" might be thought too strong to describe the emergence of competent officers from within the attenuated peacetime Canadian army. Yet Harry Hopkins, one of President Franklin Roosevelt's key aides, once said it had been a miracle that the United States — which, like Canada, had neglected its army between the wars — had produced so large and brilliant a group of military leaders competent to command troops and to deal with complex problems, as much political as military.[16] The regular U.S. Army between the wars ordinarily numbered some ten thousand officers — far too few for the demands of a world war, to be sure, but numbers enough to provide the basis of proper training and career progression. With Canada's interwar professional officer corps just one-twenty-fifth that size, no one could have expected it to produce Marshalls or Eisenhowers, MacArthurs or Pattons during the war. Even so, Canada was remarkably fortunate to find as many competent senior officers as it did, far more than its governments and people deserved. A miracle, indeed.

PERMANENT FORCE GENERAL OFFICERS shared more than their patriotism and demographic attributes. The Royal Military College at Kingston also served as a focal point, for either they had graduated from RMC, and hence were part of a club with common memories, rituals, and attitudes, or they had not, and thus resented those who had.

RMC's influence was substantial. Although fewer than a third of the general officers of the Second World War were ex-cadets, those twenty-one held most of the key positions most of the time: all four wartime Chiefs of the General Staff, T.V. Anderson, H.D.G. Crerar, Kenneth Stuart, and J.C.

Murchie; the army commander through the fighting in Northwest Europe, Harry Crerar; the Chief of Staff at Canadian Military Headquarters, Ken Stuart; corps commanders Guy Simonds and E.L.M. Burns; and division commanders such as J.H. Roberts, Rod Keller, Chris Vokes, and Harry Foster.[17] These officers and other ex-cadets to a total of 1427 had served during the war, or over 80 percent of those graduates alive and fit enough to do so. The Canadian army had 960 RMC graduates in its wartime ranks, with the artillery having most at 252, the infantry next at 191, the engineers and the Armoured Corps following with 139 and 111, respectively; then the General Staff with ninety-nine, the Signal Corps and the Ordnance Corps with thirty-one each, and the remainder in other corps. In all, 281 ex-cadets had held ranks of colonel or above; 114 had been killed during the war; and 678, or close to half of those engaged, had won decorations ranging from the Victoria Cross to the George Medal.[18] This was a strong record of service from a small college.

RMC was tiny. Founded in 1876 with eighteen cadets, RMC did not graduate as many as twenty-five in a single year until 1903, and its annual enrolment for the dozen years before the outbreak of war in 1939 was around two hundred.[19] The largest entering class, that of August 1918 when the college was running at a stepped-up Great War pace, was only 115, and as soon as the war had been won, RMC resumed its more regular tempo, allowing in only some sixty cadets a year. To June 1942, when RMC closed down for the duration of the Second World War as a cadet-training college, a grand total of 2828 cadets had been admitted in the sixty-six-year history of the college, 2788 had joined the college, and 2032 had graduated;[20] each cadet had a college number ranging from 1 to 2828, and at every military gathering, and some civilian ones as well, ex-cadets could be heard establishing contact with the query, "What's your number?"[21]

That there were so few cadets admitted to RMC between 1876 and 1942 also suggests how small the Canadian army was in peacetime. From its first graduating class to the last peacetime class before the Second World War, most graduates joined the militia rather than the Permanent Force. Statistics collected by Lieutenant-Colonel E.L.M. Burns in the late 1930s showed that of 327 graduates between 1927 and 1935, sixty-nine joined the PF, twenty-two joined the Royal Canadian Air Force, and twenty-eight joined the British army. In most years no more than two or three went to the regulars, although in Burns's sample much higher numbers took PF commissions in the years 1933, 1934, and 1935, and about as many joined the British army.[22] In 1921, just after the Great War, there were ninety-four ex-cadets in the PF and 189 in the British army; five years later there were eleven ex-cadet generals serving with British or imperial forces, as many as with the Canadian army.[23] During the 1939 war, there were 107 ex-cadets in the British and Indian armies and a further twenty-six serving with other British services.[24] It could scarcely be otherwise, so long as the PF had such a paltry strength. Still, RMC's advocates maintained, the training offered there had its value to the country, whatever its graduates did. And, as one 1921 examination of ex-cadet professions showed, RMC graduates did just about everything, from acting to engineering to farming to law.[25]

What gave the college its elan was the first year, when new cadets were subjected to "recruiting." This was a type of military hazing directed by the senior cadets when new entry cadets were made to memorize trivia about the college — obliged, for example, to rattle off in a few seconds the names of "The Old Eighteen," the first class of 1876. Punishments for failure ranged from "arse fannings" or canings to "flat P.T.," an exhausting form of exercises conducted by a senior cadet, and "shit meetings," where the entire recruit class was herded into a confined space, stood at attention, and verbally abused. Hazing also included "doubling the square," or running flat out across the parade square every time it had to be crossed, and "fagging" for a senior cadet by polishing his buttons (but not shining his boots — that was considered "menial"), running his errands, and withstanding his abuse, a practice that was suppressed in 1925, but emerged full-blown again the next year. It included initiation rituals that bordered on the demeaning and brutal, occasionally to the point where a cadet fled the college, resulting in newspaper cries of scandal.[26] The process of recruiting had existed almost from the beginnings of the college, but it had intensified in the years after the Great War, possibly because of the "adoption of certain West Point customs," Colonel Ken Stuart told the senior class in 1936, "many of which still have the flavour of their Prussian originator."[27]

Those who went through the process swearing at it soon swore by it and retained a fierce loyalty to the college.[28] One graduate from 1932 waxed about "the transformation in one year of a rabble into a class with an esprit de corps. A self-disciplining group responsible for the actions of all its members and a genuine concern for its physically and academically less gifted members." RMC, to Brigadier-General Frank Lace, was "a world in which the standards and values were as true and uncompromising as one could find anywhere. Wealth, family and politics had no place in this atmosphere."[29] The college motto, "Truth, Duty, Valour," seemed to most cadets to sum it up.* Perhaps this was so, although before the Second World War most cadets were selected from applicants from the private-school-trained Anglo-Canadian elite, with a sprinkling from French-Canadian military families, though never enough to fill the vacancies allotted to Quebec on a "rep-by-pop" basis. The fees for the four-year course were not expensive, but at roughly $1450 during the 1930s, for example, more than high enough to keep out the indigent and the middle classes.[30] The well-off homes from which they were drawn and the inherent elitism fostered by a small college tended to create a widespread belief in the PF and the NPAM that ex-cadets were snobs. This sense was reinforced by the precise drill the college taught its cadets and their assurance that no one, neither Permanent Force nor militia regiment, could march as well as they. Some were undoubtedly snobbish, while others were not.

Looking back on his entry to the college fifty years before, Guy Simonds recalled that "our class came through our recruit year with great cohesion, a great esprit and enhanced morale." This, said Simonds, had been the purpose of the ritual of recruiting.[31] It taught the necessity of working together, of teamwork, of getting along. If it broke some or brutalized others, most saw that as a small price to pay for the confidence it instilled that anything and everything could be overcome.[32] As seniors, cadets got a full taste of responsibility, learning how to handle the perquisites of power. Above all, RMC taught cadets to do impossible amounts of work in limited periods of time, and to keep their military and academic lives running smoothly in the face of the high-pressure demands of their seniors and

---

*Even Prime Minister Mackenzie King was impressed enough on a visit to RMC in 1938 to write in his diary "It was interesting to reflect that had I been a year older at the time, I might myself have received a training at the Military College. I recall father was very anxious I should take a course there, and was impressed by the value of the training. I was, however, a year too young." (NA, W.L.M. King Papers, Diary, 1 August 1938, f. 585). The idea of Gen. or even Lt W.L.M. King is, frankly, difficult to contemplate.

instructors.[33] It was valuable training for the demands of war. As Chris Vokes, commanding the 1st Canadian Division in Italy, put it when he was looking for an aide-de-camp, "I realized quickly I'd have to find someone who came from my old school, RMC, who had learned that sulking would not do regardless of apparent provocation and who, in fact, had had his sulking and pouting inclinations quite permanently removed."[34]

The academic standards of the college at best were mixed. By the interwar years, RMC offered its cadets, all of whom had junior or senior matriculation on entry, a university-level general curriculum with heavy emphasis on mathematics and engineering subjects. The classes were small, the combined military and civilian faculty underpaid and operating in mostly ill-equipped classrooms and laboratories. On graduation after four years (the course was increased from three years just after the Great War), an engineering degree, depending on specialty, could be secured by one or two years' attendance at university. There was little emphasis on military history or strategy, politics or international relations until the late 1930s, when Stuart led a drive to change the curriculum to reflect the realities of the day. At the same time as they struggled with physics, of course, cadets were also studying military subjects, learning to ride and shoot, and engaging in a rigorous program of physical training. Even if the academic standards were not the highest,[35] it was a challenging course, though more so physically than mentally.

Most ex-cadets tended to do well in the army, not least during the war. In 1994 T.C. Douglas, the CCF Member of Parliament for Weyburn, Saskatchewan, made the point that "control" of the army was "going increasingly into the hands of professional soldiers; that the R.M.C. men particularly, and naturally, since they are the trained men, have been given positions of responsibility; that civilian soldiers to some extent have been pushed aside."[36] There was some truth in that, but was it a conspiracy? Many thought so. The novelist and former officer Colin McDougall in *Execution*, set in wartime Italy, wrote about "the mystic numbers" possessed by ex-cadets "which qualified the recipient for lifetime membership in a sort of mutual-benefit club." One of his characters, an ex-cadet, pulled strings with "a Colonel who was in my class at R.M.C." to secure an appointment with the general for an officer trying to prevent the execution of one of his soldiers.[37] The old-boy net did exist, but was it a mutual benefit society? There is, in truth, no hard evidence, but ex-cadets tended to believe that others who had passed through RMC would be more likely to know something of discipline, loyalty, and soldiering than everyone who had not.[38] There was, one recalled, "instant mutual respect,"[39] and often it was justified.

THE PERMANENT FORCE that some RMC graduates chose to join was tiny, ill-equipped, underfunded, and unsure of its mission. Recreated after the Great War and designed to correct the mistakes of the prewar years, the PF was intended to be an army in microcosm with regular infantry, cavalry, and artillery units, along with the other arms and services. At National Defence Headquarters in Ottawa in the 1920s, the General Staff drew up plans for war against the United States[40] or for Canadian service as part of an imperial force operating against Britain's enemies. It laid down policy on everything from training standards to the size of bow ties to be worn with mess dress. Even with the best will in the world, the task of building a regular army in Canada after the Great War would have been well-nigh impossible. Canadian governments, however, whatever their political coloration, showed no such good will. The result inevitably was a backward-looking organization, one devoted to its own survival as its primary task. There were some fine officers and men who worked hard to improve their knowledge and skills for the day when Canada once more went to war; there were also time-servers and hangers-on, those who counted the years until their pensions came due.[41] Extraordinarily, enough of the able remained in the PF to provide a handful of capable commanders in the Second World War. Many of them had emerged from the Royal Military College.

RMC graduates who went into the Permanent Force, however well-trained they were from their college course, still had a lot to learn — as the PF officers who had not gone to the college were more than happy to let them know. Cavalry regiments professed unhappiness with the RMC riding style and often obliged new lieutenants to learn how to ride like a proper officer. Infantry regiments had their own rituals, and the Royal Canadian Engineers or Royal Canadian Corps of Signals, which usually had to wait a year or two until ex-cadets received their university degrees, had theirs. Learning to be a junior officer, learning how to take care of men, was a full-time job. So, too, was figuring out how to rise in the PF.

Officers with ambition spent much of their time studying for promotion examinations or the examinations for the British Army Staff College.[42] "Studying was the lieutenant's lot," one remembered.[43] Canada had no staff college of its own, and in the circumstances to attend the Staff College at Camberley in England or at Quetta in India was widely perceived as the route to promotion. National Defence Headquarters pressed officers to apply: "All combatant officers from the time they first join the Permanent Force should be encouraged to make Staff College a goal." But to win entry was extraordinarily difficult. Aspiring officers, all qualified as captains and with at least six years' commissioned service, were urged to attend lectures and sit examinations run for NPAM officers taking the Militia Staff Course. If they did well on these examinations, and if they were recommended at least once on their annual confidential reports as a suitable candidate for the Staff College, then officers might be selected to attend the rigorous five-month-long Staff College Preparatory Course run annually at the Royal Military College, Kingston. After finishing that course and completing the work involved in the Advanced Militia Staff Course, candidates for Camberley and Quetta could write the Staff College entrance examinations held in February each year.

The examinations consisted of compulsory papers on training for war (which included map exercises, military topography, military engineering, and military history), organization, administration and transportation, and the history and organization of the empire. For some years, and well into the 1920s and 1930s, there were optional papers on engineering, chemistry and physics, languages, political economy, business organization, mathematics, and some additional areas of history, which could be used to boost candidates' marks.[44] For candidates without much formal education, those papers were unquestionably more difficult than the straight military subjects. The results, in fact, demonstrated that substantially higher numbers of Royal Canadian Engineers, Royal Canadian Artillery, and Royal Canadian Corps of Signals officers, those generally having the strongest academic qualifications, made their way through the Staff College examinations successfully. Infantry and cavalry officers tended to be under-represented.[45] The examiners set a high standard, not least in prose style: in his comments on the 1929 examinations tried by 564 officers, the Chief of the Imperial General Staff complained mightily about verbosity, unmethodical and illogical statements, sloppy handwriting, and "a vicious use of unauthorized abbreviations." Only 141 officers had qualified — in the whole British Empire[46] — and qualification did not mean acceptance, for spaces were limited.[47]

Ordinarily between the wars there were three Canadian candidates accepted each year at Camberley and one at Quetta. The courses were considered to be rigorous and demanding and lasted two years. The first year, the Junior Wing, generally dealt with staff work within brigades and divisions. It included combined operations with naval and air forces, imperial policing, and training of officers to fill posts as General Staff Officers 2 and 3. The second year, or Senior Wing, trained officers to work within divisions, corps, and armies and aimed to produce General Staff Officers 1. Both years also stressed the practice of command through exercises designed to teach students the appreciation of tactical situations and the rapid issuance of orders.[48] Not everyone enjoyed the process, and not all thought it valuable. Historian John Keegan said flatly that the Staff Colleges' value in the interwar years "was social rather than educational."[49] Guy Simonds in 1936–8 loved the free thinking and the search for solutions to the problems of warfare, but Harry Foster a year later was "unimpressed by the bilge of Staff College . . . the jolly boy attempt to be theatrical and to waffle."[50] Still, some of the best officers in the British army instructed there, and the friendships that developed between candidates and between candidates and instructors were important in later years as they fought their wars with the same methods and under the same commanders. Harry Crerar, for example, renewed his link with Alan Brooke at Camberley, one initially formed during the Great War; when, during the Second World War, Brooke was Chief of the Imperial General Staff and Crerar was commanding I Canadian Corps and then the First Canadian Army, their close relationship was important indeed.[51]

More than half of the PF officers who rose to general officer rank before or during the Second World War had attended either Quetta or Camberley, a list that included R.O. Alexander (Staff College 1919), T.V. Anderson (1920), E.L.M. Burns (1928), Harry Crerar (1924), Harry Foster (1939), Charles Foulkes (1938), Rod Keller (1936), A.G.L. McNaughton (1921), J.C. Murchie (1930), George Pearkes (1919), Maurice Pope (1925), H.L. Salmon (1931), Guy Simonds (1938), and Georges Vanier (1924). Vanier was the sole francophone in this (incomplete) list of general officers and one of only two French-Canadian officers to attend Staff College. In all, sixty-three Canadians went to Camberley or Quetta between 1919 and 1939 and, well socialized into the British way of command, thirty-six reached the rank of Brigadier or higher. Both of Canada's wartime full generals, all but one of its lieutenant-generals (the exception being Price Montague, who was NPAM), all four of its Chiefs of the General Staff, and all but four of its fifteen PF division commanders (the exceptions being D.C. Spry, who was too junior even to have sat the entrance examinations on the outbreak of war, J.H. Roberts, Lionel Page, and F.F. Worthington) were Staff College graduates. It was the route to the top.[52]

There was one additional military school that was intended to provide the final polish for officers expected to ascend to the highest posts. The Imperial Defence College in London took a small number of students for a one-year course in high strategy and international politics. Students played at being prime ministers and chiefs of staff, argued over imperial defence questions and the interface between politics and war, and worked on such questions as whether Hong Kong could be defended.[53] The Canadian forces had only thirteen IDC graduates between 1927, the year the college opened, and the outbreak of war, but the ten army officers within that group included A.G.L. McNaughton and Harry Crerar, the two wartime army commanders; E.L.M. Burns and Maurice Pope, a corps commander and the military adviser to the Prime Minister, respectively; and George Pearkes and Guy Turner, both major-generals.[54] It is highly significant that none of the IDC graduates and only two of the British Army Staff College graduates were French-speaking Canadians (see chapter 9).

Quetta, Camberley, and the IDC attracted only the high-fliers. Inevitably most officers were content to soldier on through the peacetime doldrums of administration and "interior economy," with some spending every moment they could playing polo or entering riding competitions. Not for them the hard study involved in getting the coveted letters "psc" or "idc" after their names in the Defence Forces List; not for them the writing of learned articles or argumentative think pieces in the *Canadian Defence Quarterly*, the military's one journal. After all, they were all paid much the same and, considering the responsibilities of senior officers, not very well. The estimates of the Department of National Defence for the military staff at National Defence Headquarters for 1937–8 showed that the Chief of the General Staff, Major-General E.C. Ashton, was to receive $8000 a year. The CGS had responsibility for making army policy, for the equipping, administration, and efficiency of the PF and the NPAM, and for advising the government on all aspects of defence policy. His salary was a substantial one in the Depression, to be sure, but no more than the equivalent of $70,000 in 1990 dollars; Ashton, who was then sixty-four years old, had held his rank since the Great War. In the same estimates, Pearkes, then the Director of Military Training, was to receive $5329, the same as most other officers of his rank at NDHQ. Burns's pay was $4161. In the military districts scattered across the country, the District Officers Commanding, all brigadiers, were to receive from $5110 to $6570, while majors on their staff were to get from $3285 to $4161, the variations attributable to seniority in grade and allowances.[55]

Junior officers received much less and suffered much more interference with their lives. A lieutenant in 1938 drew pay of $4.10 a day out of which he had to purchase uniforms, from British military tailors such as Gieves and Hawks who offered long repayment terms,[56] and pay his mess bill. Officers ate in the mess and contributed — in the case of the Royal Canadian Horse Artillery — $1 a day "extra messing," a sum to cover small luxuries at table. In some regiments, the RCHA in Kingston, for one, officers were obliged to dine in the mess and dress for dinner four nights each week. In addition, there was the individual tab for bar bills which, again in the case of the RCHA, was limited to a maximum of $13 a month for junior officers.[57] That didn't sound much, but once prohibition had become but a memory, drinks were cheap enough for many officers to develop a taste for liquor and regularly become drunk. The situation was bad enough for observers to say that drink was the curse of the Permanent Force. It also affected wartime officers, including one general who was reputed to need two drinks before he could get up in the morning and others who went through a bottle a day — in the field or out of it.[58]

The army also forbade junior officers to marry unless they had ten years' service or their commanding officer's permission. Marriage offered a way out of the financial stringency imposed by the pay scales, however, and, as Foster recalled of his regimental service in the 1920s, marrying money was sometimes the only alternative to resigning from the service. "This required a very rapid courtship before the novelty of a uniform, gleaming boots and silver spurs paled and the unfortunate girl discovered what sort of lifestyle she'd be inflicting on . . . herself. Every young impecunious officer worth his salt kept a weather eye peeled for money-marrying opportunities."[59]

The apparent futility of serving in a force that had little equipment, that received only neglect from the government, and had limited public support — the Lord Strathcona's Horse were seen by Calgary citizens as "the scum of the earth . . . parasites" in the 1920s,[60] — probably encouraged both hasty marriages and peacetime drunkenness among officers. What made their situation yet more difficult to bear was that during the early years of the Depression PF pay had been made subject to the 10 percent rollback imposed by the Bennett government on public servants' salaries. The DOC in Victoria, Brigadier-General J. Sutherland Brown, was outraged by the government's action, pointing out that his duties as District Officer Commanding involved major social obligations that had cost him $2000 more than his pay and allowances in his three years in his post. Moreover, Brown fumed, soldiers were on duty twenty-four hours a day when necessary and, he added correctly, "many officers and instructors are on military duty from 50 to 150 nights a year."[61]

Night duty for most PF officers was instructing the militia. Officers and NCOs[62] on instructional cadres ran a variety of courses in armouries across the country and, because militiamen had jobs during the day, the instruction was almost always at night. The Royal Canadian Regiment in Halifax, for example, had the responsibility of assisting infantry regiments in Nova Scotia, New Brunswick, and Prince Edward Island, as well as staffing training courses for officers and non-commissioned officers. There were provisional schools at armouries to qualify militia officers and NCOs for promotion, and there were royal schools, conducted annually for the same purpose — during which candidates lived in barracks for up to a month. In the summer, concentrations took place at camps such as Vernon in British Columbia, Sarcee in Alberta, Petawawa in Ontario, or Aldershot in Nova Scotia, where the PF ran camp schools, conducted firing practices for the artillery, or ran exercises for infantry and cavalry regiments.[63] The PF were teachers as much as anything else — like teachers everywhere, some PF officers had only contempt for their NPAM students, sentiments many militia students heartily reciprocated[64] — and their task was infinitely harder because of shortages of equipment and ammunition. In some Depression years, for example, gunners could only fire five rounds a gun in their two weeks of summer training.[65] The PF's budget, $4.9 million in 1930–1, would not rise to $5 million until 1935–6 and to $6 million until 1938–9.[66] Shells were too expensive to waste by firing them.

In the Permanent Force units like the RCHA, the Royal Canadian Dragoons, and the Royal Canadian Regiment, regimental training occurred only in the annual PF concentrations in the summer, and in both the 1920s and in the depth of the Depression the government often cancelled these sessions for want of funds.[67] Only once, in 1938, did all the Permanent Force's units come together for summer training at Camp Borden, Ontario, as a "skeleton infantry brigade."[68] This one-week exercise, sloppily handled as it turned out to be, was likely the only time that officers who had joined since the Great War saw one thousand Canadian troops on parade. The RCR, for example, had its companies stationed in Halifax, St-Jean, Quebec, and London, Ontario, so officers had the opportunity to meet their regimental comrades for only a few weeks each year. It also meant constant postings back and forth between the RCR's stations. Daniel Spry, who joined the RCR as a twenty-one-year-old second lieutenant in 1934, initially found himself posted to London; two years later he went to Halifax, and in 1939 to St-Jean. In between those postings, he attended courses or summer concentrations at Kingston, London, Ottawa, Trenton, Aldershot, Niagara, and Camp Borden and instructed Canadian Officer Training Corps cadets in Guelph, Ontario.[69] That was typical for a junior officer. A young single officer, like Spry, could find the constant postings enjoyable. A married officer with a family, however, was almost certain to react differently, and his spouse, unless she was an exceptional woman inured to constant moves, was sure to object.

All this might have been tolerable if a good officer could count on promotions coming his way at decent intervals, but that was not the case. After the Great War, General Sir Arthur Currie encouraged bright young officers who had won their spurs overseas to stay in the Permanent Force, and these officers generally kept their wartime ranks. That sensible policy had created a rank and age structure for the officer corps that saw lieutenants in the early 1920s averaging 28.7 years, captains 29.8, majors 36.0, and lieutenant-colonels 42.6. But in a small force, with little turnover and no growth, promotion stagnated. Fourteen years later, the rank and age structure had lieutenants averaging 25.0 years of age, captains 34.5, majors 44.4, and lieutenant-colonels 49.2. Captains averaged 12.7 years of service, majors 20.3, and lieutenant-colonels 24.0.[70] The brigadiers and major-generals were ordinarily well into their fifties,[71] but so were many in intermediate ranks. In 1939 there were eighty-one officers in ranks higher than major who were fifty or older; there were an additional seventy-four who were over forty, and there were only twenty-two officers of the rank of major and up who were under forty. The oldest PF officer on the rolls was sixty-six; the youngest major in that year had been born in 1907.[72] This was all the more striking as thirty-two was the age of some major-generals in 1944. The system was stuck in neutral, the main reason being that promotion was by seniority, while those at the top, the senior officers at NDHQ and the DOCs, tended to rotate in and out of their posts.[73]

There were always those to defend this process. "Promotion by seniority is unsatisfactory," the Director of Military Operations and Intelligence told the CGS in 1925, "but at the same time officers who have performed good service and long service cannot be overlooked because some of their juniors may be more brilliant. Promotion by merit brings in again that human error of judgment. An officer in peacetime may appear to be a very useful and brilliant fellow and may utterly fail in war, or the reverse, he may appear to be somewhat of a dud in peace and may turn out to be a most gallant, energetic and determined officer on active service."[74] There was some good sense in those arguments, but not much. The net effect of the PF's promotion system was, as Simonds said ten years after the war, that "the senior officers played musical chairs year in and year out," producing a "demoralizing effect" on officers of junior and intermediate ranks. Not only was this demoralizing, "but it resulted in many officers being retained in the Army who, when war broke out, had lost their zest or were medically or physically unfit to serve."[75] Chris Vokes, Simonds's RMC classmate, seconded this view when he wrote that, while in 1939 the PF officers under the age of forty generally were competent, "over 50% of the then serving officers in the PF were useless for active service, either from old age, ill health or inefficiency." Why? Vokes asked: "I would say that this state of affairs was brought [about] by a feeling of security in the service which permeated the peace time army. Provided an officer, no matter how lazy or incompetent, could avoid sudden death or grave misbehaviour, he could look forward to a ripe old age in the service. This view was shared by the Canadian public at large and caused a lack of prestige."[76]

Vokes had captured the scorn with which PF senior officers were held. Colonel George Currie, Deputy Minister of National Defence under Colonel J.L. Ralston during the war, told a reporter in 1942 that he had served on the headquarters staff in the Great War and "came away from that experience with the utmost loathing and distaste for the mentality and competence of permanent staff officials. He said that he himself, like so many other men, approached the present war with the feeling that no good thing could come out of the permanent force." Currie said, however, that "his view has now considerably modified, he has come to have considerable and increasing admiration for a number of the younger permanent force men who are rising rapidly to the top."[77] Vokes, Simonds, and Currie might almost have been describing the effects produced by the system of tenure in Canadian universities. In any case, they were right, and it took the war to shake loose the dead hand of seniority and give the young their chance. D.C. Watt described the British army at the beginning of the war as bustling with "able and thrusting divisional and brigade commanders, the army and corps commanders of 1944–5. At the top, however, its leaders were slow, gallant, intellectually undistinguished, relatively unimaginative and riven by feuds."[78] Those damning phrases might have been written to describe Canada's Permanent Force, except that it was the captains and majors who were able and thrusting and who would become the corps and division commanders of 1944–5.

If these views are thought to be too harsh, too condemnatory, one might consider for contrast the comments of Lieutenant-Colonel G.T. Perkins, a United States Army officer, who toured Canadian defence installations on an inspection trip in June 1926. His report commented favourably on the "spirit of enthusiasm, interest in the work and loyalty" he found in a force "tremendously handicapped by meager appropriations." The Permanent Force, he said, was gallantly trying to stay "on its feet in spite of national indifference."[79] That indifference was so strong that if there was blame to be fixed for the condition of the Permanent Force between the wars, it lay not with the soldiers, who did their best with the paltry resources they were given, but with Canadian governments and those who elected them.

THE NON-PERMANENT ACTIVE MILITIA also coped with limited resources. Although the prevailing mood in Canada shortly after the Great War was anti-war and, to some extent, anti-empire, and although pacifism flourished in Parliament, in academe, and among large segments of the population,[80] the militia continued to have a certain social cachet. In smaller towns the armouries were a centre of social activity, and the colonel of the regiment was almost inevitably a key figure in the local elite.[81] In the larger cities, officers were drawn from the professional and business classes, and most public ceremonies involving the legislature, the lieutenant-governor, or visiting dignitaries were attended by officers in colourful uniforms, their medals glistening.

RMC was another source of militia officers. In big city units there was a good chance that ex-cadets would make up a substantial proportion of officer ranks. The 2nd Field Regiment, Royal Canadian Artillery, in Montreal, for example, had twenty-one ex-cadets among its fifty-eight active officers in 1938; on the regiment's reserve list of officers, twenty-seven of fifty-three had gone to RMC. In the city's Black Watch (Royal Highland Regiment), seven of forty-six active officers were ex-cadets.[82] Overall across Canada, however, Lieutenant-Colonel E.L.M. Burns found that in 1935 RMC graduates made up only 3.3 percent of NPAM officers and 4.3 percent of those on the Reserve of Officers, a paper stand-by force.[83] The leavening of ex-cadets, important because they had training of a kind that the great majority of NPAM officers did not, was very small.

As in the PF, militia promotion was slow. One officer in the Toronto Scottish who had joined in 1929 calculated that, given normal peacetime conditions, he would rise to command his regiment in 2032![84] For the most part, then, the militia officers were local leaders, men who believed that readiness was no sin. They enjoyed the training, the mess life, the occasional parade, and although they knew in their hearts that they and their grossly under-strength and under-equipped regiments were unprepared for war, they reckoned that devotion to their regimental traditions would see them through. In the sergeants' mess, too, there would be dedicated individuals who believed in the regiment and encouraged young recruits to join up — sometimes too young, as one PF officer from Ontario complained about the "large proportion of boys in [the] Ranks."[85]

No one joined the NPAM for the money. "The officers," Major-General W.A. Griesbach said in the Senate in 1936, "receive pay only when they are in training. They buy their uniforms and equipment in every detail, and the pay they receive does not begin to cover this cost to them."[86] Pay was meagre in any case, and in many, perhaps most, regiments, officers turned theirs over to the regimental fund. Uniforms could cost from $400 to $1400 in Highland regiments, although hand-me-downs could often be secured.[87] In the Depression years, when Ottawa's support for the NPAM began to dry up and when Great War equipment and even older armouries began to show their age, regiments scrambled to find the money to keep their men dry and in boots. The DOC in British Columbia struggled hard to get the Seaforth Highlanders in Vancouver a new armoury. "Say that this is one of the best regiments in Canada," he advised a brother officer, "and has had the worst possible quarters since its organization, and we don't want it penalized in perpetuity."[88] It was a hard job to keep the militia alive in Canada between the wars, and it should not be surprising that, generally speaking, greater success was had in urban areas, with their larger resources and concentrated populations, than in rural regions.[89]

Still, all across the country, officers, NCOs, and men turned out one evening a week around the year. There were occasional weekend training exercises and the annual summer camp, ordinarily two weeks long, where two men holding a ten-foot pole would act as if they were a ten-man section and machine guns would sometimes be represented by a rifleman with a flag.[90] As most militiamen had jobs, even during the Depression, and as most received only two weeks' vacation, it took genuine dedication to spend holidays at training camp when all that could be done was to play at being soldiers.* For most horsed units, regiments of cavalry or artillery, the summer camp was the only time they had a chance to operate with horses. When mechanization finally began to come into effect in the late 1930s, it enabled the militia officer, as Simonds later recalled, "to concentrate on his tactical or technical problem without at the same time having to cope with a noble but sometimes unfamiliar and reluctant mount."[91] Even so, until well into the 1930s, proficiency in riding remained an essential qualification for NPAM officers taking the Militia Staff Course, and cavalry units continued to train with horses until the outbreak of war.[92]

As a route to higher rank, the Militia Staff Course was the equivalent for NPAM officers of Camberley or Quetta. Consisting of two parts, one theoretical and one practical, the MSC, which began in 1902, lasted to 1914, and

* In the early years of the Depression, the Department of National Defence provided the militia with funds for only eight nights of drill per year and, moreover, sometimes cancelled the summer training period. At least one artillery battery, the 51st of Ottawa, staged a ten-day camp without pay and at its own expense at the Connaught Ranges. R.G.C. Smith, ed., *As You Were! Ex-Cadets Remember*, vol. 2: 1919–84 (np, 1984), 41–2.

started again in 1922, intended to train officers, mainly captains and majors, for staff positions. Unlike Camberley, where PF officers spent two years of intensive full-time study, the MSC, reflecting NPAM realities, consisted of lectures and exercises during the winter and practical work over two weeks in August, usually at RMC, Petawawa, or at Lennoxville, Quebec, and Sarcee, Alberta. In 1929–30, for example, the theoretical portion of the course saw candidates examined on strategy, map reading and field sketching, organization and administration, training for war and military law.[93] In 1932, sixty-one candidates attended the practical portion of the MSC course at Lennoxville and, in addition to the set exercises, observed a demonstration of the assembling and launching of an assault bridge and had the opportunity to see the "cross country performance of the Austin '7' reconnaissance car." In 1929 candidates took a brief reconnaissance flight. Such efforts showed some initiative on the part of the directing staff, but candidates' transportation on exercises was often by private automobile; in other words, money was and continued to be a problem.[94]

Militia officers taking the practical portion learned how to make appreciations of tactical situations and to issue orders. There was also the opportunity to work closely with PF officers, many of them Staff College graduates, who could talk about the role of tanks (even if Canada had none) and contemplate the use of aircraft for artillery reconnaissance.[95] PF officers preparing for the Staff College Preparatory Course often sat in on the MSC theoretical portion, as did young lieutenants who duly wrote the MSC examinations.[96] The MSC built up a substantial body of partially staff-trained militia officers — in 1940 there were 112 MSC-qualified officers in Military District No. 11 (British Columbia) alone — and, while none of those who completed the course were immediately able to step competently into staff posts on mobilization, this was a long step towards that goal. Certainly NPAM officers with the MSC were considered first for such appointments once war began.[97]

Beyond the MSC, there was from 1935 an Advanced Militia Staff Course with its month-long practical phase at RMC for majors as a next stage[98] and examinations for promotion to the rank of colonel in the NPAM. The 1938 colonels' examination, a two-day practical affair, took place at Port Hope, Ontario, and Calgary, and involved map exercises and a large-scale tactical exercise without troops. The officers in charge of the course, all Staff College graduates, included some of the PF's best younger officers, such as

Lieutenant-Colonel E.L.M. Burns and Major H.L. Salmon; among their students was Lieutenant-Colonel A.E. Walford, who rose to major-general during the war and held the most senior staff posts at First Canadian Army and at NDHQ.[99]

Despite the courses and the dedication, the NPAM as a whole was desperately weak in every respect. The organization created after the Great War was enormous and ramshackle, consisting of eleven infantry and four cavalry divisions, a force far beyond Canada's capacity to sustain. In 1931 the Chief of the General Staff, Major-General McNaughton, used the occasion of the International Disarmament Conference to announce that Canada would reduce this establishment to six infantry and one cavalry division, although the proposed changes were not put in place until 1936. Cavalry regiments, as a result, were reduced from thirty-six to sixteen plus four armoured-car regiments; 135 infantry regiments shrank to fifty-nine rifle battalions, twenty-six machine-gun battalions, and six tank battalions. At the same time, the artillery, engineers, and signals expanded. In effect, the NPAM and its 48,761 members were put on a modern footing, and the Minister of National Defence, Ian Mackenzie, congratulated the militiamen who "have rendered a high public service in sinking their personal emotions for the good of the service and their country."[100] As that remark suggested, the reaction to the changes had been sharp indeed, as regiments with honoured traditions had been combined with others, much to the chagrin of all.[101]

Budgets, pared to the bone early in the Depression when the Non-Permanent Active Militia in 1932–3 received only $1.8 million, slowly began to rise as the war drew nearer. By 1938–9 the NPAM received $2.7 million. In 1939, for example, there were 266,595 man-days of training given, more than double that three years earlier.[102] Militia units, all with strengths well under that required by their war establishments,[103] were getting ready as best they could. NDHQ had prepared its mobilization plans, making use in the first instance of PF units and the best of the NPAM regiments.[104] The United States Army's Military Intelligence Division pronounced the NPAM in 1939 the best trained of all the British Empire's militia forces.[105] That may have been true of parade-square drill, but scarcely of field tactics; if it was, providence must have helped mightily in winning the war that began later that year. A fairer assessment was that by historian Charles Stacey, when he wrote that on the outbreak of war, "Canada had no troops ready for immediate action, except for local coastal defence against very small raids. The tiny Permanent Force did not constitute a striking force capable either of counter-attack . . . or of expeditionary action. The Non-Permanent Active Militia, with its limited strength, obsolescent equipment and rudimentary training was incapable of immediate effective action of any sort."[106] Colonel Stacey might well have added that Canada's generals in September 1939 were in all too similar a condition to the forces they commanded. They, too, were unready for action, obsolescent in their thinking, and rudimentary in their training for modern war. In the chapters that follow we shall see how the old and unready took command, soon to be brushed aside by the young, those more attuned to the requirements of the day.

CHAPTER 2

THE OLD BRIGADE

T HE PRESENT OFFICERS, General George C. Marshall, Chief
of Staff of the United States Army, said in October 1939, "are for the
most part too old to command troops in battle under the terrific pres-
sures of modern war. Many of them have their minds set in outmoded
patterns, and can't change to meet the new conditions they may face." In
his post for only one month, the General made his point crystal clear: "I
do not propose to send our young citizen-soldiers into action . . . under
commanders whose minds are no longer adaptable to the making of split-
second decisions . . . nor whose bodies are no longer capable of standing
up under the demands of field service. . . . They'll have their chance to
prove what they can do. But I doubt that many of them will come
through satisfactorily. Those that don't will be eliminated."[1]

With an average of 12,000 officers during the interwar years,[2] Marshall's
U.S. Regular Army had the numbers to work with as he sought effective
commanders. The succession of defeats the United States suffered in the
six months after the Japanese attack on Pearl Harbor "produced some positive consequences for the American high command," military historian D.
Clayton James wrote, "in purging a number of senior officers who might
have been satisfactory for peacetime but not for wartime leadership, in
bringing to the forefront replacements with promise, and in preserving
worthy survivors of the prewar high command."[3]

The Canadian situation was quite different. Instead of a professional
officer corps of 12,000, the Permanent Force had only 450 officers at the

outbreak of war — and many, possibly up to one-half, were unfit for active service. These were the timeservers, the old, the ill, and the inefficient.[4] Others had become disillusioned, tired of waiting for promotion, while the PF's brigadiers and major-generals endlessly rotated through the top posts at National Defence Headquarters and in the military districts.[5] It was absolutely wrong, Major-General Harry Crerar wrote in a blistering memorandum to the Minister of National Defence on his return from Britain in the summer of 1940, to retain in senior positions officers "who are inefficient, or who are undependable, whatever their length of service may be. . . . In the present circumstances it is dangerous. . . . One reason advanced for the retention in command and staff appointments in Canada of Permanent Force officers whose indifferent past record or present poor physical condition precludes them from appointments overseas," Crerar continued, "is that on the termination of war, their retirement can then be effected and vacancies for those Permanent Force officers overseas can thus later be created." This argument was "unsound," Crerar argued, "because it assumes that second-rate officers can be accepted for appointments in Canada." Inefficiency in Canada would only produce "inadequately trained and equipped units and drafts for overseas. It will result in lack of confidence, dissatisfaction and unrest in the mobilized forces and in the civil population." What he wanted, Crerar said in words that must have struck a chord with his Minister, Colonel J.L. Ralston, who promptly named Crerar the Chief of the General Staff, was "to create a highly efficient Canadian Army *now* — the present or future economic security of the individual professional soldier, whether officer or other rank, while requiring just consideration, must not be allowed to prevent the attainment of this object."[6]

Crerar also knew that it was not only the Permanent Force that suffered from the problems caused by inefficient officers. The Non-Permanent Active Militia had its old war horses, too, the colonels and brigadier-generals of the last war who, sniffing gunpowder, gamely and gallantly wanted the opportunity to serve in action once more. With only some 5000 indifferently trained officers at the beginning of the war, the NPAM's senior leaders, and large numbers of its juniors as well, were every bit as old, ill, or inefficient as the Permanent Force's colonels and generals.

Major-General A.G.L. McNaughton, charged with the responsibility of mobilizing and commanding the 1st Canadian Infantry Division, clearly realized the problems he faced in finding the officers to command and administer his citizen-soldiers. He knew them when he moved up to command the Canadian Corps, and he remained all too aware of them when he became commander of the First Canadian Army in 1943. "It was necessary to appoint, as commanders of divisions and even of corps," historian Charles Stacey wrote, "officers who had never commanded even a battalion in action and whose battle experience, if they had any at all, was limited to junior appointments in the First World War. Some proved triumphantly successful; others gave way to other men."[7]

McNaughton is usually thought to have favoured "scientifically" inclined and intellectual commanders, but many of the officers he put into high places and whose careers he fostered and protected in the first three or four years of war — men such as Ernest Sansom, Armand Smith, Basil Price, Arthur Potts, and Hardy Ganong — scarcely fit that mould. As Lester Pearson, stationed in London on the staff of the High Commission, put it in October 1939, "I was delighted to hear that two of the three Brigadiers of the First Division are Militia; one a jam-maker [Smith] and the other a milkman [Price]!"[8] There wasn't too much science there, at least not military science. Still, McNaughton had very little to work with in the early years of war. As *Fortune* magazine wrote in January 1944: "At first McNaughton had to lean on the older militia officers, veterans of the last war, who were middle-aged businessmen rather than soldiers. In one of his homely metaphors, they served as 'a cover crop, to help the younger men through the wilting strains of the first responsibilities, in the same way that older trees are used to shelter saplings through the heat of the day.'"[9] That rural analogy was apt enough, even if McNaughton failed to understand that he, too, was part of the "cover crop," for most of the senior officers who ended the war in command of Canada's divisions and corps were young PF or NPAM lieutenants, captains, or majors in 1939, officers who had learned their trade during the long years the Canadian army trained in Britain.

Sometimes the process of removal was forced on McNaughton and the Canadians. The great housecleaner was Lieutenant-General Bernard Montgomery, in 1942 the General Officer Commanding South-Eastern Command, where the Canadian divisions in England served. The British general conducted rigorous inspections of Canadian units, watching exercises and interviewing officers and senior NCOs in infantry battalions.

His reports on personnel, sent to Lieutenant-General Harry Crerar, acting GOC of the Canadian Corps, advanced some careers and ended others. Monty's aims show clearly in the indiscreet letters he sent Major Trumball Warren, a Canadian officer who had served as his aide-de-camp for a time (and who would be with him again) and for whom Montgomery formed a genuine affection.[10] In April 1942 he wrote to Warren, in Canada for a staff course: "I hope to be sending you Pearkes, Potts, and Ganong back to Canada shortly; you will find them useful your side, I hope, you need some really good officers back in Canada."[11] Major-General G.R. Pearkes, a Permanent Force officer and a Victoria Cross winner, commanded the 1st Canadian Infantry Division, and Brigadiers Potts and Ganong, both militiamen, were brigade commanders. In June, Montgomery added another senior officer to his list: "I hope to be sending Price back to you; he will be of great value in Canada where his knowledge of the milk industry will help on the national war effort."[12] Major-General Price was GOC of 3rd Canadian Infantry Division and, as Montgomery's cruelly snide comment suggested, he had headed a large Montreal dairy before the war.

It was hard to get the changes made. Montgomery observed that "the weak point in the Canadian Corps at present is the knowledge of commanders in the stage management of battle operations, and in the technique of battle fighting generally." The weakness of the brigade commanders was impossible to rectify "unless the Divisional Commanders are themselves competent to train their subordinates, and are themselves fully conversant with the handling of a Division in battle."[13] Later he told Warren that the problem with the Canadians was that "the training of the senior commanders had not progressed in the same way as had the training on a lower level." If that could be managed, then the corps "would be unbeatable." Three of those senior officers he had targeted were still there: "I don't think it is possible to make very much of Price. We have got rid of Potts — by making him a General!!"[14] But a month later, Monty reported further success: "After much hard work I managed to get Potts & Ganong returned to Canada. But it is not my doing that they return to you as Generals!! What an Army!! . . . I do not think Price (3 Div) can last much longer; he is quite useless as a soldier."[15] Finally, in August, Montgomery had his way, and Price left the army to head the Canadian Red Cross in Britain: "I have at last got rid of Basil Price; it has taken 6 mths. He is a very decent chap, but no soldier."[16] Only Pearkes — "no good . . . has no brains"[17] — still remained on Monty's hit list, but not for long. Late in August 1942, just a few weeks after Montgomery had gone to North Africa to take command of the British Eighth Army and make his reputation, Pearkes was also relieved and returned to Canada to take command on the Pacific Coast.[18]

The phrasing in Montgomery's private letters was unnecessarily (and, regrettably, most characteristically) cruel, but he was ordinarily right in his judgments, and his methods and comments were every bit as harsh on British officers. The "nasty little shit," as Montgomery was widely known in the British army, never forgot that generals led men into situations where they might be killed and where the fate of nations might be decided; he wanted none of the incapable in charge.

Nor did anyone, in truth. Major-General J.H. Roberts, an RMC graduate, a Great War veteran, and a PF artilleryman, had gone overseas with the 1st Division and had played a notable role in rescuing his regiment's guns from the debacle of the division's brief foray to France in June 1940. By July 1940 Roberts was a brigadier; by April 1942, at the age of fifty-one, he was a division GOC, commanding the 2nd Division, one he called the "the best trained" in the army with "the first chance to do a job if presented."[19] Montgomery supported this estimation of the division, and he pronounced Roberts "the best Divisional Commander in the Corps . . . very sound, but . . . not in any way brilliant."[20] The job Roberts's division was handed was Dieppe in August 1942, where two of its three brigades were destroyed in a few hours ashore in an operation that showed the Canadians' enormous courage, if little else.[21] As the raid's naval commander noted, Roberts "had to look on, without the ability effectively to intervene, while his Division lost very heavily."[22] The tragedy of Dieppe, contrary to widespread public perception, did not immediately destroy Roberts's career, whatever it may have done to his spirit. Instead, in March 1943, Crerar, his corps commander, reported that in recent exercises Roberts had demonstrated a lack of the high tactical abilities required of a division commander in mobile operations.[23] The next month, Roberts was placed in command of Canadian Reinforcement Units in Britain, and two years later he joined the Commonwealth War Graves Commission. Goronwy Rees, a British officer seconded to the planning staff for Dieppe, wrote twenty years later that Roberts at no time revealed "either the intellectual ability nor the powers of command which would have fitted him for the terrible task which was entrusted to him."[24] Harsh as that assessment was, it was likely true, and Roberts had to go. Command in the Second World War was for the young and fit.

Once in action, the Canadians found this out for themselves, and the older officers tended to drop away under the strain of battle. As Chris Vokes put it after the war: "When the [1st] division had been mobilized in the autumn of 1939, all officers holding the rank of lieutenant colonel and above, and many other officers and senior NCOs, had seen service in the 1914–18 War." By January 1944, after the 1st Canadian Infantry Division had been in action in Italy for six months, they were almost all gone. "I was 39, the brigade commanders were below 35, and the battalion commanders all below 30 years. As far as the 1st Division was concerned it had become a young man's war."[25] Brigadier James Roberts said much the same thing when, after a late night meeting to receive orders from General Guy Simonds in Normandy, "I could not help noticing that some of the older Canadian senior officers, commanders of divisions or brigades . . . found it physically difficult to stay awake as the orders continued." Roberts was sympathetic but, he said, "evidently, war was a young man's game. . . . Failure of an operation or, worse, unnecessary loss of Canadian lives could result from the inability of older senior officers to withstand the punishment their bodies had to absorb."[26] That was the problem.

Still, the Great War veterans were essential in the first years after 1939, for new and capable generals could not be created simply by putting up the red tabs, which denoted senior officer status, on young captains and majors. Of course, many of the "old sweats" were out of date in their military thinking after twenty years of peacetime soldiering in a country that cared nothing for its armed forces and vigorously practised military retrenchment. Others had turned soft physically and mentally. Yet more had become fixed in their views and rigid in their thinking. The incoming Chief of the General Staff, Major-General T.V. Anderson, had been only half-joking when he wrote to a friend in mid 1938: "Things have changed so in the last few years that I find it very difficult to keep up to date in things military, so I go about looking wise but keeping my mouth shut!"[27]

But if Canada had to raise and train an army in September 1939, as it did, what other option was there than to use such officers? At the Royal Military College, ex-cadets who survive for fifty years after their graduation become members of the "Old Brigade." The boys of the Old Brigade in the Second World War, not all ex-cadets by any means, had survived the fighting of the Great War and the intervening and debilitating years of peace. The NPAM officers gave up their jobs, and they and their PF comrades left their families behind to rally once more to their country's defence. On them fell the responsibility for creating Canada's army — and, in truth, they did good work in difficult conditions. But once the action began, younger men had to seize the reins.

VICTOR WENTWORTH ODLUM exemplified the best and the worst of Canada's militia system. Born in Cobourg, Ontario, in 1880, he was raised both in Japan, where his father, a leader in the British Israelite movement, was president of a Tokyo college, and in Vancouver. Odlum served in South Africa as a private in the Royal Canadian Regiment, returned to Canada after being wounded, and rejoined the 3rd Canadian Mounted Rifles, this time as a lieutenant, and fought the Boers once more. On his repatriation he joined the militia first in Toronto and, finding work in Vancouver as a newspaper reporter, then in British Columbia. By 1905 he was the managing editor of the Vancouver *Daily World*, of which he later became owner, and by 1908 he was selling bonds and insurance in Winnipeg and next in Vancouver. When war broke out in 1914, he was living on the West Coast.

Odlum went overseas as the second-in-command of the 7th Battalion of the first contingent of the Canadian Expeditionary Force, and by 1916 he was a Brigadier-General commanding the 11th Brigade in the 4th Canadian Division. Wounded in action three times, twice decorated with the Distinguished Service Order, Odlum had a well-deserved reputation for courage and efficiency. His battalion became expert in trench raids, his brigade captured Hill 145 on Vimy Ridge, and Odlum, a teetotaler, was greatly admired by the troops despite their unbounded fury at his efforts to have the rum ration replaced by hot soup![28] His personal reconnaissances were fearless, and one of his former staff officers, Major Maurice Pope, wrote in September 1918 that "General Odlum, as usual, was nosing about the forward area, and for the third time was picked off by a sniper bullet through the arm and across the back."[29] According to Odlum's own account, in the summer of 1918 his friend Lieutenant-General Sir Arthur Currie told him that he "would be given command of the 1st Division, to be, as he put it, the spearhead of his operations in

1919."[30] The war ended before that appointment could be made. Still, Currie's loyalty to Odlum had undoubtedly been cemented when, late in the war, Odlum helped rescue the corps commander from scandal by putting up a large part of the money Currie owed the government for a fraudulent prewar diversion of funds intended for uniforms.[31]

With the armistice, Odlum acted as commander of the 23rd Infantry Brigade in British Columbia from 1920 to 1925, after which he went on the reserve of officers.[32] His formal military connections at an end (though he was "said to have read every war book of note published since 1920"),[33] Odlum devoted himself to business and politics. He became wealthy in the bond business, continued to dabble in newspapers, contributed heavily to worthy causes in Vancouver, and, from 1924 to 1928, sat as a Liberal in the British Columbia legislature. He was a prominent party organizer for years after that,[34] a vice-chair of the Board of Governors of the Canadian Broadcasting Corporation, and a close friend and firm supporter of Vancouver Member of Parliament Ian Mackenzie, from 1935 to 1939 the Minister of National Defence. When the Second World War began, Mackenzie, even if he was quickly relegated to the Pensions and National Health portfolio, did all he could to get Odlum a senior command post.

Even so, it took a major campaign to get him a job overseas. To one Great War friend, Odlum wrote: "I thoroughly expect to be in England before very long."[35] To another, he said, "You are quite right in supposing that I am not likely to be on any Staff. Command is my natural role . . . because I have had long training and experience along that line."[36] And to the Prime Minister, a man obsessed by fear that the conscription crisis of 1917 which had split the country and divided the Liberal party might recur in this second war, he loudly proclaimed: "I am one of the few soldiers opposed to conscription on purely military grounds — unless a grave emergency arises." Perhaps realizing that his qualifying phrase might not entirely reassure Mackenzie King, Odlum added that spirit was the key to success in war and only volunteers had it.[37] But those efforts, and letters to Norman Rogers, the new Defence Minister,[38] failed to produce results, and in December Odlum's friends were writing to the Prime Minister urging that "all senior commands should be under Canadian born citizen soldiers," notably Victor Odlum, "our ablest soldier."[39] Finally worn down, Rogers recommended in April 1940 that Odlum take command of the 2nd

Canadian Infantry Division, choosing him over three Permanent Force officers. "It was thought Odlum and McNaughton would work well together," King wrote in his diary, "and also they represent different parts of the same country, each having been in the late war. Odlum's appointment would be well received."[40] King failed to note that Odlum was a militia officer and that his appointment owed as much to that as to anything else; the army, however, drew the proper moral. Colonel Ernest Sansom, overseas on McNaughton's staff, wrote home about "the bad news of Odlum's appointment. . . . Political I should think as compensation for his assistance to Ian McKenzie [sic] in the [1940 general] election." Later he added that "judging by the appointment of Odlum N.D.H.Q. are capable of doing almost anything."[41] Another officer remembered hearing Odlum described at a meeting as "a silly old political general who knew nothing" — and another officer walking from the room in protest.[42]

Thus Victor Odlum, in his sixtieth year and fifteen years removed even from militia experience, was a major-general and a division commander. Within a few days of getting his command, Odlum was en route to England with Rogers to begin preparations for the reception of his division.[43] When he returned to Canada in mid May, as the German blitzkrieg was crushing the French and British forces on the Continent, he was pessimistic. "The Germans have 200 divisions fully equipped," he told Vancouver journalist Bruce Hutchison. "Italy has 40 divisions. We are, therefore, not only desperately inferior in equipment but are outnumbered. . . . There is absolutely no hope of making any headway against the German army this year or next."[44]

Meanwhile, Odlum had to try to get his division into shape before it went overseas. It was a daunting task, his brigade commanders telling him bluntly that the men were "essentially untrained, except in the most elementary subjects, such as arms drill and marching."[45] Worse, it was not possible to concentrate the division so it could train together, and in late May and June 1940 some units of the 2nd Division were warned for duty in Iceland.[46] Troubled by this and by equipment deficiencies, Odlum complained to Colonel J.L. Ralston, the new Defence Minister, "that units in his Division were no further advanced in training than they should have been after two months of mobilization."[47] Nonetheless, by 21 July 1940 Odlum was again en route to England, this time with 4000 of his men. The Prime Minister saw him the day before his departure: "He looks young and really radiant. Says he does not know what it is to feel tired. Has a fine spirit. Intends to do all he can to put his spirit into the officers and men, leaving as much else as he can to others. . . . He is a gallant fellow. A brave heart. A fine soul."[48]

A fine soul, perhaps, but not destined to be a successful commander. Odlum carried detailed notes on his officers with him in his notebook,[49] and he took care to acknowledge General McNaughton, still commanding VII British Corps which did not include the 2nd Canadian Infantry Division, "as our leader."[50] Nonetheless a disproportionate amount of Odlum's time seemed to be taken up with extraneous matters. He crusaded for regimental brass bands,[51] for changes in map reference codes to preserve their secrecy,[52] and for a distinctive arm patch for his division designed to recall the 2nd Division of the Great War.[53] Known to the troops as "Bugger" Odlum or "Hoodlum," where he was known at all, Odlum simply failed to make much impression as an effective trainer during divisional exercises or as a potential division commander in action. Worse yet, as the next senior officer to McNaughton, Odlum was a potential corps commander, and he acted as such on at least one exercise, Victor, in January 1941. Harry Foster, a PF and Staff College–trained lieutenant-colonel in the fall of 1941, wrote in his diary that "for a long time we have feared the promotion of Gen. McNaughton. Gen. Odlum is next senior."[54] The simple truth was that Odlum was preparing himself and his troops to fight a 1918 war, and neither he nor his division were anything like ready to face the conditions of blitzkrieg unleashed by the Nazis in 1940. Odlum was too old for his post. "Can you imagine," one distinguished officer wrote later, "what would have happened if the 2nd Division commanded by General Odlum . . . had been in action?"[55]

Such views were beginning to be widespread. General Sir Alan Brooke, the British officer commanding Home Forces, had begun to worry as early as April 1941 about the quality of Canadian senior officers. After another look at the Canadian commanders in a later exercise, Brooke wrote to McNaughton in September 1941 that while Odlum was loyal and respected, he was "too old . . . too set . . . to adapt his ideas" to modern warfare. He might have to succeed McNaughton in command of the Canadian Corps, Brooke wrote, and "I view such a possibility with grave apprehension."[56] McNaughton must have agreed, for he told the Chief of the General Staff in Ottawa that "Odlum is showing signs of advancing years to such an extent that I will have to make a change in command before the Second Cdn Div goes in the line in the second week in October." Then, probably because he was aware of Odlum's powerful political connections, McNaughton recommended that he be promoted to Lieutenant-General and made Inspector-General in Canada.[57] That did not find favour in Ottawa, and there was great concern until the Prime Minister, who had been consulted, suggested making Odlum High Commissioner to Australia. "This seemed to relieve a difficult situation very much," King wrote.[58] Armed with a letter from Mackenzie King and with newly created age limits for senior officers, it fell to Ralston to wield the axe. Odlum, the Defence Minister wrote in his diary, was "quite broken up. Wanted to end career shooting Germans. Would prefer 6 months life here to 25 yrs somewhere else." In the end Odlum accepted his removal with as much good grace as he could muster: "Tell Prime Minister ructious as ever but will of course do what he thinks best."[59]

In fact, he was deeply hurt and believed he had been the victim: "In a struggle between the Permanent Force and Citizen Soldiery in which the permanent force did all the struggling while the citizen soldiers went quietly ahead with their duty, the Permanent Force has won. My removal is the signal of complete victory."[60] This was not an entirely unreasonable interpretation, since Crerar was quickly named to replace him as GOC 2nd Canadian Infantry Division. Later Odlum wrote to his friend Ian Mackenzie that age limits were foolish when fitness was what mattered: "In fitness I was ahead of every senior officer in the Corps. . . . I am so much more physically fit than is General McNaughton that the contrast is fantastic."[61] Although he would try repeatedly to get a command once again,[62] Odlum's military career was over.

His diplomatic career, destined to be a decade long, was just beginning, and Odlum promptly caused great embarrassment to his government. He arrived in Australia in the wake of the startling Japanese advances, and the Canadian High Commissioner made his mark by urging the dispatch of Canadian troops to Australia on grounds of "high Imperial policy." The Prime Minister was horrified by these promises to Canberra, and a telegram had to be flashed to Odlum that only the Cabinet War Committee could commit itself to the disposition of Canadian troops; he was not to give the Australians "any reason to expect despatch of Canadian forces."[63] That didn't stop Odlum, who was soon quoted in the *New York Times* as saying that "Canada's interest in the defense of Australia was the primary reason for the despatching of two Canadian divisions [sic] to Hong Kong. She can do more if Australia wants. Australia has only to say the word."[64] Similar statements that flew in the face of common sense and the government's commitment to defeat Hitler first continued to be made to Australian officials,[65] and it was clear that Odlum suffered from a remarkable lack of judgment. "My mind is that of a fighting soldier," he wrote to King, "and I am making no progress in changing it. Sitting in the placid atmosphere of Canberra I expect to die of slow motion, internal explosion or spontaneous combustion." What made it worse for him was that he was still fit, walking ten miles a day, "rain or shine, hot or cold. And I am always the first in for breakfast."[66] In March 1942 Odlum sought permission "to place himself at the disposal of the Australian government, in any capacity, if and when the occasion warranted," a request refused by the Cabinet War Committee.[67]

In the fall, after a brief trip home, Odlum went to China as Canadian minister, and this was followed by a posting as Ambassador to Turkey. Not until 1952 did Odlum finally retire from government service at the age of seventy-two, impetuous as ever. In 1957 he sought permission to accept a Chinese government invitation to visit Beijing, a request that was turned down. An External Affairs official wrote that "General Odlum's political judgment is not to be relied upon . . . it would be most dangerous at the present time to give the General any encouragement to visit Communist China."[68]

Victor Odlum simply was too old to command troops in the Second World War. A brave man in the trenches, a fierce fighter with high ideals and an unquenchable will to win, his military skills were as obsolescent as the tanks with which the Allies began the war. But the Non Permanent Active Militia probably needed to have one of the first two GOC's posts, and, in 1940, so weak was the militia's senior officer ranks, Odlum was probably as qualified as any for the job. This was the tragedy of the Canadian army at the beginning of the war, and it was fortunate indeed that Odlum, at once impetuous and firmly in a rut, did not have to lead his 2nd Canadian Infantry Division's gallant charge against a German invasion of Britain.

ONE OF THE SENIOR OFFICERS passed over so Odlum could get the 2nd Division in 1940 was H.F.H. Hertzberg, a Permanent Force engineer. Halfdan Fenton Harboe Hertzberg, born in 1884, was the son of a Norwegian engineer from a distinguished military family who came to Canada in 1880 to work for the Canadian Pacific Railway. Called "Dane" by his brother Charles, whose military career paralleled his own, but "Hertz" or "H.F.H." by everyone else, Hertzberg had attended Upper Canada College and St Andrew's College and hoped to go to the Royal Military College. Money was scarce, however, and instead he studied engineering at the University of Toronto. He served in the militia and went overseas soon after the outbreak of war in 1914, transferring to the Permanent Force in 1915. His record was superb, and he ended the Great War as a colonel with a Military Cross and a Distinguished Service Order.

Then there were twenty long years in the peacetime Permanent Force, which he joined as a major. Hertzberg served in Halifax, attended the British Army Staff College, Camberley, and worked at National Defence Headquarters, where his qualities impressed his superiors; he was one of a half-dozen officers singled out by the Chief of Staff, Major-General J.H. MacBrien, as "possess[ing] qualifications fitting them for high appointments."[69] In 1925 he was posted to the Royal Military College and, in his four years there, he developed enormous affection for that institution. Then he was GSO 1 in Toronto, a posting followed by his becoming District Officer Commanding in Halifax in 1934. With three young children, a boy from whom perfection was demanded and two girls who were reputed to be hellions with a remarkable talent for cussing, Brigadier Hertzberg was near the peacetime summit of his profession.[70] He was not a military reactionary, like some others of his rank; when proposals were advanced in 1932 to reduce the proportion of cavalry and infantry in the NPAM, his response was calmness itself, though, as a member of the Royal Canadian Engineers, his corps would be a beneficiary of the changes.[71] Gruff by nature, notoriously "liverish" in the mornings, able to tear a strip off military miscreants, yet known as "one of the finest fellows to work with — or for,"[72] Hertzberg was always charming with women, had a soft heart underneath, and a gift for speechmaking. He was humanized by his wife Dorothy, a liberal-minded woman who managed the family finances and dealt fairly and sensibly with the servants they acquired at District Headquarters in Halifax.[73]

At the outbreak of war in 1939, the fifty-five-year-old Hertzberg was Quartermaster-General in Ottawa, fresh from his success in arranging the transportation for the 1939 Royal Tour, and was sometimes spoken of as a future Chief of the General Staff.[74] When the Adjutant-General, Major-General H.H. Matthews, fell ill and died in the winter of 1940, Hertzberg was drafted to fill that additional post ad interim. He was not a success, according to a probably apocryphal family legend, because he refused to appoint a NPAM incompetent to a senior post. It was wartime and that post needed an able officer, Hertzberg insisted. The CGS, General Anderson, pleaded with him: "For God's sake, Hertz, bend a little." But Hertzberg held firm, even in the face of Mackenzie King, who said, "General, I refuse to be swayed by your famous rhetoric."[75]

That was one disappointment. Another was his failure to get command of the 2nd Division. The CGS had suggested Hertzberg and two other PF officers, but the Minister, Norman Rogers, chose Victor Odlum. The Prime Minister wrote in his diary: "There was a general feeling that Hertzberg is one of the best men we have. It was felt he was needed here and should be kept in reserve."[76] That decision did not sit well overseas, where one senior staff officer wrote that he certainly would have preferred Hertzberg: "I know of no one better fitted in Canada to command the division."[77] That was not to be, nor would Hertzberg become GOC of the 3rd Canadian Infantry Division when that choice was being made in the summer of 1940. Although Hertzberg's was one of the names submitted by the CGS and although his old friend Harry Crerar told Ralston he was his choice,[78] the command fell to Brigadier Ernest Sansom. General McNaughton wired the CGS that "from past experience do not consider [Hertzberg] has the character required."[79] Earlier, the Canadian Corps' commander had told the Minister about the "development of new tactics which differ radically from old [and] require that Divisional Commanders be selected from men having current experience."[80] Hertzberg, stuck in Canada, could not get that experience, and McNaughton clearly wanted to control overseas appointments, so only those officers he favoured were promoted. Of course, McNaughton was right: the army overseas had to provide the bulk of the officers for the senior combatant posts.

Instead of getting a division, Hertzberg went back to RMC, this time as Commandant. He took over from Brigadier Kenneth Stuart, who went to NDHQ as Crerar's right-hand man. The college continued to train cadets until 1942, and before and after that year it ran a variety of staff and training courses for officers, including the Canadian Junior War Staff Course, all of which fell under Hertzberg's responsibility. He gave most of his time to the cadets, who responded to his (and his wife's) concern with affection. As the *R.M.C. Review* wrote of the ceremonies that ended the college's wartime duties as a cadet-training institution: "Under his direction, the closing exercises and the Laying-Up of the Colours in St George's Cathedral, which might have been only heartrending affairs, became heart-uplifting ceremonies, which, all who had the privilege to attend, can never forget."[81] What those ex-cadets from the last wartime graduating class who survived the war still remember is Hertzberg's sentimental and moving address at the closing ceremonies:

> Every corner I turn, every building I enter, every time I set foot on the Square and hear 'Steady Everywhere,' the thought rises, 'The last time.' As it did last Sunday in St. George's [Cathedral] when I turned my head to your gallery. It came to you all this morning when the Battalion marched off with its Colours and left an empty Square. But we are all wrong because none of these is the last time. It is simply a matter of intervals of varying duration — a postponement . . . after the long interval of war, you will all come back in body — or in spirit . . . And the Square shall again be filled with Cadets just as before and then there will be *Recruits* and they will be *running* and may you and I be here to see![82]

Hertzberg, his heart broken by his failure to secure a field command in the war, received only one consolation prize — a visit to the United Kingdom in 1943. That gave him a chance to see his son, Peder, a captain in the PPCLI fated to be killed in action in Italy the next year, and his brother, by then a major-general on the verge of being retired on grounds of age from his post as Chief Engineer of the First Canadian Army. The trip overseas let him meet a host of ex-cadets and, as he wrote his wife: "Strange but all these bloody Ex Cadets seem to like me & mine. I get great receptions from 'em all."[83] It wasn't strange at all, for Hertzberg, even if he had not been an RMC cadet, embodied much that was best in that institution.

If H.F.H. Hertzberg was a professional soldier, Charles Sumner Lund Hertzberg, two years younger, was a militiaman. Like his brother a St Andrew's College and Toronto graduate in engineering, he saw hard service during the Great War in the 7th Field Company of the Royal Canadian Engineers. Like his brother, to whom he was close, he won the Military Cross, but unlike him he was badly wounded near Vimy Ridge in 1917. Invalided home to Canada and declared "permanently unfit any service," he nonetheless finagled his way to Vladivostok with the Canadian Siberian Force in October 1918, where he remained until his return to Canada and subsequent demobilization in June 1919 as a major.[84] While building a large practice as a consulting structural engineer (including the construction of the Canadian Bank of Commerce head office in Toronto),[85] Hertzberg kept up his NPAM connections until 1930, when he went on the Reserve of Officers. On 28 August 1939, perhaps to his surprise, he was asked to "command the Engineers of the Field Force if & when it is provided,"[86] a post he accepted and one that was announced on 1 November. ("Like most Norwegians," the *Toronto Star* gushed, "he likes skiing, open-faced sandwiches and snow storms.")[87] Lieutenant-Colonel Hertzberg reported for duty on 16 November.

Leaving behind his wife Jessie (whom he would not see again) and his two sons, the elder of whom was a cadet at RMC, Hertzberg went overseas with the 1st Canadian Infantry Division in December 1939. His first task in England was to coordinate the acceptance of "the flood of offers of hospitality for the troops at Xmas."[88] Then he designed new-style huts for the troops that were better than the British army's accommodation, built roads and bridges, supervised the training of his field squadrons, and showed, as one of his officers remembered, that he was a "bit of a gadgeteer."[89] Perhaps that was why he got on so well with McNaughton, himself an engineer by training, for as the GOC rose, so did he, becoming successively the division, corps, and army Chief Engineer. It did not hurt that he was close to McNaughton's wife Mabel — "she worships Charles," his brother said in 1943. In fact when Ian, one of the McNaughtons' sons, was killed on RCAF service in 1942, it was Hertzberg who first had to break the news to her and then to the General.[90] In January 1942, when Hertzberg was Chief Engineer of the corps and over age for his brigadier's rank,[91] McNaughton asked the Minister to give him a one-year extension of service because there was "no other suitable officer available to replace Brigadier Hertzberg."[92] The next year, with the age limit for major-generals overseas set at fifty-seven,[93] and with Hertzberg, now Chief Engineer of the army, reaching that age in June ("57 today — damn it," he wrote in his diary),[94] his string ran out. McNaughton, however, argued that because of "this officer's outstanding and most satisfactory service," an appointment should be found for him in Canada where the age limit in static establishments had been fixed at sixty.[95]

In fact, Hertzberg desperately sought another active post overseas and, in September 1943, finally learned that a posting had been arranged for him in India. He was to advise the forces there on airfield construction using a prefabricated bituminous surfacing material that had been developed by Canadian engineers under his supervision and command in England.[96] His brother, in England when this was settled, wrote home: "I am so damn glad for him that he's missed the shelf for a while at least . . . "[97] Major-General Hertzberg arrived in India in October and, despite having had a smallpox vaccination in December 1939, died in January 1944 from haemorragic smallpox.

The Hertzbergs were the only two brothers to hold general officer rank at the same time in the Canadian army. Too old to see action in the Second World War, despite their wish to do so, they made their contributions to the army's wartime development. H.F.H. held RMC together and managed to infuse the speeded-up wartime classes with that institution's ethos. Charles, fortunate enough to get overseas, demonstrated that he was ideally suited for the Canadian army's tasks in Britain though, given his age, he likely would have had difficulty dealing with the demands of the battlefield. Still, he had the trust of McNaughton, he and his men developed new techniques that proved invaluable, and he, like his brother, gave all he could.

ERNEST SANSOM was another officer whose wartime rise and fall came quickly. Born in 1890 in Stanley, New Brunswick, and educated there and in Fredericton, he hoped to go to the Royal Military College but his family could not afford the tuition. Instead, he harvested wheat on the Prairies, surveyed land in the Cariboo district of British Columbia, and, on his return to New Brunswick, joined the militia. By the outbreak of war in 1914 he was a lieutenant, and he went overseas with the first contingent in 1914. He learned about machine guns so well that he was made an instructor, and he did not get to France until August 1916. By the end of the war, now married to Eileen Curzon-Smith, a woman he had met in England, he commanded a machine-gun battalion as a lieutenant-colonel with the Distinguished Service Order. Back in Canada in 1919, he joined the Permanent Force.[98]

A big man, solid, steady, convivial, and blessed with a youthful full face, Sansom rose throughout the interwar period. He attended the British Army Staff College, Camberley, graduating in 1925, and he served his time at National Defence Headquarters and in the military districts. Solid Sansom may have been, but he was not devoid of imagination. He had seen tanks in action during the Great War and when the Chief of the General Staff circulated a paper on the future of armoured vehicles in 1920, Lieutenant-Colonel Sansom of the Machine Gun Corps was enthusiastic about them. Arguing that a separate tank corps should be formed to prevent tanks from simply becoming "mere additional firepower," he saw that this new weapon could "facilitate shock tactics and manoeuvring. He also urged that the Machine Gun Corps was "the logical branch to father the tank in its infancy in Canada," its personnel having the "broad technical expertise and training" necessary.[99] None of those suggestions met favour in the straitened circumstances in which the PF and NPAM operated, however, and Canada began the Second World War with no modern armoured vehicles whatsoever. Sansom by then was a Colonel, the Director of Military Training at NDHQ. When the 1st Canadian Infantry Division was mobilized, he became McNaughton's Assistant Adjutant and Quartermaster-General, in effect the division's senior officer on the administrative side, and he went overseas in December 1939.

He left some problems behind him. His wife had died from complications following tonsilitis in 1927, leaving him with two young daughters. He had married Mary Lucy Waddell, the daughter of a Queen's University professor, in 1930, and they had one daughter. The second Mrs Sansom was a terror, the widow of General F.F. Worthington recalled, one who thought she was the queen and all other officers' wives her subjects.[100] But Sansom doted on his new wife, and she kept a close eye on him. The two eldest daughters were nearly adult in 1939, but the third child was not yet an adolescent. Nonetheless, Sansom's wife desperately wanted to join him in England, and in his letters to Canada, Sansom had to exert all his efforts to discourage her:

3 February 1940: Mrs Walford [wife of Lieut.-Col. A.E. Walford of the division staff] is very keen to come over & he realizing how little she would see of him and all the difficulties of blackout lack of gasoline scarcity of

> accommodation cold houses rationing etc is trying to dissuade her. . . . We would all like to have our wives here but the difficulties are great.

> 11 February 1940: officers are invited to lots of private houses for dinner. . . . The people whose wives are here are seldom invited.

> 1 March 1940: So many foolish wives are coming over which I consider quite wrong unless they are prepared . . . to do war work.[101]

Some officers may have discouraged their wives from coming to Britain so they could resume their freewheeling bachelor style of life; but Sansom, as he put it in his letters home, had only "my virtuous couch" in a room at the division headquarters mess next door to Charles Hertzberg.[102] Sansom had failed to make the best argument to his wife — that it was simply unfair for officers who could afford to bring their spouses to England to do so when virtually none of the other ranks could. After the fall of France, Canadian wives were ordered home, but substantial numbers found some way to remain or made their way back.[103] Sansom's wife, however, remained in Canada.

These familial concerns were secondary to Sansom's job. He worked closely with McNaughton, the GOC, accompanying him to "conference after conference with different groups of people," as he wrote in January 1940.[104] A great admirer of his chief, Sansom listened to McNaughton's troubles "with the Govt. in Canada and the Minister," and he revelled in the belief that "McN. is a real friend to me & takes me fully into his confidence."[105] He watched the interplay of personalities among the division's senior officers, and he formed a harsh view of George Pearkes, then a brigade commander, who "has made himself very unpopular with the other Brigadiers" because he was "out entirely for himself and scores off them whenever the opportunity arises instead of trying to be generally helpful as an experienced Permanent Force officer should."[106] He worried over promotions going to others, and knew his wife would as well. "Don't mind about Harry Crerar being made a Major General," he wrote in late February. "It is only while holding his present appointment" as Senior Combatant Officer at Canadian Military Headquarters, London. "He needed the rank to enable him to deal with the War Office on our behalf."[107] And in March when Pearkes fell seriously ill with meningitis, Sansom took over his brigade. "A commanding job," he said, "is a way ahead of a staff job," but the increase in pay wasn't going to amount to much: "I shall have a lot of entertaining to do to keep up my end with Basil Price & [Armand] Smith [the other two brigade commanders] who do a lot of it."[108] And at a tactical exercise without troops, Sansom's solution to the problem won McNaughton's approval. Brigadier Smith the next night said, "You old son of a gun, you stand there without any sign of nervousness and expound the problem and your solution clearly and concisely and then to cap it all the General ignores my solution and agrees with you!"[109] Matthew Halton of the *Toronto Star* must have heard the same stories, for he reported a few days later that Sansom, described as "all man," had a brain that got cooler as the action got hotter.[110]

Sansom almost had the chance to try out his brain in action in mid April. The German attack on Norway had resulted in the dispatch of British and French troops there. They were being savagely mauled, and McNaughton's division was asked to provide two battalions to join in an attack on Trondheim. Sansom had to organize the preparations and prepare the brigade for the attack and, piped aboard the train by the Seaforth Highlanders band, the force left for Scotland on 18 April. Happily, the plans changed and the assault, almost certain to have been costly and futile, was abandoned. So, too, was Norway within a few weeks.[111] From Sansom's point of view, the importance of this exercise was that he had done well. Although Pearkes returned to take over the brigade on 13 May and Sansom returned to his job at division headquarters, he was marked for promotion. In July, with the war situation totally transformed by the Allied defeat in the Low Countries and France, Sansom went to CMHQ as a brigadier.

That job, that rank, was only briefly held, for in October 1940 McNaughton tapped Sansom to become GOC of the 3rd Canadian Infantry Division, still forming in Canada. The CGS, Harry Crerar, was not pleased, telling the Minister that "Sansom is a good officer but I do not consider that he is so outstanding as to be raised from Colonel to Brigadier to Major General in three months. Incidentally," he added with his usual concern about the PF pecking order, "this will jump him over Page and Stuart," two brigadiers hitherto ahead of Sansom on the PF seniority list.[112] Nonetheless Sansom, then the country's youngest major-general at the age of forty-nine, took command of the division on 26 October 1940 and began its training at Debert, Nova Scotia, and Sussex, New Brunswick. The 3rd Division was the operational reserve for the new Atlantic Command, created in the apprehension over Canadian security caused by the threat that Britain itself might be occupied. By the time the division was ready to proceed overseas in April 1941, Sansom had left it to take over an armoured division, the 1st, which was soon redesignated as the 5th Canadian Armoured Division. In November 1941 he led the division to Britain.[113]

For a year, Sansom commanded his armoured division through the increasingly intensive training exercises the Canadian Corps staged. At one point he had to defuse an "industrial action" staged by unhappy men, many of them miners used to strikes and work stoppages, in the Cape Breton Highlanders, a job he handled skilfully. Picking out the loudest striker, Sansom "turned complaints that the new officers," a group imposed on the Highlanders from another regiment, "were completely chicken shit (regs happy) around." Regulations were necessary, Sansom got the men to concede, "if the Highlanders were to equal the glorious standards set by their forefathers in the old 85th Battalion at Vimy." As author Fred Cederberg wrote, "The snow job hit home ... then he gave everyone the rest of the day off."[114] Even so, Crerar, acting corps commander in April 1942, wrote to a friend that while it would soon be necessary to select a commander for II Canadian Corps, none of the major-generals, in his view, were up to the task, though Sansom and two others, he said, "are all quite effective in their present appointments."[115] McNaughton, however, had a higher opinion of Sansom, and in November 1942 he sought permission to create the new corps headquarters and to put Sansom in command as a lieutenant-general. The army commander listed the appointments Sansom had held, noted that "he is 52 years of age physically fit energetic and has evidenced initiative in all things entrusted to him."[116] How fit he was might have been doubtful, for a journalist reported that he "is just tall enough to carry a well-developed middle section."[117] The appointment was duly approved and came into effect on 15 January 1943.

Sansom's career trajectory had been continuously upward since the beginning of the war, but now his troubles began. In Exercise Spartan, a major test of First Canadian Army in March 1943, his command of his corps was noticeably slow and ham-handed. The comments on the exercise by the Commander-in-Chief Home Forces, General Sir Bernard Paget, were simply devastating: Sansom's corps had advanced slowly and there had been tactical and administrative errors in its handling. There was "lack of practice in command ... much to learn in the handling of armoured formations" and "one disastrous operation by 2 Cdn Corps."[118]

Captain B.H. Liddell Hart, the prominent British military thinker, noted privately that the "execution of [McNaughton's] plan was in remarkably static contrast to the conception," and he attributed this to Sansom's personality: "Shortly after the last war when I was on the brigade staff at Shorncliffe, he came there on attachment, and I got to know him well; he showed an interest in mechanisation that was rare in those days, especially among Canadian officers, but he was distinctly on the solid side in body and mind. Twenty years later he has naturally become more solid. Much as I liked him, I should never have conceived that he would become commander of an armoured corps in mobile warfare."[119] Paget took the same view and urged McNaughton to replace Sansom. But the Canadian GOC-in-C, convinced that his choice of his old friend was a good one and that II Canadian Corps was still a new formation needing time to work up to full efficiency, refused.[120] Paget returned to the matter again on 26 July "and wondered if he could not be replaced under the Age limit. I said no," McNaughton wrote in a memo for file, "and further that Sansom had been administering and building up 2 corps in a satisfactory manner. I said that his tactical efficiency was yet to be tested but that the exercises now in progress . . . would give me some opportunity to form a conclusion."[121]

The forces against Sansom were building quickly now. There were some suggestions that his happy officers' mess was too jovial and that the corps commander drank too much. "Not temperate enough for an officer of high rank," Colonel Ralston was told.[122] Some of his staff officers were dissatisfied, and years later one recalled Sansom having read about an Eighth Army corps commander who travelled with a truck full of telephone cable so he could always stay in touch. Sansom decided to try that and had his Chief Signals Officer put the corps' entire reserve of cable on a truck. But the desert was much more open than built-up Britain and the cable was cut repeatedly. That was minor, however, compared to Sansom's apparent inability to be a competent commander. On one occasion, he asked his operations staff to prepare a plan for a major exercise, was duly presented with a sheaf of paper, and, flipping through it, said it was great. That was all.[123] Another officer was devastatingly blunt in his appraisal: Sansom was "the most incompetent general" in the army, yet another product of McNaughton's inability to choose good people.[124]

At one point, incredibly, one officer in Sansom's mess was asked to get him drunk so he could be fired. The officer refused,[125] of course, but that was symptomatic of the feeling that had built up against II Canadian Corps' GOC. Once McNaughton himself was sacked, Sansom's days were numbered. He might well have known this, but it ceased to matter when he fell ill with incipient bladder cancer in December 1943. Lieutenant-General Kenneth Stuart, acting commander of First Canadian Army, saw Sansom on 5 January and wired to Harry Crerar, commanding I Canadian Corps in Italy and already designated to take over the army, that he "had interview with Sansom today and he should be replaced earliest."[126] Two days later he made clear to Ottawa that Generals Brooke and Montgomery "are equally anxious that Sansom be replaced earliest."[127] More privately, Major-General Price Montague at CMHQ told the Minister of National Defence that "Stuart saw Sansom today and had most satisfactory interview. Matter will be . . . arranged on medical grounds."[128] Behind this, it seems clear, was that General Montgomery, back in England to command the invasion of France in which First Canadian Army troops were at last to get into action, had no confidence in Sansom. As Monty told Vincent Massey, the Canadian High Commissioner, Sansom "had not the qualifications of a corps commander."[129] Sansom formally gave up his corps command to Guy Simonds, fresh from his successes in Sicily and Italy, on 29 January 1944. The battle-tried younger generation had taken command.

This was a hard blow to Sansom. He received no guarantee of future employment in Canada, and Stuart "told him we could not employ him in Canada as a Lieut-Gen but that it might be possible to find employment for him as a Major-General."[130] Sansom returned to Canada in February for treatment and, recovered, was much on McNaughton's mind when he became Minister of National Defence on 1 November 1944. He sacked Stuart as Chief of Staff at CMHQ at once, and the Minister suggested that Sansom might take over. Crerar, horrified at the suggestion given what he knew of Sansom's command in Britain, replied delicately that he doubted whether Sansom was "particularly well equipped in background and recent experiences to deal with senior officers Troopers [the War Office]." The post instead went to General Montague, who had been ensconced at CMHQ since the beginning of the war, an officer in whom Crerar had confidence.[131]

Unfailingly loyal to officers he had selected and promoted and to those who remained loyal to him through his own travails, McNaughton soon brought Sansom back into service. He was to investigate the events on the West Coast where Major-General Pearkes and several of his officers in Pacific Command had been talking to the press about their difficulties in getting home defence conscripts to volunteer for overseas service.[132] Given his task on 23 November, Sansom had not arrived on the coast before the King government reversed course and decided to send 16,000 Zombies overseas. There were soon near-mutinies of conscripts, and for a time the situation was very delicate indeed. Sansom's investigation, characterized by Pearkes as "Star Chamber tactics," led him to meet individually with and secure signed statements from each officer who had talked to the media. As Sansom wrote some years later, "the GOC Pacific Command [Pearkes] in his signed statement accepted responsibility for the actions of all the other officers." Sansom returned to Ottawa on the night of 25–26 November and prepared a report on his findings. When he gave it to McNaughton a few days later, the Minister's response was that Pearkes should be "retired at once without any pension." Sansom dissuaded him from that course; in the heated political atmosphere of the day he knew such action would only make the commander on the West Coast into a martyr.[133] Although Pearkes's actions during the conscription crisis some-times suggested political motives more than the loyalty the military was supposed to owe to the government, he was not fired. Instead, he volun-tarily retired from the army in February 1945 and ran successfully as a Progressive Conservative candidate in British Columbia in the 1945 general election.

Sansom's military service was not yet finished, however. In January 1945 McNaughton named him Inspector-General and charged him with the task of determining the actual availability of reinforcements overseas and their standard of training. His interim report, submitted on 20 March, and his final report, dated 29 March, pronounced both the numbers and training satisfactory.[134] The Minister and the Cabinet War Committee were gratified, especially so after hearing General Sansom on 11 April tell them "he had no recommendations to make for any improvement in the situa-tion as he had seen it."[135] His report effectively brought the conscription crisis to a stop, and the war in Europe ended on 8 May.

Sansom's military career had ended two days before when he was retired on medical grounds. In fact, he speeded his release so he, too, much like George Pearkes, could run as a Progressive Conservative candidate in the coming election. But, unlike Pearkes, Sansom was defeated in York-Sunbury, New Brunswick, and he lost again in a 1947 by-election.* There was some irony in this, for his investigation on the West Coast and his reinforcements report had helped the Liberals weather the conscription storm. As he said later, "There is a tradition in the Service which I have always followed viz. that one must serve our country loyally through the duly elected Government irrespective of the party in power at the time even though one might not agree with Government policy."[136] The contrast with Pearkes was clear, though Sansom's personal loyalty to McNaughton undoubtedly played its part. General Sansom died in 1982 at the age of ninety-one.

THE CANADIAN ARMY in the Second World War was fortunate that it had almost four years before any of its divisions saw sustained action and five years before all were involved. However frustrating that long wait was for the army, the time spent in England allowed the young and able junior officers of September 1939 to master their trade. Those older Great War veterans who held the fort in the early years, while they were certainly incapable of commanding troops in action in the conditions found on a Second World War battlefield, had played an indispensable role. Some of the lessons of the Great War still had validity, and Odlum, the Hertzbergs, Sansom, and others like them could teach these skills to the young men training in Britain and in Canada. Good fortune had been on Canada's side, and McNaughton's "cover crop" had done exactly what he had intended by allowing the young saplings to grow and mature out of the direct heat of the sun.

---

*Generals did not usually fare well as candidates. In addition to Sansom, Major-Generals F.R. Phelan and C. Basil Price ran and lost as Conservative candidates in Montreal, and McNaughton was defeated in a February 1945 Ontario by-election and in the 1945 general election in Saskatchewan. Brooke Claxton, a Liberal minister, wrote later that the Tories "never found out that generally speaking, generals are not political assets; there are a great many more privates than generals among the electorate." NA, Brooke Claxton Papers, vol. 8, Memoirs, 1439.

CHAPTER 3

McNAUGHTON:
THE GOD THAT FAILED

I N APRIL 1940, AS THE BRITISH AND FRENCH sought to rescue Norway from the devastating lightning strike that Hitler had launched against it, one brigade of the 1st Canadian Infantry Division received orders to prepare for a frontal assault on the port of Trondheim. A junior staff officer, Captain J. Desmond B. Smith, told to secure winter kit for 1500 troops, discovered quickly that there was nothing suitable in British army stores. Acting on his own initiative, Smith called Lilywhite's and arranged for this well-known establishment to produce fleecelined jackets, which the company promptly delivered. Fortunately for the lives of the men in the brigade, the War Office called off the operation, the sheepskin coats soon turned up on the backs of girlfriends across the south of England, and eventually the bills arrived on the desk of Major-General A.G.L. McNaughton, General Officer Commanding the division. Smith was summoned before McNaughton, who waved the accounts under his nose and said sternly that if the costs were deducted from his pay, they would take his entire Permanent Force service to be recovered. As Smith blanched, McNaughton's tone changed: "To hell with rules, get it done, that's the kind of young officer we want." The army paid the bills, Smith went to Staff College, and every time thereafter he was promoted McNaughton called him personally: "Is that Major Smith?" "No, Sir, it's Captain Smith." "Well, it's Major Smith now."[1]

That was why men worshipped Andy McNaughton. Without showing off or grandstanding, he had the knack of inspiring enormous affection verging on awe in his private soldiers and his officers alike. As early as January 1940, Beatrice Lillie put on a show for the Canadian troops and, as one officer wrote to his wife, "the G.O.C. got a tremendous ovation when he went up on the stage to thank the cast. He has certainly gained the affection of the troops."[2] In the first year of the war, McNaughton radiated energy and drive, so much so that he stood out in stark contrast with the pink-faced and cherubic British officers with grey records who had suffered defeat on the Continent.[3] In Canada the government's public-relations machinery built the General into a towering figure, and his stern, craggy face was featured everywhere as McNaughton rose from division to corps and finally to army commander.

Not everyone was uncritical. The United States military attaché in Britain, Colonel Raymond E. Lee, wrote in his diary of a visit to Lady Astor's estate at Cliveden in October 1940: "Everyone expressed unbounded admiration of McNaughton but after meeting him a number of times I am inclined to think that he is a trifle overrated. He is a very intense, academic type who never laughs or smiles and I have seen nothing yet to make me think he is as big a name as his admirers would have him be. He is, of course, tremendously energetic but I should say more eminent on the technical than on the command side. I hope that I am wrong and that he is another Stonewall Jackson."[4]

Lee continued to watch McNaughton closely. In May 1941 he said that the Canadian who "a year ago . . . [was] breathing fire and exuding energy like a dynamo, is more subdued. I think he had the idea at the time that he could 'pep up' the British Army and give them a great many new ideas." Those ideas, however, had been coldly viewed.[5] A few months later Lee observed after a meeting that "McNaughton, of course, was full of his devices for improving war. After lunch, he produced a sample of a newly captured German gun."[6] Still, there were widespread suggestions that McNaughton might enter Churchill's War Cabinet. The British Prime Minister in 1942 requested that the Canadian general prepare an appreciation of the possibility of his forces attacking northern Norway and that he fly to Moscow to see Stalin about the operation.[7] McNaughton's mission to Moscow did not take place, however, and the Chief of the Imperial General Staff, General Sir Alan Brooke, grumpily wrote in his diary after the Norway affair that McNaughton "did not rise in my estimation . . . he seemed incapable of telling Winston that an operation was impracticable."[8] The drive, the ideas, the reputation all still seemed to be there, though by 1942 criticisms were beginning to be heard aloud, and McNaughton's interests had become increasingly focused on scientific and technical subjects. Inevitably the human dynamo that was Andy McNaughton had begun to run down, and his meteoric career had hit a snag. It was, ultimately, a question of competence and character.

ANDREW GEORGE LATTA McNAUGHTON was born in Moosomin in the North-West Territories in 1887. His father ran a trading post there, and he and his younger brother grew up on the Prairies. In 1900 he went to Bishop's College School in Lennoxville, Quebec, where he did well; then he entered McGill University to study electrical engineering. Again he performed splendidly, and he took his Master's degree as well, completing his thesis in 1912 and joining the university's teaching staff. His burgeoning career was launched as he gave lectures and presented papers to the Royal Society of Canada and the Canadian Society of Civil Engineers.[9] In 1914 he went into a private engineering practice.

Like many other students in that imperialist age, McNaughton sampled soldiering on the side, in the Bishop's cadet corps and later at McGill, when he took courses intended to lead to a place in the British army; he secured the offer of a commission in the cavalry, but his mother's illness led him to turn it down.[10] Instead, in 1909 he joined the militia and, after just four years' service in those halcyon days before the Great War, he was a major in the 3rd Battery of the Canadian Field Artillery.[11] In a lecture he gave to the McGill contingent of the Canadian Officers Training Corps in 1913, the young Major McNaughton was characteristically firm in his wholly orthodox views: "Artillery," he said, "cannot itself win battles. It is the resolute advance of the Infantry which is alone capable of producing this result. . . . the sole object of [artillery] employment is to render effective assistance to the Infantry."[12]

McNaughton soon had the chance to put his theories to the practical test. He took a battery overseas in 1914 with the first Canadian contingent. Just before leaving, he took another crucial step, marrying Mabel Weir, a tough-minded woman who quickly demonstrated that she had no intention of missing her husband's great adventure. She followed him to

England, where, during his leaves, they started a family that was to number three children by the time the war was over. The leaves included convalescent time, as McNaughton was wounded at Ypres and at Soissons. Unlike many service marriages, the McNaughtons' was strong and enduring; from the beginning the distinction between professional life and home life was more than slightly blurred. "Mrs Andy" was an extension of her husband, who discussed everything with his wife.

By 1916 McNaughton was a lieutenant-colonel, and in 1917 he became Counter-Battery Staff Officer of the Canadian Corps, a post that put him in charge of locating and neutralizing enemy guns. This task was made to order for a scientifically minded soldier, and McNaughton rose to the challenge. At Vimy Ridge, to cite the most famous example, McNaughton's counter-battery fire was said to have eliminated 83 percent of the enemy guns before the Canadian troops left their trenches. By all accounts, he did extraordinarily well in his senior artillery post, working closely with British officers like Lieutenant-Colonel Alan Brooke, who had been posted to the Canadian Corps to provide it with a leavening of professional experience. Just before the armistice, McNaughton was a Brigadier-General in command of the corps' heavy artillery.

McNaughton believed that the concentrated fire of his guns could save Canadian lives, and he took as his maxim "to pay the price of victory, so far as possible, in shells, and not in the lives of men."[13] He was as good as his word, and the Canadian Corps' gunners fired some one-quarter of the shells used by the British Expeditionary Force in the last hundred days of the war.[14] McNaughton had proven himself in action, he had won the Distinguished Service Order, and he certainly merited the comment on his confidential report that he was "an officer of outstanding ability and experience" who had performed his tasks "brilliantly during the latter phase of the war. He has rendered invaluable service."[15]

When McNaughton returned to Canada in 1919, it was only natural that General Sir Arthur Currie should encourage him to remain in the army after the war — the Canadian Corps commander considered McNaughton "an exceptionally able soldier" with "strong common sense, an aggressive mind and an appreciation of the needs of the Service." Currie asked him to stay in the army for two years, which, the General said in 1920, "he has done . . . at great financial sacrifice."[16] McNaughton served on the committee struck to reorganize the militia and then as

Director of Military Training in Ottawa. In 1921 he went to the British Army Staff College, Camberley, where his confidential report was as glowing as any received by a Canadian until Guy Simonds almost two decades later. McNaughton was "an officer of exceptional attainments, with immense powers of concentration, and great strength of character," the Commandant observed with an enthusiasm that was rarely employed in describing dominion officers. "He has good tactical ability, and as a scientific gunner, he is quite outstanding. . . . He expresses himself with conviction. . . . He is tactful, and has a good manner, in which the intenseness of the man is evident. Strong and has a great capacity for hard work."[17]

Perhaps that praise led McNaughton to commit himself to remaining in the Permanent Force. By 1923 he was Deputy Chief of the General Staff. The CGS, Major-General J.H. MacBrien, noted that his deputy was "capable of filling any position, either Staff or Command. Doing splendid work in his present appointment."[18] He was also the "most outstanding" of the army's younger officers, the CGS wrote.[19] In 1927 McNaughton went to London to attend the Imperial Defence College (one of his classmates was his comrade from the Canadian Corps, Alan Brooke), where he again drew glowing praise for his "ability, knowledge, experience & enthusiasm. . . . He has shown himself to be a man of great determination & thoroughness, and an admirable debater. He has certainly left no stone unturned to add to his knowledge of the military problems of the Empire."[20] On his return to Canada, McNaughton took command of Military District No. 11 on the West Coast — he promptly built a swimming pool at Work Point Barracks that was filled and emptied by the tides[21] — almost his first experience since the war of something other than staff work. In 1929 he became Chief of the General Staff at the extraordinarily youthful age of forty-two. His rise had been simply phenomenal in a military force bound up in seniority and red tape, and he had made it to the top on ability alone.[22]

McNaughton appealed to politicians. He even believed in the militia, as every officer had to in this period. The politicians naturally appreciated a general who combined military genius with an understanding of the budgetary problems that dictated a small professional army. Perhaps the smaller the better, for, as McNaughton had written to the CGS in 1923, "To use the regular Army as the basis of expansion to national armies is I think a mistake." However much experience regulars had, "I doubt very much if they would make as much success in a war of the 'Nation in Arms' type" as militiamen, "who, while less qualified technically, nevertheless have in general a wider experience of men and affairs, and are used to getting results from semi-trained personnel. The competition of private life," he said, "is a school for training in initiative through which the regular officer does not pass."[23] At the same time, McNaughton kept a close eye on the best officers of the Permanent Force, men such as Harry Crerar, with whom he had served in France, and he worked hard to keep them in the forces.[24]He also did his best to keep himself up to date in new technologies and military ideas.[25] He was a positive force, a genuine teacher, so much so that General Kenneth Stuart, later one of McNaughton's enemies, recalled that he had learned more in those four years from McNaughton when they had served together on the West Coast than at any other time in his career.[26]

Not every politician or soldier was an admirer of McNaughton's style or ideas. Colonel J.L. Ralston, the Minister of National Defence from 1926 to 1930, resisted McNaughton's attempt to make himself a "super chief of staff," imposing unity and coordination on the Royal Canadian Air Force and the Royal Canadian Navy. For a time, McNaughton contemplated resignation, but the defeat of the Liberals and the arrival in power of R.B. Bennett's Conservatives led him to stay on.[27] Even within the army, McNaughton had his opponents. The military technologies he favoured involved the application of science to warfare, and to some he seemed willing to discount the value of infantry and cavalry.[28] Brigadier-General J. Sutherland Brown, the long-time Director of Military Operations and Intelligence at Ottawa headquarters and then District Officer Commanding in British Columbia, for one, was complaining as early as 1930 that "our Department now seems to be a one man show," by which he meant McNaughton, a man with "a fearful and wonderful brain but sadly lack[ing] human qualities."[29] That was bad enough, but Brown soon convinced himself that McNaughton was also "a vindictive and conceited man. He doesn't like advice and does not ask it and is much annoyed if anyone has differ[ent] views to himself." Moreover, he "is uncouth and slovenly in his makeup . . . and forgets that he is dealing with men, the most of them on a lower mental capacity than himself but general[ly] with more balance and knowledge of men and more business sense."[30] Brown kept up his complaints until McNaughton literally forced him out of the service, and ever after he damned his enemy, somewhat unjustly, as "a super-engineer and college professor."[31]

The difficulty likely was, as Brown surmised, that McNaughton, so much brighter and more able than most ordinary men, forgot to make allowances for human frailty — and Brown, in McNaughton's eyes, was frailer than most. Above all — here Brown was certainly correct — McNaughton had come to believe that modern warfare demanded technically competent officers, men scientifically trained and able to apply their knowledge to solving the problems of the battlefield. The infantry, McNaughton told a journalist in 1931, were still needed to close with the enemy, and the efforts of the other arms aimed to foster this engagement. "Where the change lay . . . would be in the very much larger demands for technically-trained personnel for aviation, engineers, mechanics."[32] In army terms that meant that the engineers and artillerymen, the officers able to use a slide rule with quick intelligence, were the ones he favoured. Inspirational leaders, the officers who could motivate men into assaulting the enemy by sheer force of will power and personality, took second place in McNaughton's mind to the scientifically inclined soldiers.

Still, there could be no doubt of McNaughton's ability. As CGS, he led the army into the Depression, and his fertile brain found ways to get more money for his soldiers. There were no funds for military bases or airfields in the Bennett government budgets, but because there was concern about the radical tendencies among the unemployed men drifting across the country, there might be money if a way could be found to help neutralize that threat. McNaughton devised a scheme to use these men, many of them demoralized veterans of the Great War, to construct military buildings and airfields; in return, they would be housed in camps under the control of the Department of National Defence, paid 20 cents a day, and given their room and board. It was a clever idea — too clever, as it turned out — and the "Royal Twenty-Centers," as the unemployed in the camps were quick to call themselves, became a breeding ground for revolutionaries and soon a focal point of attack on the Conservative government.[33] Even so, a British government observer visiting Canada in December 1934 pronounced McNaughton "a patriot and loyal to the Empire," and also, because of his success in using the unemployed to get funds for National Defence, "a clever opportunist." To Sir Maurice Hankey, McNaughton and his General Staff were "a kind of star of efficiency in a constellation of less efficient Government Departments."[34]

Shooting star, perhaps. In May 1935 the Prime Minister, facing an election and concerned that the CGS was just another of the many lightning rods attracting criticism to his government,[35] offered McNaughton the presidency of the National Research Council in terms that made clear this was not a request. McNaughton wavered and then accepted, but insisted on being seconded from National Defence "as by this means all my contacts with the Militia would not be severed and I had the chance of coming back in emergency if required."[36] His salary was $15,000, a good raise from the $10,000 he had received as CGS, his term seven years.[37] He was much missed at National Defence Headquarters. As Harry Crerar wrote to a friend, "From the defence point of view he is, of course, quite irreplaceable. . . . it is hard for me to see the future without him."[38]

At the National Research Council, McNaughton devoted himself to his scientific pursuits. In the mid 1920s he had developed the idea of the cathode-ray direction finder and patented this forerunner of radar.[39] He had as Deputy Chief of the General Staff and as Chief worked on "Aeroplane Location of Targets for Coast Defence Artillery."[40] Now his interests turned to the development of "a Trajectory Chart for the graphical solution of the gunnery problems of crest clearance and air burst ranging" — a solution to a hitherto difficult problem that worked, despite its complexities for troops in the field.* He also developed automatic sights for coast defence guns in cooperation with an NRC colleague.[41] His reputation remained high, and in the summer of 1939, with the sanction of the Liberal government, McNaughton led a delegation from the Canadian Manufacturers' Association to Britain to seek munitions orders.[42]

As these events suggested, and as he had insisted when he accepted secondment to the National Research Council, McNaughton had kept up his interest in and connections with Canadian defence and the army. One

---

*Brigadier William Ziegler remembered an artillery exercise at Larkhill in England where the gunners were using McNaughton's plotting board. Ziegler, then a junior officer, was leaning over the board when a voice behind him asked what was wrong. "I don't know but if I ever get hold of the SOB who designed this board. . ." It was, of course, McNaughton, who just laughed. Brigadier Ziegler interview, 23 October 1991.

officer remembered McNaughton coming to speak to the Militia Staff Course of 1938 at Connaught Ranges near Ottawa and telling the assembled officers that he was still a serving officer and expected to be in command in the event of war.[43] At the same time he kept watch on the debate on defence in the country. In 1938 he had written privately to congratulate Floyd Chalmers of the *Financial Post* for publishing George Drew's attacks on the Mackenzie King government's half-hearted defence and rearmament policies. He also told Drew that "every word is true, and I do not think you have over-emphasized any point."[44] When he returned to Canada from his Canadian Manufacturers' Association mission at the beginning of September, while the Nazi blitzkrieg was smashing Poland's defences, McNaughton took the earliest opportunity to write to King "to place my services wholly and unreservedly at your disposal."[45]

WHAT CANADA'S MILITARY ROLE IN THE WAR would be was far from clear in September 1939. The government, remembering how the conscription crisis of 1917 had pitted English-Canadians against French Quebec, was desperate to avoid a repetition of the wartime strains that had torn the country apart. If it could have done so, the King government would have preferred to send no army units overseas. Public opinion made such a course impossible, and by mid September the cabinet had decided to raise two divisions, one to proceed overseas at the earliest opportunity. On 22 September, the new Defence Minister, Norman Rogers, told King that he believed the recommendation for GOC of that division would be McNaughton. The Prime Minister was pleased. McNaughton, the scientist, preferred the use of machines in war to the squandering of human life. To King, fearful that heavy casualties would lead to demands for conscription and desperately afraid that this could split the Liberal party into English and French camps, McNaughton was his kind of soldier. "I thought no better man could be selected," King confided to his diary, "certainly not one whose appointment would meet with more general approval though it might meet with some opposition from some of those in our Cabinet who are inclined to be prejudiced against him."[46] Many Liberals still remembered that McNaughton had been close to Bennett, but, in fact, there was no opposition to his appointment.

Instead, the difficulties McNaughton faced in becoming GOC were of his own making. Quite sensibly, he held out for a division complete in all respects when he met with Rogers on 5 October. That concerned a cost-conscious government. Less sensibly, he appeared to threaten the government by telling Rogers that the public "demanded that Canada should be represented by a fighting unit in the line of battle and that public opinion would be satisfied with nothing less and that any Government which did not satisfy this desire would have difficulty remaining in office."[47]

Those unwise words worried the ministers, naturally enough, and the Prime Minister met McNaughton the next day. The most distasteful episodes in the recently published memoirs of Britain's Great War Prime Minister, David Lloyd George, King told the General, were the evidences of civil-military conflict. Obviously, "we wished to avoid anything of the kind," he said, "to have utmost confidence on both sides. The Government would have to decide its policy and take responsibility for it but would, within lines agreed upon, be solidly behind the military authorities." McNaughton won King's agreement to a complete division and, in return, accepted King's statement of the situation. In so doing he became very emotional as he talked about the terrible responsibility a commander faced in being accountable for the lives of his men. "I noticed," King wrote, "that his eyes filled with tears and the right side of his mouth visibly twitched as he spoke of what the responsibility meant."[48]

The events of 5 and 6 October foretold much that would happen in the next four years. McNaughton initially did not seem to have a clear grasp of his position as a military commander subordinate to the civil authority. The government did not seem to appreciate that an incomplete division would be substantially less powerful and less capable of operations than one properly balanced with all its arms and services. McNaughton demonstrated that, while he was properly concerned with the responsibilities he would have to meet, he could become emotional, indeed almost distraught. Certainly King sensed this, and he wrote in December: "I felt a little concern about his being able to see this war through without a breakdown. I felt he was too far on in years to be taking on so great a job."[49] Nonetheless, McNaughton was in command of the 1st Canadian Infantry Division. "The scientist in war, the mathematician in khaki," as journalist Grant Dexter, one of the first to begin the campaign of adulation that would make McNaughton the best-known general in Canadian history, called him, would have his opportunity.[50]

Part soldier, part scientist, part politician — McNaughton seemed the very model of a modern major-general when he led his almost wholly untrained Canadian division overseas in December 1939. The "penetrating force of his glance" made a powerful initial impression on those he met in Canada and England.[51] So did his "red tape be damned" approach. The commanding officer of the Royal Montreal Regiment, unable to draw boots for his unit from Ordnance stores, instead purchased them from Eaton's. Ottawa refused to pay, but McNaughton approved the purchase on the spot, confirming for his officers that the General would always do the sensible thing and thought first of the men.[52] That reputation did McNaughton no harm at all. His staff officer, Colonel Ernest Sansom, wrote privately that at a War Office meeting early in 1940, "McNaughton said he wished to mention a few preliminaries before getting down to the business of the meeting & from then on he dominated the conference & when he finished all agreed that there was nothing more to be said & the meeting ended."[53]

His judgment was more open to question. When he returned from a visit to the Maginot Line, he declared himself "greatly impressed with the morale of the French Army."[54] Of course, others made similar misjudgments in this Phoney War period, but his acumen in treating with the Canadian government was similarly suspect. In February he alarmed Ottawa by hinting at the formation of a Canadian corps overseas. The Cabinet War Committee responded that "except in the event of some unforeseen emergency, no further offers or commitments should be made with regard to Military forces," at least not until after the coming general election.[55] McNaughton took this early rebuff badly, and there were more to come. Sansom noted that the GOC was "tired out" but could not get away because "a disturbing cable" from Ottawa demanded his attention. In March the GOC finally got away for a rest; "I hope it does him a world of good," Sansom wrote.[56] Physically restored, McNaughton promptly fell victim to another fit of enthusiasm. When the War Office requested a Canadian brigade for Norway in April, McNaughton enthusiastically agreed — without first clearing matters with Ottawa. The British were delighted: "Andy played up magnificently, took responsibility of accepting," wrote Major-General Richard Dewing, the Director of Military Operations, in his diary. "Came up to the W.O. that afternoon . . . and got right down to working out all details."[57] Faced with a fait accompli, the government agreed to the commitment, but added sharply: "We feel that when consultations commenced intimation should have at once been given . . . to afford Canadian Government reasonable opportunity to pass on a disposition of such importance."[58] McNaughton promptly lapsed into a bout of depression, grousing to the faithful Sansom "all about the troubles he has had with the Govt. in Canada."[59]

A pattern had already taken shape. McNaughton's role as commander would be full of troubles, almost all self-created; others would be fixed with the blame. In the spring of 1940, however, in the midst of the disaster that befell Allied armies in France and the Low Countries, McNaughton's personal problems were minor indeed. The War Office sent McNaughton to France on 23 May to make an assessment of the situation and to determine if his division could help at Calais or Dunkirk. Before he left, he took the opportunity to tell his officers that when the Canadians got to France, this would be "our opportunity to show the stuff we are made of, it's going to be a sticky business, you must be absolutely ruthless. . . . tell the men we are not particularly interested in prisoners."[60] On his return the next day, his optimism having given way to depression as he saw the hopelessness of the military situation, he confidentially advised Vincent Massey, the Canadian High Commissioner, that "there is no use in attempting to deal with the German thrusts separately for that is what they want — they would like to defeat us piece-meal, but . . . we should conserve our resources, and cope with them by well concerted, fundamentally planned movements. I hope that that is what is being done," Massey added.[61]

It wasn't, and although the War Office on 27 May told McNaughton that any commitment of the Canadian division "would be throwing good material into a quicksand which is already engulfing too much,"[62] ten days later the Canadians were on their way to France as part of a new British Expeditionary Force under General Alan Brooke. McNaughton this time told his senior officers that the "enemy is inferior to us in initiative and will to fight."[63] This was what everyone, including McNaughton, had to try to believe, but it was something they all must have known was manifestly untrue. The Canadians landed at Brest, entrained and moved inland, then promptly returned to the coast and to safety, leaving much of their equipment behind.[64] The bitter joke among the troops, spoiling for a fight, was that the initials of the Canadian Active Service Force, the CASF, stood in truth for "Canadians Almost Saw France"; others called it "the Big Bust of Brest." The division, however, was now the best-armed and best-equipped in Britain as it awaited the Nazi invasion.

At the request of the Chief of the Imperial General Staff, McNaughton soon had command of VII Corps, a mixed formation composed of the Canadian division, a British formation, and New Zealand troops, and he was duly promoted to lieutenant-general.[65] The promotion and the added responsibility played well in Canada, which, weak as it was, was now Britain's ranking ally. McNaughton's doings dominated the press.[66] He read his clippings and found them plausible if not, indeed, convincing. Others struck up the tune: "every officer and everyone in the ranks of the Corps worship him and trust him implicitly," one officer told the Empire Club in Toronto.[67] That was not entirely true, but, riding high, McNaughton bluntly told the Minister of National Defence that his friend and protégé Harry Crerar, hitherto Senior Combatant Officer at Canadian Military Headquarters in London, should be Chief of the General Staff in Ottawa. McNaughton got his way, and Crerar clearly understood his role: "I hate going back," he wrote McNaughton. "The only argument which permits me some peace of mind is that you believe, and I sometimes think, that I can do more for the CASF at the Ottawa end than I can in the theatre of operations."[68] In effect, McNaughton, and not National Defence Headquarters, had taken control of the army's war effort.*

For the next three-and-a-half years, McNaughton and his Canadians would be based in England. His 1st Canadian Infantry Division was joined by the 2nd in late 1940, by the 3rd in 1941, and by two armoured divisions, the 4th and 5th in 1942 and late 1941, respectively. The Canadian Corps, labelled as such in late 1940 with the arrival of the 2nd

---

*Lieutenant-General Guy Simonds later wrote that this was "one of the basic faults in the whole of our conduct of Army policy during the war . . . From the very earliest beginning in 1939, the commander in the field was dictating policies to Ottawa which properly should have been made at Army Headquarters . . . there was hardly ever at Army Headquarters an influence strong enough to say to the commander in the field 'this is what you are going to get and get on with your job.'" NA, E.L.M. Burns Papers, vol. 2a, "The bodies" file, Simonds to Burns, 30 December 1953.

Division, was followed by the formation of the First Canadian Army in April 1942. With two corps in the field, one under Crerar, brought over to Britain at the end of 1941, and the other, initially led by Lieutenant-General Sansom, McNaughton commanded a powerful and balanced force of five divisions as well as ancillary units, including two additional armoured brigades.

McNaughton never forgot that he was more than a mere military commander. From his headquarters at Headly Court, Leatherhead, he was the senior Canadian officer overseas, the de facto representative of Canada in Britain.[69] His forces served with and under British command, but McNaughton could not simply be ordered by a senior British officer to do this or that; if he disagreed with the feasibility of an operation he, like Sir Arthur Currie a quarter-century before, could refer the matter to his home government. This was a real, not a theoretical power, and McNaughton treated it as such. His forces had to serve under Canadian command, and he, as the senior commander, was obliged to seek approval from and be directly responsible to Ottawa for their operational employment.

McNaughton held this view as an article of faith, and it frequently pitted him against the British, who almost openly longed for the easy, bygone colonial era when dominion troops did what they were told. Exercise Victor, one of the multitude of exercises mounted by the Home Forces in Britain, tested the defences of England in January 1941, and it involved the Canadian Corps. During the course of Victor, the 1st Canadian Infantry Division was temporarily put under British command, and at one point was divided up between four or five different British commanders. McNaughton believed, as did all Canadian soldiers, that Canadian troops fought best together and under their own leaders. The situation that had resulted was, he told Major Charles Stacey, the historical officer at Canadian Military Headquarters, "a grave 'constitutional crisis,'" for it raised "his own responsibility to the Government and people of Canada for the proper handling of the troops entrusted to his command." Moreover, "it was problems of defence and military cooperation that supplied the 'acid test' of sovereignty — the test of its reality."[70]

True enough, but there was a war on. It fell to McNaughton to make satisfactory arrangements with General Sir Alan Brooke, the Commander-in-Chief Home Forces, and his old comrade-in-arms.[71] Brooke knew

McNaughton well, but knowing him did not necessarily mean "respect" or "like." Brooke admired Canadians and appreciated their value as fighting soldiers. The fuss over Exercise Victor, however, stimulated doubts in his mind about Andy McNaughton. It was obvious from Brooke's diary that misgivings about the Canadian general were no novelty. He wrote that McNaughton had come to see him to complain that the dispersion of the 1st Canadian Division "was not in accordance with the charter governing the employment of the Canadian Corps!" He added later that this was an "example of MacNaughton's [sic] warped outlook concerning the sanctity of this charter. He had not sufficient strategic vision to realise that under conditions of extreme urgency no charter could be allowed to impede the employment of troops." McNaughton, he added, "loved to surround the employment of his Corps with a network of 'Conventions,' 'Charters' and 'Constitution' which would have rendered the employment of Canadian troops even more difficult than that of Allies."[72] Brooke's scorn, almost always confined to his diary or to conversations with his intimates, was probably justified on military grounds, even if Victor was simply an exercise. But his suggestion that Canadians were not *Allies* was insupportable. To Brooke, who was certainly intelligent enough and well enough versed in the legal situation to know better, McNaughton's men were presumably nothing so much as British colonial forces to be disposed of as the War Office wished, but that was something that no Canadian could have accepted. The battle for military autonomy had been fought and won during the Great War, and McNaughton, not Brooke, had history on his side.

Constitutional niceties apart, Brooke had a serious point: McNaughton's professional performance since coming to England in December 1939 was not what it should have been. The effects were all too obvious, Brooke believed. In April 1941 he recorded he was "depressed at the standard of training and efficiency of Canadian Divisional and Brigade Commanders. A great pity to see such excellent material as the Canadian men controlled by such indifferent commanders." He said the same thing in June, and he later put the blame for this situation squarely on McNaughton, who, he maintained, "could not see the deficiency in training and was no judge of the qualities required by a Commander." Brooke added that McNaughton "had not got the required qualities to make a success of commanding a Corps. A man of exceptional abilities where scientific matters were concerned, but lacking the required qualities of command. He did not know his subordinate commanders properly and was lacking in tactical outlook."[73] Brooke's views were clear and definite and, because he became Chief of the Imperial General Staff before the end of 1941, very important.

Was he correct in his strictures about McNaughton's control of his corps' training? Was he right in assessing McNaughton's choice of division and brigade commanders? The short answer on training was yes, though on the surface this should not have been so. The Canadians in Britain went through exercise after exercise, testing the role of the battalion in defence, the brigade in attack, the division in advance or on river crossings. The exercises were unrealistic as such exercises always were, and, while they practised commanders and troops in their roles, some questions might be raised as to how effective they were. E.L.M. Burns, the Brigadier General Staff at Canadian Corps headquarters in May 1941, explained to Crerar, the CGS in Ottawa, that the troops were in good spirits though "bored with make-believe exercises." McNaughton and his staff, he added, were "pretty satisfied with the way in which the troops can be moved across the country at any rate." Unfortunately, Burns said, "I am not sure myself what would happen after they had completed their bus move." Two months later he returned to the same subject: "It is becoming increasingly difficult to get the men in the ranks to really take an interest in these exercises."[74] Half a year on, Burns's successor as BGS, Brigadier Guy Simonds, was more critical still, telling one of General Bernard Montgomery's staff officers that he was worried about the Canadian Corps' training. The problems, Simonds said, ran through all officer ranks, with the greatest weaknesses at the battalion and brigade commander level. Simonds said very few battalion commanders were capable of fighting their regiments and that only four out of nine brigadiers could train their battalion commanders.[75] Montgomery, his new broom sweeping clean throughout South-Eastern Command, set to with a will to rectify matters.

"God Almonty," as the troops came to call Montgomery, soon had the opportunity to act, for McNaughton, again showing signs of nervous strain, fell ill and went on sick leave.[76] He would not be back at the helm of First Canadian Army until March 1942. In acting command from December was Lieutenant-General Crerar, who said later that "McNaughton had sadly neglected training," leaving the "situation in a 'hell of a state' when he came to take over from Canada."[77] Crerar claimed to be "delighted," or so the CIGS said,[78] when Monty imposed systematic training on the corps and undertook to assess virtually every officer and senior NCO in some of his divisions. The results were impressive on the training front, as extraordinarily rigorous and realistic exercises — "Tiger" is still recalled as gruelling by many participants — upgraded the corps' fighting abilities.

Monty's devastating comments on many of the division, brigade, and battalion commanders he observed forced sweeping changes on the corps. Major-Generals C. Basil Price and George Pearkes and Brigadiers Potts and Ganong were replaced or returned to posts in Canada, while heads rolled among the battalion commanders.[79] Though McNaughton on his return expressed himself deeply obliged for Montgomery's frank assessments,[80] Monty believed he detected "very curious repercussions in that I have to proceed very carefully and to be very tactfull [sic] — there is considerable jealousy in a certain quarter," that is to say, McNaughton. Still, he added in a letter in June 1942, the corps "is now beginning to become known as a good Corps (after 2 1/2 years)."[81] Montgomery exaggerated slightly — the corps as such had existed for substantially less than thirty months; his point, nonetheless, was correct.

McNaughton was not wholly to blame for the problems. His divisions had been given defensive tasks that inhibited training, and he had to work with what he was given. The tiny Permanent Force had few generals in its ranks ready to step into senior posts, and the militia officers, after years of tight budgets and inadequate training, were blessed more with spirit than expertise. Nonetheless, Montgomery's parenthetical time estimate was fatal. Thirty months is a long time in war, and at the very least McNaughton might have been more vigorous in training the younger and the more able. McNaughton had spotted many of the comers like Guy Simonds, Charles Foulkes, D.C. Spry, and Bruce Matthews. He had given them progressively more responsibility, but the senior officers were weak and they remained so for months to come. Captain B.H. Liddell Hart recorded a conversation with one British general, Sir Frederick Pile, who thought that McNaughton was a man "of first class ability and real vision," but that most of his divisional commanders were "duds."[82] Unfortunately that was all too true.

The cause of the difficulty was twofold. McNaughton had something of a Highland chief about him, and he saw people as either loyal to him or not.[83] He valued loyalty above all other virtues, and those officers he had picked in the fall of 1939 and who had worked with him on building up an army from raw and untrained levies were his friends and allies. As an assessment of McNaughton given to the Defence Minister, Colonel Ralston, in mid 1943 noted quite shrewdly: "Has chosen several very capable men but on the whole has surrounded himself with men of average ability. Does not brook opposition easily, resulting in 'yes men' having more influence than they should. Has strong prejudices and plays favourites, this being particularly noticeable in his choice of men from the Permanent Force, the 1st Division or the artillery."[84] It was hard for McNaughton to come to the realization that some of the officers he had selected were not up to the standards needed; when he did, or when this realization was forced upon him, all too often the officers were kicked upstairs — "a vicious practice," General Guy Simonds reflected, "which had grave disadvantages later."[85] All this was destructive of the fighting efficiency of the army, though where McNaughton could have found more able replacements in the early years of the war was unclear.

More seriously, McNaughton had grown increasingly distant from his army, which scarcely saw him.[86] Worse yet, he simply paid little attention to the process of training his divisions for battle. Training was the task of his staff officers, of his division commanders, and McNaughton, Simonds recalled, "would not focus his mind on training and operational problems, and for a long time we were adrift."[87] Another officer said much the same thing: "We never saw much evidence that he could come to a Corps Study period and say all the things he should about why we were there to study and what we were to study — he never showed much interest in how the corps should function and its place in the scheme of things. . . . He was always so busy thinking in technical and political terms and defending the interests of the Army at large. I find it hard to picture him being as steady as a Field Commander should be."[88]

The GOC saw as one of his main tasks the development of weapons and equipment for his army. Officers still remember McNaughton under a truck checking the transmission or in his office with a machine gun stripped down on a table and his hands covered with grease. This interest was human, it probably led to better weapons for his men, and it may even have saved lives — but it was not McNaughton's job. As one officer said, "McNaughton wasn't interested in war, only in the instruments of war."[89] A British journalist caught the spirit of McNaughton's headquarters in September 1942 when he wrote: "There is an awful predominance of engineers in his mess, and a guest feels obliged to be interested in gadgets."[90] This emphasis impressed many observers — American journalistic pundit Walter Lippmann thought the Canadian's "special gifts in connection with the relation of the design and manufacture of weapons to their use" could be very helpful in Washington.[91] However, McNaughton's obsession with scientific developments and the political side of his job, coupled with his aversion to training and his reluctance to think about operations, frightened many more who wondered if he was capable of commanding an army in the field. His headquarters, one senior officer recalled, was like a War Office in the country, not an operational headquarters.[92]

Brooke showed he was aware of this problem when he suggested to McNaughton in January 1942 that the Canadian force was now too big to be handled by one corps commander. "I feel that you require a Force or Army Headquarters which will take over the running of all the war services, workshops, base organization, etc., and thus free the Corps Commander's hands for the job of commanding & training the fighting formations. That in itself is a full-time job."[93] So it was, but it was not a job McNaughton wanted to do. The problem persisted and, eighteen months later, Crerar told the Minister of National Defence that it was impossible for McNaughton "effectively to do so many jobs — command, research and development, Undersecretary for war (political functions), and S.C.O. [Senior Canadian Officer]."[94] That the Canadian, whose title of GOC-in-C now reflected his status as an army commander, was often ill and almost always hypertense was a reflection of the strain his workload put on him. The death in action in June 1942 of his son, Ian, an RCAF squadron leader, added the terrible burden of grief to his days and nights.

Spartan, the great exercise in March 1943 designed "to study the problems arising in an advance from an established bridgehead," was the point at which all the concerns about McNaughton came to the fore. Running for two weeks from the beginning of March and pitting McNaughton's army of two corps and a third British corps against a "German" army of two corps, Spartan involved more than a quarter-million men and 72,000 vehicles across a large area of southern England. There was even a newspaper, *The Advance Post*, for the troops, the "first daily newspaper of its kind to be printed specially for the purpose of a military exercise in this country."[95] The CIGS, General Brooke, wrote in his diary that he had "started by motoring to Godalming to see Andy MacNaughton [sic] commanding Canadian Army, and proving my worst fears as true, that he is quite incompetent to command an Army! He does not know how to begin to cope with the job and he was tying his force up into the most awful muddle!" What had most upset Brooke was seeing McNaughton, engrossed in a bridging problem, order II Canadian Corps to move across I Canadian Corps' lines of communications — in battle an almost certain recipe for disaster. Brooke said bluntly: "I felt that I could not accept the responsibility of allowing the Canadian Army to go into action under his orders."[96] The official report on Exercise Spartan, prepared by General Sir Bernard Paget, the Commander-in-Chief Home Forces, was also critical of McNaughton's dilatory tactics, weak handling of operations, and what he called "a lack of confidence [which] resulted in missed opportunities, delayed decisions, changes of orders and frequent and conflicting short moves of units and formations."[97]

For his part, McNaughton professed himself not greatly concerned with the criticism of his part in Spartan. Exercises were to train officers and men, mistakes were to be expected, and so long as everyone learned from them, nothing was lost. The strictures on II Canadian Corps, a new formation functioning only since the beginning of 1943, in particular, concerned him not at all. Guy Simonds, newly promoted to major-general, looked at the Spartan report at McNaughton's request, however, and told him that while it was not always accurate on the facts, "the main conclusions indicating weaknesses in organization and training are substantiated by events during the exercise, and that is the important issue."[98] Simonds left out the army commander's ability to lead his army as, in the circumstances, he had to do. McNaughton's British and Canadian superiors, however, could not omit this criticism from their calculations. After Spartan, Andy McNaughton's fate was effectively sealed. All that was needed now was the right moment to depose him from his command.

IN ADDITION TO COMMANDING HIS MEN, McNaughton's task was to deal with politico-military questions between Ottawa and London, to press the government in Canada for the units and formations he needed to build his division into a corps and his corps into an army, and to ensure that the War Office did not push his troops piecemeal into operations for which they were unready, unsuited, or ill-equipped. The First Canadian Army was to be a dagger pointed at the heart of Berlin, and if McNaughton had his way it would be kept together until the invasion of Europe.[99] The CIGS noted that McNaughton "always informed me that the Canadian Government was strongly opposed to the use of Canadian Divisions detached from the force as a whole," but this made it difficult to find a role for the army: it was "too large," Brooke said, "to embody easily in the formations we have in the field."[100] McNaughton remained firm in his view, however. As he wired to the Chief of the General Staff, Lieutenant-General Ken Stuart, at the end of March 1943: "I do not recommend that we should press for employment merely to satisfy a desire for activity or for representation in particular theatres however much I myself and all here may desire this from our own narrow point of view."[101]

Against this understandable concern that Canadian strength not be frittered away and dispersed, other factors had to be set. One was the perceived popular desire to see Canadian troops in action. The Canadian Corps in the Great War had made a formidable reputation for itself — and for Canada — and the people at home appeared to expect something similar to emerge from this war. So did the soldiers and the politicians. Crerar, then CGS in Ottawa, told McNaughton in May 1941: "Although the public here realize the vitally important role the Canadian Corps is playing in the United Kingdom, there is a not unnatural desire to see the Canadians in the headlines these days by some demonstration of their fighting abilities."[102] This was a political fact of life and, however concerned King was about casualties and the fear they might force conscription on his government and country, he had to react to his people's craving for action and success. The defeats at Hong Kong in December 1941 and Dieppe in August 1942 had thus far been the only battles for Canada's army; Canada — including its soldiers — wanted another taste of battle, and the Canadian cabinet concerned itself with this problem from the spring of 1941. The Prime Minister bemoaned the desire of his colleagues to put men into action in order to encourage recruiting: "I do not feel that any government has the right to take the lives of any men for spectacular purposes," he wrote in his diary.[103] But that pressure was there and growing, and the Dieppe raid might well be considered one result of it.

The other key factor was that battle was the great test, the forge on which leaders and soldiers were made. The boredom of exercises in England prepared troops — up to a point; the rigours of the battle-drill training adopted by the Canadian army taught men how to react in action — up to a point. But only through combat could theories be tested and leadership proven. The British army, and especially General Montgomery — whose reputation stood sky high after his defeat of Rommel and the Afrika Korps — were convinced of this fact. As Monty wrote to a British officer, "we want all the Corps in England to be commanded by generals from the active front so that we get good battle experience in to the Army in England."[104] Montgomery, Stacey argued, "made a fetish of battle experience as a qualification for command, exalting it even beyond its very real importance."[105] Still, no Canadian officer, neither McNaughton nor any of his possible successors, could be truly tested and accepted until he was proven in operations. And to the British, no Canadian officer — with the one exception of Guy Simonds — was ever accepted as the equal of a British commander even with that battle experience.

McNaughton understood that the British tended to look down on Canadian command abilities. He failed to realize the weight of these other factors, however, as he struggled to keep his army together in the face of Ottawa's desire to see Canadian troops get into action to appease the public's yearning for heroes and the War Office's concerns about him as a commander and how best to use the First Canadian Army in action. This story has been fully told before and from different points of view,[106] and there is little point in rehearsing it here in detail. All that need be said is that the Canadian government in April 1943 prevailed upon Britain to allow Canada to participate in the Sicilian campaign with the 1st Canadian Infantry Division and a tank brigade;[107] some months later, the Canadians continued on in Italy with a force that eventually comprised I Canadian Corps, consisting of the 1st Infantry Division, the armoured brigade, and the 5th Canadian Armoured Division.[108] McNaughton had agreed to participation in the Sicilian operation if the 1st Division returned to Britain thereafter;[109] he objected to the dispatch of I Canadian Corps, which left his First Canadian Army with only one corps and hence with its existence in doubt.[110] He said he was prepared to resign if this policy were carried out. McNaughton knew that, as the Governor General in Ottawa wrote privately to Prime Minister Churchill, he had become an "idol in the eyes of his countrymen."[111] His threat was likely calculated on the assumption that his position was so strong in Canada that the government would not dare to proceed against him.

The difficulties McNaughton was raising over the employment of his army now combined with the concerns raised by Exercise Spartan. In June 1943 General Brooke, Chief of the Imperial General Staff, dropped a comment at the White House in Washington to General Stuart, the CGS, that suggested some concern about McNaughton's command capacities.[112] From that point on events accelerated, as these extracts from Brooke's diary make clear:

18 June 1943: Crerar "came to dinner in the evening. . . . He is very unhappy about Andy MacNaughton [sic] who is . . . undoubtedly quite unsuitable to command an Army. I only wish I could find some job I could remove him to but that is not easy."

5 July 1943: Stuart "came to see me. Apparently he realizes MacNaughton [sic] is unsuitable to command the Canadian Army! We discussed possible ways of eliminating him; not an easy job! Best solution is to split Canadian forces between the Mediterranean and European theatres but this is easier said than done!"[113]

3 August 1943: Ralston "came to see me and remained nearly two hours discussing how we are to get rid of MacNaughton as an Army commander. No easy problem."[114]

Between Brooke's diary entries of 5 July and 3 August, the CIGS sat next to Vincent Massey, the Canadian High Commissioner and no admirer of McNaughton, at a dinner. The talk turned to Harry Crerar, whom Brooke described as a better corps commander than McNaughton, and then the floodgates opened. McNaughton's performance on Spartan was denounced by Brooke, and Massey chipped in with an assault on McNaughton's views on the employment of the army. Brooke indicated that he felt "nervous" about entrusting troops to McNaughton's command, and Massey, knowing that Colonel Ralston was coming to Britain, suggested that Brooke and the Defence Minister should talk confidentially about the McNaughton problem. Brooke asked whether it would be all right for him to have this conversation, and Massey replied that "the importance of the question is so great that . . . he would be justified in taking it up very personally and informally."[115] The route to that 3 August conversation between Brooke and Ralston had been pointed.

As all this suggested, McNaughton was in substantial difficulty with the CIGS, with one of his corps commanders, Crerar, with the High Commissioner, and with his Minister and the CGS. On 10 July Ralston had also expressed his doubts — and those of the British — to Prime Minister Mackenzie King.[116]And when the Minister and General Stuart in early August explored the possibilities for the dispatch of the remainder of I Canadian Corps to Italy, McNaughton was furious. As King put it in his diary, "McNaughton had said: 'The die is cast' to Ralston, and said: it is clear from the conversations you have been having, you do not care anything about the Canadian army."[117] For his part, Stuart was frank in what he told the Prime Minister: "Paget and Brooke did not have confidence in him for continental operations. They both were very close friends of his and neither wished to say anything, but it was the question of the lives of the men which was at stake and no feelings could be allowed to stand in the way."[118] At Quebec City for the meeting between Churchill and President Roosevelt and the Combined Chiefs of Staff, Brooke also told King that McNaughton "seemed to have become more suited for planning and research than for action in the field. . . . Full of inventive genius but interested in study."[119] Study of military technology, in Brooke's view, was not the major requirement of good generalship.

Brooke's feelings against McNaughton had been exacerbated by the Canadian's attempt to get to Sicily to see the 1st Canadian Division in its first actions there. Although the visit had been arranged by the War Office,[120] General Montgomery, the Eighth Army commander, refused to permit McNaughton to set foot in Sicily, and his superior, General Sir Harold Alexander, backed up Monty, adding that McNaughton was "rather snotty" about the rebuff.[121] To the CIGS, Alexander explained that Montgomery wanted no visitors at all for the moment, adding that "these incidents are very upsetting when we are trying to win battles." In fact, Alexander added, Montgomery had said that Major-General Simonds, commander of 1st Canadian Division in his and its first battle, "had urgently requested that this visit be delayed." In his memoirs Montgomery was even more explicit: "For God's sake keep him away," Simonds begged.[122] Brooke offered Alexander his "heartfelt sympathy," but did point to the need to meet "Canadian susceptibilities." Later, after ninety minutes with McNaughton, who was "livid with rage," he told Alexander that McNaughton was going to protest to his government "in terms which will suggest his constitutional rights have been ignored."[123] Brooke, whose job in any case required exceptional patience, distributed the blame for this fiasco: Montgomery for trying to stop McNaughton's visit for no valid reason; Alexander for lacking the strength of character to sit on Montgomery; and, above all, McNaughton for his "ultra political outlook to always look for some slight." Later, Brooke added that McNaughton was "devoid of any form of strategic outlook, and would sooner have risked losing the war than agreed to splitting the Canadian forces. The move of one of his Divisions to the Mediterranean had not been achieved without employing considerable pressure from Canada on him, it was therefore doubly unfortunate that through Monty's foolishness he had been prevented from visiting the Canadian Division!"[124]

Word of the Commonwealth spat reached the Americans, who were, characteristically, both puzzled and gratified by the story. Captain Harry Butcher on General Eisenhower's staff wondered "how in the hell the British had ever succeeded in holding together an empire when they treat the respected military representative of its most important Commonwealth [country] so rudely." In an almost bemused way, Butcher quoted Alexander as saying that if McNaughton had been a junior officer "he would have placed him under arrest."[125]

In the light of this growing disenchantment with McNaughton, the crisis when it came was almost anticlimactic. In late September 1943 Brooke for the first time sounded as if he and the Canadians had found a way out: McNaughton "is a source of serious anxiety to me, but think I have now got his case settled."[126] Five weeks later, Ralston and Stuart came to Britain determined to force the issue with the commander of First Canadian Army. When the three met on 5 November for an acrimonious discussion on the events that had led to the breakup of the army, Ralston told McNaughton that "the question of command of the Canadian Army" had been discussed with the CIGS in the summer and that Brooke had said the commander and some of the army staff required battle experience. Had Brooke or Paget discussed this with him? Ralston asked McNaughton. Not directly, McNaughton said, apparently oblivious to the situation he faced, but he was sure that the two British officers would be agreeable to having him in command. The meeting ended there, and the next day Ralston and Stuart saw Sir Alan Brooke. "The Minister asked whether he was willing to entrust" command of the army to McNaughton. "The C.I.G.S. said that he had not changed his view, . . . [that] he was bound to say that he could not truthfully answer in the affirmative."[127] A meeting with General Paget on 8 November confirmed the British attitude: Paget said McNaughton "was not suited to command an army in the field" because he could not stand the physical strain and was temperamentally unfit for such a post.[128] Ralston and Stuart again met McNaughton later that day. The Minister "told McNaughton that he would remain in command of First Canadian Army, but this did not mean he would command it in action. Both the C.I.G.S. and Paget had stated that a change in command would be necessary before the Army went into action." McNaughton was calm but said he wanted to see the British officers.[129] The General's demeanour impressed Ralston, and he told Vincent Massey that "it was the most unpleasant task he had had to perform since taking on his present post. McN., he said, took it as a soldier."[130]

The calm lasted only two days. As Sir Alan Brooke encapsulated it accurately enough in his diary, Ralston "had informed MacNaughton [sic] that neither I nor Paget had confidence in him as an Army Commander in Action. MacNaughton [sic] had been to see Paget, and on the strength of his interview . . . had wired to Mackenzie King that Rolston [sic] and Stuart had framed up a case against him which was in no way supported by Paget, and had given a completely erroneous interpretation of his interview with Paget. It rather looks as if MacNaughton is going off his head!"[131]

For the next month, there was an extraordinary flurry of telegrams between McNaughton and Ottawa and Ralston and Ottawa and a series of hasty meetings, negotiations, and secret conversations. It was almost as if McNaughton had been monarch of an independent nation-state, rather than a soldier at the disposal of his government, so delicately were events handled. The key player was Mackenzie King, a man who liked McNaughton because of his opposition to conscription,[132] and one who did not greatly care for Ralston because of his past support for compulsory service. In the final analysis, however, King backed his Defence Minister, as he had to, and McNaughton, whose health had completely buckled under the strain, was out. The public was told nothing of the behind-the-scenes struggles, only that the General's ill-health made his retirement necessary.[133]

What now for the army in England? The British would have preferred to break up the First Canadian Army or, if that could not be done, to put it under a British officer. Those options were unacceptable to Ralston, who could see the dreadful domestic political problems such moves would surely create.[134] Instead, to replace McNaughton temporarily, General Stuart became acting army commander, but the post was destined for Harry Crerar, then in Italy getting some battle experience in command of I Canadian Corps. Crerar was both Stuart's and McNaughton's choice, as well as the officer greatly preferred by Brooke and Paget. McNaughton convinced himself that Ralston and Stuart had told the British generals he no longer had their confidence and that this had amounted to a "stabbing in the back." At the same time, contradictorily, he believed that his relief from command had been orchestrated by the British because of their resentment of his stout Canadianism.[135]

On the day he was fired as he rode in his automobile with Brigadier Elliot Rodger, formerly one of his personal assistants, beside him, McNaughton said, "I hope there won't be mutiny in the army, Elliot."[136] That was the saddest comment of the whole crisis. Not only was there no uprising of the troops, but McNaughton's ouster caused scarcely a ripple. The General, however much he had been admired by the men of the 1st Canadian Infantry Division he had brought to England in December 1939, however warm the human relationship he had once had with the soldiers under his command, had long since ceased to be a presence to the men of First Canadian Army. Absorbed in his battles with the British and with Ottawa, fixated on his search for better equipment and weapons, McNaughton had lost touch with the men he had once led. Now as the prospect of action at last neared, that command would be exercised by someone else.

A ndy McNaughton did not plan to go quietly into the dark night of retirement. True to his Highland heritage, he was plotting revenge on those who had done him in even before he left England. He took the opportunity of a courtesy call by Lord Cranborne, the Secretary of State for Dominion Affairs, to denounce Allied policy, General Montgomery, and all and sundry at home, promising to "add some scalps to his belt when he got back to Canada." Cranborne was stunned and felt obliged to warn General Brooke that McNaughton "was preparing to do a lot of harm on his return to Canada."[137] Certainly McNaughton intended to prevent any public suggestion that he was unfit to lead his men in battle and, in conversation with King in Ottawa, he indicated that "he had not yet given up the idea that he might be able to command the Canadian army."[138]

McNaughton was a loose cannon, one posing great potential danger to the ship of state and the war effort. The government, however, had carefully made its preparations to handle the publicity when the General returned. Press and parliamentary statements were drafted and redrafted, stressing McNaughton's ill-health,[139] and the Prime Minister soon let the opposition leaders see the correspondence on the matter, a shrewd device to squelch an embarrassing debate. This took the steam out of any attack on the government.[140] After McNaughton and Ralston met in June 1944, the General's leave was extended for a further three months.[141] With attention focused on the fighting in Normandy, the McNaughton affair seemed to have been a damp squib.

Still, McNaughton had plans. Starting in July 1944, he began conversations with Progressive Conservative party officials on the possibility he might play a role in producing a postwar reconstruction policy for the Tories; unstated was the implicit suggestion that he might take over from the demonstrably lacklustre John Bracken as party leader.[142] This move into politics was scuppered when Mackenzie King asked McNaughton, promoted to the rank of full General when his retirement from the army was announced in September, if he would consider becoming the first Canadian Governor General. That idea so attracted McNaughton that he broke off conversations with the Conservatives.[143] Significantly, McNaughton's discussions with the Conservatives took place after the party had begun to press for the imposition of conscription, for the use of home defence conscripts — or Zombies, as they were known in a most derogatory way — overseas.[144]

At the end of October King turned to McNaughton as the man who could find the way out of the conscription impasse; Defence Minister Ralston had been determined to dispatch the Zombies overseas to meet the army's reinforcement needs, and the cabinet had divided on the issue. McNaughton eagerly seized the opportunity offered him (see chapter 8). The chance to replace Ralston as minister and to take his revenge on Stuart was simply too good to miss. He accepted, but he failed King in his larger purpose. The Conservatives, who would have grudgingly accepted McNaughton as Governor General, found his transformation into Minister of National Defence and a Grit politician too much to bear.

"Your latest move destroys the last vestiges of respect I had for you. . . . Now I would not insult a yellow dog by calling you one," wrote Ontario's Conservative Premier, George Drew.[145]

It was all highly distressing for McNaughton, who had believed he could persuade the NRMA conscripts to volunteer to go overseas as reinforcements for his army overseas. The Zombies, inured to appeals phrased in terms of duty and service, turned a deaf ear.[146] Just as startling to McNaughton was his rude reception at a meeting in Arnprior, Ontario, on 5 November and at a Canadian Legion meeting in Ottawa the next day when his comrades of the Great War had booed and hooted at him. That shook his confidence — and ended his speechmaking efforts. The final blow came from the general officers at NDHQ and in the military districts across the country. The senior officers in Canada had been trying for years to persuade home defence conscripts to go overseas, and they knew the difficulties; McNaughton simply did not, and even if they had been willing, the generals could not implement their new minister's voluntary policy. The decision to send conscripts overseas on 22 November, forced on McNaughton by receipt of advice from the CGS and his senior staff officers that the voluntary system could not find the necessary reinforcements,[147] was yet another shattering blow.

Incredibly, however, the General, his health now restored, proved that he could rebound from this sustained battering. Mike Pearson, on the verge of taking over as the new Canadian Ambassador to the United States, reported in December that McNaughton "was full of vim and vigour, right on top of the world. He has taken to political life."[148] By most measures, he ran the Department of National Defence efficiently, though he acted too much as his own Chief of the General Staff (or so some complained), and he failed to realize that a politician, unlike a general in the field, could not simply give orders and receive instant obedience in return.[149]

Overseas, Lieutenant-General Harry Crerar, the GOC-in-C of the First Canadian Army, was initially horrified at McNaughton's "astonishing" emergence as Minister of National Defence. There would be pressure to move the troops from Italy to Northwest Europe, he told Massey, and McNaughton could turn this demand into an anti-British issue if the War Office resisted.[150] If stirring up that kind of trouble was the General's intent, he found no support for it from his colleagues in National Defence Headquarters. General Maurice Pope, the Prime Minister's Military Secretary, recorded an interview with the Minister on 18 November:

Andy spoke of the Army's unsatisfactory command position. I thereupon put my hand on his shoulder and said that I was sure that he would want me, as in the past, to speak to him with complete frankness. He replied that most decidedly he did. I therefore argued that our Army's position was not really as unsatisfactory as he seemed to believe, and he seemed impressed when I pointed out that the French Army fighting on French soil had no more to say regarding the direction of operations than our own Army. . . . was it reasonable for us to expect more?[151]

McNaughton happily did not cause the difficulties he might have, and I Canadian Corps joined up with the rest of First Canadian Army as part of a major shift of units from Italy to Northwest Europe in the spring of 1945.[152]

For McNaughton, his venture into politics ended in electoral humiliation. He lost a by-election in the rural constituency of Grey North, Ontario, in February 1945 after a campaign that concentrated on his wife's Roman Catholicism almost as much as on conscription and reinforcements.[153] In the general election of 1945, he met defeat again, this time in the riding encompassing his home town of Moosomin, Saskatchewan. After the conscription crisis of November 1944, which had sparked emotional charges all across English Canada that he had betrayed both his principles and the men overseas, McNaughton did not appear to be electable anywhere.[154] Moreover, the offer of the governor generalship also evaporated — the soldier who earlier would have been acceptable as a vice-regal figurehead had now been tainted by partisan politics (or perhaps only by his failure to win election!).[155] The remainder of his long career was spent as a diplomat at the United Nations, as the head of the Canadian section of the Permanent Joint Board on Defence, and as the Canadian chair of the International Joint Commission, in all of which he rendered distinguished service to his country. Andy McNaughton was a great man, highly intelligent, a compelling personality, one who did well in every single endeavour he took on — except as commander of the First Canadian Army.

CHAPTER 4

CRERAR: AMBITION REALIZED

I F THE TRIO OF McNAUGHTON, Crerar, and Simonds dominated the Canadian army during the Second World War, the key figure was not Andy McNaughton. It was General H.D.G. Crerar, who truly might be said to have modelled Canada's army in his own image and fashion. A Permanent Force brigadier at the outbreak of war, Harry Crerar established Canadian Military Headquarters in London in 1939 and 1940 and laid down the organizational structure that was followed overseas. Then back in Canada as Chief of the General Staff from mid 1940 until the end of 1941, he constructed the training organization that provided new divisions and reinforcements to McNaughton overseas. Returning to Britain, Crerar took over I Canadian Corps, commanded it in training there and briefly in action in Italy, and was in the ideal position to succeed McNaughton at First Canadian Army, which he did in early 1944. Crerar then led his army into Normandy and commanded it through Belgium, the Netherlands, and into Germany. Finally, when the fighting was over, Crerar defined the rules for demobilization and effectively selected the CGS who would guide the postwar army. No other single officer had such impact on the raising, fighting, and eventual disbanding of the greatest army Canada has ever known. Crerar was unquestionably the most important Canadian soldier of the war.

Yet Crerar is almost entirely unremembered today. There are innumerable books on Montgomery and Eisenhower, as might be expected, and studies of other army commanders abound. Crerar usually gets a brief entry in dictionaries of the war, though almost always with incorrect data. Alone among Eisenhower's chief lieutenants in Europe, Crerar has yet to receive detailed study in print, both of the man and his role.[1] That says volumes about the way Canadians treat their national figures. Of course, it may also say something about Crerar.

HARRY CRERAR was born in Hamilton, Ontario, in 1888. His father, a lawyer, was Scots-born and educated, and came to Canada in his twenties. He married in Hamilton and had three sons and one daughter, of whom Harry was the eldest. The boys went to private school in Hamilton and then to Upper Canada College, where one of Harry's teachers was Stephen Leacock. During the Second World War Leacock wrote an amusing piece, "Generals I Have Trained," touching on the six general officers he had taught at UCC, and on young Harry, who had arrived when he was thirteen years old:

> I recall the similar case of a general, newly arrived from Hamilton, Ontario, his home at the time, though his address just now is North Africa and Italy. He wasn't feeling so good, just sitting on the edge of his bed and looking downhearted. So I asked him where he came from and said Hamilton was a great place, and the general said it was the greatest iron and steel centre in Ontario. As he said it, the tears broke into his eyes at the thought of it. . . . I saw it mentioned in the papers the other day that he is a man of iron determination. They got it wrong — iron and steel, rolled iron, ingots and steel bullets — in other words, from Hamilton. Yet I am sure that he still keeps the softer side that I first saw. If anyone whispered, 'What about Burlington Bay in the moonlight of June?' — his iron (and steel) reserve might break.[2]

Leacock, characteristically, had hit on some of the fundamental truths about Crerar. He was loyal to his birthplace, and overseas in the Second World War would frequently go out of his way to visit Hamilton regiments. He was also an emotional man, though few outside his family would ever know, so rigid was his self-control.

Next came a year at school in Lausanne, Switzerland. The Crerar fortunes were on the rise, and Harry's father was a friend of Sir Wilfrid

Laurier's and president of the Hamilton Liberal Association in the booming years of the new century. Crerar then went off to the Royal Military College in 1906. He was a slender boy of eighteen, 5 feet 8 inches tall, and he was immediately occupied, as an article on him in the *R.M.C. Review* in 1921 noted, "in doing all the funny things which a Recruit is asked to perform."[3] He was not an academic star, neither coming in (twenty-seventh on the list of new cadets) nor going out (when he was thirteenth). But, despite a tendency to be injury-prone, he did win prizes in equitation and artillery, French and gymnastics, and, as he said later, he greatly enjoyed sailing. "I had a 16' dinghy of my own when I was 19," he told journalist Gratton O'Leary, "and spent most of the spare hours I had in it either at Kingston, or the Muskoka Lakes where my mother and father owned an island."[4]

Crerar graduated from RMC in 1909. He had hoped to join the British or Indian armies, "but on finding out that it would mean that my father would require to assist me financially and indefinitely, I gave up the ambition and decided to become self-supporting." Given the family's more than comfortable means, Crerar's decision might have been otherwise motivated, likely by his desire to be self-sufficient. He joined the Canadian Tungsten Lamp Co in Hamilton, "where I did my 10 hours a day in the factory for a year." From 1910 to 1912 he commuted between Hamilton and Austria to learn more about making light bulbs, and he was the superintendent at the plant when the first metal filament lamps of Canadian manufacture were produced. In 1912 he joined the Hydro-Electric Power Commission of Ontario — Sir Adam Beck, its powerful chairman, had married Crerar's sister — as an illuminating engineer, and the next year he was put in charge of Ontario Hydro's testing laboratory.[5]

His burgeoning career in industry, however, was almost secondary to his interest in the militia. Crerar had joined the 4th Field Battery, Canadian Field Artillery, in Hamilton on leaving RMC, and he became a captain two years later. Even when his business career took him overseas, he made it a point to be in Canada for summer camp at Petawawa. When the Great War broke out, Captain Crerar went to Valcartier as part of the first contingent and proceeded overseas in the 11th Battery of the 3rd Brigade, Canadian Field Artillery. He had a distinguished war record, served in the first actions of the Canadian Division at Ypres, became a staff learner, and then took command of a battery in 1915. By 1917 he was an acting lieutenant-colonel in command of the 3rd Brigade, Canadian Field Artillery, "and the last of the original officers of that Brigade who had left Canada in 1914." He went for a staff course in England in 1917, then joined the 5th Canadian Divisional Artillery as Brigade Major. He came into close contact and became friends with a brilliant young artillery officer named Andy McNaughton, the Canadian Corps' Counter-Battery Staff Officer; together they organized trench mortar batteries for counter-mortar work. As Crerar wrote later, "I decided what [McNaughton] was doing to the enemy batteries could be accomplished in respect to enemy mortars by the mortars of the 5th C.D.A. In the course of a few weeks by a bit of organization and by 'scrounging' and borrowing Signals equipment and personnel to establish the necessary communications . . . we found ourselves in a position to concentrate fire from several of our mortar positions on any enemy mortar within a few minutes of it opening fire."

McNaughton was delighted and saw to it that Crerar went to corps headquarters in the summer of 1918 as the understudy to and, for a time, successor of Lieutenant-Colonel Alan Brooke, the British staff officer, Royal Artillery. "Brookie," as he was ever after to Crerar, was "a great fellow. . . . We often used to tramp the front line of battery positions together." As acting SORA, Crerar had to plan the artillery support for the corps' great advances in August 1918, a task he admitted openly he could not have handled without Brooke's assistance.[6] Crerar ended the war as Counter-Battery Staff Officer of the corps in the rank of lieutenant-colonel, his confidential report pronouncing him "an all-round capable officer who had made good in every capacity."[7] He had won the Distinguished Service Order in June 1917 and was mentioned in dispatches.

Crerar himself had emerged from the war unscathed, but one of his brothers was killed in action in the Royal Air Force; the other, Alistair, who had followed Harry to RMC, served with the Royal Canadian Dragoons in France, was severely wounded in 1918, and won the Military Cross.[8] The war intensified his already serious outlook on life, but it was not all tragedy. Crerar had married Marion Verschoyle Cronyn on a brief leave to Canada in January 1916. Always known as Verse, his wife was stunningly beautiful and came from a distinguished and wealthy family in London, Ontario. Their first child, Peggy, was born in November 1916; a son, Peter, followed six years later.

Offered back his job with Ontario Hydro, Crerar also had to consider a suggestion from General Sir Arthur Currie and McNaughton that he join the Permanent Force. "I thought it out," he said, "and decided to carry on with the work which I had always mainly been interested in." His decision was eased by the annual income produced by a substantial inheritance from his mother, who had died in 1919. Now he could support his family well *and* do what he wanted. Crerar joined the PF artillery as a major and was soon promoted to temporary lieutenant-colonel. He would remain in that rank for almost fifteen years as promotion in the Permanent Force slowed to a crawl. That frustrated Crerar beyond measure, for he was always acutely conscious of his rank, his place on the army gradation lists, and his pay and allowances.[9]

Yet his appointments were the right ones. He was Staff Officer Artillery in Ottawa initially, working on the reorganization of the army.[10] He sat the Staff College preparatory course at RMC and passed the examinations, winning him entrance to the Staff College in Camberley in 1923, where he excelled.[11] His instructors there included such able British officers as Ironside, Gort, Fuller, Brooke, Haining, and Adam. Instead of returning to Canada at the end of his course, Crerar was posted as General Staff Officer 2 at the War Office in London, the first Canadian officer sent there since the Great War, where he was in charge of a section dealing with Home Defence, helped put down the great General Strike of 1926, and sat on subcommittees of the Committee on Imperial Defence. His boss at the War Office was Archibald Wavell, one of the army's brightest general officers. "Wavell had a glass eye," Crerar said later, "but he didn't miss much."[12] The friendships he solidified with his British brother officers were to be important; moreover, his confidential reports from his War Office superiors were superb.[13]

Crerar wrote occasional articles in the *Canadian Defence Quarterly* (including one on "The Difficulties of Unified Control of Allied Operations," which had a ring of prescience about it).[14] He also delivered a lecture to the Royal United Services Institute in London on "The Development of Closer Relations between the Military Forces of the Empire." That talk drew the stern comment from the nationalist Dr O.D. Skelton, Undersecretary of State for External Affairs in Ottawa, that it "was an out and out advocacy of Imperialist policy in defence." That was a fair assessment. Crerar had said: "It is not enough that the Imperial Forces should be allies. We must make them far more than that; they must be parts of one and the same Imperial Army."[15] Such a proposal was anathema to Mackenzie King, who saw the Skelton memorandum, but Crerar's career did not seem to suffer for his views. Most important, Crerar's lecture demonstrated that he was thinking about international questions, and that alone marked him out from most of his PF comrades.

Back in Canada in 1927, he had a spell of regimental duty in Kingston in command of B Battery of the Royal Canadian Horse Artillery — one of his subalterns was a recent RMC graduate, Lieutenant Guy Simonds. He was also at RMC a brief time as professor of tactics, where he was popular with the cadets even if he would have preferred another post.[16] Then, in 1929, Major-General McNaughton became Chief of the General Staff, and "Andy," as Crerar always called him in their correspondence, set out to get "Harry" on his staff. "He wanted someone to get down to real consideration of the defence problems of Canada," Crerar said later, "to be free from routine office work, and to produce for him the results of his appreciation[s]."[17] Crerar was "tickled to death over his new appointment," another officer noted,[18] as he became General Staff Officer 1 at National Defence Headquarters and began his productive career as the pre-eminent staff officer of the interwar years.

For most of the next decade, while his family settled into a comfortable existence in Ottawa,[19] Crerar worked on planning. He produced the papers that led McNaughton to press for a major reorganization of the militia, changes that roused the ire of cavalrymen and infantrymen across the country who saw the artillery and engineers coming to the fore.[20] He drafted major papers on "The Defence of Canada" (1935) and on "The Requirements of Canadian Defence" (1935) that set out the General Staff's ideas of what was needed.[21] He wrote able papers on the defence of the West Coast in the face of an aggressive Japan and the possibility of a war between Japan and the United States in which a neutral Canada might have to protect its territory against one or both nations.[22] He joined the Canadian Institute of International Affairs and, as his grasp of international relations grew, he found himself increasingly able to comment on British policy during the Italo-Ethiopian War,[23] for example, to write sharp critiques of neutralist-nationalist views on Canadian foreign policy,[24] or to talk knowledgeably to an officer on the staff of the United States minister to Canada about Canadian-American defence relations and the state of public opinion in Quebec on imperial questions.[25]

His imperialism also had begun to come unglued as the 1931 Statute of Westminster changed the legal foundations of the empire and as British policy drifted aimlessly in the face of the dictators. When the King government stopped the liaison letters long exchanged between the Chief of the Imperial General Staff and the CGS in Ottawa, Crerar's response was infinitely more sensible, in the light of Canada's new sovereignty in foreign policy, than that of the CIGS. The British officer harrumphed incorrectly that "they are not even 'staff conversations' in the accepted sense since we are all one staff," while Crerar told a British diplomat in Ottawa, "there is, however much we may regret the fact, no such thing as a Canadian section of the Imperial General Staff."[26] Harry Crerar, it appeared, did not regret it very much.

Crerar, in other words, changed as Canada changed in the interwar years. He repeatedly demonstrated he was a political soldier in the best sense, one who understood that in Canada, as elsewhere, military questions had much to do with domestic and international politics. Commonplace as this might be now (and it is not always common in the Canadian Forces), Crerar was one of two or three officers in the interwar Permanent Force who took their imaginations out for the occasional airing. That he was also careful, methodical, and precise in word and deed (so much so that he carefully maintained a file of stories and jokes for speeches) only increased his worth.[27]

His superiors, and most notably McNaughton, recognized these qualities in him. In 1934 he was selected to attend the Imperial Defence College in London for a year's advanced military schooling, where he again studied under his friend Brooke.[28] He did well, his assessment declaring him an officer of "outstanding ability" with "all the attributes for high command,"[29] and he returned home to become Director of Military Operations and Intelligence at NDHQ. This post, essentially the army's senior staff planner, was a critical one.

His long service in Ottawa had brought him into contact with officers in the Department of External Affairs. Alone among PF officers, Crerar sought out and befriended such rising stars as Lester Pearson, Norman Robertson, and Hume Wrong.[30] His personal and political instincts again served him well. He represented the army at the Disarmament Conference in Geneva in 1932,[31] and advised the Canadian delegation at the Imperial Conference of 1937. He even thought of joining the Department of External Affairs in 1931 and serving with W.D. Herridge, the minister to the United States, but decided that securing a rank appropriate to his age and experience through political channels would inevitably irritate his diplomatic colleagues. As he put it, "I might find that the presently secure base on which my diplomatic career would largely be supported, had vanished."[32] Never a man to move far from a secure base, Crerar opted to stay in the army. After all, he reasoned, another war was on the way.

At NDHQ, Harry Crerar was a somebody, recognized as one of the army's brightest lights.[33] Yet his progress through the ranks was glacially slow. Over such places as there were he kept an anxious gaze. When an officer junior to him was promoted to substantive colonel in 1937, he wrote to the Chief of the General Staff to protest: "I am in my fiftieth year. The time during which I can apply the knowledge I have gained through the somewhat exceptional military education which has come my way cannot be long." The CGS, now the lacklustre Major-General E.C. Ashton, returned a dusty answer, merely assuring Crerar that "your service and your qualifications would be kept in mind when selections were being made for higher appointments."[34] Not until August 1938 was he promoted to temporary brigadier, when he became Commandant of the Royal Military College. Even then, he was not the CGS' first choice for that post.[35] In the seniority system that gripped the PF in an iron vice, doing the job well was insufficient to overcome the inexorable and lock-stepped processes of slow promotion and retirement at advanced age.[36]

CRERAR WAS DESTINED to spend only a short time as Commandant of RMC. He was briefly recalled to Ottawa in March 1939 to put the finishing touches on the army's war mobilization plans,[37] and as soon as the war began he started to lobby his superiors in Ottawa for a place overseas. As he wrote to a friend just before Canada declared war: "We are now at the outset of another World War. For the last twenty years I have been training to fill an appointment of trust and responsibility in that event. But a year away from Ottawa has placed me a bit upon the sidelines and it may be that my qualifications will not be remembered when Ministers get around the Cabinet table."[38] Not to fear. There was a new Minister of National Defence on 18 September 1939: Norman

Rogers, formerly Minister of Labour. Rogers was the MP for Kingston, where Crerar's RMC duties often brought them together, and they had been next-door neighbours in Ottawa's fashionable Rockcliffe for years. Crerar sent congratulations, knowing he had a friend at court.[39] In fact, he had another friend, for the new Chief of the General Staff, Major-General Victor Anderson, had not forgotten Crerar. Instead of the expected role as chief staff officer to the General Officer Commanding an eventual overseas Canadian Corps,[40] Crerar was pencilled in to be BGS at the "Overseas Headquarters," soon to be renamed Canadian Military Headquarters, in London.[41] Merit had won.

What followed, however, was a little less meritorious. Crerar asked Anderson for a promotion to major-general so he could deal on a more equal footing with his former British officer colleagues at the Staff and Imperial Defence colleges. Reasoning that overseas service decreased his chances of survival, he suggested that the higher rank would give his wife a larger pension if he were killed.[42] The request was denied. Crerar went anyway, proceeding overseas in October as Senior Combatant Officer. His wife followed in November, and his daughter, engaged to a young officer, came as well. She would be married on 6 January 1940, in a large ceremony billed as the first Canadian war wedding in the United Kingdom.[43]

Before he left, Crerar had prepared a memorandum on "Higher Organization for War" for General McNaughton with his proposals for the organization of Canadian Military Headquarters.[44] Eminently sound, his guidelines were quickly put into place, not least by Crerar himself. As soon as he arrived in London, he set about getting established and contacting his friends at the Canadian commission and the War Office. Pearson, serving at the commission, found him "as of yore, serious, hardworking, capable."[45] He noted admiringly, "he doesn't want an 'Argyle House' in this war," a reference to the patronage-ridden overseas headquarters of the Great War. "Most of the Canadian staff can be at the training camps and that which is required in London can become a sort of Military Department of Canada House. For that purpose he wants to establish his organisation in close touch with ours."[46] Crerar told Vincent Massey, the High Commissioner, the same thing and established a close relationship with him, while his wife took care to do the same with Mrs Massey.[47]

He saw his good friend Major-General Richard Dewing, the Director of Military Operations at the War Office and an officer with whom he had gone through Camberley, on 6 November. "Harry explained why he couldn't come and lodge with me," Dewing noted. "It would lay him open to Canadian suspicion that he was in the pocket of D.M.O."[48] Given that Mackenzie King was Prime Minister and the nationalist McNaughton was GOC, this was a prudent consideration. Crerar was always prudent.

The job he faced had many challenges and few charms. He had to persuade the War Office that Canadian troops should train in England and not in France,[49] get CMHQ organized properly, work out how the costs of feeding and housing Canadian troops in Britain would be covered, sort out public relations for the army overseas, and make sure that this time the accommodations provided for Canadian troops were not leaky tents on muddy Salisbury Plain. Above all, he had to keep himself and his headquarters out of trouble, something that required cautious words in ministerial ears. T.A. Crerar, the Minister of Mines and Resources and no relation, in Britain to sell Canadian foodstuffs and grain, noted approvingly after one such incident that his namesake "not only is discreet but has, I think, a very sound judgment."[50]

The Mines Minister's favourable report renewed Crerar's ardour for promotion. This time he had McNaughton's support for his argument that it was difficult to deal with his War Office opposite numbers as a mere brigadier.[51] Ottawa initially hesitated, but late in January Crerar was promoted to the acting rank of major-general "while holding his present appointment."[52] To McNaughton, Crerar complained: "I suppose that the acting rank arrangement is the best that Defence Council feels it can do — though the inference is that the job merits the rank and not that I deserve it by the way I have done the job."[53] To Norman Rogers, however, he professed to be delighted: "You must know . . . what my promotion has meant to me" both in London and because "it has indicated your confidence in what I have accomplished and your faith in my ability to tackle what lies ahead." Gratitude, even excessive gratitude, is no vice, but Crerar once again showed a certain disregard for the proprieties. He begged Rogers "for the sake of my personal security, and my future career" to see to it that his acting rank was made substantive "as soon as any other promotion to substantive Major-General amongst my contemporaries . . . comes up for approval."[54] When Rogers visited the troops Britain, Crerar again lobbied for his pay and allowances to be increased — and, to be fair, for that of other officers in London to be raised as well.[55] Able and diligent as he was, Crerar never neglected his personal interests. The quality of selflessness, said to be what Dwight Eisenhower looked for in those he put into responsible command positions,[56] was largely absent from Harry Crerar's makeup. His ambition was unbounded, his self-seeking unlimited. What was worse was the piety with which his demands were couched. He explained to McNaughton in February 1940: "As you know I have no personal aims to serve, but simply desire to carry out this job with a maximum of service to the several 'parties' involved."[57] For Crerar, the service of personal aims was a constant concern.

Events soon propelled Crerar to greater responsibilities and to the service of new and tougher masters. The blitzkrieg and the stunning Nazi successes of May and June drove Britain from the Continent and forced the surrender of France. Wholesale change was now necessary in Ottawa. Norman Rogers, tragically killed in an air crash on 10 June, was replaced by Colonel J.L. Ralston, the Minister of Finance. Crerar was quick off the mark. He sent Ralston a copy of a letter he had been drafting to Rogers, one that admittedly "cut corners" by criticizing the Chief of the General Staff, Victor Anderson, whose lax administration at NDHQ had produced intolerable delays in getting answers to critical questions for the troops overseas.[58] This was the same CGS who, a few months earlier, had championed Crerar and got him his key post overseas. Anderson was also thought to have failed to produce the kinds of crisp, detailed advice the politicians wanted when the National Resources Mobilization Act was being drafted. The NRMA, passed into law in June 1940 in the panicky mood produced by the fall of France, called for a national registration and the call up of single men for thirty days' military training.[59] Fresh on the scene, Ralston presumably saw the problems at National Defence Headquarters himself and, encouraged by McNaughton, decided to recall Crerar to Ottawa as Vice-Chief of the General Staff.[60] Crerar did not doubt what this meant. As he told his friend Dewing, he was "quite obviously to take over C.G.S. from Victor Anderson very shortly." That was the plan. Dewing added generously and truthfully that "having Harry at head of Canadian Mission during the past months has been the best possible insurance against any serious misunderstanding between Ottawa and the W.O. We were close enough friends to speak frankly without danger of damaging relations."[61]

Before he reached Canada, Crerar took care to protect his rear, telling McNaughton he hated returning to Ottawa. "It seems like turning my back on the front line and on the men. . . . The only argument which permits me some peace of mind is that you believe, and I sometimes think, that I can do more" for the army overseas "at the Ottawa end than I can in the 'theatre of operations.'" If he found he could not do so, Crerar added, "I'm hot after the 3rd Division — and count on you to help me."[62] Crerar made no bones about it: he wanted to command a division.

Making National Defence Headquarters run more effectively was the first step. On the slow boat to Canada in July 1940, Crerar wrote a memorandum, "Observations on Canadian Requirements in Respect to the Army," that set out his concerns. "The urgency of the situation," he wrote, "does not permit of large-scale reorganization. The best we can do is to obtain greater efficiency out of the existing organization by the substitution of more efficient Commanders and Staff for those who have failed to measure up." To Crerar, the inefficient had to go, whether they were Permanent Force officers or not. The incompetent should not be put into training or administrative posts, for inefficiency there would only produce "inadequately trained and equipped units and drafts for overseas." And the NDHQ organization had to be geared up to produce decisions faster.[63]

Events moved faster than Crerar. Ralston promptly appointed him CGS two days after he arrived. Then, at his first meeting with the minister, Crerar won Ralston's agreement to the outline he had proposed. He wrote to Pearson that "the pressure on the Government developed by recent events has completely blown off the previous restrictive lid on the Canadian military effort." The difficulty was that men were being enlisted with "no clothes to put them in let alone adequate weapons to give them and with no military object to serve even when enlisted."[64]

Crerar's job was to bring order out of chaos. Alarmed at the way everyone was working intensely without enough sleep, he ordered all officers at NDHQ to take one day's rest each week, to work no more than three nights a week, and to have one long weekend each month. The staff officer, Crerar was fond of saying, is the servant of his troops, not the master, but staff officers couldn't do their job if they were overtired and overworked.[65] That was sensible. He had Colonel E.L.M. Burns, one of the officers he valued highly and one he stuck with through thick and thin, taken from the 2nd Division staff to work with him on reorganization;[66] he snatched his old friend and successor as Director of Military Operations and planning, Brigadier Ken Stuart, from his post as RMC

Commandant to be his VCGS;[67] and he persuaded a senior industrialist, Philip Chester, to become Master-General of the Ordnance.[68]

Before he could get NDHQ functioning to his satisfaction, however, Crerar faced another challenge. The National Resources Mobilization Act, as we have seen, imposed conscription for home defence on the country. With conscripts about to arrive, Crerar had to organize reception, training, clothing, and arms. "It was too late to change the basis of the training scheme which had already been announced," he lamented to McNaughton, "but I made it plain . . . that this scheme must be regarded as purely an interim measure and that in the course of the next few months the Government would need to face the entire problem of the future organization of military service for Canada." At the same time, the Permanent Joint Board on Defence had been organized after the Ogdensburg meeting in mid August of President Roosevelt and Prime Minister King. "I did what I could to push matters along," Crerar said. The army overseas and the plight of Britain remained his prime concern, however, and he had tried to counter the "panicky outlook, the tendency . . . to look inward and think in terms of strict 'continental' defence. I believe that I have been able to correct that defeatist attitude," he claimed, and the "fortress Island" was now seen as "our first line of defence rather than the Atlantic seaboard."[69]

Crerar put these views to the Minister and others. He and Burns prepared a major paper, "The Canadian Army," that called for highly mechanized forces and radical changes in the use and training of NRMA soldiers.[70] He followed that with a call for an end to the thirty-day training scheme and its replacement with a four-month plan. "While there are military grounds for preferring volunteers in an overseas army. . . . this does not affect the principle that service in the defence forces *in Canada* should be compulsory for all fit male Canadians."[71] The four-month training scheme duly came into force in February 1941 and was followed in April by the decision to keep conscripts under arms for the duration of the war.[72] Crerar was equally blunt in a confidential conversation with Grant Dexter of the *Winnipeg Free Press*. "Of what possible utility could it be to train men for 30 days? None. We now had in Canada a direct conflict in policy — compulsion at home, voluntary enlistment for overseas. These were mutually destructive and in combination they must hamstring our industrial effort." Over the next year, and in spite of criticism from the government's political opponents at the slow progress, Crerar created an effective training plan for junior officers and other ranks and set up the reinforcement pipeline to expand and sustain the army overseas.[73] It was an impressive achievement.

Administrative achievement was not yet matched by political skill. Crerar seems to have decided that his minister did not measure up, and he ventilated his opinions to his friends — and others. Ralston, Crerar maintained, was taking advice from every direction, and he and his executive assistants were interfering in military policy. "The Chief of the General Staff," Crerar told Dexter, "was the military expert of the minister. . . . The deputy minister had no business interfering in policy, nor had he any business interfering with the heads of the fighting services. . . . When he had come to the department he had actually found that the minister and three executive assistants met each morning in the minister's office and decided policy — in the absence of the chief of staff. He had stopped that," Crerar said, adding that policy was now discussed "chiefly between himself and the minister." Crerar believed that soldiers knew about war and politicians knew about politics.[74]

Ralston would not have differed, but Crerar made it impossible to agree.[75] Inevitably word of Crerar's views got around, and inevitably Ralston formed negative conclusions about Crerar. "He thinks Crerar is perhaps as good a soldier as we have available for the job in Canada," Ralston told Victor Sifton, the Master-General of the Ordnance in succession to Chester, "but finds that he has very grave weaknesses of character. He is immensely ambitious and is constantly seeking to arrogate to himself the whole business of the department. He even demands copies of letters coming to Ralston personally." According to the Minister: "Crerar is bound he is going to get himself made a lieut. general, so as to be the indisputable top of the heap. But Ralston will never agree to this."[76] A few months later, Ralston was making clear that he "*hates* Crerar; despises the general staff from top to bottom. But who can he get to succeed Crerar? Odlum?"[77] That Odlum, then still commanding the 2nd Division overseas, could even be thought of as CGS suggested that Ralston's idea of military competence was very strange indeed.

Nonetheless, his assessment of Crerar, was generally correct. The CGS was pressing hard to be promoted so he would have unquestioned primacy over the senior army officers at NDHQ. In a long campaign that he began in October 1940 and that lasted for more than a year, he tried repeatedly to get the Minister to make him a lieutenant-general. When the Chief of the Naval Staff, Percy Nelles, was promoted to vice-admiral, the equivalent of lieutenant-general, in March 1941, Crerar was almost beside himself. "Quite apart from my personal feelings," he wrote to Ralston, "it seems to me not only illogical but highly undesirable that the Chief of the Army Staff should remain inferior in rank to the Chief of another Canadian Service, the operational responsibilities of which are measurably less in scale."[78] Crerar's reasoning was sound: the navy was still tiny, and Crerar's responsibilities were vastly greater than Nelles's. He would almost certainly have been promoted in the ordinary course of events — if he had not pressed so hard and if he had held his tongue about his minister.

Still, Crerar's personal ambitions and his personality conflicts with Ralston do not seem to have interfered with the development of the army's program. On a visit to England in December 1940, Crerar told the British that the objective was a complete Canadian Corps, first of two divisions and ancillary and supporting units, and then of three.[79] The next month, the cabinet accepted the three-division scheme, adding as well an army tank brigade and promising the dispatch of an additional armoured division later in the year. This was a big army, big enough to set the ever-cautious Prime Minister worrying.[80]

But Crerar's plans for the army overseas were not yet complete. As early as June 1941 there were ideas floating around National Defence Headquarters for a truly "big" army, one that would have six infantry divisions and two armoured divisions, all commanded by an army head-quarters.[81] Crerar himself, poring over the sometimes slapdash studies of Canada's available manpower, had concluded that numbers would not "be a restrictive factor for some time yet," and that there were sufficient men to maintain an army of eight divisions, two of which would be kept in Canada, for six more years of war. What that meant, he wrote to McNaughton, was that a fourth and a fifth division could be dispatched overseas in 1942. "This would result in too large a corps," he said ingenuously, "but have you ever considered the pros and cons of a Canadian Army comprising 2 corps each of 2 Divisions and an Armoured Division?" That was an ambitious scheme, given the numbers of supporting troops required, but, Crerar said, "I do not think that the picture is an impossible one."[82] This grandiose plan, with the elimination of one infantry division and the addition of two armoured brigades, would eventually be accepted by the government early in 1942.[83] It was a triumph of argumentation and lobbying (but not of fact, alas) for Crerar, a victory of major proportions for the army. That it eventually proved to be more than the country could sustain with a voluntary system of recruiting, however, was primarily the politicians' problem.

At roughly the same time as he won his battle for the big army, Crerar faced attack because of his role in encouraging Canadian acceptance of a commitment to send troops to Hong Kong. The British Crown Colony near Canton had long been seen as impossible to defend adequately and impossible to abandon politically, and the prewar British Chiefs of Staff had agreed to a low standard of defence for reasons of "prestige rather than strategy."[84] Defended, therefore, by only four battalions, Hong Kong looked to be easy pickings if the Japanese decided on war against Britain, a situation that prevailed into the late summer of 1941. In August Major-General A.E. Grasett, the retiring Hong Kong garrison commander, passed through Ottawa on his way back to Britain. Although his mannerisms were almost a caricature of those of the British upper class ("particularly," one distinguished American historian noted, "his habit of saying what-what in a fashion I have only seen in the movies"),[85] Grasett was a Canadian. Most important, he had been an RMC classmate of Crerar's, one who had graduated in 1909 as the Battalion Sergeant Major, the top cadet, with the Sword of Honour. The chummy conversations between the two ex-cadets, both now general officers, undoubtedly led Britain to ask Canada for two battalions of infantry to bolster Hong Kong's defences.[86] The Canadians, London reasoned and Ottawa foolishly agreed, could boost morale in Hong Kong and show Tokyo that Britain was serious about defending its possessions. The request, once made, with the opposition regularly claiming that Canada was not helping Britain to the maximum of its strength, could not easily be refused. Told to proceed, Crerar picked the Winnipeg Grenadiers and the Royal Rifles of Canada, two regiments that had seen garrison duty of the kind anticipated in Hong Kong, for dispatch.[87]

As it turned out, unfortunately for Crerar and more so for the Canadians sent to Asia, the Japanese swallowed Hong Kong whole in the first three weeks of the Pacific war. The garrison's troops (some of the Canadians with limited training) were killed, captured, and brutalized by the superior Japanese forces. The two Canadian battalions' motor transport had not been loaded on the transport carrying the troops, thanks largely to staff incompetence at NDHQ. When someone tipped off Colonel George Drew, the opposition leader in Ontario and a loud critic of the army's training efforts, a major political furore erupted.[88] By the time the storm blew up, Crerar was in Britain as acting commander of the Canadian Corps. For a time, it seemed he might be brought back to Canada to testify before a royal commission, but the exigencies of war made this impossible and he gave his answers to questions in London instead.[89] As he almost always did, Crerar escaped censure,[90] though some of the higher staff at NDHQ were not so fortunate and were summarily sacked. The Hong Kong tragedy, whatever else it was, was a reminder that Canada's military planners were still not prepared to deal with the conditions of modern war.

MUCH TO THE SURPRISE of those who knew him, Harry Crerar yearned to be a commander in the field. When he returned to Canada in July 1940, he made it clear he wanted to command a division. That goal remained foremost in his mind. In the fall of 1941 when he went to England with Ralston he had a conversation with Colonel G.S. Currie, the Minister's executive assistant, which Currie recorded in his diary:

> Conference with Gen. Crerar re personal situation. Would serve where he can be most useful. Would like 2nd Division — is physically fit — Need a Force Commander in England — should be two corps — McNaughton should be pulled back to Command Forces. Brook[e] and other [War] office officials think McNaughton is a genius and that his best role would be scientific. Crerar wants to be appointed Lt.Gen. and then will revert to go Overseas as Major General — would be placed in invidious position, etc.[91]

That was a revealing conversation, one in which Crerar referred openly to his intentions. He wanted a division and he wanted to be promoted, though he was, he maintained, willing to give up his promotion to get overseas. Those were past themes. What was new was Crerar's hint that there were concerns about McNaughton in the War Office. Genius the GOC may have been, but his "scientific" interests were not best employed in commanding the Canadian Corps, or so Crerar seemed to be implying.

Instead, McNaughton could be force commander, presumably some largely honorific title, while another — Crerar? — would exercise command in the field.

This interpretation is strengthened by the fact that, on this trip, Crerar also raised his concerns with the High Commissioner. At dinner, Massey wrote, "I had a good talk with him on many subjects — e.g. McNaughton and his virtues & faults."[92] One of McNaughton's major faults, in Crerar's eyes, was his insistence on keeping the Canadian divisions together and under his control. McNaughton simply refused to countenance the employment of all or part of the Canadian Corps in operations abroad, and possibly in the Middle East.[93] His eye was fixed on Europe.

For the moment this was not a major problem. Crerar's immediate aim was to return overseas, and he had already prepared the ground for this objective. Major-General Victor Odlum, the GOC of the 2nd Canadian Infantry Division, had failed as a senior commander and had to be replaced. Crerar had already asked McNaughton for the job and, after some slight hesitation because of Crerar's lack of field experience, McNaughton agreed.[94] After conversations with Crerar, the Chief of the Imperial General Staff, Sir John Dill, added his mite in conversation with Ralston: "Let us have Crerar over here . . . why not make Canadian Army put Crerar in charge"?[95] Dill's phrasing also seemed to suggest that McNaughton's services could be dispensed with and that, too, hinted at the content of Crerar's talk with him. Ralston went along with the military advice and, when he returned to Canada, he told the Cabinet War Committee that, "All things being considered," Crerar was the most suitable officer for GOC 2nd Canadian Division. At the same meeting, the cabinet agreed that the three services' Chiefs of Staff should be lieutenant-generals or the equivalent rank,[96] and Crerar was duly promoted on 19 November 1941. When McNaughton fell ill and went on an extended sick leave, Crerar became the beneficiary. As McNaughton told the new CIGS, General Sir Alan Brooke, Crerar "will be the senior officer next to myself in our forces here and, in consequence, I propose that he should then take over acting command of Canadian Corps from [Major-General George] Pearkes, who is his junior." McNaughton added that, because Crerar had just been made a lieutenant-general, "I will ask for authority for him to continue in this rank whilst acting in command."[97] Crerar, in other words, was to command a corps, not a division, and he was to remain a lieutenant-general. As he wired McNaughton in gratitude, the army program was well in hand and his work in Canada had been largely completed. "I therefore feel that I can hand over my present appointment and gratify my personal ambition to serve in the field under you without a sense of shirking other responsibilities."[98]

Crerar took over the Canadian Corps two days before Christmas 1941, donning the battledress now worn overseas for the first time. He cut an unwarlike figure; battledress was not kind to the middle-aged, especially those not blessed with trim figures. Academic in appearance,[99] Crerar mixed his learning with a dash of practical soldiering. Training, for instance. That was one of McNaughton's defects, but it was an area Crerar thought he knew something about. It did not take him long to discover that training had been sadly neglected and that many of his senior commanders were less than adequate. Some were also downright rude. One of his early visits was to the 1st Division for a tactical exercise without troops; Major-General George Pearkes, the GOC, created a scenario involving a staff officer fresh from Canada who messed up a battle situation.[100] Crerar would not forget.

Fortunately, his corps was serving under Home Forces' South-Eastern Command; his friend Brooke wrote, "Do you know Montgomery who commands S.E. Command? He is a first class commander and can be of great help to you, I have the greatest confidence in him. . . . He is worth consulting. He is a first class trainer and a grand fighter."[101] Perhaps because he was more nervous at being in command than he let on, Crerar took the CIGS' advice, saw Montgomery, adopted his suggestions on training, and gratefully accepted Montgomery's offer to assess the senior officers in the Canadian divisions.[102] As Brooke told Montgomery, Crerar was "delighted with all your help, and all set to play to the utmost."[103] Play he did, and, with Montgomery's help, Crerar succeeded in getting rid of a number of inadequate officers and in greatly improving the corps' training. He and Monty got on well in the months before Montgomery went to the North African desert to win his first battles and make his reputation,[104] and the British general was more than pleased with Crerar's handling of the corps. After the tough Exercise Tiger in the spring of 1942, for example, Montgomery congratulated Crerar on his role in the operation: "You did splendidly. As you know, I always say what I mean." He said the same privately to Trumball Warren, formerly his Canadian ADC,[105] and he was later more than happy to invite Crerar to Africa to see him in operation against the enemy.[106] For his part, Crerar admired Montgomery while fully aware of his peculiarities. When he returned from the African front, he observed that "'Monty's' definition of an army with good morale was an army commanded by 'Monty'" — which said it all.[107]

The two did have a clash in July 1942 when "Rutter," the first plan for an attack on Dieppe by the 2nd Canadian Infantry Division, was in its final stages. Montgomery had barred McNaughton and Crerar from the operation headquarters, and Crerar confronted him, pointing out that Canadian commanders could not "avoid our separate responsibility to the Canadian Government concerning the employment of Canadian troops, no matter who the Senior British Commander might be." Montgomery, who had only a limited responsibility for the operation and the plans for it, eventually saw the light.[108] Once Rutter was scrapped, this contretemps scarcely mattered. It did matter in August when the operation, now called "Jubilee," was carried out. Montgomery was already in North Africa, but Crerar was in place and on the spot to exercise his "separate responsibility." The responsibility for Canadian participation in the Dieppe raid was largely his. He had come to England convinced that the army had to see action soon, both for its own morale and for domestic Canadian consumption.[109] As acting corps commander, once he had heard of the prospect of a major raid, he exercised his status as a national commander to demand of Combined Operations Headquarters and the British Chiefs of Staff that it should be carried out by Canadian troops. When McNaughton returned to take command of the First Canadian Army in April 1942, the decision had already been made and the GOC-in-C simply concurred in it. Crerar's was, as Lieutenant-General Guy Simonds later said, "the decisive part in getting the operation launched."[110] There was nothing remotely improper in Crerar's actions, for he was in command while McNaughton was ill. Moreover, he was almost certainly correct in his assessment of Canadian morale in Britain and at home.

The raid on 19 August turned into a debacle, not a triumph. This time Crerar's political instinct did not fail him. He immediately adopted the "positive" line that, in Simonds's phrase, "though the raid had been costly, it had been well worthwhile because of what had been learned from it."[111] His approach ever after has been the favoured rationalization of the Dieppe raid, and it may even be right. McNaughton, for his part, told

Massey that "he had examined the plans carefully and assumed full responsibility for the Canadians taking part."[112] That was honest. The certainty is that neither responsibility nor blame then or since attached to Crerar, again demonstrating that this general led a charmed life.[113] McNaughton, in contrast, did not.

As we have seen, McNaughton suffered from serious flaws as a commander and trainer. His unwillingness to countenance the breakup of his force so that officers and men could get battle experience was a grave error, and there can be little doubt that, if the Canadians had been sent into action under his leadership, the results could have been disastrous. Politically and militarily, Crerar was a far better army commander, and in that sense he was more than justified in his actions. In that sense only.

It is amply clear that, while professing his loyalty to McNaughton, Crerar repeatedly and continuously undercut him with Brooke, Ralston, and Massey. We have already followed his actions in the fall of 1941.* In June 1942 he was at it again. Crerar dined with Massey and complained about McNaughton's rigid attitude towards and opposition to the possible use in action of the First Canadian Army. As Massey wrote in his diary: "Harry says that military expediency for the more effective prosecution of the war should come before national prestige and shouldn't it?"[114] He said much the same to Brooke some months later in "a long harangue . . . as to the necessity of getting some Canadians fighting soon for imperial and political reasons,"[115] and he repeated the message after another private dinner with the CIGS: Crerar "poured his heart out to me as regards his worries. . . . He is very unhappy about Andy MacNaughton [sic]."[116] To Ralston, his old antagonist, he was more discreet, confining himself to noting the impossibility of McNaughton effectively handling all his manifold military, political, and constitutional duties.[117] When in October 1942 McNaughton decided that Crerar had spoken behind his back to Ralston, Crerar was simultaneously angry and unctuous in attempting to dispel his

*Crerar, however, was loyal to McNaughton when former prime minister R.B. Bennett, living in England, denounced him vigorously. "Crerar tried to stop him and failed. Then, taking Bennett by both hands and looking at him with kindness, Crerar said: 'You mustn't, you really must not — not to me.' Bennett's response was immediate: 'Of course not, Crerar, I should know better." Lord Beaverbrook, *Friends* (London 1959), 107.

commander's concerns. In their twenty-five years of service together, Crerar wrote, "I have served my Chief, whoever he may have been, loyally and thoroughly. It just is not my habit to 'talk out of turn' . . . or knife people behind their backs." Reassured, McNaughton was quick to withdraw and to "dispel any remaining idea . . . that I feel a lack of confidence in you." He trusted Crerar's discretion "implicitly," he said.[118]

Exercise Spartan in March 1943 brought matters to a head. McNaughton did poorly commanding the First Canadian Army, in the estimation of Generals Brooke and Paget, the GOC-in-C of Home Forces. Crerar, commanding the I Canadian Corps, performed well. "His Corps H.Q. a real good show," Brooke wrote. "He has improved that corps out of all recognition."[119] After Spartan the British, too, were actively interested in seeing McNaughton replaced. On 31 March Crerar dined yet again with his friend Brooke and, the CIGS recorded, "I had a long discussion with him as to which was the best method of having MacNaughton [sic] recalled back to Canada to avert his commanding a Canadian Army which he is totally incapable of doing!"[120] Crerar presumably said much the same thing to Massey in a long private dinner about "Can. Army affairs. . . . Harry is however never disloyal to his chief & talks to me privately & intimately as he can to no one else."[121] There was perhaps just a hint that Massey felt vaguely guilty about hearing Crerar's complaints about McNaughton; there might have been more if Massey had known just how "intimately & privately" Crerar spoke to Brooke. Nonetheless, Massey had no hesitation in encouraging Brooke to raise the McNaughton problem with Colonel Ralston, the first major step in bringing Andy McNaughton down.[122] Harry Crerar had helped to prime both men well.

What must be said in Crerar's defence, however, is that his criticisms of McNaughton were correct. McNaughton had neglected the training of his men, and he had failed to fit his senior commanders for battle. His refusal to use the Canadians in battle in anything but corps or army strength meant that battle experience could never be gained, something that would cause unnecessary casualties when the First Canadian Army finally got to grips with the enemy. And McNaughton had so personalized matters with the War Office and with Ralston that he had become an impediment to the smooth functioning of the war effort. Still, Crerar's personal interest in all this was too clear and his disloyal methods of getting at McNaughton too underhanded to be readily countenanced. It was one thing to gossip maliciously about one's superior, but it was quite different for Crerar to undercut so consistently and with such force the man who had fostered his career — and in such high places. Unfortunately, and despite his protestations of virtue, it *had* become Crerar's habit to knife his superior in the back.

Incredibly, when the crisis broke in November 1943 and McNaughton at last became aware of the British and Canadian political and military forces arrayed against him, he continued to think highly of Crerar. In one of the climactic meetings with Colonel Ralston and General Stuart, the question of who might succeed McNaughton at the head of the First Canadian Army arose. "We spoke of Crerar," McNaughton wrote, "and I told him of my endeavour to shield him from the controversy in which I had necessarily been involved." Ralston's account of the conversation was very similar: "He recommended — had trained Crerar to 'keep away from these important things'. Would recommend him — only man we have. . . . Came back to Crerar. The man to succeed him."[123]

While these events were unfolding in England, Crerar was in Italy. He had just arrived there with his I Canadian Corps headquarters and the 5th Canadian Armoured Division, which was to join the 1st Canadian Division, in theatre since the invasion of Sicily. He learned of McNaughton's pending ouster from a note sent by his friend General Price Montague, in charge at CMHQ. Then Ralston arrived in Italy to see the troops — and to sound out Montgomery, who was expected to lead the invasion of France, about Crerar and to determine Crerar's interest in the army commander's post. Montgomery's word was that Crerar still had the "necessity for battle experience — nothing can substitute."[124] Monty had said much the same to Crerar almost a year earlier:

> It is a poor game sitting in England and doing nothing, with vital battles going on all over the world. And the real trouble is that the army in England is not really battle worthy. . . . Many of the generals have never seen a shot fired in this war — most of them in fact; they are not in touch with 'the feel of the battle'; they cannot possibly teach their subordinates if they themselves do not know the game. . . . Not only the theoretical side of it, but the stern practical side, and the repercussions that arise if you do NOT know what you are doing.[125]

It was that battle experience Crerar hoped to get in Italy, though he had to refuse Montgomery's suggestion at the end of October that he take command of the 1st Canadian Division to get it. His orders from McNaughton — that he consolidate all Canadian forces in the Mediterranean under the I Canadian Corps — did not permit him to consider that idea.[126]

In any case, it was soon clear that Crerar's time in the Mediterranean theatre would be limited. When he saw Ralston on 29 November, he handed him a memorandum that covered "his possible future position vis-à-vis Stuart (characteristic)."[127] It was characteristic of Crerar to put everything down on paper, ensuring that his own position was both clear and protected, and Ralston clearly had not forgotten his difficulties with the ambitious General when he was CGS. In fact, Crerar had produced a very sensible paper that proposed a division of labour between Stuart, expected to become Chief of Staff at CMHQ, and the army commander, one that would relieve Crerar of much of the non-military work that had worn McNaughton down. He was wise to insist that matters be clarified as soon as possible so that "all ranks of the Canadian Army Overseas should know, without any delay, that I am the GOC-in-C designate, even though temporarily remaining in command of 1 Cdn Corps." Crerar also suggested sweeping changes in command, proposing Guy Simonds, E.L.M. Burns, and Charles Foulkes for promotions to corps and divisional commands.[128] Crerar was letting the Minister know in no uncertain terms that he intended to put his stamp on the overseas army. In the end, matters worked out much as he had suggested, though the announcement of the change in command was delayed until early March.[129] Stuart minded the store as acting army commander until Crerar returned from Italy in March 1944, and then became Chief of Staff at CMHQ.[130] Simonds became GOC of the II Canadian Corps in England, with Foulkes as GOC of the 2nd Canadian Division. Burns took over the I Canadian Corps in Italy.

Crerar had also made clear to Ralston "that if he could not make good in battle he didn't want the job" of army commander.[131] The CIGS, Brooke, was aware of the political problems he would face if McNaughton's designated successor failed the test of command, but he also had to deal with the inexorable timetable that pointed towards D-Day and the invasion of France. First Canadian Army's commander had to be in place as soon as possible. On 4 January 1944 he wired to General Sir Harold Alexander, in overall command in the Mediterranean, that "it is essential that Crerar should gain maximum possible battle experience in next two months. Can you therefore arrange that Canadian Corps HQ takes over a sector at earliest possible date"?[132] There were problems, however, in the supply and tactical situations that made this impossible to arrange. There were difficulties as well with the Eighth Army commander, General Sir Oliver Leese, Montgomery's much less gifted successor. Before his departure, Montgomery had watched Crerar fall into quarrels with Guy Simonds (see chapter 6) and had begun to have doubts about Crerar as a field commander. So, too, did Leese. A big, guffawing Guardsman, Leese took a supercilious attitude to Crerar: "I am having a big problem with Canadian Commanders. Harry Crerar is here — & of course knows nothing of military matters in the field — but is presumably the commander designate of the Canadian Army in England." Worse, Simonds, the one good Canadian commander in Leese's view, was to return to England. "So I have to teach Crerar for a time — and then change again to another totally inexperienced commander." It was all Montgomery's fault, he told his wife: he had "shelved the necessity to teach Crerar . . . & refuses to take him as Army Commander till I've held the baby."[133] There was some justification in those complaints, however patronizing the tone.

In the end, Leese had no opportunity to teach Crerar anything. When he returned to England in March, the First Canadian Army's new commander had little more battle experience than when he had left. All he had done operationally was to institute a policy of intensive patrolling that was unsuccessful.[134] What most soldiers remembered, however, was that the corps commander imposed rigorous discipline on the 1st Canadian Division, a battle-tested formation that had adopted the Eighth Army's casual but efficient ways and resented what it saw as parade-square make-believe in an operational theatre. As General Chris Vokes, Simonds's successor in command of the division, wrote later, Crerar "had an outstanding administrative and organizational ability and was a disciplinarian, but there was all the difference in the world between the make believe of training in England and the real thing in Italy." He added that the new corps commander had been "meticulous in his observance of the clothing regulations. If he was improperly dressed I'm quite sure he felt naked."

Discipline might be difficult to bear, but Vokes and his staff also resented the flood of paper that soon emanated from corps headquarters, and he objected to Crerar's insistence on standing by a preconceived idea "even though it had been found unworkable or unreasonable in contemporary practice. His whole outlook on tactics was influenced by

his experience as a junior officer of artillery in the 1914–18 war." Crerar
believed the tactical methods of attack employed in Italy were wrong and
should be brought in line with those used in France and Flanders in the
First World War. Certainly Crerar was affected by the dreadful mud in
Italy that sometimes made the front look like Passchendaele, but his comments on the subject, delivered to the corps' officers on 11 February,
"were heard in stony silence by that battle-hardened galaxy."[135] Vokes was
overstating matters and far too condemnatory in his criticisms, as he was
wont to be, but he was at least partly right: Crerar was undoubtedly a
rigid man, wedded to the artillery-based doctrines of fire support he had
helped to develop in France and Flanders in 1918.

Nonetheless, the CIGS was delighted when Crerar returned to England to
take command of the First Canadian Army. "I have had to get rid of Andy
MacNaughton [sic], give Crerar sufficient war experience in Italy and get
Monty to accept him with very limited active experience," General Brooke
wrote. "All has now been accomplished with much anguish and many difficulties, but I have full confidence that Crerar will not let me down."[136]

QUICKLY ESTABLISHING himself in command,[137] Crerar professed astonishing optimism about the future course of the war when he
took over the First Canadian Army in March 1944. He told Vincent
Massey he felt "that German resistance may well be broken in a month or
six weeks,"[138] and he said much the same to George Currie, now Deputy
Minister of National Defence. "Crerar forecasts that if the first assault" in
Normandy "succeeds the remainder of the Canadian Army will not see
action as the Germans will fold up. If the first assault fails the remainder
of the Canadian Army will not be committed for some time thereafter."
Nevertheless, he had "supreme confidence" that D-Day would be successful. Crerar also talked freely to Currie about Montgomery, the army commander for the invasion. Monty "played for publicity," Crerar claimed,
"but is absolutely sound tactically." His fear, however, was that the
American public and military would turn on him "and slay him at his
first failure."[139] Except in his assessments of German resistance, Crerar's
judgments were shrewd, if not wholly accurate. He was right, however, to
focus on Montgomery, for his relations with the British commander
under whom he was to serve in the 21 Army Group would be difficult in
the coming months.

The trouble began before D-Day and continued for some time after 6 June when Crerar and Stuart were trying to sort out the constitutional and legal position of the First Canadian Army within Montgomery's 21 Army Group. Stuart saw Montgomery initially and ran into a buzzsaw. As Montgomery wrote in his diary, "I have had to be firm with STUART. . . . He wrote a letter to the C.I.G.S. about CRERAR's right to be consulted in the planning stages; I have a feeling that CRERAR put him up to it . . . I made it quite clear that I could not admit that CRERAR had any operational responsibility for Canadian troops serving temporarily in another Army.[140] Responsible to Ottawa for all Canadian army troops overseas, including the 3rd Canadian Division under command of the Second British Army for the invasion, Crerar was horrified. He scribbled on Stuart's letter setting out Monty's position, "Impossible. . . . Cdn administration must be Cdn responsibility and must [be exercised], in field by Cdn Army Comd."[141] He was correct, and the CIGS, his friend "Brookie," confirmed it to him: "notwithstanding anything Monty might say, I was bound to be responsible to the Canadian Government, in the last resort, for the operational employment of all Canadian troops in 21 Army Group."[142] Crerar put that position to Montgomery on 19 June, and Montgomery professed himself satisfied that the "air was properly cleared."[143] As one of Montgomery's British staff officers later put it, "I feel Monty was astonishing in his relationship with all the Dominion troops. He ordered them around like British troops, ignoring the devolution of the British Empire. . . . he was completely out of date."[144]

The significance of this contretemps was that it reinforced Montgomery's growing perception that Crerar was less a commander than a nit-picking legalist, someone so nationalistic that he could throw difficulties in the way of the effective prosecution of the war. "He is a most awfully nice chap," Montgomery said to Brooke, "but he is very prosy and stodgy, and he is very definitely not a commander."[145] On one level, Montgomery was right; on another, his cocksure ignorance of the Canadian constitutional position was simply staggering for the leader of an Allied enterprise, and it showed precisely why he would have difficulties with the Americans, too, much as Crerar had predicted. The CIGS understood the problems clearly, much more so than his field commander, and he expressed his alarm at Montgomery's strictures on Crerar:

I had about 1 1/2 intimate years with the Canadians in the last war & know well what their feelings are. They will *insist* that Canadian forces should be commanded by Canadians. I have already had MacNaughton [sic] kicked out & if we don't watch it we shall be accused of throwing out Canadians to try and make room for British Commanders. For that reason, I want you to make the best possible use of Crerar, he must be retained in Command of the Canadian Army, and must be given his Canadians under his command at the earliest convenient moment. You can keep his Army small & give him the less important role, and you will have to teach him.[146]

Monty backed off after he received this letter. He pointed out that Guy Simonds's II Canadian Corps had all the Canadians in Normandy under its command, that it would be wrong at this point in the bridgehead battle to put the First Canadian Army into action, and that he would teach Crerar "his stuff, and I shall give him tasks within his capabilities. And I shall watch over him carefully. I have a great personal affection for him; but this must not be allowed to lead me into doing unsound things."[147] Thereafter, in Montgomery's eyes, Crerar would have "executive" command of the First Canadian Army, but not true command. Even before this dispute, Montgomery would never have considered consulting the Canadian commander about his strategy for the conduct of the Normandy battle or, later, about his disputes with General Eisenhower over the plan to secure a quick end to the war with a massive strike into northern Germany; more to the point, after the dispute he would frequently bypass Crerar to deal directly with Simonds on matters affecting the II Canadian Corps whenever he pleased. There was little Crerar could do about it.[148]

Crerar had already sensed Montgomery's attitude. He wrote about British attempts to have Burns replaced as the I Canadian Corps commander in Italy in words that covered his own situation as well. The British views, according to Crerar, were influenced by two factors: "the Englishman's traditional belief in the superiority of the Englishman" and the "military inconvenience" of restrictions on the ready interchangeability of Canadian formations with British ones. What it all amounted to, Crerar said, his nationalism bursting forth, was "that no Canadian, or American, or other 'national' Comd, unless possessing quite phenomenal qualities, is ever rated as high as the equivalent Britisher."[149] Certainly that was Montgomery's attitude.

Crerar almost immediately fell into difficulties with the British general when his headquarters belatedly assumed its operational role on 23 July.

As the Army Group commander noted, "Harry Crerar has started off his career as an Army Comd by thoroughly upsetting everyone; he had a row with [Lieutenant-General J.T.] Crocker [the commander of the I British Corps, fighting under the First Canadian Army] the first day, and asked me to remove Crocker." There were faults on both sides, Montgomery admitted, but the problem was largely caused by Crerar: "I fear he thinks he is a great soldier and he was determined to show it the very moment he took over command at 1200 hrs on 23 July. He made his first mistake at 1205 hrs; and his second after lunch."[150] For once, Montgomery's judgment was objective. Crerar had earlier taken a dislike to Crocker[151] and, when the British officer refused to follow Crerar's overly detailed orders, Crerar had him put his complaints into writing.[152] There was room for a major blowup here, and Crerar, his approach overly academic in a Staff College way, had probably tried to interfere too much in the corps commander's battle. Montgomery had to step in to smooth over matters, to read the riot act to Crocker, and to tell Crerar politely but bluntly that "an Army Commander must stand back from the detailed tactical battle; that part is the province of his corps Commanders."[153] The lesson was learned, Crerar and Crocker began to forge a good relationship, and Crerar did not slip up in this way again.

If Montgomery had intended to keep Crerar away from the large battles, however, he failed to do so. The First Canadian Army was handed the lion's share of the struggle to reach Falaise in August, although the II Canadian Corps, led by Simonds, handled the detailed planning. Montgomery was condescending when he spoke of Crerar and his troops on 9 August:

> The Canadians should be able to fight their way to Falaise; they will not have the easy time they fancied, but they should get there; at present their forward movement is not making rapid progress. . . . Harry Crerar is fighting his first battle and it is the first appearance in history of a Canadian Army H.Q. He is desperately anxious it should succeed. He is so anxious that he worries himself all day. I go and see him a lot and calm him down. He will be much better when he realizes that battles seldom go completely as planned, that great patience is required, that you keep on at it until the other chap cracks, and that if you worry you will eventually go mad!! He seemed to have gained the idea that all you want is a good initial fire plan, and then the Germans all run away!![154]

The Falaise Gap was finally closed some two weeks later. The First Canadian Army and, notably, the II Canadian Corps had done well in very difficult circumstances, though its operations were certainly slower and more hesitant than Montgomery and Eisenhower would have wished. Still, much of the German army in France had been destroyed in the Falaise pocket. As Crerar wrote to a friend: "I believe the toughest fighting is now over. Indeed, if we were not at war with a government of fanatics, an unconditional surrender would have taken place a week or so ago."[155]

In the full flush of victory, Crerar once more found himself in an unpleasant situation with Montgomery. As the Canadian forces turned to the coastal ports and towards the Seine,[156] Crerar directed the 2nd Canadian Division to liberate Dieppe, that city of unhappy memories from two years before. After his men had occupied the town, Major-General Charles Foulkes, the GOC, asked Crerar to attend a religious service there on 3 September. Crerar, well aware of the significance of Dieppe to the division and to his country, accepted. A few hours later, Montgomery asked Crerar to come to a meeting at his headquarters at the same time. Crerar replied that the Dieppe service was important and, suggesting that the time of meeting at Montgomery's tactical headquarters be altered, attended the ceremonies. Montgomery was outraged, and when he finally saw Crerar he asked him abruptly why he had failed to follow his instructions. Crerar explained again why he had had to be at Dieppe and, according to his account, "the C-in-C intimated that he was not interested in my explanation — that the Canadian aspect of the DIEPPE ceremonial was of no importance compared to getting on with the war." Crerar replied that he had Canadian responsibilities which sometimes might run counter to Monty's wishes: "There was a powerful Canadian reason why I should have been present . . . at Dieppe that day," he said. "In fact, there were 800 reasons — the Canadian dead buried at Dieppe cemetery. I went on to say that he should realise, by our considerable association, that I was neither self-opinionated, nor unreasonable, but that, also, I would never consent to be 'pushed about' by anyone." When Montgomery persisted and said that "our ways must part," Crerar said he would report the matter to his government. Then, to Crerar's surprise, Montgomery backed off and declared the matter closed. So it was, and Montgomery sent an apologetic letter.[157]

This was one of Crerar's finest hours. As senior Canadian officer, he had stood forthrightly for the national interest in the face of Montgomery's bullying. The meeting he had missed was not of great operational importance and the Dieppe ceremonial was — to Crerar, to the 2nd Division, and to every Canadian. The one flaw in this triumph, however, was that Crerar, aware that Montgomery might try to reach him when he was en route to or at Dieppe, had left firm instructions with his Chief of Staff, Brigadier Churchill Mann, "that in no circumstances was he to receive any further communications from Monty until it was too late to cancel his role in the Dieppe ceremonies"![158] A clever man, Harry Crerar.

A few weeks later Crerar fell ill with anemia and dysentery and had to be evacuated to England for treatment.[159] Guy Simonds took over the army, much to Montgomery's gratification, and led the Canadians in the bitter fighting to clear the Scheldt estuary. If Crerar was a Quartermaster-General, in Montgomery's eyes, Simonds was a first-class field commander. The Field Marshal could treat with Simonds without the necessity of bypassing Crerar.[160] Not until early November did Crerar return.[161] Although he received a welcoming telegram from Montgomery, the Field Marshal's true feelings were quite different. When the new Defence Minister, General McNaughton, decided to promote Crerar to full General, Montgomery urged the CIGS to "arrange that announcement conveys impression that it is a normal promotion and NOT repeat NOT in any way for distinguished service in the field." God Almonty could control many things, but McNaughton was beyond his reach now, and the announcement in Ottawa talked of Crerar's "outstanding services . . . skilful leadership . . . outstanding personal qualities."[162] As that suggested, McNaughton continued to be Crerar's strongest supporter. But the leopard that was Crerar also had not changed its spots. On 6 November he dined with Massey in London and talked with him about "McNaughton's astonishing appointment as Minister of National Defence" and his fear that this might lead to pressure from Canada on the War Office to move I Canadian Corps from Italy to Northwest Europe. "If this were resisted as it might well be, on the valid grounds of operational and administrative difficulty," Massey recorded, "McN. he thought might well seize upon this and make an anti-British issue out of it. This appalling possibility is not to be excluded."[163] Pressure on London was a possibility, and it was typical of Crerar to foresee it; unfortunately, it was also entirely typical that he should gossip with Massey behind his old friend's and new Minister's back.

Crerar's war was not yet over. The First Canadian Army spent a long period after the Scheldt battles recuperating, and it was not until February that it moved into action once again in the great battle for the Reichswald, Operations Veritable and Blockbuster. Crerar's headquarters was a smoothly functioning organization on which the GOC-in-C depended, its "A" Mess a relatively happy and comfortable place with its tone set by Crerar's abstemious style. There were no surplus staff, no officers in corduroy pants or wearing scarves there.[164] Army headquarters did less commanding of the battle, however, than did Montgomery's headquarters above it or the corps and division headquarters below; the basic tasks of Crerar's headquarters were to coordinate air support for the corps under its command and to handle logistics, the trucks and tankers under its control carrying the vast tonnages needed for modern war. Crerar's own job was to visit his commanders, show the flag, and smooth out disagreements.[165] His conferences with his senior commanders, mercifully infrequent, tended to be over-rehearsed and uninspiring, and the difference in command style between him and Simonds was sharp for those who had been galvanized by Simonds's energy when he was in command.[166]

Nonetheless, Veritable was Crerar's finest hour. The battle, military historian Bill McAndrew has said, was "the epitome of the Canadian way of war: large scale orderly preparation, accumulation of massive resources, and meticulous planning. It was another Vimy Ridge."[167] Crerar's army, expanded with additional Allied troops, was 450,000 strong, the task was difficult, and the enemy fiercely defended its homeland, not least by breaching the Roer River dams and creating a horrid quagmire. Lieutenant-General Brian Horrocks's XXX British Corps was under Crerar's command, and he recorded the army commander's frequent visits to him. "He was always very well-informed because, in spite of the bad weather, he made constant flights over the battlefield in a small observation aircraft."[168] Those flights were dangerous, but Crerar, knowing he was sending men to their deaths, did not hesitate to expose himself to enemy fire.[169] Veritable was concluded successfully, though at terrible cost, and the Canadian troops participated with great distinction in the final battles of the war. Unwilling to be forced to shake hands or exchange salutes with the Nazi generals, Crerar left the surrender negotiations to his corps commanders. "The business we Canadians came over here to do," Crerar said without grandiloquence in his V-E Day message to the troops, "is virtually finished."[170]

Montgomery, who (astonishingly in light of the difficult relationship from 1944 on) told Crerar at war's end that "no commander ever has had a more loyal subordinate than I have had in you," recommended Crerar for a knighthood (KCBE), but Canadian government policy forbade the acceptance of such honours.[171] Instead, Crerar was made a Companion of Honour, an award of greater distinction. On his return to Canada in August, Crerar received a full government reception, a cross-country tour, and a number of honorary degrees.[172] The Prime Minister in 1946 also offered him the post of lieutenant-governor of Ontario, but Crerar decided "he did not feel that that was his line of country."[173] Instead, more than a little resentful that his accomplishments were not better recognized,[174] he filled a few minor diplomatic roles for the government in Czechoslovakia, the Netherlands, and Japan and, other than calling for conscription in the face of the Soviet threat, lived quietly in retirement in Ottawa. He died in 1965 at the age of seventy-seven, largely forgotten.

Harry Crerar had shaped the Canadian army. He built up its overseas headquarters, gave it an efficient training organization in Canada, and began the process of turning the I Canadian Corps into an effective military organization. In Northwest Europe he led the army effectively and cautiously, and he represented Canada with care and circumspection in Allied councils. He more than merited the honours he received. Though he had less original genius than McNaughton, he was a far abler field commander and national representative in an Allied war effort where Canada was but a junior partner. Humane as he usually was in his dealings with ordinary soldiers and junior officers, his flaws in character and his overweening ambition made Crerar a much less attractive human being than the equally ambitious McNaughton. Men loved McNaughton; at most, they had a grudging respect for Crerar.

TOMMY BURNS: PROBLEMS OF PERSONALITY

"I HAD KNOWN BURNS FOR MANY YEARS," wrote Major-General Christopher Vokes, the General Officer Commanding the lst Canadian Division in Italy for most of 1944, in a section of his memoirs that failed to find its way into print. "He had taught me as a cadet at the Royal Military College [and] . . . he had been highly regarded in Canadian military circles as one of the military intelligencia [sic]. . . and a 'comer.' . . . I had always admired him for his great ability as an officer." Vokes went on that, from the time Burns assumed command of I Canadian Corps in Italy early in 1944, "I never felt comfortable in his presence. His manner was shy, introverted and humourless. He seemed most unfriendly and distrustful. Perhaps he resented my more extensive experience in operational command and [feared] I might prove difficult to handle. For old time's sake I determined to tread warily and give him my loyal support." It was clear that the problem went beyond Burns's relationship with Vokes. Burns's introverted manner was always in evidence and "was construed by senior commanders outside the corps as a lack of confidence in himself." If he lacked confidence in himself, or seemed to, how could he inspire confidence in his subordinates? Vokes added that a cheerful manner was always necessary in a field commander and that the troops, quick to give nicknames to their generals, called the dour, glum Burns "Laughing Boy" or "Smiling Sunray," the latter tag based on the standard wireless-code name for the senior commander. "No names," he said, "were ever more negative in their meaning."[1] Before the year was out, Burns had been relieved of his command, and he never again would command troops in the field. What had gone wrong?

Burns's ability was great, his intelligence formidable. A commander has to be able to lead and to inspire, however, and the somber, introspective Burns, a man virtually without personality in the eyes of those who served under him, seemed incapable of this role. Yet to his friends outside the army and to the historian, Tommy Burns was easily the most interesting, complex, and intelligent of the Canadian generals, one of the few who thought deeply about the profession of arms and who published many articles and book reviews in the *Canadian Defence Quarterly*. At the same time, Burns led a secret life that saw him write frequently for H.L. Mencken's *American Mercury*, the best journal of the day, and even publish a creditable novel. Moreover, he was also something of a sexual adventurer, and his wartime career was nearly destroyed in 1941 when letters to his mistress were intercepted by the censors and brought to his superiors' attention. A man without personality? Hardly. But would it have made any difference to Vokes and others if Burns could have brought himself to reveal his personality to them? The question, unfortunately, is academic, for Burns's rigid military formation had not made him the kind of leader who could build consensus and carry his subordinates willingly with him into battle.

EEDSON L.M. BURNS was born in Montreal in 1897. His ancestry was Protestant Irish, his father working as a Canadian Pacific Railway investigator in Montreal and serving with the militia, and his mother coming from St Thomas, Ontario. His parents' marriage was stormy, troubled by the father's drinking, and it eventually broke up.[2] Young Burns went to school in St Thomas and at Montreal's exclusive Lower Canada College. After serving for a year in the ranks of the militia, he applied to the Royal Military College, stood second in the entrance examinations, and travelled to Kingston on 31 August to join the fifty-four-strong recruit class of 1914.[3]

The Great War had just begun when the seventeen-year-old Burns arrived at RMC, and the excitement in the country was especially sharp among his classmates. Not in Burns, however. As he wrote later, in 1927, "I had a powerful objection to dying for my country, or for anything else. . . . The incentive of a soldier's glory was quickly extinguished by the thought of filling a soldier's grave." The "usual crowd-compulsion," however, changed his attitude towards the war without his perceiving it. "The older students all went off to serve in one capacity or another . . . and the best ones went first."[4] Clearly he wanted to join them, and Burns took a commission in the Engineers as soon as he turned eighteen in June 1915. He left the college with a "Special War Certificate," an entry in the registrar's ledger that his character was "very good," and the comment, "Plenty of ability & has done well," on his academic report. Burns had the highest aggregate of grades in his class, standing first in artillery, tactics, and English, and second in mathematics, military history, field sketching, and military administration.[5] He had also helped to smuggle a cow into a senior cadet's room.[6]

The young officer had a "good" war. After training in Canada, he went to England with the 3rd Division's signallers in March 1916 and to France with the 4th Division in August 1916. Twice wounded in action, he won the Military Cross for personally laying and repairing signal cables under heavy fire. Soon after the end of the war he was a Staff Captain — at twenty-one the youngest in the Canadian Expeditionary Force — attached to the 12th Canadian Infantry Brigade and serving its acting commander, Colonel J.L. Ralston.[7] His mother, who went overseas herself and served on air force headquarters staffs, wrote to RMC's commandant in 1919 that "his generals all spoke well of his work he got his staff job at 21 — quite young for that I am told." She added: "They say he looks more like 35 than 21,"[8] the best indication that the war had taken its toll on young "Tommy" Burns — the nickname he had picked up from the famous Canadian heavyweight boxing champion who ruled the ring from 1906 to 1908.

As might be expected of a well-read young man who had noted that some senior British army officers had written about military subjects, Burns began to put something of his wartime experiences on paper. In an account of his front-line participation in the great Canadian victory of Vimy Ridge in April 1917, he acknowledged his fear and his difficulty in forgetting "that from five to twenty percent of the men got killed in big attacks." But, he said, "once the business of getting my crowd into the jumping-off trench was under way, the nervous tension was relaxed, and as I recollect it . . . my principal emotions were curiosity and a not unpleasant excitement." Burns went on to recount his actions in the assault that left him the sole unwounded officer in his unit; he concluded in a wholly conventional fashion that "this experience was a valuable one" because it taught him that "while fear may clutch, it does not necessarily strangle. . . . What am I likely to experience that will be harder to bear than that which I have borne? Or, put otherwise, I feel that I possess resources which will enable me to contend honorably against whatever adversities or calamities God is likely to throw in my way."[9]

In another article, Burns offered his assessment of the ideal soldier: "a primitive, honest fellow, uncomplicated by elaborate thought-machinery or superfluous ideas. He makes a simple and reliable tool which, though perhaps limited in its applications by its simplicity, will not get out of order at critical moments or commence to function erratically." The tone was as sardonic as the style Mencken's magazine demanded, but the scorn with which Burns wrote about five divinity students in his signals section rang loud and clear: "They were full of the sense of duty and the righteousness of the cause for which they were fighting. They wrote interminable letters, which I had to censor, filled with the most elevated and patriotic and humanitarian sentiments. But when we started to fight . . . the men I depended upon to go out at all hours of the day and night . . . were not the five theologians, but my red-headed Irish sergeant and two or three godless fellows who spent a great deal of their time in hospital from the wounds inflicted by lady snipers." [10] The preachers, he sneered, were only fit for employment as "hello girls," or switchboard operators. For all his intellect, Tommy Burns was a soldier who placed courage and the manly virtues ahead of everything else, or so he claimed for public consumption.

Burns had joined the Permanent Force as a captain in the Royal Canadian Engineers on 1 April 1920. He seemed to fit into the postwar army as if it had been made for him. Allowing for the appallingly slow pace of promotion, he moved ahead as rapidly in his career as any of his contemporaries.* A captain in 1920, Burns got his majority in 1927 and a

---

*"No, unfortunately there is more to getting promoted than passing the examinations," Burns wrote to a friend in August 1924. "Otherwise I should have been a Major-General long ago. I will probably have to wait several years before I put up my crowns. Forever, if the Liberal Government stays in power and holds to its present policy in military affairs." NA, Madge Macbeth Papers, Burns to Macbeth, 21 August 1924, ff. 1061–3.

further promotion to brevet lieutenant-colonel in 1935, although that was not confirmed until 1 September 1939.[11] At the same time, he was taking the right courses for promotion: the School of Military Engineering in Chatham, England in 1920-1, the British Army Staff College, Quetta, in 1928-9, and the Imperial Defence College from December 1938 until the outbreak of war. In the tiny Permanent Force, Burns was clearly someone who had punched all the proper tickets.

More to the point, Burns had made the right impression on his superiors. At Chatham, his report from the School of Military Engineering pronounced his ability "very good" and declared him especially so at surveying. That would have importance for his career, leading to his posting to RMC as an instructor in 1924 (where he became known for singing rude ditties while playing the piano).[12] He also became head of the geographical section of the General Staff in Ottawa from 1931 to 1936, where he was one of the pioneers in aerial mapmaking, the inventor of machines for plotting maps from air photographs, and the author of published technical articles.[13] In an army led by the scientifically inclined Andy McNaughton, those qualifications did him no harm.

Nor did his annual confidential reports. Although Brigadier C.F. Constantine, the commandant of RMC, found him shy and reticent and simultaneously sarcastic and cynical in 1926, that was almost the only black mark on his record. The Staff College report of December 1929 declared him the possessor of a "strong and imperturbable" character, mental quickness, and the ability to express himself well. Strikingly, it reported him to be a "very popular officer" with "a great sense of humour." Burns had clearly impressed his instructors and colleagues with his intellect and ability, and he continued to do so in Canada, McNaughton in 1935 pronouncing him "very capable and efficient," a man of "energy, vision and decision." Harry Crerar in 1936 was even warmer, calling Burns "exceptionally able . . . well above the average of his rank."[14] To have the two key officers in the Permanent Force so firmly on his side certainly helped his burgeoning career.

While his military life progressed satisfactorily, the enormously energetic Burns was continuing to develop the other sides of his character. Although his mother had noted in 1919 that "he isn't really a ladies' man,"[15] Burns had a lively interest in women. Yet it was not until 1927, at the age of thirty, that Burns married. His bride was Eleanor Phelan, a doctor's daughter he had met while instructing at RMC. Like him, she was Irish; unlike him she was Catholic and religious — "in an Irish way," her daughter Mary recalled.[16] The marriage was quickly followed by the journey to the Staff College at Quetta, India, an exotic locale for the couple to begin to learn how to live together.* Burns reported to a literary friend that his wife "likes it here and we both find married life quite tolerable." Later he added that they had not yet come to blows. "Married life among the British domiciled in India isn't always ideal. There is a large surplus of men, and if a woman looks like slipping there are lots ready to fling banana skins in her path."[17] There is no indication that Eleanor slipped in India (or at any time thereafter), and none that Burns strayed very far, but the marriage became troubled after their return to Canada. The difficult pregnancy and caesarean birth of their daughter in 1933 left Eleanor nervous and in frail health.

While his home life was taking shape and his military career progressing rapidly, Burns began to write articles for *American Mercury,* the magazine published by H.L. Mencken, the greatest interwar critic of American life. He had sent Mencken an argumentative letter after the magazine published an article prophesying Canada's eventual absorption by the United States, an idea that seems much more likely today than in the 1920s; Mencken, impressed by his argumentation and style, suggested he write for his magazine. "This really set me up on a cloud," Burns recalled years later, for "I admired Mencken for his iconoclastic blasts against the stuffy Victorian-Edwardian mores and literature of North America."[18]

In effect, Burns became the *American Mercury's* military writer, publishing articles under the pseudonym Arlington B. Conway, a device that protected him from the wrath of his superiors and obviated the necessity of attempting to clear publication through them. He drew on his own wartime experiences, but more often offered his speculations on trends, tactics, weaponry, and the military policies of the Great Powers. An article in 1925 on "The Cavalry of Tomorrow" shot great holes in the arguments advanced by those who maintained that the Great War experience of

---

*The servant problem required getting used to at Quetta. A single officer had six or seven servants — two personal ones, two grooms, one untouchable for menial tasks, and one gardener. University of Victoria Archives, Brigadier G.R. Bradbrooke interview, 22 May 1980.

121

trench warfare had done nothing to minimize the future value of the horse in battle. Burns advocated the creation of "an automobile that can go anywhere [the horse] can go at the same or better speed." The argument Burns advanced, in effect a call for the development of the jeep or the armoured personnel carrier, was so compelling that there ought to have been no doubt about its immediate implementation. Why was no country doing what he suggested? Burns asked. Because the cavalrymen "regard any reflections against the usefulness of their idolized beasts as the most impious kind of blasphemy. The smell of the stable is an incense to their nostrils. . . . They look on the horse as a romantic symbol of personal superiority."[19] A good example of what Burns called his "imitatio Menckenii style."[20]

Another article four years later on "The Training of Soldiers" noted that no training could inculcate initiative in infantrymen: "if the ranks of the infantry were filled with intelligent men, it is unlikely that they would long submit willingly to being used as it is intended to use infantry."[21] In 1932, he argued forcefully and with genuine independence of mind against those who believed that air power could destroy whole cities. "Never again will civilians sleep safe in their beds while the boys watch in the trenches. But . . . air forces by themselves will never do to great cities what Rome did to Carthage, or what the Assyrians did to Jerusalem."[22] He was wrong, but only a few air-power theorists by 1932 had anticipated the Lancaster and B-29 bombers that little more than a decade later levelled the cities of Germany and Japan so thoroughly.

Burns thought of himself as more than a commentator on military subjects in the *American Mercury*. He was also writing short stories, plays, and even a novel.[23] What appears to have moved him from dabbling towards active publication was his friendship with Madge Macbeth, in the 1920s a widow in her mid forties who was a widely published and well-known writer, most notably for a *succès de scandale* she published on Ottawa life during the Great War, *The Land of Afternoon*, written under the pen name of Gilbert Knox. The first of Burns's letters to her that survives, dated in June 1924, reveals that they were collaborating on a novel set in Quebec. Burns, surveying in the Eastern Townships of Quebec that summer, recounted a meeting with a Mme Payette who operated an illegal still and invited him to sample her wares. "We had quite a little discussion about the relative merits of her product and Scotch, and parted with assurances of mutual esteem."

That incident, he said, could be used in the novel.[24] The novel moved along slowly, both authors being busy with other writing and Burns fully engaged in his military life, which he recognized had to take precedence. A young officer's pay was small, however, and like his comrades he was always short of money. In October 1925 he wrote to Macbeth that he was studying for his Staff College entrance examinations in the spring of 1927,

> and as it will affect my future career very much, I don't want to take any chance I can avoid of failing them. There is an immense amount of work — principally reading — to be done for it; geography of the British Empire, Imperial organization, political economy, a subject called transportation, and the strictly military parts, which involve much practice at writing orders, and working out tactical and strategical problems from the map. When that is done, I haven't very much time left — what I mean, is that if I do anything else, it means stealing time from this important business. . . . What it amounts to, is, what are the prospects of cash returns from the novel if we write it? I need the money now — I mean when the thing is issued — but can afford to let glory wait.[25]

Burns duly scored the highest marks of all candidates throughout the empire in the entrance examinations,[26] but it had been a hard slog. Although he and Mrs Macbeth continued to correspond and comment regularly on Canadian literary life and personalities, the novel was not published until 1929, under the title *The Great Fright: Onesiphore Our Neighbour*, at two dollars a copy. The publisher, the house of Carrier in Montreal and New York, had been "harassed by fears of the action of the church," Burns said and, as he told Macbeth, "I think it could bear some bowdlerising. It is a little more outspoken than I remembered it." In fact, *The Great Fright* reads very tamely today and is noticeable only for being written in places in a mock-William Henry Drummond *habitant* style of speech that jars badly, though it would not have in the 1920s. Burns had intended that only his pseudonym would be employed,[27] but he was at Quetta when the book appeared, and Macbeth handled all the details of publication and publicity. As a result, although the book appeared under the joint byline of Macbeth and Conway, Burns was identified in the advertising by name, with a photograph, and as a serving officer. Happily, no one at National Defence Headquarters seems to have noticed, but to the authors' chagrin, neither did many in the English-Canadian literary community.

Indeed, few of Burns's colleagues in the army seem to have read anything he published except his professional articles in the *Canadian Defence Quarterly*, the semi-official journal of the Canadian forces in which Burns appeared with great regularity from 1925 on. He reviewed books in wholesale lots, his tastes ranging from military history to memoirs to strategy. He looked for good writing, he railed at the pompous and foolish, and his judgments were clear and forthright.[28] It was his articles that made his reputation — for good or ill — and Burns published more than a dozen between 1924 and 1938. Some reflected the arguments he had made in the *American Mercury*, such as "The Mechanicalization of Cavalry" in 1924 and "Speculations on Increased Mobility" in 1926, the latter based on close observation of the results of Britain's major military exercises in September 1925. Burns recognized that Canada's pathetically underequipped forces were unlikely to find solutions to the problems of mobile warfare thrown up in those exercises, but "when war does come, those who have thought about the problems will be better able to face them than if they presented themselves entirely strange, bristling with the menace of the unknown."[29] He, at least, was thinking about them, in contrast to one critic in the cavalry, Captain Roy Nordheimer, who more than merited the criticism that he "had learned nothing from his experiences at Moreuil Wood, where 300 troopers and 800 horses had gone down in ninety minutes."[30] Burns himself wrote, only half-jokingly, that the sentries at the Royal Canadian Dragoons barracks "had instructions to bayonet me on sight."[31] Horses would not finally be put out to pasture in the Canadian army until just prior to the outbreak of war.

Other subjects also consumed Burns. He ranged from "The Principles of War," that staple of military thinking, to the subject of military uniforms, advocating radical rethinking of the soldier's garb.[32] That article angered many traditionalists in the militia and the Permanent Force,[33] but it won the praise of Captain B.H. Liddell Hart, the leading British military thinker and writer who was also calling for changes in the uniform soldiers wore to fight. Burns, greatly flattered at praise from this quarter, replied that he had needed little moral courage to speak out for the new: "Our present Chief of the General Staff [McNaughton] is not much in favour of fuss and feathers. He was once detected proceeding to a formal inspection wearing a civilian hat with his uniform!"[34]

The articles that drew the most attention appeared not long before the outbreak of war in 1939. They can justly be put in the same category as the writings on armoured warfare of Charles de Gaulle or Heinz Guderian. In the April 1938 issue of the *Canadian Defence Quarterly*, Burns's "A Division That Can Attack," written while he was the General Staff Officer in Military District No. 4 in Montreal, appeared. The 1936 reorganization of the British army had left a three-brigade division of infantry without armour, the tanks concentrated in tank brigades. Convinced that this meant a return to Great War tactics, and heavy casualties, Burns instead called for fast medium tanks to be the focus of battlefield penetration tactics with the infantry confined to fire support and consolidation. An assault of such tanks, Burns wrote, "will have far greater chance of achieving real success than an infantry assault, or an infantry-cum-tank assault, because it moves much faster, is less dependent on artillery fire, and is immune to the weapons with which the bulk of the enemy troops are armed." To accomplish this role, the standard division ought to be formed of one armoured and two infantry brigades.

Burns's piece drew a spirited reply, "An Army That Can Attack — A Division That Can Defend," from Captain Guy Simonds of the Royal Canadian Horse Artillery. Arguing that it was wasteful to disperse tanks to all divisions when, of necessity, many divisions would always be on the defensive, Simonds called for tanks to be held in reserve. The division, Simonds suggested, was no longer a balanced formation of all arms; an army was now. The division was designed to hold a defensive position and, if required for an army assault, it would be reinforced with the requisite armour and artillery. For Simonds, the tanks were the key weapon in the army commander's hands, and armour could not be decentralized permanently. Burns and Simonds had another article each to continue their argument, the absolute high point of interwar military thinking in Canada.[35] Both future corps commanders had made good points, and the coming war would see both conceptions of divisional organization put into practice. Neither was proven right — or wrong.

When Burns's second article in the debate with Simonds appeared, he was a student at the Imperial Defence College, taking the one course that was thought to provide a guaranteed ticket to high command. He had impressed his superiors in the Permanent Force with his ability as a hardworking staff officer and an original thinker, and he seemed ideally placed to move ahead quickly when the Second World War began. Still in his early forties, Burns was one of the handful of Canadian officers marked for the highest positions of command.

WHEN THE FIGHTING BEGAN in September 1939, Burns was between terms at the Imperial Defence College. Like other Canadian officers in Britain on course, he reported to the High Commission in London. He soon persuaded Mike Pearson that he should be assigned as GSO 1 at Canada House, in effect the senior military representative, until such time as Canadian Military Headquarters was organized the next month under Brigadier Harry Crerar.[36] His first important task was to work out what to do with the 1800 offers of service that had been received at the High Commission from Canadians in Britain, a task he handled well enough for Vincent Massey, the High Commissioner, to begin referring to him warmly as Burns "of my staff."[37] He was also playing a liaison role with the War Office in these early days, trying to persuade the Imperial General Staff to give more information to Ottawa about its planning[38] and working out arrangements for the reception and accommodation of the Canadian Division, then in process of formation at home.[39]

Once CMHQ was up and running, Burns worked as General Staff Officer there under Crerar and his Senior Administrative Officer, Colonel Price Montague. The work, he recalled, "was heavy and without respite. There was so much to be done to bring the armament, equipment and training of the Canadian troops in England up to the standard which would fit them for battle against the Germans. We all thought we would enter the kind of war which had ended in 1918 . . . a static period of 'trench warfare'" followed by an eventual offensive.[40] In other words, Burns, the advocate of armoured warfare, recognized that the time — and equipment — for the ideas he had pressed had not yet arrived. In the interim, Burns did a staff officer's job, sitting in on meetings of the brass and politicians, taking minutes, and preparing memos on a multitude of topics.[41] He did his work well enough for Crerar, who well knew his value, to press Ottawa to promote Burns to colonel;[42] this promotion duly followed on 4 May 1940 by which time Burns was commanding the Canadian reinforcement unit at Aldershot.

As Hitler advanced, so did Burns's career. In the new atmosphere of urgency, able staff-trained officers were suddenly in great demand. Crerar was called back to Canada to become Chief of the General Staff and to plan the army's growth. Burns, slated to become GSO 1 of the 2nd Canadian Infantry Division under Major-General Victor Odlum, instead was posted back to Ottawa as Crerar's special assistant* and then as Assistant Deputy Chief of the General Staff.[43] Drafting and redrafting submissions in long-hand, his first task was to reorganize the General Staff's branches at National Defence Headquarters, hard work that won him Crerar's praise.[44]

There was a streak of stubbornness in Burns that sometimes put him in difficulty. He knew Colonel J.L. Ralston, the Minister of National Defence, from their shared service in 1919, and perhaps Burns thought that connection, as well as his intelligence, gave him special licence. At a morning conference in November 1940, as Ralston's assistant wrote in his diary, "Minister had long argument with Col Burns — Burns opposed to giving parliament statistical information as to men and armament — Minister states democratic parliament must have much of it."[45] Ralston won the argument, of course, but he was also right and he knew it. He began to form a dark view of Burns, telling Victor Sifton, the newspaper chain owner he had made Master-General of the Ordnance, that Burns and another staff officer were "as stupid as wooden Indians."[46] Or was it only that Burns, as Ralph Allen wrote later in the *Globe and Mail*, suffered from "the habit of putting his personal version of fact ahead of tact"?[47]

Perhaps the confrontation with the Minister was one reason why Crerar failed in December 1940 to get Burns the command of the armoured division for which planning was in progress in Canada. That post instead went to Major-General E.C. Sansom, brought back from England for the job.[48] In February 1941, however, Crerar reluctantly agreed to release Burns — an officer of "outstanding ability" with a "keen analytical brain,"[49] — so he could become Brigadier General Staff of the Canadian Corps in Britain three months hence. That posting entailed a promotion for Burns. Crerar told McNaughton that Burns still had particular responsibilities for the

---

*Not everyone was happy that Burns was at Crerar's right hand. Brigadier-General J. Sutherland Brown, then in retirement, wrote a friend that Burns "is one of those clever fellows who writes articles and passes examinations with 90–100% but is not fit to command two men and a boy." Queen's University Archives, Sutherland Brown Papers, box 1, f. 16, Brown to Billy [W.W. Foster], 16 August 1940.

organization of new formations for the army and was the key staff planner putting together an Army Tank Brigade for early dispatch to Britain as well as establishing the basic organizational plan for Canada's first armoured division. "It will not be possible for me to replace him for some weeks,"[50] Crerar said. At the same time, Burns was also travelling regularly to Montreal to work on the development of the Canadian-designed Ram tank.

Burns's rise towards the highest ranks was about to be stopped short. During his frequent trips to Montreal, he had met a married woman and begun an affair. A sergeant who worked with him in Ottawa during this period remembered a half century later that Burns regularly referred slightingly to his wife and found every opportunity to go to Montreal.[51]

The military had no reason to be concerned about this liaison so long as it did not interfere with Burns's work. But when he went to England to become BGS, Canadian Corps, in May 1941, the affair suddenly became known to the British authorities and to General McNaughton. As BGS, Burns was the chief planner for the corps commander, the essential staff officer who was privy to everything. Discretion was the watchword for a successful staff officer at such a high level, and Burns was ordinarily tight-lipped. But not sufficiently so, for in late July one of his long letters to his lady friend in Montreal was randomly intercepted by the British postal censors, opened, read, and sent to the War Office. Passed to McNaughton on 5 August with the dry comment, "I am sure you will agree that it contains indiscretions," the British left the corps commander to act. The next day, McNaughton told the War Office that Burns had been removed from his post and was to be returned to Canada forthwith.[52]

What could Burns have written to have tossed his career so completely into the dustbin? Not his love talk, but his references to people and policy. First, he referred to C.G. Power, the Air Minister who was visiting Britain in July 1941 and who drank heavily, as being in a "disgusting state."[53] That was likely true — Power was often a falling-down drunk — but it was not what a staff officer ought to have said, and it showed a certain personal disloyalty, for Power was an old family friend and godfather to Burns's daughter Mary.[54] Then Burns criticized British generals for having lost the initiative in the war, and he commented that McNaughton did not appear to like General Claude Auchinleck, the British commander in the Middle East. Moreover, he told his friend, "I have urged McNaughton not to have anything to do" with raids that sacrificed lives in "minor operations. . . . I understand the CinC and PM are of the same opinion. But the urge to take some action may be too strong — and the contrary view may win the day. Don't blame me too much if this occurs." There were additional comments on advice he had offered and further ruminations on air and land strategy, the tone intellectually arrogant and just as sardonic as his writings for Mencken had been.[55] None of it was recriminating (except for the comment on McNaughton's opinion of Auchinleck, which could have embarrassed the Canadian commander's relations with the War Office), but the GOC had no choice other than to act as he did. In fact, McNaughton's initial thought had been to court-martial Burns, but after discussing the case with the Judge Advocate General, Price Montague, he had "deemed it unwise in the public interest that this course be followed."[56]

The case was not concluded. Burns was suspended from duty upon his return to Canada, and Crerar, the CGS, interviewed Burns and heard him "come clean." As he noted shrewdly, "I am of the opinion that his actions in writing the way he did are almost entirely due to an excess of professional vanity and are not the result of inherent disloyalty."[57] Burns was paraded before the Minister of National Defence, Colonel Ralston, and told that "his serious offence is the disregard of the obligations of trust and confidence and of secrecy which were the foundation of his fiduciary responsibilities. . . . I have informed him of my grave displeasure." Burns was also advised that he could not be employed at his present rank and pay should he wish to remain in the army. Ralston held out some hope, however, saying that Burns's abilities were needed: "I assured him that I believed if he continued in the service he could retrieve himself and regain the confidence of his associates which was bound to be severely shaken by his action, and that he would have every chance to do this."[58]

Severely chastened and depressed by his fall from grace, Burns was reduced in rank to colonel and named Officer Administering, Canadian Armoured Corps. Nothing of these events found its way into the press or Burns's later memoirs, naturally enough, but rumours of the "defeatist" letters or remarks Burns had made were widespread among officers during and after the war. Surprisingly, the affair with the Montreal woman appears to have continued, and when Burns went back to England in 1943 she, too, found her way there.[59]

Burns spent the period from August 1941 until February 1942 administering the fledgling Armoured Corps.[60] He was then promoted to brigadier once more and given a brigade in the 4th Canadian Armoured Division, a formation he had been largely responsible for creating.[61] When his promotion was announced, General McNaughton wired from England, "I would like Burns to know that Crerar, Montague, Sansom and Worthington as well as myself are all happy in the new opportunity which is being given to him."[62] Gestures like that made many love Andy McNaughton, and Burns put that telegram in his scrapbook. He soon took his brigade to England.

The process of redemption was completed on 1 May 1943, when Burns was promoted to major-general and given the 2nd Canadian Division. The selection committee that made that choice was chaired by McNaughton, by then army commander, and had as one of its two members Harry Crerar, commanding I Canadian Corps.[63] So Burns had successfully recovered from his indiscretions and made his way back into the good graces of his superiors. His was a remarkable achievement, attesting to his courage in a time of great personal difficulty and to the ability his superiors could not do without. But the seeds of future trouble were already there. In mid 1943, someone in Ralston's confidence prepared assessments of virtually all the senior officers overseas for the Minister's private contemplation. The appraisal of Burns pointed unerringly to his weak points: "Exceptionally high qualifications but not a leader. Difficult man to approach, cold and most sarcastic. Will never secure devotion of his followers. Has probably one of the best staff brains in the Army and whilst he will lead his Division successfully he would give greater service as a high staff officer."[64]

An almost identical opinion was offered at roughly the same time by a British corps commander who had served at the Royal Military College just before the war and had some knowledge of the Canadian senior officers. Most were dismissed as "rather poor," or so General G.C. Bucknall told Basil Liddell Hart, but there was "more promise in some of the younger Canadian commanders, particularly in Simmonds [sic]. . . . Burns is technically clever, but not such a good personality."[65] With Bernard Montgomery and Dwight Eisenhower setting the standard for personality in the Allied armies, a winning smile and a knack for talking with the men was a plus with the public and, more importantly, the troops.

Burns was not long in command of the 2nd Canadian Infantry Division. At the beginning of January 1944 General Sansom, commanding II

Canadian Corps, was replaced by Guy Simonds, who was brought back from Italy to take over the corps. Burns took command of Simonds's 5th Canadian Armoured Division.[66] There was yet more to come. Within days of Burns's arrival in Italy, his future was already mapped out. Harry Crerar, tapped to succeed the sacked McNaughton as commander of the First Canadian Army and preparing to leave Italy, where he had briefly commanded I Canadian Corps, had already decided on 25 January 1944 that "if Burns acts up to expectations he will undoubtedly be my recommendation for Corps Commander."[67] The climax of Burns's extraordinary wartime career was set to begin.

BURNS TOOK OVER COMMAND of the 5th Canadian Armoured Division, which had been in Italy for about ten weeks, on 23 January.[68] The 11th Brigade of the division had staged its first operation on the Arieli River on 17 January with disastrous results; even so, it was more battle-tested than its new commander, who had never commanded so much as a company, let alone a division, in action in this war. In that sense he was in exactly the same position as every Canadian division commander with the exception of Major-General J. Hamilton Roberts, who had been in command at Dieppe; Guy Simonds, who had successfully led the 1st Division since July and briefly commanded the 5th; and Chris Vokes, who had taken over from Simonds on 1 November 1943. Even Crerar had yet to lead his two divisions in action. Still, it mattered to those who had led brigades successfully, to those who had driven the German paratroopers from Ortona, that an untried commander was put in command of a newly arrived division. ("There was a certain disposition," Burns said later, "to assume that the history of modern warfare had begun on 10 July 1943," the day Canadians landed in Sicily.)[69] Battle experience in Montgomery's Eighth Army was deemed to be the key to everything and, if Monty had already left for England to command the armies preparing to invade France, his successors continued to share his approach.[70]

In the eyes of his superiors and subordinates, therefore, Burns had to prove himself — and quickly. General Sir Oliver Leese, the Eighth Army's bluff and hearty new commander, made this clear in his letters to his wife. "I am just off to see the Canadians again — a new general by name Burns. . . . I hope he will be allright [sic]," he wrote on 20 February. Two weeks later he sounded pleased enough: "I think he will be good. I will be glad to get rid of Harry [Crerar] and get Burns installed & to get down to some degree of permanency."[71] That same search for permanency was also evident in a personal letter from Lieutenant-Colonel W.C. Murphy, the GSO 1 of the 5th Armoured Division. "We have still another general," he told his family on 5 February. "General Burns has joined us. He is very nice to work with and all goes well from that angle. No doubt I'll find a general that I consider good enough to keep on the job one of these days. I hope we'll settle down with no more changes for a while because things always have to be adjusted a bit with each boss man's viewpoint."[72]

Change was inevitable in wartime, and more came quickly. Now definitely ordered to return to Britain to take command of the First Canadian Army, Crerar had held to his conclusion that Burns ought to be his successor. "Burns is showing up very well, indeed, and gives one a feeling of great confidence," he wrote to General Ken Stuart, the Chief of Staff, CMHQ, and acting army commander in England. "Vokes has certainly reached his ceiling but, providing he is told very clearly what he is to do, and is guided, in his actions, from above, can be regarded as fit for the responsibilities of his appointment."[73] Vokes was a tough-talking officer who had done well in action as a brigade commander through the Sicilian fighting, but Montgomery had formed the view that division command was his limit and he probably communicated that to Crerar. Moreover, his constant and colourful cursing and womanizing may have offended the staid and slightly prissy Crerar.* As was so often the case, Crerar's wishes prevailed. "It was a great surprise" to be promoted to corps commander," Burns wrote.[74]

Though still untested in a major battle, though his experience commanding a division in action was limited to six weeks of static operations, Burns was put in command of the corps, initially on a temporary basis, at the beginning of March; his appointment was confirmed on 20 March and he was then, in his forty-seventh year, the oldest of Canada's active field commanders. As he wrote feelingly to Crerar, his most constant supporter, "I am not very articulate in these matters, but I think you know I am profoundly grateful to you for your unfailing confidence in me; and especially at the time when I might well have forfeited it."[75] Crerar's confi-

---

*There is an old army saw that if "fuck" and "frontal" were removed from the military's vocabulary, the Canadian army would have been left both speechless and unable to attack. Vokes, some maintained, had been the inspiration for the saying.

dence in Burns remained just as high when he landed in Britain. In two private conversations early in April with the Deputy Minister of National Defence, Colonel Currie, Crerar said that if anything should happen to him, Burns, not Simonds, was his choice for army commander.[76] He repeated much the same advice to Stuart a month later. Simonds already had a reputation in the field, while Burns "has yet to establish himself in operations."[77] He admitted that Simonds was "more brilliant," but pronounced Burns "the better balanced" and one who "looks further ahead." Leese's impression of Burns had also solidified. In mid April he wrote the Assistant CIGS, General J.N. Kennedy, that "the Canadians under Burns are developing into a very fine Corps. He is an excellent commander and will, I feel sure, do well in battle. . . . I liked Crerar very much as a man but I am sure that Burns is a better soldier." Leese added that "he also gets on better with the Divisional Generals."[78]

At the time Leese wrote, I Canadian Corps was just a month away from attacking the Hitler Line in its first major operation. Burns now had the opportunity to make his mark. The initial stages of the attack on the main Nazi position in the Liri Valley south of Rome went very well. Preceded by a massive artillery barrage (810 guns firing on 3500 yards of enemy defences!), the 1st Canadian Division opened a hole in the line and the 5th, now commanded by Major-General Bert Hoffmeister, began to pour through on 24 May, hampered substantially by a tangle of traffic-snarled vehicles. The Canadian casualties were terrible with 789 killed and almost 2500 wounded, including high rates of battle exhaustion, along with 4000 sick and injured, in the three weeks of fighting. This was easily the equivalent, Terry Copp and Bill McAndrew wrote, of a huge disaster in a large city.[79]

Despite the advance, Leese's initial responses were critical: "It is their first battle as a Corps and the joints are creaking rather to start with." A week later, he noted that the corps was "a bit rusty at first in their staff work, inter-communication and traffic control. They realize their difficulties and are improving daily." Then, most positively, Leese said to his wife: "I am very glad that Burns and his Corps staff have had a success their first battle. It will give them confidence and poise."[80] The pursuit of the fleeing Germans, however, was hampered by inexperience at the 5th Canadian Armoured Division headquarters and by terrible traffic jams as two corps of five Canadian, Indian, and British divisions competed for road space on a one-corps front and soon gridlocked the inadequate single highway running through the Liri Valley.[81] Whether this was the fault of the I Canadian Corps headquarters, the Eighth Army, or the commander of the 15th Army Group in Italy, General Sir Harold Alexander,[82] was moot, for Burns got the rocket for the delays from General Leese: "Burns came to see me today and I read him the Riot Act about the staff work and control of the Canadian Corps. I hope very much he can improve it. He is, though, a man of no personality and little power of command but I don't see at the moment who else they have got."[83]

Leese wrote to Montgomery in much the same vein a few days later, saying he had had to take the Canadian Corps out of the line to train. "It broke down in method of command, staff control, and conduct of the battle. In particular, there was a lack of coordination of Engineer and Traffic resources. The troops fought magnificently but were hampered by the lack of co-ordination and control from above."[84] The Eighth Army commander was even more blunt in a letter to the Assistant CIGS on 8 June: "I have had a difficult problem with Burns. He is a highly intelligent man and quick in the up-take. But he lacks personality, initiative, tactical sense and power of command." The General watched the problems that arose because Burns and his corps staff were new to battle, while Vokes and Hoffmeister, the two Canadian division commanders, were very experienced. "Burns realises his difficulties," Leese continued. "He has had a poor B.G.S., and as a result the staff organization and method of command has broken down in the stress of battle . . . it is not easy as neither Burns nor his Corps staff are up to 8th Army standards."[85]

Whether Leese himself was up to Eighth Army standards was not a question its commander put either to himself or others; certainly some critics then and later believed that Leese was to blame for the misallocation of roads, that he had mishandled operations south of Rome and been outshone by the French led by General Juin, and that he had needlessly fallen into politico-military wrangling with the American commander, General Mark Clark. Like too many senior officers of limited ability, like too many British officers when dealing with "colonials," Leese was not averse to blaming his Canadian subordinates for his own and his headquarters' faults. His early praise for Burns and his corps had been forgotten and was now replaced with the desire for Canadian heads.[86] In the circumstances, Burns had to sack his BGS, Nick McCarter, fire one brigade commander and caution another, and speak sternly about their failings to his Chief Signals Officer and Chief Engineer (the latter also being replaced before the end of July).[87]

Under this severe stress, Burns also became far too concerned with his troops' dress and discipline. One of his ADCs remembered that Burns called on a tank workshop to congratulate the commanding officer for his unit's repair work during the Liri battle. Unfortunately, the GOC became distracted when he saw one soldier wearing the wrong headgear and, instead of congratulations, the officer got a stern lecture.[88] Additional stories abound of Burns disciplining troops coming out of the line with their battledress jackets unbuttoned, and another senior officer remembered that this coldest of cold fish always seemed to be criticizing someone or something. Part of the problem was that Burns believed, rightly enough, that war was a serious business; unfortunately, his dour personality kept his mess a silent place, and he made his officers uncomfortable by refusing any light conversation, by not drinking, and by conveying that if he did not, none should.[89] Smiling Sunray's frigid style did not wash well with his two division commanders, his staff, or with the fighting men, any more than his austere personality succeeded in striking a chord with the more extroverted Leese.[90]

Overall, Burns wrote to Crerar, "I think we can be well satisfied with our performance. We did what was asked of us from the start, and the troops fought exceptionally well." He admitted that when the pursuit began "we were too slow and several opportunities were missed," but the failures were outweighed by the successes, "considering it was the Corps' first time in action, and a complicated operation with an untried fmn [formation] was given us to do."[91]

If Burns was now well satisfied with his performance, Leese had definitively concluded he was not, and he was making his complaints known to his superiors. On 28 June, Leese discussed Burns with General Alexander, and the Army Group commander duly cabled the CIGS, Sir Alan Brooke:

> I am very concerned about the future of the Canadian Corps. I had a long talk to Leese on the subject yesterday and there is no doubt at all that the present position regarding Command is most unsatisfactory. . . . The weakness does not lie in the Divisions but in the Corps H.Q. and more particularly in the Corps Commander. The B.G.S. has been changed and Leese is now satisfied that given a really good commander the Corps staff will be all right. I am not sure if you know Burns well. He is intelligent and easy to work with but he is

sadly lacking in tactical sense and has very little personality and no (repeat no) power of command. It might be possible in time to develop a tactical sense in him but personality and power of command are as you know qualities which simply cannot be taught to a man of his age. Burns' short comings as a Corps Commander place Leese in a very difficult position regarding the employment of the Canadian Corps since he must either give them a task beyond the powers of the Commander or below the capacity of the troops.

Alexander said, "These are the facts. The conclusions are obvious." Burns had to be replaced by a first-class commander but, Alexander added, he knew of none in the Canadian army other than Simonds. If no competent commander was available, then the corps had to be disbanded. "Between ourselves," he added, probably reflecting the gossip that Leese had heard from Canadian senior officers, "I believe the Canadian Divisions out here have no opinion of or feeling for their Corps, and would I am sure, though they might not admit it if questioned as soon be in a British Corps if they would not in fact prefer it."[92]

Whether Alexander was right about the opinions of the troops on corps headquarters, something far removed from the platoon and regiment that constituted their home in the army, was almost immaterial. There were issues of high policy at stake. To break up the corps because no suitable commander could be found might conceivably lead to a political crisis in Ottawa. The opposition's questions could be easily foreseen: After almost five years of war, Canada still had no competent commanders? After fighting to get the Canadian commitment in Italy expanded from a single division to a corps, it was to be broken up? Most important of all, after the struggle over the Italian commitment had embittered relations between McNaughton, Stuart, and Ralston, the sacked army commander was to be proven correct (after a fashion)? With McNaughton in uneasy retirement in Canada, such things were simply inconceivable. Moreover, men like Crerar who had gone out on a limb for Burns, who had declared him to be an army commander in waiting, had their professional judgment at stake. As soon as Crerar had seen the message, he wrote to Stuart that he did not doubt the honesty of Alexander's and Leese's views. He did not doubt, however, that they were governed by the British officers' view that no one, whether a Canadian, American, or other national commander, could do the job as well as an Englishman.[93] "In practice," Crerar said flatly and with substantial justice, this "also means that to a British Army Comd, such as Leese,

the Canadian cohesiveness created by the existence of a Canadian higher formation, such as a Corps, is a distinctly troublesome factor." Burns was "not a
member of the Club," as General Vokes put it,[94] and very few Canadians ever
could be.

Crerar maintained it was essential to find out if Burns — who, he said,
"has a lot of personality though it does not show on the surface" — still
had the confidence of his subordinates. If he had lost it, then he had to go
and Major-General Rod Keller, the GOC of the 3rd Canadian Division
then fighting in Normandy, was a prospective successor; if Burns had
their confidence, then Leese and Alexander had to be persuaded to temper their views. Above all, the British had to be told "at the outset. . . .that
the dissolution of 1 Cdn Corps is not a prospect even worth discussing."[95]
Stuart accepted Crerar's argument in its entirety, and he won the support
of the Chief of the General Staff in Ottawa for his proposal to visit Italy to
investigate and to make the Canadian case. Lieutenant-General J.C.
Murchie, the CGS, added the sensible comment that Stuart had to "realize
the difficulties involved in consulting Divisional commanders on the question of confidence because if the post is retained . . . [the] officer might be
in the unfortunate position of appearing to be beholden to divisional
commanders for his position."[96] Stuart's task was a delicate one indeed.

The General began his mission with a visit to Oliver Leese on 11 July.
Leese rehearsed his complaints against Burns, adding only one of critical
importance: "That he felt the Divisional Commanders and principal staff
officers had lost confidence in their Corps Commander." He also maintained that Burns should be replaced either by "a well tried Canadian
Commander or by the best British officer that could be made available."
Stuart's rejoinder was that if the criticism of Burns was justified, he must
be replaced; nonetheless, he intended to conduct his own investigation at
I Canadian Corps headquarters. In any case, "the replacement of Burns by
a British officer would be a mistake and could only be considered as a last
resort in the event of it being impossible to find a suitable Canadian
replacement." Stuart then set off to see Burns.

The corps commander offered his side of the story, admitting that he
and his headquarters had made mistakes. He and Leese had discussed the
problems, and Leese, in response to a direct question, had agreed that
Burns could correct matters and make a success of the corps. Leese had
told Stuart of this admission, but suggested he had been in error. Stuart

told Burns he was going to talk to his two division commanders and his two principal staff officers, a proposal Burns professed to welcome. If they "had lost confidence in him, Burns said, corrections would have to be made. Either he would have to be replaced or some of his subordinates would have to be replaced."[97]

The next day Stuart met individually with Major-Generals Vokes and Hoffmeister, the GOCs of the 1st and 5th Divisions, respectively, and with Brigadier J. Desmond B. Smith, the BGS, and Brigadier J.F.A. Lister, the DA&QMG. Admitting that his method was unorthodox, Stuart asked their opinions of Burns:

> Both [GOCs] were quite outspoken about the Corps Commander. They respected his tremendous fairness in all his dealings with their Divisions. They respected his tactical knowledge and found no fault whatever in any tactical decision he had made during the last operation. . . . They expressed themselves as being quite happy to go into the next operation under Burns and his present staff. They both hoped that I would speak to Burns regarding his manner and personality, and such was the only criticism I got from either of the Div Comds. My conversation with the two principal staff officers were productive of exactly the same results.[98]

After additional discreet conversations with other senior officers at corps and at the divisions, Stuart concluded that the "alleged" lack-of-confidence issue was a "washout."

Stuart told the same thing to General Alexander the next day, quickly ascertaining that Alexander scarcely knew Burns and had filed his complaint at Leese's instigation. When Stuart made it clear that he wanted Burns to stay in command and to have another chance, Alexander replied, or so Stuart recorded it: "You are a sensible fellow, Ken, and I respect your judgment. You know my views in this matter but it is primarily your decision. I will not only accept any decision you make but I will back you up in that decision."[99]

Stuart then made his way back to Leese. After a "stormy" conversation, Leese grumpily accepted that Burns would stay. Leese wrote to his wife that Stuart "was not helpful about Burns. I shall, I am afraid, have to keep him which will make this much more difficult as he is not up to standard & I do not believe in him." Later he would call Stuart "tiresome" and "very odd,"[100] and say that he had come to Italy "with the avowed intention of forcing me to give Burns a second chance, rather like a second helping of suet pudding!"* He was careful to send Alexander a copy of his terse letter to Stuart recapitulating the substance and tenor of their discussion.[101] Leese had his reasons to be unhappy. He was stuck with Burns and, if he was genuinely convinced that the Canadian was not competent to handle the corps, his ability to employ all his troops was limited. He would be hesitant to put other divisions under Burns's command, for instance. Because Stuart was so adamant about keeping the corps together, Leese also felt that his tactical flexibility was hampered; he could not split the two divisions into different sectors whatever the military situation. But Leese was simply wrong in not recognizing that there was a Canadian national interest in having the country's troops fight together. As far as Canadians were concerned that issue had been settled in France and Flanders in an earlier war when the success of Sir Arthur Currie's Canadian Corps had proven the value of cohesiveness.

Crerar was delighted with Stuart's success "in pouring oil on the troubled Canadian waters,"[102] and he took the earliest opportunity of telling the CIGS so. "I mentioned that it was quite conceivable that the operation which GOC-in-C Eighth Army had called on Lt-Gen Burns to carry out . . . had not been well thought out at the Army level." For his part, Brooke took the opportunity to point out that it was just as well Burns would get another chance, since Keller, Crerar's choice for the succession, "had not proved himself as a suitable substitute."[103] Keller was on the verge of being fired from his command of the 3rd Canadian Infantry Division in Normandy.[104]

In fact, Brooke's private judgment was unhappily realistic about the whole Canadian situation. As he wrote to Alexander:

> As I was with the Canadian Corps for 1 1/2 years in the last war, and have had the Canadians under my orders during the whole time I had Home Forces, I know pretty well the difficulties connected with them.
>
> In the last war Bing [sic] was replaced by Currie in command of the Canadian Corps in spite of the fact that we had few better Corps commanders than Bing and that Currie was hardly fit to command a Corps. The

---

*A different suet pudding reference was also in use. Oliver Leese, said one Canadian officer, was a "smooth-faced baronet with about as much personal appeal to Canadian troops as a suet pudding in a Sam Browne belt." Strome Galloway, *The General Who Never Was* (Belleville, Ont., 1981), 180.

> Political and National feeling is so strong that it is quite useless going
> against it. The Canadian Government and the Canadian Army insisted in
> finding their own formation Commanders, and it is up to us to *train* them
> and make the best of them. I feel however that Oliver does not realize his
> responsibility as regards training Corps commanders.

Brooke added that from what he had heard it ought not to be impossible
to make Burns into a commander. If it couldn't be done, then of course he
must be replaced but, he said, "to replace him by a British Command[er]
at this stage of the war is looking for trouble both within the Corps itself
and with the Canadian Government." Brooke concluded his letter by
sharply criticizing Leese: "I may be wrong but he gives me the impression
of stickiness and lack of thrust. . . . He is not a thruster and I feel that he
requires the application of considerable stimulus from behind."[105] The
CIGS was simply wrong in some of his Great War judgments and memories, but events would vindicate his comments on Leese. He might have
added, though it was implicit, that Sir Oliver had no political sense, a trait
essential to every good general.[106]

The whole affair had been "pretty shaking to me personally," Burns
said, probably just as much so as his narrow escape from being court-
martialled three years before. As he wrote to Crerar, "I feel that it is fairest
to judge a person or organization's competence by results. Everyone says
the breakthrough of the 'Hitler' line was a good operation." It was, and
Burns remained convinced that success would not have occurred if "I or
the Corps HQ were as inadequate as has been made out. However, I look
to the future to put the matter out of question."[107] Burns's behaviour in
this crisis of command had been exemplary and, after one more interview
with Leese,[108] he had survived the British assault against him — for a time.
But his position as corps commander had been gravely weakened. His
subordinates had been told there were questions about his competence,
and they knew, if they had not before, that their confidence in his abilities
was the key to Burns keeping his command.[109]

This was soon to be critical. In late August and September 1944, I
Canadian Corps played the major role in attacking — and breaking —
the Adriatic anchor of the Gothic Line, the main German defences in
northeast Italy. The Canadian objective was Rimini, a city that could only
be reached if six river lines, each strongly defended, could be breached.
Hoffmeister's 5th Canadian Armoured Division distinguished itself in the

fighting, but not until 21 September did I Canadian Corps reach its objective — at a cost of 2511 casualties.[110] The north Italian plain now lay before the Allied armies.

Showered with praise from Oliver Leese, congratulated on the "leading role" played by his troops, and told that "under yourself, the B.G.S. and Staff at your Corps headquarters controlled the battle well at every stage," Burns basked in the limelight.[111] Leese wrote to Ken Stuart: "I have entrusted General Burns the 4th British and the New Zealand Divisions."[112] This was surely a sign of confidence after his refusal to do any such thing a few months earlier. General Alexander told Stuart that "Burns has really done very well," adding that he had just signed an order awarding him an immediate Distinguished Service Order.[113] Burns said later that he took that decoration, naturally enough, "as a sign that the generals had decided that I could handle my command and that confidence had replaced the doubts."[114] Unfortunately, the advance stalled in the cold mud of a harsh Italian autumn,[115] and before a month had passed the old complaints against Burns were raised with new fury.

Leese had been posted to the Far East in early October (where he promptly fell into difficulty), and his successor in command of the Eighth Army, Lieutenant-General Sir Richard McCreery, wrote to Alexander on 24 October that Burns lacked "the attributes of a Higher Commander. I find that he is indecisive, and appears to lack that grasp of the whole situation which is essential in battle, in fact he does not lead." He had never commanded units and lower formations in battle, McCreery added, and he lacked "that knowledge of the many factors that must be weighed up in any tactical problem. This prevents him from ever making any constructive proposal, and causes his opinions to change, and puts him at a great disadvantage with his subordinate Commanders. . . . His manner is depressing, diffident and unenthusiastic, and he must completely fail to inspire his subordinate Commanders."[116]

That was putting it mildly. Chris Vokes, the GOC of 1st Canadian Infantry Division, had reached the breaking point with the corps commander and, some weeks after the Gothic Line battle, he let fly in a hand-written letter to a friend at CMHQ:

> Things have reached a crisis here . . . but whether any action is taken by the parties responsible at your end is impossible to predict. If nothing is done & done quickly, Bert [Hoffmeister] & myself plus Pres [Gilbride], Des

[Smith], Johnny [Plow], and Collie [Campbell, respectively the DA&QMG, BGS, CRA, and CE at corps] are prepared to adopt the only course possible. Personally I am absolutely browned off. In spite of no able direction we have continued to bear the cross for an individual who lacks one iota of personality, appreciation of effort or the first goddamn thing in the application of book learning to what is practical in war & what isn't. I've done my best to be loyal but goddammit the strain has been too bloody great.[117]

That laid out the problem with characteristic Vokesian style. Burns's frigid personality, his quick dismissal of ideas with which he disagreed, and his sarcastic comments in doing so had led to arguments and misunderstandings. His senior commanders and staff officers had become irritated beyond measure by the scholarly intellectual at their head and, as far as Vokes and Hoffmeister were concerned, there remained serious doubts about his ability as a tactician and commander. The course of events also showed that some senior Canadian officers had been complaining behind Burns's back to the Eighth Army headquarters.[118]

The issue, raised once more and in this fashion, was no longer in doubt. Crerar had had an inkling of the coming trouble from the CIGS in late October, and he and General Montague had talked about Burns with Brigadier J.F.A. Lister, the former DA&QMG of the corps who had come to the First Canadian Army to fill the equivalent post there. Lister reluctantly admitted that there were problems; the main reasons, he said, were a "lack of personality" on Burns's part and his failure to "inspire affection and confidence." Incredibly, Crerar's faith in Burns remained largely unshaken, and he blamed the departed Leese for the problem. Exactly as in July, he wanted the situation investigated. In fact, that investigation had already been undertaken on his own initiative by Brigadier E.G. Weeks, the Canadian officer in charge of the rear area and reinforcements in Italy. His cabled report at the beginning of November revealed the depth of the problem between Burns and his subordinates:

On 16 Oct Hoffmeister informed me relationship with Burns was becoming intolerable. During recent ops Hoffmeister stated had lost all confidence in Burns. Gave as examples remarks at conferences tendency interfere forward commanders.

Hoffmeister found himself in spite best intentions inclined to be insubordinate to Burns with result Hoffmeister feels that either he or Burns should be relieved. On 18 Oct I proceeded Corps by air. On arrival Gilbride informed relationships between Hoffmeister and Vokes with Burns becoming intolerable. Des Smith Gilbride Plow Campbell informed me individually that they were considering formal parading before McCreery in order to bring attention Burns attitude and remarks conferences arguments with Hoffmeister and Vokes lack dignity unpleasant embarrassment. Also tendency on part Hoffmeister and Vokes ignore Burns direction.

The damning report continued in the same vein, and Weeks added that he had seen McCreery, who stated that the situation was "intolerable" and had arranged for Weeks to see Alexander. It was Alexander's order that had led to McCreery's letter of 24 October. Weeks, whose own relationship with Burns had been good, had expressed his "repugnance" at his part in the discussions from the point of view of loyalty, but Alexander, quite properly in the circumstances, said "loyalty to service" was more important than to an individual.[119]

The brigadier's cable settled the matter beyond any chance of intervention by Harry Crerar. Burns, who was on leave, was out.[120] Before departing from Italy, he wrote Alexander a gracious note thanking him for his "personal kindness" and his consideration of his feelings. "It has helped a great deal."[121] McCreery and Alexander both recommended that Vokes succeed him, but here at least Crerar could direct the course of events: "I consider Foulkes, *not* Vokes, definitely the better prospective Corps Comd."[122] Major-General Charles Foulkes was Crerar's man, and he took command of I Canadian Corps on 10 November. Vokes, who despised Foulkes, was transferred to command the 4th Canadian Armoured Division in Northwest Europe.

Although he was naturally angry at the time of his ouster, Burns was remarkably calm later about the events that had destroyed his career as corps commander. As he wrote to Crerar, "whatever my defects of personality as a commander, I did my duty under difficult circumstances, and . . . 1 Cdn Corps, under my command, and acting on plans I made, fought two successful battles, breaking through the very strong Hitler and Gothic Lines; defeated the best German divisions in Italy . . . [and] advanced farther and faster than any British Corps."[123] True enough, but the victories had not saved Burns or won him the confidence of his senior officers. His "defects of personality," his dour manner, his sarcasm, his diffidence, had done him in. He was, one of his brigadiers later reflected, "an example of a good man in the wrong appointment."[124] Burns was a staff officer by nature, not a field commander.

The rest of Burns's war was anticlimactic, a posting eventually being found for him in major-general's rank as General-Officer-in-Charge, Canadian Section, General Headquarters, 2nd Echelon, 21 Army Group. In effect, Burns was to be responsible for Canadian rear area units.[125] He handled this task successfully, however great a comedown it was.

After the war Burns was seconded to the Department of Veterans Affairs in 1945, eventually becoming its deputy minister from 1950 to 1954. On one occasion he dressed in seedy clothes to find out how his department treated veterans and, unhappy with what he learned, raised hell. "I looked after the boys during the war," he said to his daughter, "and I should look after them postwar too."[126] Important though it was for veterans, DVA was a political backwater, and Burns seemed to be lingering in relative obscurity until, in 1954, he was asked to take command of the United Nations Truce Supervisory Organization, a small peace-keeping observer force operating on the Israeli-Arab borders. He did, and because he was on the scene when the 1956 Arab-Israeli war erupted, Burns became the head of the United Nations Emergency Force, a major responsibility he held until 1959. That peacekeeping service made his reputation with Canadians in a way the war had not, and in 1960 the Canadian government gave him the rank of ambassador and appointed him its adviser for disarmament, a field he worked on and wrote about for more than a decade.

While he was commanding UNEF in January 1958, Burns was visited by John Bassett, the Toronto newspaper publisher and prominent Progressive Conservative who, for a time in Italy, had been Burns's military secretary. When Bassett said he was surprised Burns was still a major-general, Burns replied he would never be promoted. "Yes, you will," Bassett promised. He went to see Prime Minister John Diefenbaker on his return to Canada and easily persuaded him to promote Burns to lieutenant-general.[127] There was a retrospective vindication in that recognition, a triumph of competence and devotion over the problems of personality.

CHAPTER 6

SIMONDS:
MASTER OF THE
BATTLEFIELD

TINY AS IT WAS, the interwar Permanent Force had its stars, its thinkers, its officers who were thought to be candidates for high command if — many soldiers said "when" — war came again. These were the officers who, instead of drinking themselves into a stupor every night in the mess, pored over the new books on tactics and strategy and studied the British, Canadian, and European military journals for ideas on how mechanized war might be waged. These officers took the long hours necessary to prepare themselves to write the examinations for the British Army Staff College and, once selected for the staff course, worked hard to excel.

Not surprisingly, there were few such officers in a regular officer corps of approximately four hundred men. Officers like Harry Crerar or Tommy Burns, thought by their peers to be better potential staff officers than field commanders, stood out because they had good intellects and could use them. Others like Rod Keller, Chris Vokes, Harry Foster, and Dan Spry perhaps had less academic brilliance but more leadership potential, more of the ability to make officers and soldiers follow them and carry out their bidding. Born after the turn of the century, too young for the killing fields of the Great War, these men were junior in rank at the beginning of the war in 1939. Nonetheless, they were the leaders to whom the army turned when Canadian troops went into action.

Of these men, all roughly peers on mobilization, one stood out. Guy Simonds was the officer Field Marshal Montgomery called the only Canadian "general fit to hold high command in war."[1] To General Omar Bradley, he was the "best of the Canadian generals,"[2] to General Sir Miles Dempsey, he was "the best of my Corps Commanders" in Normandy;[3] and to General Sir Brian Horrocks, he was "a first-class commander with a most original brain and full of initiative."[4] Military historians have tended to agree. Max Hastings said Simonds "was to prove one of the outstanding leaders of the [Normandy] campaign — a dour, direct, clever sapper [sic] upon whom Montgomery increasingly relied."[5] These assessments may be overstated, and they may yet be revised by later scholarship, but they exist. The accolades they contain were offered to no other Canadian soldier. In the eyes of his contemporaries and later historians, Canadian and foreign, Guy Simonds was the best soldier Canada produced in the Second World War.

GUY SIMONDS WAS BORN IN ENGLAND in 1903. His father was a major in the Royal Artillery; his mother, Eleanor Marion Easton, an American from a well-off Virginia family. The two had met in Bermuda, where Major Simonds was stationed as a gunnery instructor and where the whole Easton family went to winter in a large house overlooking Hamilton harbour. Mrs Simonds went through money at a great rate, far more than the major's pay could support, and by 1912 the family had emigrated to British Columbia to attempt to recoup their fortunes overseas. On the outbreak of war in 1914, the War Office recalled Major Simonds to duty, soon promoted him to lieutenant-colonel, and posted him to France, where he served with distinction. The war did nothing to improve his fortunes, however, and the Simonds family — there were two more sons and a daughter — would continue to exist in straitened circumstances.[6]

This penury had substantial impact on Guy Simonds. He went to school in England and in the public and high schools of Victoria, British Columbia, but that was not enough. The boy had always wanted to be a soldier. The best preparation for admission to the Royal Military College, the family agreed after much calculation of the cost, was two years' seasoning at a boarding school. Simonds duly arrived at Ottawa's Ashbury College, a society school of no great academic distinction, in the fall of 1918 and made some small reputation as a school athlete (football, soccer, track) and as a debater.[7] Finances intervened, however, and he had to drop out for a year to work in a law office.[8] He was therefore one year behind his friends.

He sat the entrance exams for RMC in 1921 and ranked second in the country. When he arrived at the college on 22 August, he was eighteen years of age and a slender youth with black hair and striking grey eyes.[9] Warned by an ex-cadet to "keep smiling" through the hell of "recruiting," Simonds turned up with a big grin, only to be greeted by the Battalion Sergeant Major, RMC's senior cadet, with a shouted, "Wipe that Goddam smile off your face!"[10] That rude introduction aside, the singleminded and dedicated Simonds made a mark at RMC, surviving his first year in good style and surmounting a series of hazing and other scandals that beset the college and his class.[11] Dubbed "the Count" because of his aristocratic bearing and appearance, Simonds performed in RMC entertainments like the annual "Cakewalk" and the Minstrel Show (where in a sketch called "The Ventriloquist," the *R.M.C. Review* observed, he "did very well and got off some quite original jokes"), and participated with some success in track and field.[12] His grades were generally very good, and his reports stated with monotonous regularity "Conduct excellent." The one warning note, sounded by the Commandant, Major-General Sir A.C. Macdonnell, the much-loved "Batty Mac" of 1st Canadian Division fame in the Great War, was that Simonds "must keep himself in hand and not get a swollen head [and] avoid flying suddenly off the reel." Even that criticism was softened by the added comment that he was "a fine man in the making."[13]

Simonds finished the entire course in superb fashion, earning a diploma with honours, winning a silver medal for standing second in his class academically, and taking prizes in tactics, artillery, civil engineering, and general proficiency in military subjects. Most important, he won the Sword of Honour, the college's highest prize for conduct and discipline, and, by selection of the entire body of cadets, the Victor Vander Smissen award for "the best all-round cadet, mentally, morally, and physically." That prize attested to his popularity and to the widespread admiration for a man who, the *R.M.C. Review* observed, was "a model of discipline and smartness on the parade ground," while off parade "he was much given to blowing smoke rings, and plunging himself into many separate and distinct female entanglements."[14] Cadets admired all such attributes. Simonds had also decided to join the Permanent Force in the Royal Canadian Horse Artillery and, with confidence in his star, he told his cadet colleagues, "I will be Chief of Staff of the Canadian Army."[15]

The prizes he won (especially the Vander Smissen award, which was worth $150) and the career he mapped out for himself perhaps began to make up for the hard time Simonds had had at RMC. The problem again was money, or the lack of it, for in those days the annual tuition at the college was $450, and Simonds's parents, now effectively separated and living in genteel poverty, proved unable to provide this sum. Fortunately, General Macdonnell could see that Simonds was "a boy of an excellent type" and, taking a personal interest in his problem, persuaded Colonel R.W. Leonard of St Catharines, Ontario, to lend $300 to cover his first year's fees. The Commandant found Simonds work in the summer of 1922 with the Canadian Pacific Railway in Kingston and gave him free quarters at the college. This let him save more than a hundred dollars to put to his next year's fees, and most of the remainder again was provided by assistance from Colonel Leonard's foundation. There were still arrears, and the family proved unable to assist until Mrs Simonds resorted to selling off some of her possessions and scraped together $264.

The same desperate situation continued for the next two years, and Simonds's file at the college is full of pathetic letters from his parents, from various clergymen and acquaintances, and appeals to all and sundry, not excluding the Governor General, Lord Byng of Vimy, for assistance. As Colonel Simonds, out of work and supporting himself and his family on his military pension of $133 a month, wrote in February 1923, "had I known at first how I stood it would have been clear to me that Guy could not have gone to the R.M.C. and I then would not have been so crippled as I am already on his behalf." In the end, thanks to Macdonnell's efforts, there was just enough to cover the tuition bills. When Simonds graduated in the summer of 1925 he was obliged to work as an instructor at the military camp at Petawawa until such time as National Defence Headquarters confirmed his Permanent Force commission. His pay at the camp was barely enough to cover his mess bills. Again Macdonnell provided a loan from college funds to meet his incidental expenses, arranged for the sale of his RMC winter kit to an incoming recruit,[16] and granted time for Simonds to pay off the amount that remained on his college account. As he wrote to Colonel Simonds, "The sums derived from these sources should enable him to carry on. . . . He will, of course, have to practise economy, but should I feel be able to manage fairly well."[17]

Guy Simonds was a fiercely proud man. That he had had to carry the burden of this humiliating situation with him at RMC — where a large proportion of the cadet body came from well-off and socially prominent families — only magnifies his success.[18] To have stood so high both academically and militarily in his class, to have won the respect of his cadet peers and of General Macdonnell, was a triumphant achievement. The Commandant must have thought so, for the Sword of Honour was in his gift and he awarded it to a man who had coped with adversity. "This boy impresses me as a winner if he can be given a chance,"[19] Batty Mac had said in 1922. His judgment would be confirmed by Simonds's standing on graduation in 1925 and reconfirmed repeatedly in the years to come — much to the army's and the nation's great benefit.

SIMONDS JOINED the Royal Canadian Horse Artillery in 1925. His pay was small, his uniforms expensive, and the work sometimes far removed from traditional soldiering. The Permanent Force frequently found itself called upon to act in aid to the civil power, all too often in labour disputes where strikers insisted on viewing the "brutal licentious soldiery" as strike-breakers. When Simonds finished his instructional duties at Petawawa in the summer of 1925, he went to Sydney Mines, Nova Scotia, where the RCHA struggled to control a tense labour situation. "In the early part of the strike," Simonds wrote later, "the miners and their families were very hostile to the troops . . . we would get stones and bricks thrown down on us from the many rail 'over passes' in the area, (tin hats were necessary equipment!) and abused and insulted." It took time, he recalled, but eventually "we were able to convince the striking miners that we were not on anybody's 'side' — we didn't represent the owners, but were there to protect lives and property." That was a naïve representation of the benign role of the forces of order in a labour-management conflict, but Simonds added that the RCHA squadron formed a soccer team and challenged the miners to meet in a game. "This, with other measures, broke the ice, hostility and violence ceased, and at the end of the strike when the troops were withdrawn, the miners and their families lined the streets and cheered us as we left."[20]

For the gunners and the officers, such duty was a break from routine, and any such change was welcome. As Simonds said, "Idleness and boredom were ogres of which one had to be constantly aware and continually and consciously fight." Military life in peacetime, he went on, "possibly offers greater opportunity for drifting than other careers and the temptation to do nothing wrong by the simple process of doing nothing beyond daily routine is ever present."[21] For Simonds, riding became his way of fighting ennui. He competed for and won prizes at jumping, tent-pegging, and shooting from the saddle, he played polo, and he participated in his regiment's musical drive, which was a featured event at fairs across the country.[22] Sometimes these activities were dangerous. In July 1929 a horse fell backwards on him; Simonds fractured a lumbar vertebrae and was strapped to a bradford frame for weeks, struggling with a cast for months to come.

Such activities were an integral part of an officer's life, but there was more. He was posted to the RCHA's Winnipeg battery in 1928. There, some garrison officers' wives thought he was very superior, with his nose in the air as if he had smelled something unpleasant. He was never one of the crowd of pleasant young officers, Mrs F.F. Worthington recalled.[23] Perhaps he was too shy. Still, his annual confidential reports were excellent, and he kept busy studying for promotion examinations where again he did well. He became a brevet captain in 1929, very speedy promotion by PF standards. There was an engagement in 1931 and marriage in 1932, something only achieved on appeal after his commanding officer initially refused permission. His blonde bride was Katherine (known as "K" or Kay) Lockhart Taylor, the daughter of a prominent Winnipeg stockbroker, and the wedding, with Major J.C. Murchie, a future wartime Chief of the General Staff, as best man, made the social pages in Winnipeg and Victoria; the Simondses were even pictured in Toronto's *Saturday Night*.[24] Immediately after the honeymoon, the couple left for Britain, where Simonds was to take the Gunnery Staff Course at Larkhill. After a year abroad, it was Winnipeg again for two more years of regimental duty. The Simondses soon had two children, a girl born in 1933 and a boy in 1935, for whom Kay was the principal parent.[25] There was also an effective end to the financial problems he had laboured under since RMC. By 1933 his annual income, as reported on his income tax, was just under $2900 — no fortune, to be sure, but in the depth of the Depression years enough to live on.[26] For Captain Simonds, his Winnipeg posting was a time filled with preparing to write the Staff College examinations; then, success achieved, there came a two-year stint at Camberley in 1936 and 1937.

He did brilliantly. "The essence of teaching at the Staff College," Simonds said later, "was not to indoctrinate officers with preconceived theories, but to make them think and come up with their own solutions to the problems of modern war."[27] Under a directing staff that included British officers such as Gort, Adam, Slim, and Gale, Simonds studied hard, mastered the preparation of military appreciations and operation orders, and wrote papers on assigned topics. There were papers on the lessons of Gallipoli and other combined operations, on the press and the nation, and on "The Task of the Army in Defence of Imperial Communications." Often the comments offered by his "syndicate leader" sounded a familiar refrain: "an excellent paper . . . impressive style."[28] At the end, his assessment by the Commandant of the Staff College was superb, an appraisal full of genuine commendation. Simonds had not received one of the "courtesy passes" that, rumour had it, were often given to dominion officers. Colonel Georges Vanier, serving at the High Commission in London, wrote to congratulate Simonds on his "wonderful results. . . . You were a credit indeed to the Service."[29]

When Simonds returned to Canada to join the instructional staff at RMC in the spring of 1938, he came back definitely marked as a man to watch.[30] His reputation was further enhanced when, in July, he wrote a rejoinder to Tommy Burns's article on organization for armoured warfare in the *Canadian Defence Quarterly*. "An Army That Can Attack — A Division That Can Defend" was one of the best articles that journal ever received, and it provoked a reply from Burns. Simonds in turn offered another riposte in "What Price Assault without Support?" and published a third piece, "The Attack," just before the outbreak of war.[31] The Staff College experience had exposed Simonds to new ideas about mechanized warfare and the problems of most effectively coordinating the action of infantry and armour. He had had the opportunity in Britain, as he could not in Canada, to see large bodies of troops on exercises with modern weapons. He had spent a summer attached to the British 2nd Division, commanded by one of the great British soldier-scholars, Major-General Archibald Wavell. His interest in the complexities of armoured warfare had been sparked, and Simonds's articles quickly demonstrated that he could think with the best. He was also promoted to temporary major.

His year-and-a-half stint on the staff at RMC kept Simonds's mind working. Initially appointed as professor of artillery, his title, thanks to the successful efforts of Colonel Ken Stuart to modernize the curriculum, was soon changed to professor of tactics, with a mandate that included teaching international affairs, strategy, and tactics. The library's holdings were expanded in these areas, and Simonds conducted discussions and set papers on current problems. Tactics he taught on the ground or on the sand table.[32]

He also commanded a half-battalion of cadets with whom he was far from popular. None of his cadets, one remembered years later, would ever have thought of going to Major Simonds with a personal problem.[33] The aloofness for which he had been known in the officers' mess in Winnipeg and for which he was to be famous as a division and corps commander a few years later had become fixed. His time at RMC also brought Simonds into close contact once again with the college's new Commandant, Brigadier H.D.G. Crerar. Crerar was a fellow RCHA officer, and Simonds had served under him as a subaltern when Crerar commanded B Battery, RCHA, in 1927. The two were not friends — a major and a brigadier could not be friends — but the older man developed some sense of Simonds's worth. That would be important in the war that began for Canada on 10 September 1939.

At once NDHQ ordered Simonds to report to Ottawa for "special duties," a cover phrase for his appointment as General Staff Officer, Grade 2, in the 1st Canadian Infantry Division. The GSO 2's duties covered operations and training, Simonds's areas of expertise and, in the first weeks, the organization and equipping of the division. Simonds went overseas in December, and his job was all-consuming then and for months thereafter, so much so that Kay Simonds in Kingston complained that she never heard from her husband. "I am not surprised," Colonel Ernie Sansom of the division staff told his own wife, whose ear had been filled with Kay's laments. "He is working very hard and doing an excellent job as GSO II."[34] Simonds's duties put him in close contact with General McNaughton, and he was with the GOC on 16 May 1940 when he attended a conference called by the Chief of the Imperial General Staff on the rapidly disintegrating situation in France. The briefing, very full to judge by Simonds's notes, pronounced the situation critical but not hopeless, called on commanders to use the methods developed during the Great War to teach bayonet fighting to imbue their men with "ruthless fighting spirit," and urged that enemy paratroopers not be made prisoners of war.[35]

The fortunate rescue from the debacle of the elements of the Canadian division that had been sent to Brest after the Dunkirk evacuation gave Simonds his next task. He was made commanding officer of the 1st Field Regiment, Royal Canadian Artillery, in July. The situation he found was not promising. The regiment had been to France and, thanks to its CO, Lieutenant-Colonel J. Hamilton Roberts, had returned with all its guns — and even with one additional twenty-five-pounder abandoned by a British unit. Much of the remaining equipment had been lost, however, and morale was in tatters. Simonds took over very firmly and began anew with basic training. His Adjutant, a Permanent Force RCHA officer, Captain Robert Rothschild, remembered that Simonds had been an excellent pre-war gunnery instructor, and he proved to be a fine Commanding Officer. He related well to the gunners, but he terrified the junior officers, Rothschild included. Rothschild remembers him picking out one bad apple in a group of reinforcement officers and refusing to accept him. Still, he was fair. When he told Rothschild to prepare a training plan, the Adjutant who had had no staff training had to admit that he had no idea how to do so. Simonds then took a half day explaining what was required, and thereafter Rothschild was expected to know the job.[36] That command lasted until November 1940 and was Simonds's only stint of wartime regimental duty.

His new task was to find a way to help fill the Canadian need for trained staff officers. Able young officers like Rothschild had to learn to do the jobs involved in training and fighting a large force. As early as September 1940, McNaughton had realized the shortage of staff-trained officers and was considering setting up a course;[37] to run it, he selected Simonds. Simonds's job was to create the syllabus for the Canadian Junior War Staff Course, find the instructors, arrange for the selection of students, and run the course. He managed the task with his customary efficiency, putting the course together quickly to include message writing, military appreciations, operational orders, tactics, familiarization with the arms and services, intelligence, combined operations, and tactical exercises without troops. It was a Camberley course in miniature, designed to last three months instead of two years, but it suited wartime needs.[38] The directing staff included young officers like J. Desmond B. Smith, Holley Keefler, and J.F.A. Lister, all men who rose to senior positions, and the first class of sixty-one at the CJWSC had among its number promising officers like

Robert Moncel, Pres Gilbride, C.H. Drury, and Rothschild from Simonds's 1st Field Regiment.[39] One officer who took the course, J.W. Bishop, remembered it as a "straight tactical course" designed to teach officers to think militarily and to appreciate problems. He also remembered Simonds as "a very, very strong man."[40] Another, John Page of the Toronto Scottish, recalled Simonds telling the class on its first day that half would fail.[41]

In fact, fifty-nine officers completed the CJWSC course, thirty-six receiving staff qualification and seven conditional passes.[42] "The mere fact that we come from Canada," Simonds said, "does not make us first-line soldiers; a Canadian does not become an excellent soldier by the mere process of putting on uniform." That was a direct shot at the "militia myth" that had been created in Canada to suggest that every Canadian was a natural soldier and that professionals were unnecessary. What was needed was discipline, training, and loyalty. "Loyalty," Simonds said, "is an important quality in a staff officer; but this doesn't mean being a 'yes-man.' In appreciating a situation, be sure to place all the facts before your commanding officer; let there be no 'special pleading'; don't conceal a fact that does not support your own argument. And remember that the commander has to take the ultimate responsibility; whatever his decision, it must be loyally enforced." Then Simonds added, "Should you find yourself out of sympathy with your commander, resign your appointment. If the disagreement is in principle, this is the only honest thing to do."[43] Words to live by.

Simonds ran only the one course at the CJWSC. In May 1941 he was posted as GSO 1, in effect the principal staff officer, to the 2nd Canadian Infantry Division. His GOC was Victor Odlum, and Simonds was fortunate to spend only three months with this senior officer who had little understanding of the differences between the present conflict and the Great War of 1914–18. He may not have enjoyed the experience, but Odlum admired him. In August, when Simonds left the 2nd Division to become Brigadier General Staff at Canadian Corps headquarters in place of Tommy Burns, Odlum told McNaughton of Simonds's "splendid work. . . . I have never had an officer on my staff who gave better service."[44]

Simonds's appointment as McNaughton's principal staff officer meant that for the next year he was in charge of planning for the corps' training and possible operational roles. He was not happy with the state of training in the corps and said so to Lieutenant-General Bernard Montgomery's

BGS, under whose South Eastern Command the Canadians fell. He blamed McNaughton's absorption in political matters and his near-obsessive interests in weapons development. When McNaughton fell ill in late 1941 and Lieutenant-General Harry Crerar took over as acting corps commander, however, matters initially worsened from Simonds's standpoint. A gossip had told him that Crerar had strongly opposed his appointment as BGS and intended to seek his removal. That, Simonds wrote later, seemed to be confirmed when Crerar told him he wanted to post him to the command of a brigade.[45] Nonetheless, it was some months before his posting and, in the critical area of training, matters improved substantially, not least because of Crerar's and Montgomery's interest in and attention to the subject. The heads that rolled, the dead wood that Montgomery cleared away, began the process of replacing the Great War generation of senior commanders and opened the door for the younger men. Simonds's own prospects improved, not least because Montgomery noticed him. For his part, Crerar worked Simonds hard and benefited from his ability, but, as he commented critically in a private letter, his BGS "forms definite views and is inclined to express them somewhat forcibly."[46] That squared entirely with Simonds's view of the proper role of a staff officer.

Happily for him, his duties did not include planning for the Dieppe raid of 19 August 1942. What had removed Simonds from all but the earliest stages of the ultimate tragedy was his involvement in July and August with McNaughton in preparing an appreciation — at Winston Churchill's request — of the possibilities of a Canadian attack on Norway. The whole scheme, codenamed "Jupiter," was as immensely foolhardy as any of the Prime Minister's self-conceived military plans, and Simonds's schema for the assault required so many troops and so much air and naval support that it proved impossible to contemplate even for Churchill.[47] The project was abortive, but Simonds's work was noted, the UK Chiefs of Staff Committee telling McNaughton that "this was one of the clearest and most ably worked out appreciations which they ever had before them."[48]

Simonds's work as a staff officer was now at an end. In September 1942 he became the commander of 1st Canadian Infantry Brigade in the 1st Division. In April 1943, at the age of forty, he was promoted to major-general and given command of the 2nd Canadian Infantry Division, then still recuperating from the mauling it had received at Dieppe. His rise had been spectacular — from major to major-general in three-and-a-half years — and no other officer in the army, PF or NPAM, had risen so far and so fast to that point. The Defence Minister, Colonel J.L. Ralston, was told by a senior officer that Simonds was a "most outstanding officer but not a leader of the type that will secure the devotion of his followers." Instead, he was "similar in characteristics to General Burns and would give his best service as a high Staff Officer. Has undoubted ability and will fight his Division and make few mistakes."[49] Burns was often viewed as a dour intellectual by fellow officers; as this appraisal suggested, Simonds had a similar reputation. He had been austere and cold, a no-nonsense, business-first planner, and now he had a chance to prove himself as a division commander — but not of the 2nd Canadian Division. When Major-General Harry Salmon, the 1st Canadian Infantry Division's GOC died in an air crash en route to the Middle East, McNaughton immediately named Simonds to replace him on 29 April 1943. Guy Simonds would become the first Canadian officer in the war to lead his troops in an invasion and a sustained campaign — the forthcoming attack on Sicily. His reputation, and to some extent the military reputation of his country, now was in his hands.

THE 1ST CANADIAN INFANTRY DIVISION and the 1st Canadian Armoured Brigade, their inclusion in the Sicilian operation in direct response to Canadian political imperatives,[50] were to serve as part of General Sir Bernard Montgomery's Eighth Army in the Sicily operations. Simonds had already had some dealings with the British general, and Montgomery had pronounced him "a first class B.G.S." after Exercise Tiger.[51] He had even made a brief visit to the Eighth Army to study its operations in the final phase of the North African campaign. Simonds's detailed report of that visit, covering a range of questions from the movement of anti-tank guns with infantry on the attack to the organization of an army headquarters, was carefully studied by First Canadian Army.[52] Then, once he had been named to replace Salmon, Simonds again flew back to the Middle East for discussions on the Sicily operation. He was, therefore, well known to Montgomery and his staff.

The officers of the 1st Canadian Infantry Division also knew him well. Simonds had commanded its 1st Brigade, now led by militiaman Howard Graham, until the beginning of 1943; his RMC classmate Chris Vokes commanded the 2nd Brigade; and his PF gunner colleague, M.H.S.

Penhale, led the 3rd Brigade. The GSO 1, Lieutenant-Colonel George Kitching, had been on the corps headquarters staff when Simonds was BGS, and the division's chief administrative staff officer, Lieutenant-Colonel Pres Gilbride, was Simonds's choice to replace an officer killed in the air crash with Salmon.[53] These familiar officers helped Simonds in the frantic rush to prepare the division for its long sea voyage to Sicily.

Although German U-boats attacked some of the ships carrying Canadian troops to Sicily, with serious losses of men and equipment, the invasion on 10 July went well and the Canadians made their way inland for the first few days without meeting serious opposition from Italian troops. Simonds scratched out a diary note on D-Day that began "Heavy firing on shore," but he added that prisoners were "brought in by the dozens." The next day, as things continued on course, he wrote, "Although the fruit is not all ripe some apricots and melons are — Are they ever good."[54] The Germans soon made their appearance — after the Italians "that is a different kettle of fish," an officer in the Princess Pats wrote home[55] — and on 16 July, near Piazza Armerina, Simonds came under fire for the first time. The historical officer with the division wrote admiringly: "General Simonds certainly believes in staying close to his fighting troops. This morning he came under mortar fire and had two or three close calls." When a mortar bomb exploded a yard away from Simonds, sheltering in a slit trench, the officer with him asked, "What would the people of Canada say if they knew that they were paying him $24 a day to be where he was at that moment. The General," the historian noted, "took the remark good naturedly."[56] After one such personal reconnaissance, Simonds would be recommended for and duly receive the Distinguished Service Order.

There would be some serious fighting in the extraordinarily difficult terrain of Sicily that greatly favoured the defending Nazis. Although he made mistakes — as at Nissoria on 24–25 July when he committed his battalions piecemeal and adhered to a rigid fire plan — Simonds, almost always issuing orders verbally, showed substantial and increasing skill in putting together his armour, artillery, and infantry in attacks on the road to Agira and Regalbuto.[57] His British superiors were pleased. The corps commander, Lieutenant-General Oliver Leese, wrote repeatedly about his "mad keen" Canadians and their commander, "a young Regular Canadian soldier and very intelligent." "They have been very well commanded by

Simonds," Leese added later, "who is young and forceful."[58] Montgomery was a bit cooler in his comments. To McNaughton, he wrote that when the division landed "they were a bit soft and felt the heat very much and the hot sun; their operational discipline was not too good." Since then, however, they had done well. Of Simonds, the Eighth Army commander said he "has got to learn the art of command just as his Division has got to learn the art of battle fighting. I shall teach him; and he is learning well. He will be a 1st Class DIV. Commander in due course."[59]

Monty's reference to the art of command undoubtedly had to do with a sharp difference of opinion on an operational question between Simonds and Brigadier Howard Graham on 15 July. It resulted in Graham deciding to resign his command of the 1st Brigade because of the GOC's interference. Montgomery had heard of the situation and wrote to Leese: "This is a great pity. Graham is an excellent fellow and much beloved in his Bde; I expect Simmonds [sic] lost his temper. Simmonds is a young and very inexperienced Divisional general, and has much to learn about command. He will upset his Division if he starts sacking Brigadiers like this." Monty added that Simonds "would be well advised to consult his superiors before he takes violent action in which he may not be backed up."[60] Montgomery saw Simonds and Graham separately and patched matters up, and the two Canadians carried on from there. As the division's historical officer recorded in his diary, "the G.O.C. sent for Brigadier Graham. I happened to be standing near the G.O.C.'s vehicle at the time when I heard him say to the Brigadier: 'Good afternoon.' Brigadier Graham replied: 'Good-afternoon, Sir.' Without further ado both then were deep in conversation over a map presumably on operational matters."[61] There were also difficulties between Simonds and Brigadier R.A. Wyman, the commander of the 1st Canadian Armoured Brigade.[62] The Canadian public knew nothing of these matters but, as the newspapers noted, Simonds was the youngest Canadian ever to lead a division into action.[63] Sometimes it showed.

Simonds soon wrote to General McNaughton with his assessments of his senior officers and of the campaign. He found the portly Brigadier Penhale too old and unfit, and reported that Graham had reached his ceiling. Brigadier Bruce Matthews, his senior artillery officer, was good but not yet ready for a division. Only Chris Vokes was pronounced an excellent brigade commander, one who drove forward with resolution. He ranked his lieutenant-colonels in order for promotion to brigadier: George Kitching, his GSO 1; Bert Hoffmeister, the CO of the Seaforths; Geoffrey Walsh, his Chief Engineer; and Pat Bogart, the CO of the West Nova Scotia Regiment. All those officers would rise, two to command divisions, but there was more than a hint of Montgomery-style hubris in Simonds's note to McNaughton after the Canadian victory at Valguarnera on 17–18 July: "I succeeded in enveloping and cutting off [the German] rearguard. The slaughter was terrific."[64] That early battle, in fact, had not been uniformly well handled, and Simonds's attitude, then and later, annoyed officers such as Hoffmeister. Simonds's orders groups, he remembered, were cold and formal, ending with a curt "Any questions?" Simonds paid no attention to the psychology of the situation, unlike the best British officers, and he showed no understanding of his subordinates' problems.[65] Vokes, who had known Simonds much longer, seconded that assessment in his usual blunt, crude fashion: Simonds was "the finest Canadian general we ever had," but as "a leader of men" he wasn't worth "a pinch of coonshit."[66]

Still and all, Simonds and his division had done well in Sicily for a commander and a formation seeing action for the first time. Although a pleased Montgomery seemed to feel that he now needed a rest,[67] Simonds led his men onto the toe of the Italian boot on 3 September 1943, where they advanced with great speed against light opposition. Now very confident in his tactical abilities, Simonds did not hesitate to express his opinion on plans laid down by his new corps commander, General Miles Dempsey, an officer he knew well from his service with the Canadians early in the war. On 22 September he objected in strong terms to the routes for the advance, separated by seventy miles of rough country, that Dempsey had assigned to his division: "I consider advancing a single division on such widely separated axes objectionable from both a tactical and administrative point of view." Simonds lost the argument, but the significance of the incident was that he felt sure enough of his position and his abilities to dispute calmly the orders he had received.[68]

Simonds fell ill with jaundice in the third week of September and was out of action for a month. By the time he was fit to return, General McNaughton had already decided to place Simonds in command of 5th Canadian Armoured Division which, with the I Canadian Corps headquarters, was being sent to Italy to join the 1st Canadian Infantry Division.

Lest anyone feel that Simonds had done poorly in fighting with his division — Simonds himself apparently interpreted the move this way[69] — CMHQ advised journalists that Simonds's switch to the 5th was "a definite promotion and the result of brilliant handling of his former command."[70] Vokes, promoted to major-general, succeeded him in command of the 1st Canadian Division.

Wearing a black beret just like Montgomery's, Simonds greeted the first units of his new division when they reached Naples in November to begin their training. He ran a sand table exercise for the division officers, one engineer remembered, sitting on his throne like God.[71] As one of his padres noted in a letter home, "I am working again for Guy Simonds who used to command First Div. He is no easy man to work for. . . . He has already stepped on a good many toes and I expect to see the Div. at a high standard of efficiency in double quick time." Being a padre, the officer also approved of Simonds's putting brothels off limits to the division's personnel.[72] Simonds was putting into practice his firm belief that Canadian soldiers — the "best in the world *bar none*" if they have proper leadership — merited the best commanders that the army could provide. As he wrote soon after, "We have the material to provide the standard of leadership required. Only outworn prejudices prevent it being used to the best advantage . . . seniority, position on 'lists,' the fact that so and so has done such and such a job for a certain time and 'hasn't done anything wrong' (probably because he hasn't done anything at all!) . . . I consider that before going into action it is not sufficient to remove only the 'bad' C.O. The 'indifferent' must be replaced by the 'better' and the 'not quite good enough' by the 'best.'"[73] Unfortunately, it was often difficult to find officers who were better than those who had demonstrably failed.

Now he was to face a new problem in the person of Harry Crerar. A few weeks earlier, Crerar had arrived in Italy to await the arrival of his I Canadian Corps headquarters, and he and Simonds soon clashed. Their first conversation on 30 October stimulated some harsh words, and when Crerar appropriated vehicles intended for the armoured division for his own headquarters, matters worsened. Crerar doubtless reasoned that as corps commander he needed and deserved a proper establishment, but he seemed to have forgotten in the process why his troops were in Italy. Short of trucks, Simonds's training program suffered and, lacking training, his division's move to the front was likely delayed. Then early in December,

Crerar added fuel to the fire by sending an officer to the armoured division's headquarters to measure Simonds's caravan so a similar one could be constructed for him. Although an officer on Simonds's staff gave permission in the GOC's absence for this to be done, Simonds became outraged at the intrusion, sending the officer away with a rocket. Crerar's desire for his creature comforts, it seemed, had been more than sufficiently indulged. At roughly the same time, Simonds had summarily sacked Brigadier R.O.G. Morton, the Commander Royal Artillery of his division, after earlier indicating that he would consult Crerar before taking action. The two events combined to create an extraordinary situation over the next three weeks. Crerar even consulted a visiting army psychiatrist and his own senior medical officer about Simonds's stability and queried Montgomery about Simonds's suitability for higher command. Simonds had upset the normal order of deference — and deference was founded upon respect. Simonds for his part made it clear he would not "take troops into battle" under Crerar's command if he had lost his confidence. "When that time comes . . . I shall have to ask to be relieved."

Lieutenant-Colonel John English has examined this extraordinary affair in his fine book, *The Canadian Army and the Normandy Campaign*, and he comes down firmly on Simonds's side. Crerar's "puerile" desire to have a caravan like Simonds's was exceeded only by his determination to make an issue out of what Crerar called the "personal discourtesy" Simonds had shown him by chasing off his ruler-wielding officer. English's conclusion focuses on "the malevolence of Crerar," who increasingly envied the rising fortune of his once junior subordinate. Crerar, he says, was guilty of "simple jealousy."

There is some reason to agree. Crerar *was* extraordinarily ambitious and ruthless in the race to get — and stay — ahead. Without question, the characteristics of vanity and self-seeking perched on his epaulets, but Crerar had other qualities, too. He knew that Simonds was his best field commander, and frankly admitted as much. Writing to Montgomery, he said that Simonds had always been an excellent soldier, but one who "has also always been high-strung and with a tendency to be introspective, rather than objective, when faced with acute problems." That was certainly true, and so was his comment that Simonds in December 1943 was "tensed up," as might have been expected after a serious illness and six months' command in action.

It may well be that Crerar was genuinely concerned about Simonds's fitness to take on the command of the II Canadian Corps in Britain, for which he would recommend him on 6 January 1944. That day he wrote to Simonds. His only purpose in their long, bitter exchange of letters had been to try to discover whether "the incident which occurred meant you were admittedly 'on edge' and needed a change. I wasn't out to 'knock you,' but, if I could, to help you. That was my whole motive." Moreover, Crerar said, "You have always had my confidence as a Staff Officer and Commander and if you had definitely lost that confidence you would not have had the *chance* to take troops into battle under my command." There seems no reason to doubt Crerar's statements. Simonds's letters boil with suppressed rage and perceived slights, and no senior officer could have received them without having concerns about the stability of their writer.[74]

Where Crerar himself went off the rails was in tattling to Montgomery, in writing for file a five-page single-spaced analysis of Simonds's rejoinder to his complaints, and in sending copies of the correspondence to Lieutenant-General Ken Stuart, the acting GOC-in-C of the First Canadian Army, "as 'background' to be locked up now, but to be read over again at some possible future time when the further appointment of this brilliant, and comparatively young, man comes up for consideration."[75] A few months later, Crerar told Mackenzie King that Simonds, though "a very good soldier . . . might not be the best man for post-war planning,"[76] a role for which tact and balance were essential. That comment was to prove important in the future.

Each of Crerar's actions could be justified individually as necessary for someone with his personality. Together, they smack of nothing so much as spite and a determination to ensure that Crerar's point of view in this argument would prevail with his Canadian and British superiors. The tragic irony of the situation from Crerar's point of view was that Montgomery, probably as a result of the corps commander's letter to him on Simonds's fitness, for the first time began to express serious doubts about Crerar's own ability to command the First Canadian Army, the post for which he had already been tapped after McNaughton's ouster.[77] To Monty, Simonds was much the better soldier, and he would frequently bypass Crerar to talk directly to Simonds during the year-long campaign in Northwest Europe. As he told Vincent Massey, the Canadian High Commissioner, Simonds "had the makings of a future army commander.

Although he did not inspire his troops they had immense respect for him and his great ability was fully recognised."[78]

THE FIGHTING BETWEEN the generals did not interfere with the progress of the real war, and Guy Simonds was from late January 1944 the GOC of the II Canadian Corps, at forty-one years of age "the youngest corps commander in the Empire," or so one Canadian journalist maintained.[79] His 3rd Canadian Infantry Division had been detached to form part of the Normandy invasion force, but Simonds still had the 2nd Canadian Infantry Division and the 4th Canadian Armoured Division, both scheduled to form part of the follow-up invasion force, under his command.

His first task was training, and for training, as for combat, he needed a staff and commanders in whom he had confidence. Major-General Charles Foulkes, who had been BGS of First Canadian Army, commanded the 2nd Division, which he took over on 11 January 1944. Major-General "Fighting Frank" Worthington, fifty-four years old, commanded the 4th Armoured until 1 March, when Simonds's pressing for a change led, ostensibly on grounds of age, to Worthy's return to Canada; to fill his place, Simonds had Brigadier George Kitching promoted and given command.[80] With his own HQ staff, a group inherited from Lieutenant-General E.W. Sansom, who had been relieved of command in January, he wielded a very stiff broom with great vigour. Simonds met the officers on his arrival: "Good morning, gentlemen. There are some of you in whom I have not much confidence. I will see you all individually the next day and tell you why." The Chief Engineer, the Chief Medical Officer, and the Commander Corps Royal Artillery, were sacked. Others stayed. The DA&QMG, Brigadier Dan Laing, went for his interview and returned: "I've been through and I'm staying. What about you?" he asked the Chief Signals Officer, Brigadier S.F. Clark. Clark stayed, too.[81] Lieutenant-Colonel Robert Moncel was the GSO 1, the junior member in Simonds's A Mess, and his recollection was that each morning at breakfast another senior officer was gone. Finally, Moncel, who had first met Simonds on the Canadian Junior War Staff Course he had run and who had stood first, was one of the few originals left, and Simonds smiled and said, "You're staying." He brought in his own people from Sicily and Italy, Moncel said, and he was right to do so. They performed well. The new corps staff included Brigadier Bruce Matthews as CCRA, Brigadier

Geoffrey Walsh as Chief Engineer, and Brigadier Elliot Rodger as Chief of Staff (a term picked up from the Americans that had replaced BGS), a man who had been at RMC in Simonds's last year and who had worked with him at the First Canadian Army headquarters. Additional changes were made at the brigade level, too, Simonds again putting as many trusted and proven officers in command as he could. It was a first-class group, notably so at corps headquarters, but even the first class needed stimulation. Simonds moved the headquarters out of its comfortable billets and into the field. Everything was on "a caravan and camp basis" now.[82]

Simonds then laid down policy for his corps. At his first staff conference he explained how he worked. "In brief," his new Chief of Staff noted, "he will COMMAND and we, his staff, will provide him the information on which to base his decisions and will also implement in detail his commands and decisions. A staff officer," Rodger said, "could hardly ask more of his commander!"[83] Ideas were welcome, Simonds's reputation for not tolerating those of others notwithstanding. Naturally he had his own definite views. He wrote a string of papers on operational policy, efficiency of command, and honours and awards,[84] initially in his own hand, and all typed word for word by his clerks, watched over by senior officers lest a single typographical error provoke an explosion. The operational policy paper laid out his understanding of the role of his corps — "to pass through a beach-head which has been secured by assaulting forces and attack, wear down and destroy German troops which oppose it, within the corps 'corridor' defined by the Army Commander." It distilled what he had learned in his six months of action against the enemy and set out his ideas with admirable clarity:

the weight of artillery support must NOT be divided . . .

When the Germans decide to stand and fight a defensive battle, attack without adequate reconnaissance and preparation will not succeed . . .

The success of the offensive battle hinges on the defeat of the German counter-attacks with sufficient of our own reserves in hand to launch a new phase as soon as the enemy strength has spent itself . . .

A sound, simple plan based upon: (a) The ground (b) enemy dispositions and probable intentions (c) The Support available (d) The characteristics and capabilities of our own arms and troops and pressed home with resolution, will usually succeed. Complicated, involved plans seldom succeed.[85]

Assessing this document, historian Terry Copp observed that "Simonds did not attempt to lead; he sought only to command. His directive . . . is brief, coherent and all-encompassing. There is no room for discussion; it is an outline of a procedure which is to be followed."[86] He might have added that some of Simonds's plans in Normandy suffered in their implementation because of their complexity.

Simonds also ran a study week in mid March for his senior officers to rehearse the key points his operational policy anticipated: forcing the crossing of an obstacle, night attacks, clearing towns, cooperation with the air force, and the role of the infantry and the armoured division in the attack.[87] His paper on efficiency of command was similarly straightforward, replicating much of what he had said on the subject a few weeks before in Italy: "Officers who commanders or commanding officers consider unsuitable to their posts will be recommended for removal on an adverse report. . . . I require that these reports shall be strictly honest."[88] His first few weeks at the II Canadian Corps more than justified General Stuart's comment to Ottawa that Simonds was a "very strong" character "in whose judgment I have the greatest confidence."[89]

Confidence was the word others used. When Colonel G.S. Currie, the deputy minister to Colonel Ralston, visited Britain, he had dinner with Generals Crerar, back from Italy to take command of the army; Stuart, now Chief of Staff, CMHQ; and Simonds. "Impressed with the absolute confidence they have in success," he wrote in his diary. After only Crerar remained, however, the discussion turned to Simonds's personality and military qualities. As Currie scribbled in his diary, Crerar had said that "Simonds needs guidance, particularly politically, our very best tactical commander but he must be ridden like a temperamental race horse with soft but firm hands. Stuart," Currie added, "had already told me this same thing." The race horse now was champing at the bit.

D-Day, 6 June 1944, saw the Allies establish themselves on the Continent. The 3rd Canadian Infantry Division, commanded by Major-General Rod Keller, performed with distinction in the first day of the invasion, but then, in the eyes of senior British commanders, things began to go awry. The commander of the I British Corps was unhappy with Keller's division in the bitter fighting for Carpiquet in early July. So was the British Second Army commander, General Miles Dempsey, under whom the Canadians were serving until the II Canadian Corps and the

First Canadian Army went into action. There was "immense dash and enthusiasm" on D-Day, followed by "the rather jumpy, highly-strung state" of the next few days, and then "a rather static outlook." Keller himself, Dempsey said, "seemed to go through exactly the same phases. . . . It will never be a good division so long as Major-General Keller commands it. Had it been a British Division I would recommend most strongly that he be removed from command at once." Montgomery agreed on 8 July, adding that as the 3rd Canadian Infantry Division would in a few days come under Simonds's corps, he had ordered that nothing be done for the moment as "I would prefer that any official action that may be necessary should be taken by Canadian generals."[90] The problem of what to do about Keller thus had landed squarely in Simonds's lap. The general who had expressed time and again his views on the required qualities of commanders now had the opportunity to put thought into practice; thought and practice, it turned out, could be far apart.

Rod Keller had graduated from RMC in 1920 and had joined the Princess Patricia's Canadian Light Infantry in the Permanent Force. A Staff College graduate, he went overseas in 1939 as a brigade major, commanded the PPCLI in 1941, and became a brigadier in the same year. McNaughton promoted him to command the division in September 1942. Popular with the troops who, many claimed, admired his military smartness and tough-talking demeanour, Keller was much less highly regarded by his senior officers. His brigadiers and many of his senior staff officers had been unhappy before D-Day with his excessive drinking and with his violations of the strict security measures in force before D-Day. Some felt he was absent so often visiting his married mistress that the GSO 1 was running the division. These concerns increased once the division landed in France, where Keller was noticeably jumpy and so concerned for his own safety that several of his senior officers began to claim then and since that "Keller was yeller."[91] Some of this, especially Keller's drinking, had been known to Crerar since 1942, and Crerar had talked to Keller about it in 1943; but on Keller's denial of over-indulgence, his word was accepted.[92] Probably Keller ought to have been sacked then. In July 1944, with his weary men engaged in the vicious fighting on the outskirts of Caen, Keller had a critical role to play.

Simonds saw Keller on 13 July, ironically dealing first with Keller's determination to sack one of his brigade commanders, Brigadier Ben

Cunningham. Then Simonds showed his hand. First he gave Keller the adverse reports. Simonds reported what happened next: Keller's reaction surprised him in that "Maj-Gen Keller also indicated that in any event he did not feel that his health was good enough to stand the heavy strain and asked that he be medically boarded as he felt that he would be found to be unfit." Logically, Simonds should have agreed. Instead, surprisingly, he urged Keller not to make a hasty decision. The next day, after recovering his sang-froid, Keller said he wanted to continue in command of his division.[93] Simonds agreed and let another ten days go by before he reported to General Dempsey on Keller. His conclusion focused less on Keller and more on problems in his division, so much so that he said "the individual qualities of General Keller are unimportant at the moment in comparison with the bigger problem of maintaining the morale of 3 Canadian Division." Simonds said he had spoken frankly to Keller and had come to believe "he has it in him to command" the division "successfully. I am NOT prepared to recommend his removal on evidence at present available to me."[94] That ended the matter for the time being, the British acceding to Simonds's judgment. After watching Keller for the next ten days or so, however, Simonds apparently changed his mind, coming to Keller's headquarters and letting slip to two of the division's brigadiers and the GSO 1 that there would be a change of command. A few days later, when American bombers, supporting the Canadian attack in Operation Totalize, dropped their bombs on Canadian troops, Keller was among the wounded.[95] He saw no further action, and Brigadier Dan Spry, promoted to major-general and flown from Italy to the Normandy battle front, took over the division on 18 August and led it for the next six months.

What is one to make of Simonds's actions here? While he was almost certainly correct in his assessment of the morale problem in the 3rd Canadian Infantry Division, it is hard to understand his urging Keller to reconsider his suggestion that he could not stand the strain. Given Simonds's views on effectiveness of command, Keller should have been replaced that day and likely would have been had he not been a popular PF officer. But there were few successors in evidence as yet in either Normandy or Italy, the troops liked their GOC, and it was unquestionably difficult to get the division's senior officers, bound to Keller by a loyalty he did not reciprocate, to speak out against him. Simonds's decision remains difficult to understand unless he was so absorbed in operations that he simply could not devote sufficient time and thought to the question.[96]

Certainly he was now actively involved in the fighting, and he and his Staghound armoured car were regularly seen close to the lines.[97] In the course of his first five weeks in operations with the II Canadian Corps, Simonds directed four separate major attacks against the Germans, and his corps played a major role in closing the Falaise Gap, albeit more slowly than it might have, and in helping to destroy a large portion of Nazi strength in France. Operations Atlantic, Spring,[98] Totalize, and Tractable were major affairs — "which included some of the most costly and tragic moments in the history of Canadian military action," Terry Copp and Robert Vogel wrote[99] — and, although Simonds has not wanted for critics then and later, his high reputation as an effective and notably innovative commander was confirmed in July and August 1944.

Totalize, which began on 7 August and of which Simonds had first advised his division commanders on 31 July in one of his polished, precise orders groups, was the *pièce de résistance*. His plan called for the attack to be launched at night under "artificial moonlight"[100] with a variety of navigation aids to help the troops, organized into a huge armoured box of six closely packed columns, keep direction as they broke out down the road to Falaise. The attack was supported by heavy bombers, which, in Phase II of the plan, dropped some of their loads on Canadian and Polish troops with serious losses. It featured the first operational use of armoured personnel carriers — an idea Simonds had had in North Africa. Using "defrocked" Priests (self-propelled artillery from which the guns had been removed), the carriers transported the leading infantry protected from enemy fire.*

---

*A later British study noted that "Gen. Simonds was insistent that infantry accompanying the armour in the initial phase must go straight through with the armour and themselves be protected. He therefore arranged that all available Priests should be stripped of their armament (less Browning machine guns) and made available as armoured personnel carriers . . . there were approximately sixty." (PRO, Cabinet Records, Cab 106/1047, British Army of the Rhine, Battlefield Tour "Operation Totalize," September 1947.) After the war Simonds tried unsuccessfully to register a claim for his invention. NA, Crerar Papers, vol. 8, Simonds to GOC-in-C, First Canadian Army, 10 June 1945; Guy Simonds Papers, 1945–9 box, 1947 file, Simonds to Secretary, Awards Committee, [U.K.] Ministry of Supply, 7 February 1947.

Totalize was a brilliant, if too complicated, attempt to neutralize the superiority of German armour and anti-tank weaponry. That it was at best a very limited success was partly Simonds's fault. Three of the divisions in his corps, the 2nd Canadian Infantry, the 4th Canadian Armoured, and the 1st Polish Armoured, were still relatively green, and Simonds ought to have taken that into account in formulating his complex plan. His innovative plan, precise as it was, fell apart almost as soon as the action began. The result, as Kitching noted, was chaos, the end result of "putting some 50,000 soldiers into an area approx 2 miles by 4 miles . . . particularly as there was a battle going on in the middle of it!!"[101] Immeasurably adding to the difficulty was the stout resistance offered by the superbly led and numerically inferior Germans, the casualties suffered by senior Canadian officers, and the heavy losses inflicted on the attackers. Still, Simonds's forces had 700 tanks by 10 August, while the Germans had only thirty-five remaining runners; even so, the attack ground to a halt.[102]

With Totalize stalled, Simonds followed up on 14 August with Tractable. Covered by a smokescreen and once more preceded by heavy bombing (some of which again with damnable luck fell among the attacking troops), Tractable initially made substantial gains. Kurt Meyer, commanding the 12th SS Panzer Division, later told a Canadian officer that the attack of the 4th Canadian Armoured Division was "so rapid that I could not withdraw my Infantry and the Canadian Infantry completely passed all of my Infantry Battalions, and when they reached their objective and held up they were halfway between my Infantry and Armoured Columns. It took my Infantry two days to rabbit-leap back to my armour."[103] Desperate, the SS men fought for survival and made the Canadians pay dearly. In vicious fighting that lasted until 21 August, elements of the Polish Armoured and the 4th Canadian Armoured finally plugged the Falaise Gap and the retreating Germans were killed in huge numbers by relentless assault from the ground and the air.[104] Two German armies had been savagely mauled, their casualties amounting to some 60,000 men and most of their equipment. The Canadians, too, had paid a price, Simonds's three Canadian divisions losing 1479 killed, 4023 wounded, and 177 taken prisoner from the beginning of Operation Totalize to the day the Falaise Gap was finally closed.

Nonetheless, there was criticism from the Americans (and later from historians) that Simonds's attacks towards Falaise had not been pressed forward with sufficient resolution to prevent the escape of some quarter-million Nazi troops. The II Canadian Corps had had huge numerical and materiel superiority, and the German units in its way had already been reduced to skeleton strength. Heads had to roll. On 21 August, Simonds sacked his friend George Kitching, an officer he had served with since Sicily and one he loved like a brother, from command of 4th Canadian Armoured Division. Reduced in rank, Kitching was soon dispatched to Italy, where he became a successful BGS of the I Canadian Corps. In his place came Harry Foster, a PF cavalryman, who had commanded a brigade in the 3rd Canadian Division since D-Day. Other lower rank officers who, in Simonds's judgment, had failed the test of battle also were replaced. As one officer remembered, some senior commanders failed to realize "that war is a two-sided affair, and that, particularly when the enemy is the Germans, even very good commanders cannot be expected to win every battle." That was so and, to make matters worse, "owing to the limited number of experienced Canadian commanders, those that were removed tended to be replaced by someone more inexperienced."[105] Still, some Canadian commanders *had* failed. Simonds's judgments might have been incorrect on occasion, but this time he had no choice but to act.

There was scant respite for Simonds, his commanders, or his troops. The retreating Nazis were pursued across the Seine[106] — it was like "cutting through cheese," Simonds said — and when he came across an abandoned enemy 88-millimetre gun in perfect working order and with its ammunition neatly stacked, "I knew that we would win. It was the first time I had ever seen a German gun position abandoned without a fight."[107] By 4 September British troops had entered Antwerp. There seemed to be every possibility that the war might be finished quickly and, in the middle of the month, Montgomery launched Operation Market Garden, the huge airborne assault that aimed to take the bridges over the lower Rhine at Nijmegen and Arnhem.

The attack failed, however, the high hopes of a speedy victory faded, and the fact that the Allies had neglected to clear the Scheldt River approaches to Antwerp now became critical. Without that great port city's facilities, supplying the vast Anglo-American-Canadian armies was problematical. "Right now," Eisenhower said, "our prospects are tied up closely with our success in capturing the approaches to Antwerp. . . . if we can only get to using Antwerp it will have the effect of a blood transfusion."[108] Belatedly, Montgomery gave the First Canadian Army this task. At precisely this time, Crerar fell ill and was evacuated to England, Simonds became acting army commander on 27 September, and Charles Foulkes replaced him as acting commander of the II Canadian Corps. Guy Simonds was now to have the responsibility for one of the crucial battles of the war.[109]

When he took over command of the army, Simonds had already received the appreciation prepared by the Plans Section at First Canadian Army headquarters for Operations Switchback and Infatuate — the plans to clear the Scheldt approaches. His reply to this appreciation, sent on 21 September, shredded the "hypothetical" army plan and pointed to all its misconceptions about German strength and to the advantages held by the defenders on Walcheren Island and South Beveland. To take strongly fortified Walcheren, Simonds said, an assault across water could not be ruled out, however uninviting it might be, and the necessary military and naval forces should be readied and trained for this eventuality.[110] The key was bombing the dykes on Walcheren to flood the island and deny the enemy the advantages provided by the ground.* This idea had apparently been considered by Crerar's planners, but it had been rejected by the Royal Air Force. Winston Churchill opposed any more bombing of Dutch and Belgian towns, and the RAF wanted to concentrate its efforts against targets in Germany. Moreover, the Chief Engineer at the First Canadian Army had argued that it was impracticable to flood Walcheren by breaching the dykes. Crerar had agreed, but Simonds had insisted that an attempt be made — if it failed, nothing had been lost. When Simonds took over the army, he pushed the bombing idea hard with the Royal Air Force in a meeting in the caddy shack on the golf course at Ghent and, through sheer force of argument, carried the day.[111]

The fighting in the Scheldt estuary was as hard as anything Canadians encountered during the war. In dreadful conditions of water, mud, and

---

*Two days later, probably because he had received inklings that Crerar was unhappy with his attack on the planners, Simonds wrote to the Army commander to assure him of his "complete and continuing loyalty. . . . I have never had the feeling that the submission of a suggestion would be interpreted as showing any disloyalty. Your decision is final and will not be argued here." Crerar Papers, vol. 7, 958C.009 (D169), Simonds to Crerar, 23 September 1944.

cold, the troops had to clear the Breskens Pocket and attack across the Leopold Canal, the latter accomplished with the aid of massed flamethrowers. Then the struggle to get across the narrow "peninsula" to South Beveland was followed by vicious fighting over the even narrower causeway to the eastern end of Walcheren. British troops of the First Canadian Army successfully launched an attack from the sea against western Walcheren, by now almost wholly under water and with the few acres of land remaining under constant attack from the air and artillery, though with serious losses among naval forces and the assaulting troops. In all, almost 13,000 officers and men of the army were killed or wounded in the fighting to clear the Scheldt. Bad as those figures were, they could have been much worse if Simonds's tactical skills had not prevailed. Antwerp was open for Allied use by late November.

Simonds's performance as acting army commander was the pinnacle of his wartime career. Montgomery had been pleased with his vigorous direction of the First Canadian Army, so much so that in mid October he asked the War Office to ascertain what Crerar's plans might be: "It is highly important that he should NOT repeat NOT return here until he is able to stand up to the rigours of a winter campaign in a damp and cold climate. . . . advise me as to the real form regarding Crerar's health and stamina." The Vice Chief of the Imperial General Staff knew what Montgomery really meant and reported that Crerar was likely to be fit enough to resume command shortly. "In these circumstances," he went on, "there is nothing further we can do although I know well what you would have preferred to happen."[112] On Crerar's return, to Monty's disappointment, Simonds resumed command of the II Canadian Corps, a post he would hold through much additional combat in the Rhineland and until the end of the war.

Guy Simonds's command of the 1st Canadian Infantry Division, II Canadian Corps and First Canadian Army in Italy and Northwest Europe had been outstanding. He was prepared to see casualties suffered if, by taking an objective, this would save lives in the long run. Perhaps because of this cold ruthlessness, neither his officers nor his men loved him, but at all levels there was undoubted respect for his competence.[113] Brigadier James Roberts put it simply and well in his memoirs: "Simonds was a tough baby. Of the Montgomery type, he brooked no sentiment and demanded results. I felt toward him as I did to Montgomery, an admirable battle commander but not a man one could love. In my heart I knew, however, that I would rather serve under the Simonds-Montgomery type than under a more kindly but less driving commander; the former is much more likely to win the battle."[114]

Montgomery's view of Simonds — a Canadian he regarded as one to whom he had taught the art of war[115] — was glowing. General Miles Dempsey wrote to Simonds that "months of experience have taught me that you always produce the goods — without fuss!" One of his staff at corps noted in his diary: "I will say this for the Old Man. He believes in getting his own HQ as far forward as possible, and frequently he is well up in advance of the Division HQs. This really burns them up." Simonds's aunt and uncle in Sussex wrote to say, "Your success is all the more striking since you had at the beginning neither money or influence and all your successes — great commands and decorations in the field — have come through your own ability and perseverance."[116] That was fair comment. No Canadian commander rose higher and faster in the Second World War, and none did as well in action. Simonds owed his success wholly to his own abilities and efforts — and those of the men who served under him.

YET IT WAS LIEUTENANT-GENERAL Charles Foulkes and not Guy Simonds who became the dominant figure in the Canadian army in the postwar era. In July 1945, two months after V-E Day, General J.C. Murchie, the Chief of the General Staff in Ottawa (and thirteen years earlier Simonds's best man) asked Harry Crerar for advice on the future employment of Simonds and Foulkes, both then corps commanders. Given his run-in with Simonds in Italy, Crerar's reply was judiciously phrased:

> Lt.Gen. Simonds. An outstanding officer of exceptional professional ability whose record in field as a Div and Corps commander in this war is second to none. A keen soldier of determined character. Of commander type but has proved himself an excellent senior staff officer. Fully qualified for any appointment of high military responsibility.
>
> Lt.Gen. Foulkes. A very able intelligent and thoughtful officer who has been definite success in the field both as Div and Corps commander. Above the average of his rank. While he has proved to be an excellent commander consider his particular qualities make him specially suitable for very senior staff appointment.[117]

As Crerar well realized, Murchie was seeking a successor as CGS. Thus his recommendation of Foulkes as "specially suitable for very senior staff appointment" could only have been intended to scupper Simonds's chances — and it did. Foulkes became CGS in August, and Simonds remained in command of the dwindling Canadian forces in Europe. He was subsequently sent to the Imperial Defence College, became an instructor there, and then took command of the National Defence College in Kingston, Ontario Not until 1951 did Simonds become CGS, and only when Foulkes moved up to the newly created post of Chairman, Chiefs of Staff Committee. It was almost as if Simonds, arrogant and contemptuous of politicians, was too hot to handle in peacetime.

The victor in this behind-the-scenes struggle, Charles Foulkes, was the same age as Simonds and, like him, had been born in Britain.* After briefly attending university, Foulkes joined the Royal Canadian Regiment in 1926. He served as a staff officer in various of the military districts; he was one year behind Simonds at Camberley, where his confidential assessment ("Sound and competent . . . Should make a good commander though possibly not a very sympathetic one") was much less glowing than his compatriot's;[118] and he was a major when the war began. His rise was only slightly less spectacular than his rival's, however. Brigade major in the 3rd Brigade of the 1st Division, he became GSO 1 of the 3rd Division in September 1940, a brigade commander in August 1942, and then BGS of the First Canadian Army — a post that let him push major-generals around, or so one senior artillery officer remembered.[119]

Certainly, Foulkes's record seemed good, though not as outstanding as Simonds's. Crerar had spoken highly of him as GSO 1 of the 3rd Canadian Division, noting his "exceptional ability, sound tactical knowledge, a great capacity for quick, sound, decisions, energy and driving power."[120] In August 1943 when Crerar's corps needed a Brigadier General Staff, Crerar told McNaughton that "the BGS I should be happiest to have as my 'right hand man,' would be your own," Charles Foulkes.[121] Two months later,

---

*Some readers may be properly concerned at the brief treatment Charles Foulkes receives in this volume. The author's intention was to devote equal space to Burns, Simonds, and Foulkes, corps commanders all, but the surviving Foulkes papers and gleanings from interviews unfortunately proved too thin to make this possible. Foulkes's postwar career, however, is much better documented.

when Foulkes was still a brigadier, Crerar suggested that "Foulkes might be a good selection to replace Burns as Comd 2 Cdn Div. Foulkes will not make a better Div Comd than Vokes, but he *might* make a Corps comd. I don't think Vokes will."[122] That was a prescient comment. Colonel Ralston, the Minister of National Defence, was also favourably disposed towards Foulkes. In November 1943 he had a long talk with the BGS and came away "impressed with his knowledge of characteristics of officers in army, right down to Lt.-Cols."[123] Charlie Foulkes had the knack of impressing senior officers and politicians; Guy Simonds frightened them.

Still, doubts were often expressed about Foulkes, doubts serious enough that none of his contemporaries could ever quite account for his wartime rise. He was a dour man, short, pudgy, unapproachable, and as Charles Stacey noted, a "cold fish," in a high command that seemed to have whole schools of them.[124] In the prewar PF he had not been popular, Harry Foster considering him "mean and narrow" with "a hard-shelled Baptist mind" and "a sneering supercilious attitude toward anyone his own rank or below" while simultaneously "grovelling to everybody over the rank of major."[125] As a brigade major, GSO 1, and brigadier, Foulkes was criticized by staff officers for his lack of attention to training and his unwillingness to seek advice. On at least one occasion, Simonds was displeased with Foulkes's knowledge of his officers.[126] When Foulkes became GOC of the 2nd Division in January 1944 and in the Normandy fighting, officers complained that his orders lacked clarity[127] and, after his division's performance on Operation Spring, Simonds came close to sacking him. "GGS mad at CF," Kitching noted in his pocket diary on 2 August, "said he was NBG [No Bloody Good]."[128] Yet, despite this somewhat problematic record, Crerar and Simonds picked Foulkes to take command of the II Canadian Corps when Simonds temporarily took over the army from the ailing Crerar; and the two again chose him to command the I Canadian Corps in Italy in place of Burns.[129] Perhaps there was no one else. Nonetheless, Brigadier Elliot Rodger, Simonds's Chief of Staff, visited the Italian Front in January 1945 and recorded in his diary that "Foulkes was in particularly good form and had apparently taken charge and was *running* the show with a firm hand — and the Divs were happy about it."[130] The point Rodger was making, of course, was that when Foulkes had replaced Simonds on the Scheldt, he had neither taken charge nor run his divisions with a firm hand.[131]

His command record in Italy and then in the Netherlands was not in the same league with Simonds's, but there could be no doubt he was a much smoother man than his abrupt rival. Foulkes played the army political game as well as any man, and it was simply inconceivable that Foulkes would ever have argued, let alone fallen into a slanging match, with Crerar sufficient to lead that officer to question his sanity. Nor would he, as Simonds did, sweep by the Minister of National Defence in Ottawa's Château Laurier in 1946 with a covey of ADCs in such a way that the Minister felt obliged to remind Simonds that the war was over.[132] Despite Simonds's better fighting record, Foulkes, at 42 the youngest CGS to that point in Canadian history, was, in fact, the better choice for that supremely political job in 1945. Crerar had made the right recommendation, though probably for the wrong reason.[133]

The treatment Simonds received, however, was almost cruel. In November 1945 Foulkes told the Chief of Staff at CMHQ that he had suggested a number of possible positions for Simonds: Inspector-General or commander of the reserve army in Canada; CGS; or that he be transferred to the British army permanently or loaned to the British for four years. The Minister rejected the first two proposals, and the British stepped in to find Simonds a student's place at the Imperial Defence College. "This officer's record and ability entitle him to be kept on in a military career," Foulkes said. "Regret there is no place in our organization but feel that in case of emergency or at a later date an attractive opening for this officer may be available."[134]

When Simonds completed the IDC course, what then? Field Marshal Montgomery, the CIGS, told Foulkes he could give Simonds a corps in Malaya, but the CGS replied "it would be much more in keeping with Canadian policy" if Simonds could be in a training establishment where Canadians were involved. Thus Simonds stayed in exile at the IDC as an instructor.[135] In 1949, finally, NDHQ permitted Simonds to come back to Canada to command the National Defence College at Kingston; this, as Foulkes wrote Simonds in detailing "the plot" for his employment, "will allow you to get into the Canadian atmosphere and see some of the Canadian problems, and for the Minister to have a chance of seeing you at work."

Minister of National Defence Brooke Claxton refused, however, to commit himself to appointing Simonds as CGS when Foulkes's term expired.[136] There would be difficulties along the way and Simonds, frustrated at being on the shelf at the NDC and as explosive as ever, accused Foulkes in January 1950 of not acting "in frankness and good faith," a charge the CGS flatly denied.[137] Not until 1951 did Simonds receive the CGS' position he might have expected in 1945. With the efficient, organized, cold Charles Foulkes, a man who lived for compromise and conciliation,[138] still his superior as a full General and as Chairman, Chiefs of Staff Committee, the CGS' job must have been frustrating for Simonds.

Simonds nonetheless found the men and equipment for the growing army in Canada, for Korean War service, and for the Canadian brigade group with the North Atlantic Treaty Organization in Europe, and he whipped the expanded army into shape.[139] It was the most rapid military expansion in peacetime Canadian history, and he was in his element. Typically, however, he made speeches that upset his minister when they leaked into the press and, when his term as CGS ended in some public controversy in 1955,[140] there was nowhere for him to go. Foulkes tried unsuccessfully to find Simonds a spot with NATO in Europe, but NATO's Supreme Commander, General Alfred M. Gruenther, could offer nothing.[141] Gruenther's briefing notes on Canadian officers noted that Simonds, highly praised for his command attributes, was "resolutely outspoken" and preferred to keep Canada close to British standards and methods "at a time when consideration was being given to standardizing on U.S. organization, equipment and tactics." That was a fault in American eyes. Foulkes, in contrast, was painted as "pleasant but unimpressive, restrained and thin-skinned. He is not a forceful leader nor is he endowed with any great amount of brains. He appears to think highly of US military leaders and enjoys associating with them. In dealing with him a little flattery and personal attention on a 'first name' basis would be helpful."[142] The double meaning in that assessment of Foulkes apparently slipped by its drafter.

Retired from the army, Simonds promptly went public with his arguments for a radically overhauled defence policy. Canada needed peacetime conscription, he said, and the big budgets going to the Royal Canadian Air Force had to be cut.[143] He made no headway. More realistic, much more political, Foulkes stayed on as Chairman of the Chiefs of Staff and took Canada into the North American Air Defence Command, masterminded the scrapping of the Avro Arrow, and led John Diefenbaker's government into its politically fateful decision to accept nuclear weapons. He retired in 1960, more than two years before the controversy over the Bomarc blew up in Diefenbaker's face and destroyed his government.

The tortoise and hare analogy is not inappropriate for the race between Guy Simonds and Charles Foulkes. Simonds clearly outdistanced Foulkes in wartime, but Foulkes more than made up the ground and retained his lead in the postwar years. For all his undoubted military ability, Simonds lacked Foulkes's political sense, and it was Foulkes, not Simonds, who became Canada's most powerful military mandarin and the creator of the postwar Canadian armed forces.

The relationship between General A.G.L. McNaughton and Prime Minister Mackenzie King was criti-
cal to the war effort. King liked McNaughton for his opposition to conscription, but he fretted about
McNaughton's ability to withstand the strain of war. The two are pictured on King's visit to England in
August 1941.

McNaughton thought of himself as a strategist and, sitting with Winston Churchill and poring over a map in February 1941, he was in his element.

McNaughton's successor as GOC-in-C of the First Canadian Army was Harry Crerar *(centre)*, a much smoother and more political officer. But even Crerar had difficulties dealing with Colonel J.L. Ralston, the Minister of National Defence *(right)*, and General Sir Bernard Montgomery *(left)*, then Eighth Army commander. Here Monty demonstrates that he, at least, had enough sense to get out of the Italian rain in November 1943.

It fell to Crerar to command the First Canadian Army in Northwest Europe. Here, Crerar *(right)* and the staff of his headquarters attend a church service aboard HMCS *Algonquin*, en route to France on 18 June 1944.

The impact of five years of war on Crerar can be seen by contrasting this photograph, taken when he was a Brigadier and Commandant of the Royal Military College in 1939, with the one above.

As army commander, Crerar had to deal with the British. In the Hochwald Forest in March 1945, the Canadian GOC-in-C hosted Churchill, Field Marshal Sir Alan Brooke, the CIGS and his friend from the Great War, and Field Marshal Montgomery, the C-in-C of 21 Army Group.

Crerar's relations with Montgomery worsened after he avoided attending a conference at Monty's HQ to participate in the 2nd Canadian Infantry Division's commemorative service at Dieppe in September 1944. Crerar, Major-General Charles Foulkes, and Lieutenant-General Guy Simonds pay homage to those killed in the abortive raid two years before.

Major-General Victor Odlum was a sixty-year-old militiaman when he took command of the 2nd Canadian Infantry Division in 1940. Here, standing next to Crerar and listening to Colonel Ralston in December 1940, Odlum looks his age.

Major-General George Pearkes, VC, had been a fierce fighter in the Great War. But as GOC of the 1st Canadian Infantry Division, he had powerful critics, British and Canadian. Pearkes here inspects one of his division's RCAMC units in December 1941. Note that he is shaking a soldier's hand, something generals did not ordinarily do.

This portly Lieutenant-General Ernest Sansom, here watching one of his units pass by in March 1943, commanded II Canadian Corps in Exercise Spartan. His tactics were severely criticized by British observers, and he remained in command only until the end of the year.

Major-General J.H. Roberts led the 2nd Canadian Infantry Division in the Dieppe raid of August 1942. The casualties there probably broke his spirit, but he hung on until after Exercise Spartan, where his role was criticized. Roberts here inspects the Queen's Own Cameron Highlanders in November 1942.

Canada's only generals from one family were the two Hertzbergs. H.F.H. *(top)* was Commandant at RMC for most of the war; Charles, here talking with a Sergeant-Major from No. 1 Tunneling Company, RCE, in 1942, was McNaughton's Chief Engineer until 1943, when he was obliged to retire on grounds of age.

Lieutenant-General E.L.M. Burns led the I Canadian Corps in Italy. His difficult personality caused him problems with superiors and subordinates alike. In the photograph below, Burns (centre) listens as the Eighth Army GOC-in-C, Oliver Leese, talks to a Canadian officer. Between Leese and Burns is Major-General Bert Hoffmeister, GOC of the 5th Canadian Armoured Division and probably the best fighting general Canada produced.

Lieutenant-General Guy Simonds was the one Canadian commander esteemed by the British and the Americans. Abrupt and aloof, Simonds's closest army friend was George Kitching *(left)*, whom he put in command of the 4th Canadian Armoured Division before D-Day. Here the two (with Kitching's tailored battledress in sharp contrast to Simonds's off-the-rack issue) watch troops of Kitching's division. A few months later, after the struggle to close the Falaise Gap, Simonds relieved Kitching of his command.

Charles Foulkes's rise to high command puzzled observers. Shrewd and political, Foulkes made the best of his opportunities. In the top photograph, he is being welcomed to Normandy in July 1944 by the 3rd Canadian Infantry Division GOC, Rod Keller *(left)*. As GOC of the I Canadian Corps, Foulkes had the honour of accepting the surrender of the German army in the Netherlands on 5 May 1945.

Senior staff officers exercised tremendous power. Overseas, the key figure was General Price Montague *(left)*, here greeting the CGS, Ken Stuart *(centre)*, and the Adjutant-General, H.F.G. Letson, on their arrival in Britain in August 1942. General Maurice Pope *(second from the right)*, shown below with his colleagues on the Canadian Joint Staff, Washington, in June 1944, differed with Stuart about conscription in October and November 1944; Stuart was sacked but Pope, who had supported Mackenzie King's position, survived and prospered.

Major-General Chris Vokes was a tough-talking, hard-driving commander. He got on well with those troops who appreciated plain talking. From his jeep, Vokes here addresses men of the PPCLI at Riccione, Italy, in November 1944, just before he moved to Northwest Europe to take over the 4th Canadian Armoured Division. Note that the censors blanked out the soldiers' cap badges to confuse the enemy — and people at home.

Bert Hoffmeister and Bruce Matthews were two NPAM officers who rose to divisional command. *(Top)* Still a brigadier here, Hoffmeister *(centre)* listens to his GOC, General Vokes, talking to the commander of the 1st Canadian Armoured Brigade on the Moro River in Italy in December 1943. Like Hoffmeister, Matthews, GOC of the 2nd Canadian Infantry Division, his car flying his divisional pennant, practised a more consensual leadership style than most PF officers.

Major-General Dan Spry rose from lieutenant in 1939 to command the 3rd Canadian Infantry Division in 1944. Here, just prior to his reassignment in March 1945, Spry *(centre)* confers over his map with Chris Vokes, by then GOC of the 4th Canadian Armoured Division.

Grievously wounded in the Great War, Georges Vanier filled both military and diplomatic roles in the Second World War. Here General Vanier inspects a RCASC unit in Italy in April 1944.

The army tried hard to find French-Canadian generals, but met limited success. One able officer, eliminated from combat by heart problems, was the plump Major-General P.-E. Leclerc *(top)*. More politically inclined was Major-General Léo LaFlèche, a former Deputy Minister of National Defence, who made his way into the cabinet in 1942. LaFlèche, here being welcomed back to Ottawa by Justice Minister Louis St Laurent after winning a by-election in Outremont in December 1942, was despised by many of the country's military chiefs.

The First Canadian Army's leaders, gathered together at war's end. Sea *(from left)*: General H.S. Maczek of the Polish Army, whose men frequently served under Canadian command; General Simonds, GOC II Canadian Corps; General Crerar, GOC-in-C First Canadian Army; General Foulkes, GOC I Canadian Corps; General Hoffmeister, GOC 5th Canadian Armoured Division. Standing *(from left)*: General Keefler, GOC 3rd Canadian Infantry Division; General Matthews, GOC 2nd Canadian Infantry Division; General Foster, GOC 1st Canadian Infantry Division; Brigadier Moncel (representing General Vokes, the GOC 4th Canadian Armoured Division); and another officer.

CHAPTER 7

MATTHEWS AND HOFFMEISTER: MILITIA SUCCESSES

C HARLES FOULKES was arguably Canada's greatest military bureaucrat, but certainly he was not the most successful or most admired field soldier Canada produced during the Second World War. Always a better politician than a commander, there might have been some politics in the notes Foulkes prepared in 1945 for speeches in Canada on "The Last Battle of the British in Holland." After a conventional account of the battles in which his I Canadian Corps had participated, Foulkes's notes turned to what he called the "Contribution of Canada's Citizen Army." In a few simple statistics, he said much:

60% of Div commanders ⎫
75% of Bde Commanders ⎬ Citizen Force[1]
90% of Comd Officers ⎭

The Non-Permanent Active Militia, Foulkes said, had produced the vast majority of Canada's wartime commanders.

Although his numbers focused only on the senior officers and ignored the junior officers and soldiers who did most of the fighting and dying, the data were simply astonishing. From its 1939 paper strength of 52,000 largely untrained officers and men, the NPAM had produced from within its ranks three of the five division commanders in the field in May 1945, three-quarters of all the brigade commanders, and nine in ten of the regimental and unit commanding officers. Over almost six years of war and just two years of sustained action, the one-night-a-week soldiers became the officers who led Canada's armies to victory.

Some militiamen raised in the Sam Hughes tradition of distrust of professional soldiers had been convinced from the outset of the war that all the key appointments in Canada's army ought to go to "Canadian born citizen soldiers."[2] That did not happen, as we have seen, for the Permanent Force officers took their full measure of the key slots. Other NPAM supporters during the war were convinced they had made their way in the face of the opposition and sabotage of Permanent Force officers, eager to see that the best and most prestigious posts went to them. There was, of course, some evidence to support this attitude. Unstated in Foulkes's numerical accounting was the army commander, Crerar, a PF officer; omitted as well were the two corps commanders at war's end, Simonds and Foulkes, also PF. All the wartime Chiefs of the General Staff at National Defence Headquarters in Ottawa had been PF. Nor did Foulkes make any mention of the host of PF officers who had been given division, corps, and army commands between 1939 and 1945, only to lose them for sins ranging from political incompetence to military ineptitude. Brigadier William Murphy, a Vancouver lawyer who began the war as a junior officer, expressed the militia attitude in a letter he wrote to his family when he took command of the 1st Canadian Armoured Brigade in Italy early in 1944: "I feel I have got about as far as a militiaman can in this war."[3]

That may have seemed correct when Murphy wrote, but it wasn't true for long. As the war went on, as they gained experience and proved themselves in action, militia officers moved into some of the most senior army posts. In Italy and Northwest Europe, as Foulkes had observed, three NPAM officers, Major-Generals Bruce Matthews, Bert Hoffmeister, and the much less well-known Holley Keefler, emerged in 1944 and 1945 to command divisions. Hoffmeister, in fact, would become the best Canadian fighting general of the war.

BRUCE MATTHEWS was in many ways the embodiment of the pre-war militia ethos. His father was a prominent and powerful stockbroker and investment banker with Liberal party connections, important enough to be named Lieutenant-Governor of Ontario in 1937. Born in 1909, Matthews went to Upper Canada College, where he showed interest and talent only in cricket and the cadet corps (in his last year he failed French, Latin, English literature, ancient history, algebra, physics, and chemistry). When he also narrowly failed his entrance examinations for admission to the Royal Military College in 1927, he went to Europe, where he sat in on a few classes at the University of Geneva.[4] He returned to Canada and went to work in his father's firm, then he decided he wanted to join the naval reserve. Matthews turned out to be colour blind and was rejected by the navy. A neighbour, adjutant of a Toronto artillery regiment, then suggested he join the NPAM. In 1928 he signed up in the 30th Field Battery, 3rd Field Brigade, Royal Canadian Artillery, as a provisional lieutenant. That year, already in love with military life, he took the "long course" at Kingston that qualified him as a lieutenant, was promoted captain in 1933, and took the Militia Staff Course over two years from 1933 to 1935. That course, he said, gave him a good sense of what was involved in making military appreciations, drafting orders, and learning staff duties, and the PF officers who instructed him impressed him greatly. Matthews impressed them, too, and their assessment noted that he was a "first rate type of officer" with quick intelligence.[5] The work world and the militia had knocked the apathy and spoiled-son attitudes out of Matthews.

Matthews's militia unit was a typical city regiment. The 7th Toronto Regiment, of which he became adjutant in 1936, was under-strength and under-funded throughout the Depression. Many officers and men turned over their pay to the regiment; on occasion, that was the only way boots could be purchased, for the Department of National Defence was unable to provide them. A substantial number of officers were RMC graduates, who were eagerly sought out by his regiment. The devotion of officers and men was real — the regiment's training took one or two nights a week as well as time in the summer, and most of the work of necessity was theoretical. Even at summer camp, where his unit's guns initially were pulled by horses, ammunition was sometimes so short that there was scarcely any firing practice. Still, Matthews remembered, the realism of training had begun to improve by the mid 1930s. Instead of artillery shoots being comparable to rifle-range target shooting, the gunners now fired on "natural" targets such as spurs or hill features, woods, or groups of buildings represented by dummy structures on the ranges. Exercises were developed to force artillery observers to engage targets in a realistic fashion and, instead of pin-point aimed firing as had been done in the 1920s, units received a tactical narrative telling them where the enemy and their own troops were and obliging them to provide artillery support for a further advance. Lieutenant-General Guy Simonds, who spent many summers from 1925 on teaching militia gunners, recalled: "They were given free scope as to their route of advance, selection of gun position and when in action, the gunnery instructor, acting as an infantry commander, described the artillery support he needed to implement his 'fire plan.'"[6] By 1938 the summer encampments for Matthews's regiment provided realistic and effective training. Though the field dress still featured pith helmets and Great War–style uniforms, the unit was at least mechanized.[7]

Matthews realized there was some tension between the PF and the NPAM, but less in the artillery than elsewhere. "They embraced us," he recalled, adding that gunners stuck together,[8] perhaps as a reflection of the artilleryman's adage that there were only two types of people in the world: gunners and targets. By 1938 Major Matthews commanded the 15th Field Battery and was considered "a very good officer" by his regimental CO. After his father exercised some political pull on his behalf, he went overseas with the 1st Division in this rank.[9] Matthews may not have known of his father's efforts — certainly he was adamant that his subsequent rise in the army had nothing whatsoever to do with his family's position.[10]

Of medium height, well-nourished, and good-looking in a broad-faced way, the already balding Matthews had married an American woman, Victoria Thorne, in 1937, and they had one son before the war. As soon as she could, his wife came overseas in early 1940, leaving their child behind. Matthews and another well-off Toronto artillery officer whose wife had come to England made plans to rent a villa in the south of France, where they could go on leave from the front lines in France.[11] The course of the war tossed those plans in the discard, and Mrs Matthews returned to Toronto in the late summer of 1940 when service wives without wartime employment were evacuated. The next year she delivered twins — Toronto gossips who had not realized she had gone overseas, Matthews remembered, counted months on their fingers and whispered. Matthews did not see his wife and family again until war's end.[12]

His rise overseas was steady, but initially not spectacular. A battery commander in March 1940, he was soon 2nd in command of the 1st Medium Regiment, still as a major. After a brief period in command of an experimental battery working with new 5.5" medium guns, his capabilities, to Matthews's surprise, were recognized in September 1941 when General McNaughton offered him promotion to lieutenant-colonel, his first jump in rank since the beginning of the war two years earlier, and command of a new medium regiment, the 5th. He accepted, and was allowed his pick of forty men from his old regiment and forty more from another. Initially the 5th Medium had been equipped with old steel-wheeled 60 pounders, but Matthews and his officers and NCOs devised a way of moving them on tank transporters which let them be brought into action almost as fast as rubber-tired modern guns. McNaughton, a gunner himself, appreciated initiative of that sort, and in September 1942 Matthews became Counter-Battery Officer at headquarters, I Canadian Corps, a job that let him roam around as the eyes and ears of the Commander Corps Royal Artillery. He was more than slightly dismayed at the slackness he observed, something that confirmed him in his developing view that the Canadians' training standards were not up to the mark.

His next appointment in January 1943 was as Commander Royal Artillery, 1st Canadian Division, as a brigadier, at thirty-three the youngest then in the Canadian army.[13] The CRA commanded the three field regiments of artillery as well as more specialized anti-aircraft and anti-tank units in the division, and he served as the GOC's artillery adviser. He found the GOC, Major-General Harry Salmon, a difficult man to work for and no innovator. In April 1943 Salmon died in an air accident on the way to the Middle East, a flight that Matthews had initially been scheduled to make.[14] The lucky man found himself working with a new division commander, Major-General Guy Simonds, in preparing the 1st Division for the invasion of Sicily. Also a gunner, Simonds understood the artillery's problems, but he was brusque and demanding, a no-nonsense commander. En route to Sicily, Matthews's divisional artillery headquarters lost its vehicles and equipment when the ship carrying them was sunk. When he landed on 10 July after a heavy storm that left him retching and ill, Matthews had only his Brigade Major and two clerks with one typewriter to coordinate the division's artillery support. He had to borrow a spare artillery headquarters from the Eighth Army, and the Brits, he remembered, ribbed him unmercifully. How could someone so young be a CRA? How could a militiaman do the job? Matthews was philosophical about these jibes — and grateful, too, for the tactful way the British gunners, experienced in battle in North Africa, gave advice. As far as he was concerned, the Canadian army's growth meant that someone had to do the job. Nonetheless, the first time Simonds ordered all three of the division's artillery regiments to engage in a coordinated fire plan, Matthews had the difficult task of telling him he could not deliver it when planned. "When will it be ready?" Simonds asked. "Three hours later," Matthews responded. "Then make it so," came the command. The pressure of working under the driven Simonds was intense, and Matthews, a careful man who wanted the time to check the lay of the land and make his plans with care, always felt pressed.[15] He also demonstrated substantial courage prior to the capture of Agira, going forward under observed German fire to reconnoitre ground for his gun positions. He was awarded an immediate DSO.[16]

Matthews landed in Italy with Simonds early in September and continued to impress his GOC. When Simonds left to take over the 5th Canadian Armoured Division on 1 November 1943, Matthews worked with his successor, Major-General Chris Vokes, in another good relationship. Vokes was likeable and full of energy, but he was a worrier, very nervous at times, and given to ringing up Matthews in the middle of the night because of some enemy shelling. Most important, however, Matthews delivered artillery fire where and when Vokes wanted it, including one massive barrage in front of Ortona.[17]

Meanwhile, major changes were taking place in Britain, where Generals McNaughton and Sansom were out and Harry Crerar and Guy Simonds were in as First Canadian Army and II Canadian Corps commanders, respectively. The new broom swept away many of the old senior staff officers, and Simonds quickly asked for Matthews to become his CCRA, to "stiffen up formation and units in UK with those having operational experience," as a telegram from Lieutenant-General Ken Stuart put it. The request was promptly granted.[18] The Eighth Army commander, Oliver Leese, was sorry to see Matthews go: "a nice man whom I shall miss — He is always cheerful."[19] Matthews was that, but he also had "an amazingly clear and modest 'thinking machine,'" as his friend Brigadier Elliot Rodger, characterized by many as the finest staff officer produced by the Canadian army during the war, wrote in his private diary.[20] Academically undistinguished as his schooling might have been, Matthews had matured into a disciplined, organized, clear-headed soldier.

He had also risen to the second most senior job for a gunner in the Canadian forces, only the Brigadier Royal Artillery at the First Canadian Army headquarters outranking him. His was an extraordinary ascent, even in an army that tended to give first place to the artillery. No doubt his personal abilities had most to do with it, not to say his ability to get along with the demanding Simonds. Moreover, as a 1st Canadian Infantry Division veteran, one who had fought his guns through Sicily and Italy at a time when no other formations of the army had experienced sustained operations, he was in the right position. The right time, the invasion of France, was now at hand.

Matthews's war in Normandy did not begin until Simonds's II Canadian Corps went operational on 11 July 1944. From then on, the pace was frantic, as the corps was involved in some of the hardest and costliest battles of the war. A series of operations — Atlantic, Spring, Totalize, and Tractable — tested commanders and troops to the limit as the Canadians struggled to break the German defences south of Caen, open the road to Falaise, and destroy the Nazis in the Falaise pocket. The innovative Simonds decided to use his armour at night in Operation Totalize, and Matthews, charged with preparing the fire plan for the advance, had to use a variety of devices. His guns had to fire a rolling barrage moving at a pace that kept it just ahead of the advancing armour; at the same time, because the attack was to take place in darkness, tracers and coloured shells were employed as direction guides. There were problems with supplies, Matthews recalled, coloured shells being in scarce supply and arriving from the beaches only at the last moment. But the real difficulty was that everything had to be done at once, and there was never enough time to plan and to reconnoitre. Such haste bothered this organized man, who always struggled to ensure that he delivered the goods on time. Worse still, the old ideas of registering targets ahead of time had to be scrapped, and most artillery shoots were done by grid reference, a problem because the maps were frequently inaccurate. "The pressure," Matthews said, "the magnitude of the operations, was unbelievable."[21]

In November 1944, with the First Canadian Army emerging from the operations that had cleared the Scheldt estuary at such great cost, Simonds recommended that Matthews be promoted to major-general. He wanted him to succeed Charles Foulkes in command of the 2nd Canadian Infantry Division, now that Foulkes had gone to Italy to replace the fired Lieutenant-General Tommy Burns at the head of the I Canadian Corps. Crerar agreed, although he was ordinarily reluctant to put artillery officers into brigade or divisional commands, both because Montgomery was dubious about this practice and because the perception was widespread in the First Canadian Army that a "gunners' union" ruled the roost. Matthews, Crerar said to CMHQ, "has done excellently has sound judgment and is generally well equipped to assume div comd."[22] Less formally, Elliot Rodger, Simonds's chief of staff, wrote that it was "a well deserved promotion for Bruce — with his ability and personality it had surprised me he had not earlier had a chance to prove himself" with an infantry brigade. "Now I see it all. We'll miss Bruce here very much."[23]

The 2nd Division had had a hard time. It had taken more than a year to recover from the costly debacle of Dieppe in August 1942, and its early actions in Normandy under Foulkes, a lacklustre divisional commander, notably at Bourguebus Ridge south of Caen and in Operation Spring in July 1944, had also been bloody.[24] Then the gruelling fighting for the Walcheren causeway and in the remainder of the Scheldt operations had cost the division 207 officers and 3443 other ranks as casualties. Such losses could not be readily made up, especially with the reinforcement system running into enormous difficulties, political and military. When Matthews took over, he quickly realized that his division needed careful handling, more training, and a boost in morale. Fortunately, with the Scheldt estuary cleared, he had a period of six to eight weeks largely free of operations, and he used the time to run training schools and to get to know his units. He visited them all, talked to troops, tried to offer reassuring but honest answers to questions, and worked to see that reinforcements were trained and integrated into their new regiments. He paid special attention to his two French-speaking battalions and his one francophone medium regiment, speaking to them in the passable French he had learned in Geneva and not hesitating to give them anglophone replacement officers when the supply of French-language replacements dried up.

Of course, Matthews had to learn his new job. As an artilleryman, he had had no direct experience commanding infantry, and he had never led an infantry brigade in action. He was green, in other words. But Matthews, confident after five years of full-time soldiering, recalled that he wasn't awed by his new responsibilities. As a CRA in Italy and a CCRA in France and Belgium, he had had intimate relations with the infantry, watching them fight in battle under the fire plans he had created, and he knew their problems better than they did. After all, fire and movement meant artillery and infantry working together and, he maintained confidently, "artillery officers knew more about planning proper infantry operations than any infantry officer."[25] The turnover in infantry commanders was also such that his experience was at least as great as that of his three brigade commanders.

Artillery, almost by definition, required an understanding of all-arms' cooperation, something a division GOC had to recognize and master. An intelligent man, a shrewd student of leadership, Matthews knew that his brigade commanders would resent an artilleryman imposing his version of the proper way to fight the war on them. Instead, his command technique was to seek advice from his brigadiers in finalizing a division plan and then to delegate, to give them as much free rein as the situation allowed. That was very different from Charles Foulkes's method; Matthews's predecessor had neither consulted nor delegated. The GOC's primary job, as this gunner general saw it, was to allocate artillery and armoured support to the brigadiers, who, he recognized, were personalities, too, men he had to negotiate with like minor potentates while building good rapport. One, W.J. Megill, a PF signaller in command of the 5th Brigade, was notoriously idiosyncratic and difficult, but Matthews did his best to keep him happy and in harness. He also had to resist the temptation — which he did successfully — of interfering with his CRA, Brigadier Frank Lace, an officer from his own Toronto militia regiment.[26]

In addition, Matthews had to deal with Simonds and Crerar, his corps and army commander, respectively. In Italy, a GOC had something of a free rein, but in Northwest Europe one division was just a cog in a gigantic machine. The corps commander drew up the overall plan, allocating areas and tasks to the divisions, and Matthews and his staff worked out their particular plans, his GSO 1 negotiating with the other divisions' and corps' staffs. Then Simonds would ask his pointed questions. In action, Matthews tried to model himself on Simonds, going forward to the brigades frequently, rather than bringing the brigadiers back to his divisional HQ. When an attack was scheduled, he would invariably try to get to the battalion start lines to ensure that the company and platoon commanders had a grip on their objectives before the attack went in. Again his major problem was time: the hours for reconnaissance were never sufficient for this conscientious soldier, and there were always enemy mines or resistance points that no one knew about to disrupt the best-laid plans. After the battle there were the casualties. Matthews tried to avoid making hospital visits, something relatively easy to do because evacuation was ordinarily so prompt. He was appalled by the carnage, and weakened in spirit and resolution by seeing it; his job as a commander was to minimize casualties to the greatest extent possible.[27]

Matthews fought his division into the Rhineland in Operations Veritable and Blockbuster in February and March 1945. His operations characteristically featured careful planning and, one avenue blocked, a willingness to pull back and try another approach. Matthews had in him none of the "blood and guts" rhetorical excess that sometimes seemed to characterize exhortatory commanders like Vokes. War may not have been a rational exercise, but Matthews tried his best to impose rationality upon his small part of it. By May and the Nazi capitulation, Simonds's opinion of him, always high, had risen still further. In a brief assessment, the corps commander declared Matthews a "very able divisional comd and potential Corps comd."[28] Matthews could have had an important career in the postwar army, but he told Simonds he wanted to be demobilized "at the earliest opportunity."[29]

His wish was granted, and Matthews returned to Canada in October with a letter from Simonds attesting to his "loyal and able services" and praising his division for its "enviable record."[30] Matthews took a month to get to know his family — his twins had asked their mother "Who is that man?" when they met their father for the first time at the age of four[31] — and to get his discharge.[32] Then he rejoined the family firm, Matthews and Co. The adjutant-general sent him on his way with a letter offering the thanks of the Army Council for his wartime services. "May I also add," wrote General A.E. Walford, himself a militiaman, "that the members of the pre-war Non Permanent Active Militia consider your brilliant record as a most excellent tribute to that small but vital group, whose services have meant so much in the war effort."[33]

Bruce Matthews's postwar rise in public life and business was as impressive as his climb in the army. He became a power in Lester Pearson's Liberal party as president of the National Liberal Federation, a major fund-raiser for charity, the chief executive officer of Argus Corp., a giant

conglomerate, and a major player in a number of insurance and investment companies. Shortly before his death in 1991, he said that what he
missed most as a civilian were the two ADCs and the batman he had had
in the army as a GOC, and he reflected ruefully that the military in some
ways was easier than the business world. Soldiers did what they were told;
in business or in charities, it wasn't that way at all.[34]

THE OTHER IMPORTANT divisional commander to emerge from
the militia, and by far the most remarkable, was Bertram Meryl
Hoffmeister, an infantryman from Vancouver. His courage and daring in
action saw him advance from a battalion commander in July 1943 to
brigadier early the next year, and then to division commander in March
1944. After leading the 5th Canadian Armoured Division through to the
end of the war in Europe, National Defence Headquarters selected
Hoffmeister to lead the division Canada had promised for the war in the
Pacific. For a prewar militiaman, that was an extraordinary rise, and
Hoffmeister's career encompassed other factors that make his ascent more
remarkable still.

Born in 1907, his father a low-ranking manager in the H.R. MacMillan
timber empire, Bert Hoffmeister came from a German family with a long
military tradition. His first exposure to the military came in 1919, when he
joined the cadet corps run by the Seaforth Highlanders, one of the great
Vancouver regiments. As he recalled: "I found that the Seaforth Cadets provided me with a very good opportunity to associate with people in a different kind of a way, to build up some self-confidence. I was quickly given
stripes and became a corporal and sergeant and so on up the line. I was
responsible for a group of cadets and had to get out in front of them and
explain the close order drill in which we specialized. . . . To some extent it
was a substitute, I think, for university. It furthered my education and built
up my self-confidence."[35] As that comment suggested, because of his family's straitened circumstances, Hoffmeister had to go to work when he graduated from high school, and he had no university education. He worked in
the lumber mills for the Rat Portage Lumber Co. Ltd for twenty cents an
hour and eventually made his way up through the office staff until, in 1939,
he was sales manager for Canadian White Pine Co. Ltd. At the same time,
he was well known in British Columbia as an athlete, rowing competitively
and playing football. He had also married in 1935 and had a child.

But the undoubted centre of his life was the Seaforths. Hoffmeister had left the cadet corps in 1927 and taken a commission in the regiment. This was a big step for someone without money, for the Seaforths, even if their armouries were inadequate, drew their officers from the professional classes of the city. The Highlanders' uniform, which officers were obliged to pay for themselves, was expensive — a minimum of $400 to $600 was the usual estimate.[36] The regimental adjutant looked him over and pronounced the big, athletic, good-looking Hoffmeister as officer material; the regimental selection committee, headed by the prominent Tory politician, lawyer, and financier Brigadier-General J.A. Clark, agreed. With the help of his father, Hoffmeister scraped together enough money to get into kilts.[37]

For the next dozen years, Bert Hoffmeister soldiered in the NPAM. His regiment, like the PF units, was equipped with obsolete weaponry and spent most of its time perfecting its drill and staging elaborate ceremonial parades and athletic demonstrations. He took courses to qualify as lieutenant and captain, and his training at least introduced him to infantry tactics. The PF provided two PPCLI staff sergeants as instructors, and they lived on in Hoffmeister's memory as "sad, lethargic" types who "just sort of let us go on our own and kept a roving eye around for the sergeant-major."[38] Naïvely, Hoffmeister had assumed that regular army NCOs would be better than the scrimshanking Princess Pats, and this experience began his continuing disaffection for the Permanent Force.

The Seaforths were his hobby. "It was a very pleasant way of life," he said, "and we all put into it what we could. It did get a little boring at times and my interest lagged a bit for a year or so, particularly just around the time I was married." Then, Hoffmeister added, "when war was declared, most of us resigned from our jobs that day, and the whole thing swung into action down at the Seaforth Armoury. They moved in a very orderly way, people took over and carried out their responsibilities and the standard of discipline that had been developed in the prewar period was pretty obvious."[39]

Promoted major, Hoffmeister went overseas with the Seaforths in December 1939 as part of the 1st Canadian Infantry Division. For the next fourteen months, Hoffmeister's unit was in constant training. To him, it seemed more than a little ineffectual. "We were told that as soon as we arrived in Britain we would be given training and instruction and taken away from the regiment for this purpose. In the meantime," he remembered, "the troops would be trained by people who knew what it was all about and that we would come back and then we would have trained troops." That didn't happen, however, and the Canadians were left to their own strictly limited devices. Under Brigadier George Pearkes, the 2nd Infantry Brigade, of which the Seaforths were a part, learned about trench warfare, something Hoffmeister remembered thinking completely passé in light of the Nazi blitzkrieg. He had little sense of what would be required of him or his men in combat, he knew nothing of how to write an operations order, and he did not believe that his troops could stand up to the Germans in their present state of training. "My mind reverted to the farewell party in the armoury," Hoffmeister said years later, "when the wives and sweethearts . . . came up and said; 'Now my boy is in your company, look after him, we have every confidence in you'. . . . these thoughts kept coming back to me . . . and it disturbed me no end to realize that here I was, a company commander responsible for 120 or 130 men and I didn't know how to look after myself in a battle, let alone how to look after this number of men. "

Hoffmeister's frequent requests to his commanding officer to be allowed to take courses that would fit him for his battle responsibilities were turned down: the CO believed he had the best company commanders in the army* and he didn't want to lose any of them to courses where they might be noticed by higher formations and stolen away.[40] For the conscientious Hoffmeister, serious about everything he tackled and especially about his responsibility for the lives of his men, this sense that he was unprepared for his military tasks led to a nervous crisis in January 1941.

One foot forward, Hoffmeister stepped into the bath in his billet one day and felt nothing. When his other foot touched the water, he realized that the water was scalding, and that he was virtually without feeling on his left side. Within days he was a patient at the army's No. 1 Neurological Hospital — No. 1 Nuts, it was called — under treatment from a psychiatrist, Dr H.H. Hyland, for what in retrospect must have been hysteria. Flexible and practical, Hyland rebuilt Hoffmeister's psyche and philosophy

---

*General Montgomery agreed that the Seaforths' company officers were good. After an inspection, he proclaimed them "excellent, the best I have seen in the Corps." NA, H.D.G. Crerar Papers, vol. 8, 958C.009 (D182), "Notes on Infantry Brigades of Canadian Corps — No. 5, 28 Feb 42 — 2 Inf Bde."

in three weeks of intensive therapy, persuading him that if he was given a task to do it was because his superiors thought he was capable of it. All they expected of him was his best efforts, Hyland said. Do your best and then don't let the worries accumulate.[41] Simple as it was, that philosophy changed Hoffmeister's military life, his symptoms disappeared, and he returned to his regiment with his confidence restored. That the army allowed him to rise through the ranks despite his brief psychiatric illness was a testimony to military broadmindedness — or, more likely, to the fact that almost no one knew how close Hoffmeister had come to his breaking point.* Once the war was over, Hoffmeister sought out Dr Hyland to thank him for what he had done.[42]

After another period of regimental duty, Hoffmeister went to Brigadier Joe Potts's 2nd Brigade headquarters as a staff learner, in effect an understudy to the Brigade Major, and in March 1942 he returned to Canada to take the Canadian Junior War Staff Course at the Royal Military College. Thanks to his regiment's reluctance to train its officers in the broader aspects of war, Hoffmeister was totally unprepared for Staff College. With its key instructor a British officer who had substantial North African battle experience, the CJWSC was a deliberately contrived high-pressure atmosphere that sought to simulate the stresses of battle on staff and commanders and to inculcate the lessons learned in three years of war against a first-rate enemy. Hoffmeister's first weeks in Kingston saw him

---

*The army viewed psychiatric disorders in senior commanders quite seriously. Major-General C.R.S. Stein, an RMC graduate and PF officer who became GOC of the 5th Canadian Armoured Division in January 1943, was summarily relieved of his command in October 1943. A medical board diagnosed him as suffering from "progressive anxiety neurosis." At the same time and after being observed in exercises, Stein had been commented on most adversely by General E.W. Sansom, II Canadian Corps commander, for lacking the "tactical ability and strength of character to comd an armd div in battle." Though the timing was suspicious, there was no apparent link between the adverse report and the medical board finding. Despite his protests — "Why was I practically railroaded out of the Service with such apparent speed?" — Stein received no further military appointments. NA, DND, vol. 10033, file 9/Sr Appts/1, Montague to Stuart, 18 October 1943; NA, A.G.L. McNaughton Papers, file PA6-1, Minutes of Special Meeting . . . 13 Oct 43; ibid., file 785-70, Stein to McNaughton, 19 June 1945.

struggling vainly to cope with the course's demands. But then Dr Hyland's philosophy reasserted itself and, instead of staying up all night working on solutions to the tactical and staff problems presented to the course, he relaxed, began to enjoy himself, and sailed through, standing first in his class with a rare "A" grading and glowing recommendations. When he was offered command of the Seaforths at the end of the staff college course, he leapt confidently at the opportunity.[43]

Chris Vokes, who commanded the 2nd Brigade of the 1st Canadian Infantry Division in which the Seaforths served, had heard about Major Hoffmeister. "There is no such thing as a born soldier," Vokes was told, "but he is the next best thing to it. He takes to soldiering like a duck to water." It was Vokes who had arranged for Hoffmeister to take over the Seaforths.[44] The regiment was not in good shape when Hoffmeister returned in October 1942; indeed, Vokes told him it was now the worst battalion of the three in the brigade, and he wanted it to be the best.[45] There were problems with some of the senior officers, morale and discipline had slipped among the rank and file, and, Hoffmeister believed, "damned bad leadership and administration" were to blame. He made changes in personnel, began to send officers and NCOs on courses, and stepped up the pace of training. Morale improved dramatically, proving the adage that troops who are worked hardest are happiest. The brigade and division commanders thought highly of Hoffmeister. Major-General Harry Salmon, the GOC, recommended him for promotion (though ranking him fourth on a list behind Foulkes, Vokes, and Kitching), citing his "ability to think clearly & quickly. Good leadership qualities. Will make a good G staff [operations] officer and with more experience a bde comd."[46] Staff College had prepared Hoffmeister for battle, and when the 1st Division was detailed for the operations in Sicily, Hoffy's men, for so the Seaforths now thought of themselves, were ready.

Aboard ship en route to the Mediterranean, the CO ensured that he went to each and every platoon in the regiment to brief them on the coming assault. He knew other battalion commanders didn't do this kind of all-ranks' briefing, but he cherished the thought that the men looked on him as a friend. Such a relationship would require him to stick his neck out in action, to show himself, or else morale would fall. But he realized that unless he understood the conditions the soldiers had to face, the Seaforths' confidence in him could waver. A man of powerful personality

193

and striking magnetism, Hoffmeister was the classic leader, someone men wanted to follow. In all likelihood, they would have followed him if he had not briefed them so well; taken into his confidence, however, knowing his mind and their place in his plans, the Seaforths were ready for anything. There was nothing new in this Hoffmeister approach, nothing innovative. His was the classic technique of man management as taught to officers, the approved method of securing the "willing compliance" necessary to make soldiers risk their lives; unfortunately, it was all too often neglected by less conscientious and less sensible officers.

The worth of Hoffmeister's approach was shown in action. The Seaforths fought their way through the rugged countryside with "fire, movement and plenty of guts," taking casualties but learning quickly and besting the Germans. Hoffmeister himself narrowly escaped death near Leonforte when four Canadian artillery shells fell short and exploded near the spot where he was giving his orders on 21 July 1943. There were thirty casualties, but Hoffmeister escaped unscathed, though severely shaken.[47] The next month, Hoffmeister led his regiment in a succession of attacks against Nazi positions north of the Salso River. The attack on the enemy's 3rd Parachute Regiment north of Carcaci on 5 August, staged in conjunction with tanks of the Three Rivers Regiment and with heavy artillery support coordinated by the CRA, Brigadier Bruce Matthews, was deemed "a model infantry-cum-tank action" by Major-General Simonds, the GOC, who watched the battle from a vantage point on a nearby hilltop. So it was, for Hoffmeister rode in the armoured regiment commander's tank and kept control of the action. The paratroopers fought "to the last man and the last round," and the Seaforths in this one action lost eleven killed and thirty-two wounded.[48]

Hoffmeister and his regiment had proven themselves in action. Simonds, however, was not Hoffmeister's favourite commander, then or later. The GOC's concept of man management was not Hoffmeister's. Simonds was too cold-blooded. His orders were issued in an abrupt manner, his plans snapped out, and the session ended in a way that almost forbade comment. Simonds offered few pats on the back and, in Hoffmeister's view, made no effort to see or understand the problems of the battalion commander and his men.[49]

His initiation to battle in Sicily had confirmed Hoffmeister's view of Permanent Force officers. They were often too old and too fat, and some drank too much. The PF "protective net" that surrounded them could sometimes be hard to take. One brigadier in whom he had no confidence would later be forced upon him, the Canadian corps commander telling Hoffmeister, by then a division commander, that he was a PFer and had to be given his chance. There was also pressure to award decorations to PF senior officers who, he believed, did not deserve them.[50]

Hoffmeister merited his decorations, and he won the first of his three DSOs in Sicily. (There was an apocryphal story that his batman was recommended for the Victoria Cross simply for following Hoffmeister around!) It was not long before he was promoted to brigadier. On 1 November 1943, with the 1st Canadian Infantry Division now fighting on the Italian mainland, Vokes became a major-general and GOC in place of Simonds, who took the 5th Canadian Armoured Division then en route to Italy. To replace Vokes, Hoffmeister got the nod. He had been recommended by Simonds and Montgomery for a brigade command in September and, though the initial intent at CMHQ was to give him a brigade in Britain, General McNaughton decided he should have the 2nd Brigade in the 1st Division.[51]

In fact, Hoffmeister was already an acting brigadier, filling in for Vokes who had temporarily replaced Simonds on 29 September when the GOC was evacuated with jaundice. Vokes had found Hoffmeister at a brigade sports meet at Potenza and told him he was promoted. Following the same philosophy he had adopted more than two years before, Hoffmeister simply said, "That's fine, I'll turn over [command of the Seaforths] immediately, pack up my stuff and be at your headquarters within an hour."[52]

Hoffmeister's initiation during the rapid advance of the division in the early days of the campaign on the mainland was not without its moments. His headquarters had lost touch with one of his battalions, the Princess Patricia's Canadian Light Infantry, and Hoffmeister and another officer drove forward to find them. "I couldn't see or hear a sound around any place. . . . Suddenly I looked over my shoulder and there was a German position up on a hill, an O[bservation] P[ost] obviously manned by four or five people. In those days," he went on, "I carried a rifle and tried to look like a private soldier," a sensible way of not being singled out by the enemy. Then Hoffmeister spotted a line of panzers, found some of his missing Patricias, and used their wireless to call up his own armour. Getting away soon turned into a series of mad dashes as he and the other officer took turns running and going to ground, chased by tank gunfire. "I saw the Patricias the next day," Hoffmeister's companion on this adventure wrote later, "and heard how they had sat up on the hill and laughed at the spectacle of the Brigade Commander . . . doing hundred yard dashes between the shellbursts."[53]

If that affair had its comic side, the battle for Ortona around Christmas 1943 had none. A small fishing port on the Adriatic about halfway up the Italian peninsula, Ortona had little strategic significance itself. It was held strongly by the Germans, however, and the Canadians had been ordered to take the town. To advance from the Moro River, 5 kilometres south of Ortona, to the Riccio River, 4 kilometres north of the town, took a month and cost heavily in casualties — 253 officers and 3703 men by the GOC's estimate at the time[54] — or almost half the fighting strength of the division's infantry when the battle began in the second week of December 1943.

For Hoffmeister's 2nd Brigade, orders to take Ortona were orders. In his recollection, as in that of everyone who was there, it was "a desperate struggle" even to reach the town, so strongly were the rugged approaches defended; then the battle in Ortona itself involved the troops in house-to-house fighting as they mouseholed their way from one connected dwelling into the next. So vicious was the battle that Vokes, alarmed at the decimation of his infantry, asked Hoffmeister if he wanted to quit. The Brigadier believed his troops were at last making progress against the German paratroopers, and he said "absolutely not, to quit at this time would be letting the brigade down and the effect on the morale of the brigade would be such that it would be just shocking."[55] That may have been true, though the impact of the slaughter at Ortona left the bruised survivors reeling. Moreover, perhaps Vokes's tactics were not appropriate, some historians commenting that the division's attacks faltered because they lacked weight, often being launched by single battalions. The terrain also could have lent itself to the bypassing of the town, thus sparing Hoffmeister's brigade much of the terrible difficulty it experienced. "But Vokes, for all his bluster," historian Brereton Greenhous commented, "was never a man for daring or momentum. Or for small leaps of logic. So he sent his long-suffering 2nd Brigade to take the town."[56] Take it they eventually did after the world press painted the fight as a "Stalingrad in Italy," the Nazis pulling out finally over the night of 27–28 December.

Hoffmeister's reward for the capture of Ortona came in March 1944 when he was promoted to major-general and given command of the 5th Canadian Armoured Division. The division had arrived in Italy before the new year and had had both Simonds and General E.L.M. Burns as its GOCs in the intervening few months. Hoffmeister had won the job on merit, but it had not hurt that he was a militiaman. The defence minister, Colonel J.L. Ralston, made that clear when he wrote to Lieutenant-General Ken Stuart at CMHQ: "Comparing Hoffmeister and [Brig. T.G.] Gibson both impressed me as excellent. Hoffmeister more magnetic personality. If Hoffmeister reasonably equal in tactical ability would think his personality and the fact that he would give representation on divisional level to the N.P.A.M. might warrant giving him the call."[57] Crerar, the corps commander in Italy, and Burns, his designated successor, agreed,[58] and so did the British. General Sir Oliver Leese, commanding the Eighth Army, thought "Brigadier Hochmeister" "excellent," "a grand chap — full of fight," a commander of "immense drive" who "is turning out [to be] a very good Armoured Divisional Commander."[59] Hoffmeister himself learned of his promotion when Harry Crerar, who had summoned him to meet him at a bridge asked, "How would you like to command 5 Armoured?" "Very much," Hoffmeister replied. "When can I start?" "Well," Crerar retorted, "you're a cool one, aren't you?"[60] He was, indeed, and his rise from battalion to division commander without any intervening period of staff employment was certainly unprecedented in the Canadian army in the Second World War.

The 5th Canadian Armoured Division had only two brigades at this point, one armoured and one infantry. Hoffmeister ran it just as he had run his battalion and his brigade. He won over his senior officers quickly by, for example, telling Brigadier J. Desmond B. Smith, the commander of the 5th Canadian Armoured Brigade, that he knew "bugger all" about handling armour and asking for his help.[61] With the troops, he exerted his personality and showed himself. The 11th Canadian Infantry Brigade, his other brigade, had suffered a bloody repulse in a daylight attack on the Arieli River in January, and the troops still had not recovered their morale. The new GOC visited each unit, inspected their quarters, and demanded improvements where necessary. He informed the officers that their responsibilities included looking after their men, and morale began to rise. It literally soared after Hoffmeister organized divisional exercises to demonstrate the tremendous array of weaponry that the division had. "The punch, the clout this division had was just tremendous," he said, "and no person, private soldier, NCO, or officer could fail to be impressed."

His exercises included teaching the infantry how to advance behind artillery fire — Hoffmeister personally took every infantry company in turn to show them how to lean into the barrage. This was always a calculated risk, and when the inevitable round fell short on one such demonstration, he remembered the infantrymen looking at him: "What do you say now, wise guy?"[62]

One of his battalions, the Perth Regiment, a unit that had been hard-hit on the Arieli, was not responding and seemed so sullen and unresponsive as to be close to mutiny. Neither the brigade commander nor the battalion commander could suggest how to deal with the difficulty, so Hoffmeister arranged for two men from each platoon to meet with him with no other officers or NCOs present.

> I explained to the men exactly what the problem was, and the danger of going into battle with this lack of confidence and the poor morale that existed . . . and [said] that we were going to stay there until I had the answers. I said 'I don't have the names of any of you men and I don't want to know your names; nothing you say here is being recorded, this is for my information . . . only, so that I in turn may take the necessary action to get this unit in shape to fight.' So we sat there and looked at each other, not a word was said and this went on, it seemed, like a long time. . . . Finally a bit of dialogue started to develop and we worked this around by question and answer to the point where four officers were named as having performed very badly in the Arieli thing . . . [and] the men had absolutely no confidence in them and were reluctant to go into battle with them. That was the reason for the low morale. . . . I dismissed the meeting, went back to my HQ, called in the brigade commander and battalion commander and ordered him to dispose of these officers to the holding unit forthwith.[63]

This was not the usual general's way of dealing with unit morale, but it worked, and the Perths became an excellent fighting regiment.

How was it Hoffmeister knew the way to deal with such problems? Part of the answer was instinctive in the man, a simple sense of understanding how soldiers thought and reacted and how they wanted their officers to treat them. But it was also that only six months earlier he had been commanding a rifle battalion in action, and he understood what an infantry battalion could and could not do. As a brigadier and as a major-general, however, he knew that he could no longer influence events on the battlefield by seizing a rifle and joining the fray. Now as a GOC he had to stand back and find different ways to motivate soldiers, battalions, and staffs. To his great credit, he found the way, and he was one of the few senior officers in the Canadian army who thought seriously and systematically about such problems, one of the few who did not simply rely on the authority conveyed by his rank to get his way. Hoffmeister led as well as commanded.[64]

The beginnings of Hoffmeister's impact on his division became apparent in its first major action. When the II Canadian Corps attacked the Hitler Line in the Liri Valley on 23 May, the plan called for the 5th Armoured, now beginning to think of itself as "Hoffy's Mighty Maroon Machine" after its coloured divisional arm patch, to pour through a gap in the line opened by the 1st Canadian Division. The plan worked well, though not without heavy fighting, casualties, and delays, and the armoured division drove through the hard-won breach with great panache. For Hoffmeister's headquarters staff, the only problem caused by their GOC was his habit of going forward too far and too often. Useful as that could be and necessary as it was for Hoffmeister to see what opposition he was sending his men to meet, it put him out of touch and left the staff to fight the battle. That caused difficulties.[65] There were others, too.

Unfortunately, the Eighth Army's planners had clogged the limited road network in the valley with too much traffic and horrendous jams resulted that slowed the pursuit as the Nazis retreated towards the north. General Burns, the Canadian corps commander, received the blame, and there was a natural tendency on his part to look elsewhere for scapegoats. Hoffmeister's division took its share of the rap, his headquarters making the corps staff very angry: "It is a hopeless task to try and get anything out of HQ 5 Cdn Div," Brigadier Nick McCarter, the BGS, wrote in his personal diary. "They are behaving like complete amateurs." Worse, the division was using routes designated for other units.[66] Then, the commander of the 11th Brigade, T.E.D'O. Snow, a PF officer, had to be pushed to exercise command of his troops in action, something that angered and disturbed Hoffmeister. For his part, Snow, who was replaced in the next month, also wrote critically of the division headquarters' conduct of the operation.[67] The problems aside, the 5th Armoured had performed well in its first major operation,[68] and Hoffmeister had learned much. Certainly Burns was pleased. As he wrote privately, "Bert Hoffmeister did an excellent job and fought his green division with all the drive we expected of him."[69]

As we have seen, Burns's command of his corps in the battle was not admired by General Leese, and it took extraordinary efforts by General Stuart, the Chief of Staff of CMHQ, to see that he kept his post. Hoffmeister and Vokes, the two division commanders, were questioned by Stuart about Burns and they found the interview exceedingly distasteful. But Hoffmeister, despite a number of experiences that made him doubt Burns's good sense, held his tongue and did his duty.

That duty took his 5th Armoured to the Nazis' Gothic Line that protected northern Italy and the Po Valley. The Canadian Corps was to attack the Adriatic hinge of the line, and the date for a massive set-piece attack was fixed for the night of 1–2 September 1944. But initial patrol reports on the night of 29–30 August suggested a strange lack of German activity, and the corps headquarters decided to move against the enemy on 30 August. Hoffmeister's division now had been strengthened with an additional brigade of infantry, and his battalions once more struggled to open a hole in the line for the tanks. Although the reports were confused and confusing, Hoffmeister made the "gutsy decision" to commit his armoured brigade at once.[70] By this time his staff's work was first-rate, Hoffmeister sought advice and took it, and the change in the meticulously prepared plan was implemented without difficulty.[71] After fierce fighting, the Germans, one division in danger of encirclement, began to pull back on 1 September. There was much more fighting before the line was cleared, but Hoffmeister's courageous seizure of the initiative had helped greatly to win the battle.

Oliver Leese fairly bubbled when he told Montgomery: "The troops fought very well, especially the 5th Cdn Armd Div. This Div, led by Bert Hoffmeister, has the terrific dash of 7th Armd [the British army's famous Desert Rats] in the old days. They have really done extremely well."[72] More concretely, Leese told Hoffmeister that he had earned a vacation and gave him his personal aircraft to take him to Cairo.[73] LCol. John English, a severe critic of Canadian army training and operations, agreed with the Eighth Army commander's assessment. The 5th Canadian Armoured Division's operations on the Gothic Line, he said, "may have been the finest by any Canadian formation in the Second World War."[74] Praise from English is praise indeed.

Fresh from this triumph, Hoffmeister found himself plunged into army politics. The criticism of the corps commander, Tommy Burns, muted since the summer, flared up again, and this time Burns had to be replaced. Major-General Chris Vokes took the lead in demanding a change in command, but Hoffmeister had had his own run-ins with the GOC and shared Vokes's objections. He bluntly told a senior officer sent to investigate matters that he "had lost all confidence in Burns."[75] Unhappy as he was to be sacked, Burns nonetheless told Harry Crerar that Hoffmeister "definitely has the ability required in a potential Corps Commander."[76] That was not to be, and Burns was replaced by Charles Foulkes, who had led the 2nd Canadian Division in France. To Hoffmeister, Foulkes was just another PF type, a vain, egotistical man whose primary interest was looking out for himself. The new corps commander also drank too much on occasion, something Hoffmeister never did. He especially resented Foulkes's summoning him from a hard-earned leave in Positano to supervise the move of the 5th from Italy to Northwest Europe in February 1945, something his staff was well able to handle.[77]

In the Netherlands, Hoffmeister's division now formed part of the First Canadian Army, and the operations were much vaster in scale and much more lavishly supplied than in Italy.[78] What stands out in his mind was the fight at Otterloo in the early morning darkness of 17 April 1945 when a strong German force, seeking to withdraw, ran into Hoffmeister's headquarters. The mad scramble, highlighted by Hoffmeister's organization of the defence in his "very colourful pyjamas," or so one of his staff officers remembered them, saw an artillery regiment firing over open sights and flamethrowers used to mop up.[79]

When the war in Europe ended on 8 May, Hoffmeister was determined to say thanks to his men. He organized a massive parade of the division, with every vehicle on display, and he forbade officers to follow standard operating procedure by having units on parade hours ahead of time. Instead, trucks were laid on to get the troopers to their designated spots twenty minutes early. Hoffmeister took care to see that Ordnance and Service Corps personnel were included — in his division they were fighting troops, too.[80] This was a man who knew how to lead, and the Mighty Maroon Machine, the 5th Canadian Armoured Division, was the only division in the army that had an identity and pride of its own.[81]

NDHQ quickly tapped the reluctant Hoffmeister to command the division-strong Canadian Army Pacific Force, slated to fight with the Americans in the invasion of Japan. The Minister of National Defence, now General A.G.L. McNaughton, had indicated he would accept Foulkes, Simonds, or Hoffmeister. General Crerar recommended Hoffmeister, if the post was to be filled by a major-general, and Simonds and Foulkes, in that order, if it could go to a lieutenant-general.[82] The brass in Ottawa talked the matter over, and the Chief of the General Staff, Lieutenant-General J.C. Murchie, pronounced it a "Damn shame" for a lieutenant-general to have to drop in rank to get the job. Moreover, he said, "I feel that it would be a very useful thing to have an N.P.A.M. fellow command the show."[83] It was Hoffmeister, then, and, after winning Crerar's permission to have his choice of staff officers, he rounded up many of his 5th Canadian Armoured Division staff.[84] Shrewdly, Hoffmeister intended to give the regiments in his division the names of those in the 1st Canadian Division, a plan that appealed to McNaughton's sentimental streak because those, of course, were the units he had taken overseas in 1939.[85] The surrender of Japan, hastened by the use of atomic bombs in early August 1945, put an end to all such plans, and Hoffmeister went onto the Reserve of Officers in September.

He rejoined the business world as vice-president (production) of H.R. MacMillan Export Co. Ltd and soon was president and then chairman of MacMillan and Bloedel. But he did not forget the men who had fought with him. In the House of Commons in December 1945, a Member of Parliament quoted Hoffmeister as having said that "men who dug slit trenches for their lives in Europe do not want to dig ditches for their livelihood in Vancouver." The people who stayed home and had their living standards improve during the war "are the ones who should be digging ditches. . . . If men saw fit to place their lives in my hands overseas, the least I can do is try to find an answer to their problems here."[86]

Now in his mid-eighties and ill, Hoffmeister remains a commanding presence in his wheelchair. His eyes still fill with tears when he talks about men stopping him on the street to say proudly they had served under him. That, he says, was all the thanks he ever wanted.[87]

WHY HAD MATTHEWS and Hoffmeister risen so high and so fast? There was an element of circumstance and luck for both, of course.

Circumstance saw to it that Matthews was posted to the 1st Division as CRA and that Hoffmeister was a battalion commander there when that division became the first Canadian formation to see sustained action. Both men got their battle experience early, and this helped ensure their ascent. Both were officers who did not hesitate to expose themselves to danger, Hoffmeister because of his infantry responsibilities more so than Matthews, and they were lucky to escape the death and injury that felled other good men. Matthews was also fortunate to work for Simonds, who took his key officers with him when he rose. Hoffmeister was in a position to be promoted rapidly because he was on the scene, first when Vokes got a division and then when Burns became a corps commander. Luck mattered, but the key for both was ability. In a meritocratic army, not many incompetents found their way into command positions or held them for long once the test of battle was applied. Both Matthews and Hoffmeister, young and vigorous men, discovered they had a talent for war, and both turned out to be intelligent, flexible commanders who sought advice and, in effect, led by consensus. In an army whose high command was dominated by professional soldiers, their consensual style set them apart, and it may well have been responsible for their success then and later in the corporate world. As Major-General Elliot Rodger put it almost a half century later, Bruce Matthews "came cold from business and rose on straight ability."[88] That could be said of Bert Hoffmeister, too.

It is important to note that Rodger mentioned "business." Matthews and Hoffmeister — and thousands of other officers whether they had experience in the NPAM or not — came into the fighting army once the war had begun. Coming from a broader base than the old PF, entering the army in vastly greater numbers than the regulars, it was inevitable that some of them would prove to have great talent. That many became brigadiers and unit commanders was only to be expected in an army that expanded from 4000 to 750,000 in a few years. That three became division commanders and that two, Hoffmeister and Matthews, took their place with the best Canadian officers of the war was, however, extraordinary. Commanding large numbers of men in action is a special skill, usually found only in those who have studied war for their entire professional lives. Such talent for war is rare indeed among militiamen.

CHAPTER 8

POPE AND STUART:
SOLDIERS AND
POLITICIANS

THE IMAGE of the red-tabbed staff officer that emerged from the Great War was inordinately harsh and perhaps deservedly so. For example, Lieutenant-General Launcelot Kiggel, Chief of the General Staff at Field Marshal Douglas Haig's General Headquarters in France, was notorious — in the front-line Tommies' popular imagination and in that of subsequent writers — for never going near the front. He and his staff colleagues lived in rear-area chateaux in safety, eating and drinking well while they sent the infantry in hopeless attacks against uncut wire and enemy machine guns. There was demonic mythologizing here, of course, but there was enough truth in this perception to affect the way survivors viewed their wartime experiences. The staff was never seen at the front line, one officer recalled, and the British soldier "gained the impression that the Higher Command looked on him as cannon fodder, but considered their own lives too valuable to be risked."[1]

Canadian soldiers seem to have shared the Tommies' views. The best Canadian novel to emerge from the Great War, Charles Yale Harrison's aptly titled *Generals Die in Bed*, makes good use of parodied versions of the song "Mademoiselle from Armentieres":

Oh, the generals have a bloody good time
Fifty miles behind the line.
Hincky, dincky, parley voo.[2]

Probably that perception was unjust. Canadian staffs, from General Sir Arthur Currie down to the staff captain at a brigade headquarters, tended to be much more visible and more exposed to danger than their imperial counterparts at Haig's headquarters. In fact, one of the Canadian Corps' division commanders, Major-General M.S. Mercer, died in action and a brigade commander, Brigadier-General Victor Williams, was taken prisoner, while Currie himself regularly went forward on reconnaissance. Still, the perception of General Staff insouciance and incompetence persisted. Maurice Pope, one of the senior staff officers in the Second World War, wrote to his parents in September 1916 from the front that he had had "a good opportunity today to size up the Staff Officers. . . . they have been greatly worried about their own personal comforts and about nothing else. . . . I shudder to think that my life and those of my men are in the hands of these men. As the army says, they know damn all."[3]

Such powerful attitudes were not countered when, in the Second World War, the growth of Canadian Military Headquarters in London and of National Defence Headquarters in Ottawa seemed to outpace the increased size of the army overseas. With the exception of General Harry Crerar, none of the most senior staff officers at either headquarters ever went from a staff billet to field command, though a number, proven wanting in action, went from field to staff. CMHQ and NDHQ were where the unfit and the incompetent went, or so it seemed to the casual military observer.

Again, there were elements of truth in this attitude, especially as it focused on the unfit. The Chief of the General Staff in Ottawa at the beginning of the war, Major-General T.V. Anderson, for example, had only one arm, and the Adjutant-General from 1942 to 1944, Major-General Harry Letson, had one leg. Those were the result of wounds honourably suffered in battle, however, and, despite the fighting soldiers' intolerant perceptions, neither officer was necessarily incompetent simply because he served in Ottawa or at CMHQ in London.

Indeed, some of the staff officers at NDHQ and CMHQ were among the most efficient in the army. Price Montague, a judge on the Manitoba

Court of King's Bench before the war, became a lieutenant-general and the Chief of Staff at CMHQ in November 1944. His was the highest rank achieved by a militia officer during the war, a tribute both to Montague's politicking for promotion and to the smooth fashion in which he ran his headquarters. Major-General Howard Kennedy, Quartermaster-General in 1943–4, was a leading Ottawa engineer before the war and one who took a substantial cut in pay to join up in 1939. Major-General J.V. Young, Master-General of the Ordnance from 1942 to 1945, was an RMC graduate and a leading Hamilton industrialist who had served as a Great War lieutenant and took his general officer rank only on a pro forma basis. Yet another was Major-General A.E. Walford, for a time the highly successful senior administrative staff officer (DA&QMG) at the First Canadian Army and the Adjutant-General from 1944 to 1946. Walford had been an executive with Morgan's department store in Montreal, and he was widely considered to be one of the two or three most able staff officers in the army. That all these officers were from the NPAM also suggested that the senior staff posts were as open to the militia as were the higher ranks in the army. Even the absence of francophone senior staff officers reflected the same imbalance that afflicted the army as a whole.

Two of the most effective officers of the General Staff, however, came from the Permanent Force. Both Lieutenant-Generals Maurice Pope and Kenneth Stuart spent most of their war service in North America at the interface between politics and the army. The distance between National Defence Headquarters in its shabby wartime temporary buildings on Elgin Street and the cabinet chamber in the East Block on Parliament Hill was not more than a kilometre or two, but the gulf ordinarily seemed enormous. Only a few senior officers managed to operate successfully both at NDHQ and with the politicians during the war, and Pope and Stuart proved notably skilled in getting the government's support for what they and their service wanted.

Pope was a diplomat by nature, a fluently bilingual officer who had grown up within the circles of power in Ottawa and instinctively understood the politics of Parliament and the bureaucracy. Catholic, half French Canadian, married to a Belgian aristocrat, his overriding goal during the war was to keep the country together, an attitude that put him firmly behind Mackenzie King when the manpower question exploded into crisis in October 1944. Stuart was a clergyman's son who had worked behind the scenes and out of the public eye for almost all his military service. Politicians in 1944 and historians since have often fixed him with the blame for causing the conscription crisis of 1944 by his actions at CMHQ in the spring and summer of 1944. When the crisis arose he stood with Colonel J.L. Ralston, the Minister of National Defence. Officers and gentlemen both, in the final analysis their conception of their duty to their country and the army diverged sharply.

MAURICE POPE, according to J.W. Pickersgill, the key official in the Prime Minister's Office during the war, was the best educated and best informed of Canadian generals and the one with the most inquiring mind. Unlike most of his colleagues, Pickersgill said, Pope knew there were French Canadians in Canada, and this realization coloured everything he did. It wasn't that there were red-neck attitudes to Quebec in the military, only that there wasn't much understanding.[4] Pope, in other words, was different, something of an outsider among the khaki, someone who understood and accepted that even in a great war, the army was not all there was to the nation and the national interest.

Pope was born in Rivière-du-Loup, Quebec, in 1889. His mother was a Taschereau, a member of one of the most powerful political and judicial families in Quebec; his father was Sir Joseph Pope, the son of William Henry Pope, a Prince Edward Island politician and Father of Confederation, and himself a prominent official in Ottawa as Sir John A. Macdonald's private secretary and Undersecretary of State for External Affairs. Pope's godparents were Sir John Thompson, the Minister of Justice and later Prime Minister, and Isabelle Daisy Macdonald, the twelve-year-old granddaughter of John A. No one in Ottawa had a better lineage and more propitious sponsors.

The Pope household was religiously devout and functionally bilingual, the children always speaking French to their mother and English to their father; as Pope remembered, "in conversation within the family we could switch from a French to an English point of view effortlessly and, perhaps, even unconsciously."[5] Raised a Roman Catholic in Ottawa, with his summers spent in Quebec, he had none of the biases against French Canadians that afflicted many of his Anglo compatriots.[6] After attending McGill University to study engineering and working for the Canadian Pacific Railway for four years, he joined the Canadian Engineers soon after the outbreak of war. He was helped along by Major-General W.G. Gwatkin, Chief of the General Staff, who was "a good friend of my father who gave me my commission (in those days good clean patronage in deserving cases was acceptable). He asked me if I wanted a captaincy. I laughed and replied: 'I'll be more than pleased to become a subaltern.' "[7] Three of his brothers also served overseas and one, Billy, had joined the Permanent Force before the war.

Lieutenant Pope had a good war. Serving in France and Belgium, he saw substantial action and, perhaps to his surprise, enjoyed the experience enough to seek and secure appointment to the Permanent Force in 1917, again with the help of his father.[8] That year, he was made a staff captain, but he saw more action, winning the Military Cross in February 1918. Brigadier-General Victor Odlum, in whose 11th Brigade Pope worked as Staff Captain Intelligence, wrote to Pope's father to say that Maurice was "a splendid chap. I not only have great confidence in him, but I have become very fond of him." When Pope left to become brigade major of the 4th Canadian Engineer Brigade, Odlum told him that "you were much more to me than many a staff officer — you were a friend."[9]

Surprisingly, given his origins and his strong views in the Second World War, Pope was a militant conscriptionist in 1917. "It is good news that the Government has at last decided to put into effect compulsory measures in order to maintain our strength in the field," he wrote his father on 25 May. "If the leaders of the French be so short-sighted that they oppose it, I fear worse than a second Ireland in Canada." A month later, after Sir Wilfrid Laurier's opposition to compulsory service was clear, Pope noted that "feeling is becoming very bitter" in the Canadian Corps; so was he, for a letter on 31 August proclaimed that "the French are surely playing a very poor game and I for one am finished with them." During the election in December 1917, Pope was Deputy Presiding Officer for his brigade's headquarters, sending "down to the Base a bag containing 410 [votes] of the very best." As he told his father, "How gratifying is the result of the election" in Canada. "It is the best news we have ever received."[10] Maurice Pope may have been half French Canadian by birth, but the war had brought his English Canadianism to the fore.

Pope had also learned how to look after himself well, perhaps demonstrating his fitness for the staff. After the armistice, Major Pope sent his staff captain to find suitable billets in a nice Belgian chateau and, as he put it, preferably one with a marriageable daughter. The choice, the Château de Gistoux, was just the ticket, and in September 1920 Pope, posted back to Belgium as a member of the Canadian Battlefields Memorials Commission, duly married Simonne Marie Louise Henriette du Monceau, comtesse de Bergendal.[11] The title was grand (the first count was a Napoleonic general), but there was no great wealth accompanying it; aside from small inheritances, the Popes lived on Maurice's army salary.[12] Their first son was born in July 1921; they would have three more children and, despite Pope's frequent crotchetiness at home, a long, successful marriage.

His peacetime service in the Permanent Force was virtually indistinguishable from that of any other officer who rose to wear general's badges, although Pope probably worked harder than most. He had not attended the Royal Military College and felt himself excluded from a club that bound together ex-cadets.[13] Pope set out to succeed, nevertheless. He sat the examinations for Staff College in 1923 and ranked first. His friend and fellow engineer officer, H.F.H. Hertzberg, wrote with praise, adding "it is quite right and proper that a sapper should lead the list."[14] At Camberley, where Harry Crerar and Georges Vanier were in the Staff College's senior division when he arrived, he received the usual array of invitations from dukes, duchesses, and Buckingham Palace. He wrote papers and studied hard, and like others before him he gave a lecture on Canada to his classmates in November 1924, noting that except for the United States, a very large exception, Canada's geographical and strategical position was secure. His confidential report in December 1925, signed by General Ironside, the commandant, observed that he was "an exceptionally good type of officer. Pleasing open personality. He possesses average ability. Has proved himself a hard and keen worker. Very popular. Well fitted for command or staff."[15] Pope wrote to his father in March 1925, "We are kept quite busy but the conditions under which we live make hard work a pleasure. I shall awaken from a very pleasant dream next January when I return to Canada and come down to humdrum duty once more."[16]

Humdrum it was, a routine of postings every few years to the various military districts, summer training periods, and the long wait for promotion. It took almost fifteen years before he was promoted from the majority he had at the end of the war, and, for a man of thirty-seven years, there was little pleasant about camping out in the rain: "Papa is living in a tent [he wrote his son Harry in August 1926 from Calgary]. A number of other officers and also some soldiers are living in tents close by. . . . For two days the weather has been unpleasant. We have had a good deal of rain with the result that all my clothes are wet and it is difficult to dry them."[17] Uncomfortable as some aspects of his military life were, there were tactical exercises with some talented officers like Harry Crerar or Dick Dewing of the British army, in Canada on an exchange posting.[18] There were occasional speeches, prophesying that "mechanized armoured forces, highly protected from the air and ground alike, may well be the future land force."[19] And there were innumerable book reviews, articles, and the prize essay of 1930 in the *Canadian Defence Quarterly*.[20] The winning paper, for which he received $100, advocated the reorganization of the unwieldy and ill-balanced militia so as to produce a corps of four divisions, each of which should proportionately represent the various sections of the dominion.[21] The assumption throughout was that Canada would be fighting, as in 1914, with the British in Europe.

In 1931 Pope was seconded for two years' service at the War Office in London, the first officer of the Royal Canadian Engineers to be selected. This brought him into close working contact with some of the senior — and soon to be senior — officers of the British army. His officer's confidential report of 1932 noted that he was "an agreeable personality who gets on well with everybody," and added that he was "very keen," "reliable and thorough," "an excellent staff officer." The Chief of the General Staff in Ottawa, Andy McNaughton, took the time to write Pope's mother about the report; Lady Pope noted on the letter, "N'est-ce pas gentil de sa part!"[22]

He returned to Ottawa to serve first in the Directorate of Military Training and then as GSO 1 Operations, filling in while Crerar, the Director of Military Operations and Intelligence, attended the Imperial Defence College. National Defence Headquarters was not a happy place in the mid 1930s with Colonel Léo LaFlèche, the Deputy Minister, meddling in everything, but Pope still had time to instruct his juniors. Captain Elliot Rodger worked for him on the mobilization plans to be employed in the event of a major war; Pope, presumably dissatisfied with his junior's prose, directed him to read Macaulay's *Essays*, "in furtherance of his efforts to instill in me some of his respect for and ability to use the English language."[23] Rodger was not troubled by this criticism and he remembers Pope as a "great administrator."[24]

Pope worked hard under Crerar and McNaughton, both notorious slave drivers. McNaughton, he told his wife in a letter written in the summer of 1934, was of "une amabilité rare" during a meeting; nonetheless, he had given Pope a bundle of work that obliged him to go back to the office at night.[25] With McNaughton's "tornado-like intellect," Pope said, "working was in the contract."[26] By now, twenty years a soldier, Pope had begun to take a slightly sardonic view of his colleagues. When National Defence Headquarters closed down for an afternoon in November 1935 so everyone could help greet the new Governor General, Lord Tweedsmuir, on his arrival at Ottawa's railway station, Pope refused to go, so appalled was he at the prospect of so many officers on parade "dans un pays si peu militaire que le Canada."[27] "The Canadian military were not soldiers," Pope remarked later, "although we had many experts on the King's dress regulations."[28]

There was some relief from the hard work and tedium of NDHQ the next year when he was selected to attend the Imperial Defence College. An earlier IDC graduate had advised a friend going to the college to "be moderate in your views. Stick up for Canada, squelch any uninformed criticism and . . . they will appreciate you."[29] Pope, never a wild-eyed nationalist, certainly stuck up for Canada. In one exercise on imperial defence, he made the point very strongly that the "highly centralized Empire" advocated by British officials did not exist, that no Canadian prime minister had ever supported it, and that it would be useful to look at the reasons why this was so. Those reasons, he went on, were historical and geographical. Canadians would not rouse themselves to greater activity in defence unless there was a credible menace that could galvanize public opinion. The college commandant was not amused, Pope said, pointing to the "threat to the existence of the British Empire" posed by Germany. As Pope wrote to Crerar, who added his tick of agreement, "They can only look at the Commonwealth from the central point of London."[30] Pope was no isolationist, however, and he noted approvingly that Mike Pearson at the High Commission had said that Canadian foreign policy was directed by the "P.M., Lapointe and Skelton. 'Two isolationists,' I observed. 'Three you mean,' he retorted."[31]

Once more back in Ottawa, Pope found himself pegged by Crerar to be secretary of the Chiefs of Staff Committee and delegated to work on the array of interdepartmental committees slowly preparing Canada for war. "To my mind," Crerar wrote to the CGS, "there is nothing of such fundamental importance to the successful evolution of measures required for the defence of Canada as the work of these Committees," and Pope, "with his intellectual qualifications," was "the only possible choice" for the task.[32] Thus, in between his walks to and from work each day, Pope laboured on the war book, the compilation of directives to come into effect on the declaration of war, on the Committee for Defence Coordination preparing plans for the internment of enemy aliens and the Defence of Canada Regulations, on censorship, and on a host of additional secret interdepartmental committees, six in all.[33] Although Pope believed from the beginning that the Japanese Canadians were treated shamefully by the government in 1942 and after, his committees — and his own efforts to toughen the regulations — laid the legal groundwork for the evacuation of thousands and the internment of hundreds that followed.[34]

When war came in September 1939, Pope was a colonel, slated to become the Director of Military Operations and Intelligence. In that post, it fell to him to put into effect the plans he had helped make in the 1930s. He argued for sensible methods of mobilizing the units to make up the Canadian Active Service Force, and in October 1939 he warned the Chief of the General Staff that "conscription in this country does not appear to be a matter of practical politics." Wisdom, therefore, "appears to point to the expediency of keeping our army expansion within the limits of what is possible under a system of voluntary enlistment."[35]

In May 1940, just as Hitler launched the blitzkrieg, Pope went to London to become senior staff officer to Major-General Harry Crerar at CMHQ. As he told his wife, living in Ottawa with their children, he arrived to find everything "tout à fait perdu."[36] The war had turned against the Allies, and a terrible desperation hung over the War Office, only slightly relieved by the miracle of Dunkirk. Although this brilliant staff officer worked hard and survived the Blitz, Pope's life, at least as reflected in his deliberately soothing letters home, seemed to be a round of lunches and meetings. When Crerar returned to Canada to become CGS, Pope was convinced that his past, present, and future boss deserved the promotion for his "magnifique travail à Londres," and he ventured the hope that he himself might be promoted as a result. He was — to brigadier — and that, as well as the fact that he was now exempt from income tax, allowed him to increase the monthly pay allotment he sent his wife to $375. He must have done his tasks well, for Crerar decided to make him Assistant Chief of the General Staff in Ottawa. He returned home in March 1941.[37]

At once he replaced Ken Stuart, the VCGS, as the army member on the Permanent Joint Board on Defence, created in August 1940.* He liked the Americans and they liked him, the Military Attaché at the legation in Ottawa pronouncing him one who "has always been friendly towards the United States [and] has been more helpful than any other officer of the Canadian Army in giving the Legation confidential information of a military nature."[38] His duties brought him into the high-level meetings where Canadian officials tried to secure a place at the Allied table, something the Americans, still neutral, were often reluctant to concede and to which London, convinced that only it could represent British and dominion interests, was unabashedly opposed.[39] Pope was promoted to major-general in December 1941. When Crerar returned to Britain to become a corps commander and Stuart took over as CGS, Pope became Vice Chief of the General Staff.

In early 1942 Pope went to Washington to set up and head the Canadian military mission, a post of substantial importance, but one that removed him from NDHQ and from the struggles over the size and development of the army overseas and at home. That posting also effectively eliminated Pope as a candidate to become Chief of the General Staff. His task as the representative of the CGS and of the Cabinet War Committee[40] was to treat with the American military, with the British army representatives in Washington, and simultaneously to be the Canadian link with the Combined Chiefs of Staff, the British-American strategic directorate.

For the next two-and-a-half years, Pope played diplomat and devoted himself to worming his way into his allies' good graces. He fended off the British efforts to absorb him into their military organization in Washington;[41] he read secret papers at the offices of the Combined Chiefs; he regularly saw American, British, and other dominion officers; and he stayed in close touch with first Hume Wrong and then Mike Pearson of the

---

*After one PJBD meeting in the royal suite of the Windsor Hotel in Montreal, Pope asked his sergeant-clerk to destroy the secret papers from the meeting. The NCO found there were too many to flush down the toilet, so he tried to set them alight in the bowl. But the bathroom curtains caught on fire and fire extinguishers had to be used to put the flames out. Pope swore the sergeant to secrecy. Harold Morrison telephone conversation, 27 June 1991.

Canadian legation. Pearson said he was "a good person with whom to co-operate," and, moreover, he "has established admirable relations with the top U.S. and U.K. Service people here."[42] Pope was, as the British noted correctly, "on the fringe of the Combined Chiefs of Staff," consulted by them only "on matters that affect Canadian interests."[43] Even so, he was remarkably successful at his work. The British Joint Staff Mission reported to London that "Pope keeps more closely in touch with current problems than probably any of the other Dominion service representatives; he comes daily and makes touch with his various contacts in the J.S.M. building and undoubtedly gleans a lot of information which would otherwise not be available to him."[44] With Canada shut out of the key conferences, barred from any share in making the great decisions, Pope did what he could with what little he had. He and his small staff "became complete snoopers and based our opinions and judgments on a stray remark here, an obvious reticence several days later, and so on."[45] This surveillance was assisted by his managing to find a talented cook-batman-servant and turning the dinner table in his Washington apartment into yet another source of information.[46]

Pope also made certain that "when things directly concerning us are up for discussion we are afforded an opportunity of speaking our piece." In truth, that was all Canada could have expected to secure, for, as Pope said, "the higher direction [of the war] must, of course be entrusted to the Big Two. Any wider representation would be quite unmanageable."[47] There were occasional opportunities to go beyond his constrained role, as, for example, when he attended a British Chiefs of Staff meeting in May 1942. A staff paper suggested that if the war in Russia went badly in the summer, it might be necessary to stage a landing operation in France to relieve the pressure on the Red Army. Pope said, as he wrote in his diary, "that, so far as I could see, such an operation would simply have the effect of our losing valuable formations and thus jeopardizing our chances of intervening successfully the following year." The disaster at Dieppe with its virtual destruction of much of the 2nd Canadian Division more than proved his point.[48]

Within his sphere, he was very skillful. In October 1942 the British Joint Staff Mission, without malice but with complete assurance of their ability to understand the dominion, monkeyed with the Canadian army strength figures projected for 1944. Pope argued the numbers with the staff and won his case. He then took the opportunity to speak "very frankly" and to protest against "the casual way in which the British planners took it upon themselves" to change the figures "without calling us in to discuss them. They had made blob after blob through their natural ignorance of the Canadian situation. I suggested . . . that a procedure of this kind could have no other result than to drive us into the hands of the Americans." After all, Pope said, he was in the Combined Chiefs offices every day "and we feel that there is therefore an obligation for them to consult with us in respect of Canadian questions, and it should not be necessary for us to act like sleuths."[49]

In addition to fighting off the incompetent imperial centralizers and protecting his own turf, Pope also made himself into a good source of advice to his masters in Ottawa — and, occasionally, to London. In a conversation with Field Marshal Sir John Dill, the British Chiefs of Staff representative on the Combined Chiefs in Washington, in September 1942, Pope raised the question of unity of command in Newfoundland. The Canadian army had units there, as did the U.S. army, and the Newfoundland government wanted to see a Canadian in charge. "I urged that this would be a bad step," Pope said. "The Command System of Newfoundland," divided between Canada and the United States and sometimes the subject of delicate negotiations between generals who acted like tribal chiefs, "was admittedly à la Heath Robinson, but in view of the absence of communications, the barrenness of the territory and the minimum scale of attack, it was adequate." Pope added that "it was impossible for us to push the Americans around in this connection, and if we were foolish enough to do so I was convinced that the Newfoundlanders would find themselves in a Unity of Command all right, but under a U.S. commander, which apparently they did not want." Pope quoted Lord Melbourne: "Why can't they leave things alone?"[50]

There was eminent good sense there, a quality Pope showed in all his dealings on Canada–U.S. relations. In March 1943, for example, he was in Ottawa to attend a meeting of the Canadian section of the PJBD with the Chiefs of Staff; they were to advise the government about an American request for permission for their troops to use the Alaska Highway in the postwar years. "It was a thoroughly bad meeting," Pope wrote. The cabinet wanted advice on the defence aspect "and even to a blind fool it should have been obvious that there is no military aspect to it whatsoever. The question is purely political." When the Chief of the Air Staff, Air Marshal L.S. Breadner, "whose anti-American bias is developing into a phobia," worried about the United States filling the West with troops, Pope "was dying . . . to ask him . . . about the rest of the three thousand miles of unprotected frontier, the only occasion . . . I can remember . . . that any reference to the unprotected frontier would have been apposite."[51] He held his tongue.

This apostle of common sense still might have hoped that he could become Chief of the General Staff in May 1944. The post had been left vacant since Stuart had taken over as Chief of Staff at CMHQ and as acting commander of the First Canadian Army when McNaughton was sent back to Canada at the end of 1943. In Britain, Stuart and Crerar, the army commander, talked about the problem and decided that Pope was their choice for CGS. Instead, General J.C. Murchie, the VCGS and Crerar's and Stuart's recommendation for Adjutant-General, became the government's man.[52] Pope had some regret at being passed over for the top job,[53] but Murchie was a "very shrewd, first class soldier," Pope said, who had profited enormously from attending Staff College. He was one of "the best Canadian *military* minds" he had ever encountered. That eased the pain, as did his knowledge that "I wouldn't have lasted three months as Ralston's CGS."[54]

There were other, more familial concerns. Pope's nephew, Major J.H.W.T. Pope, while second in command of the Royal Canadian Regiment, was killed in Sicily. His eldest son Joe was in the artillery; his next son Harry, who had graduated from RMC in 1942, was slightly wounded in the Royal 22e Régiment's attack against the Hitler Line in Italy and then taken prisoner when he went back unarmed into the enemy position after the battle to recover his wounded men. Lieutenant Pope soon escaped by jumping from a truck over the head of his guards, spent seven weeks with partisans behind the lines, and then rejoined his regiment. Pope, his daughter remembered, showed no emotion (though his letters to Harry did),* but his wife worried fearfully.[55]

---

*The exuberant Harry Pope was frequently a trial to his father. Eight years later, Pope's old friend Major-General W.H.S. Macklin, the Adjutant-General, wrote to him that his "stormy petrel" was doing "exceedingly well" with the Canadian brigade in Korea and attributing this to his [Macklin's] "forceful instructions . . . to keep quiet and get on with soldiering." Pope told his son that he doubted his being told off "has caused you to act in such a way as to earn his or anybody else's commendation," but "I beg of you, my dear boy, to act as if this was the case." Harry Pope must have listened to some of this advice, for he won the Military Cross in the fighting. Harry Pope Papers, Maurice Pope to Harry Pope, 5 November 1952.

At the end of August 1944, at Ralston's suggestion, Pope was called back to Ottawa to become Military Staff Officer to Prime Minister King. That post also made him Military Secretary to the Cabinet War Committee and a member of the Chiefs of Staff Committee.[56] "This contact with external affairs," King wrote in his diary, "would give us the benefit of his wide and general knowledge and be helpful to keep under review the work of all departments that should be related." King took care to tell Pope about the relationship "of confidence and mutual trust" he expected, and explained "that I wanted someone to whom I would not have to tell what to do but who would tell me what was required, why and how it should be done, and who would keep me fully informed on everything I should know."[57] Pope's view of his new appointment was clear-eyed: if "I am burning my bridges behind me . . . that is of little importance as the last one leads me to new and lusher pastures."[58] His testing time, as we shall see later in this chapter, was yet to come. So, too, was the country's.

EARLY IN 1944, when Lieutenant-General Kenneth Stuart was Chief of Staff at CMHQ in Britain, *Saturday Night* published a long article about this "scientific soldier," a regular description applied to virtually every officer who, like Stuart, was an engineer and had published articles. Little had been written on "the 'mind' of the Man, the Soldier, the Citizen," the Toronto weekly observed. "After the war the floodgates will go down, and a spate of reminiscences and appreciations will flow from the pens of his intimate friends and military colleagues, of his political chiefs and army subordinates, whose lips are now sealed."[59] Unfortunately, it was not so, for Stuart, who died soon after the end of the war, faded into almost total obscurity, his services forgotten and his name remembered only by journalists and historians who fixed responsibility for the manpower crisis of 1944 on him.

Stuart was born in Trois-Rivières, Quebec, in 1891. His father was an Anglican clergyman, the rector of St James Church and the author of a history of *The Church of England in Canada, 1759–1793*. There was little money, but Stuart was sent to Bishop's College School in Lennoxville, the school from which his father had graduated and where the young Andy McNaughton was one of his upper classmen.[60] In 1908 he applied for entry to the Royal Military College and, although he did not do especially well on the entrance examination, standing twenty-eighth of the thirty-eight successful applicants, he was admitted. Gentleman Cadet Stuart, not yet seventeen years of age when he went to Kingston, changed in his three years there. He grew an inch-and-a-half to just under six feet, his chest measurement increased by four inches, he played in the backfield on RMC's Canadian intermediate championship rugby team, he made close friends that he kept all his life, including Major-General J.V. Young and Liberal cabinet minister Colin Gibson, and he did better at his studies than might have been anticipated, his standing on graduation being fifteenth in a class of thirty-three.[61] Stuart joined the Canadian Engineers of the Permanent Force on graduation and was almost at once sent to the School of Military Engineering in Chatham, England, for training. In 1913 he returned to Canada as an officer in the Engineers' First Fortress Company at Halifax.

Like Maurice Pope, Stuart had a good war, though for the young PF engineer it began slowly. At the onset of fighting and for months afterward, Stuart found himself in command of a battery of searchlights overlooking the great harbour of Halifax. It took until November 1915 before he was able to get himself overseas. There he had his fill of action with the 1st Army Troops Company, Canadian Engineers, one of the first mechanized engineering units in France; then he joined the 7th Field Company in the 3rd Canadian Division, with whom he won the Military Cross at the beginning of 1917 and, promoted major, was slightly wounded. The next year, as an acting lieutenant-colonel commanding the 7th Battalion, Canadian Engineers, he won the Distinguished Service Order when he led his unit in bridging a river under heavy fire on 8 August 1918, the "black day" of the German army.[62] Stuart had made a distinguished record for himself, but he knew all too well the horror of war. His brother had been killed in action and, despite searching for his body for four days, Stuart could find no trace.[63]

When Stuart returned to Canada after the armistice, he began his peacetime career as an engineering officer. Married to Marguerite, a Haligonian he had met in England in 1916, where she was a volunteer in the Folkestone hospital, he moved in the usual pattern from military district to military district, notably in Winnipeg, Calgary, Quebec, and Victoria. His domestic service was punctuated by two years at Camberley, where his eagerness to fly led him occasionally to drop messages to his family from the observer's seat of Royal Air Force aircraft.[64] Then he served four years at National Defence Headquarters as an intelligence officer.

At Victoria, he had served under Andy McNaughton, the DOC, and the two men and their families became close, a relationship that deepened during his time in Ottawa when McNaughton was Chief of the General Staff. Stuart's children and the McNaughtons' brood played together at Work Point Barracks. Most important, Stuart's widowed mother, living with the Stuarts for eighteen years, grew close to all the McNaughtons, a family without a grandmother. Old Mrs Stuart would alternate Christmases in Victoria and later in Ottawa between the Stuart and McNaughton houses. "She loved Andy," Stuart's daughter remembered, and when she died shortly after the outbreak of war she was found in her nursing-home bed holding two photographs, one of McNaughton and one of her son, on her breast.[65]

Stuart's postwar career was typical for an able officer of his rank (he remained a major until 1931). What made Stuart different was his conviction that the professional stagnation of PF soldiering had to be countered by education. His vehicle was the *Canadian Defence Quarterly*, of which he became editor in 1929. The *Quarterly*, begun in 1923, was published by a committee of officers in Ottawa, mostly from the militia, though it was unofficially sponsored by the Department of National Defence and received a subsidy of some $400 a year.[66] It featured original articles on military and foreign policy questions and military history, reprinted pieces from British and other service journals, and published book reviews.

Stuart was the heart and soul of the *CDQ*, a labour of love that absorbed his evenings and many weekends.[67] He began the essay prize competition that Maurice Pope was the first to win in 1930. He wrote editorials in each issue, articles in many, and book reviews without number. Scarcely an issue appeared without two or more pieces by him, and some were very good. In an editorial in June 1930, for example, Stuart complained that military history is top heavy, always focused on the generals and their great campaigns. "The object of a junior officer should be to fit himself for the rank he holds and for the next senior rank. . . . The field of study for the junior subaltern," he argued, "should be limited to the actions of the platoon, the company and similar sub-units."[68] He confidently took on the arguments of such as Liddell Hart, countering his discussion of the Great War in *The Real War* (1930) and then giving the British author space for a rejoinder — which he then rebutted in an editorial.[69] Stuart, in other words, tried to inject both discussion and controversy into his pages, and his efforts met some success.

219

Sometimes the criticism of the *Canadian Defence Quarterly* became loud. After an article by Major Pat Hennessy of the Army Service Corps called for a substantial reduction in the Non-Permanent Active Militia's cavalry and infantry units,[70] Brigadier-General J. Sutherland Brown, the DOC in Victoria, was outraged. Brigadier H.H. Matthews, the original *CDQ* editor, told Brown he had held off from publishing the article in question, "but Ken Stuart was all for publishing it and must have talked the C.G.S. over as soon as I left Ottawa."[71] To Brown, this was all part of "an intrigue by the Artillery Association which has been running the Department, or trying to, for a good many years."[72] It was McNaughton's and Stuart's fault, Brown believed, the former "a super-engineer and college professor," the latter "a sapper who does not believe in the P.F., only super-staff officers and super instructors."* Stuart, he added, "sees eye to eye with McNaughton in everything."[73]

If "Buster" Brown's attack came from the reactionary military right, the *CDQ* could also be fired on from the radical political left. Stuart's editorials and the articles his journal published almost always assumed that Canada would be part of an imperial effort in any future war. That provoked the neutralist CCF stalwart, Professor F.R. Scott of McGill University, to denounce the *CDQ*'s editorials as "opposed to the whole idea of the collective system and . . . strongly jingoist in character." Stuart denied the accusations and stated his editorial philosophy quite simply: "My purpose is not to force my own views on anybody," he wrote, "it is merely to promote thought within the Canadian defence forces. Experience has taught me that one of the best means of promoting thought is to provoke it, hence the somewhat aggressive style adopted in some of my editorials." As for the imperialism for which Scott chided the *CDQ*, Stuart was firm in his opinion: "though sentiment in Canada may be imperialist in character, there is a large and fast growing body of opinion within the Services

---

*Stuart did not want to eliminate infantry, of course, but he was sensitive to the casualties infantry suffered. E.L.M. Burns recalled a discussion of tactics on a Militia Staff Course in this period when George Pearkes, VC, and a British officer who also had the VC, both favoured a frontal attack. Stuart, who advocated a flanking approach, said that he felt their proposed course "suffered from having too many V.C.s in the planning." University of Victoria Archives, G.R. Pearkes Papers, Acc. 74-1, box 22, file 36, Burns to Professor Reg. Roy, 21 December 1970.

whose views, though perhaps influenced by sentiment, will be governed by reason, and whose advice . . . will be motivated primarily, not by Imperial but by Canadian requirements."[74]

Stuart's educative purpose was apparent in every page of the *CDQ*, but he was also thinking about education in other ways, too. In 1931 he published a brief article in the *R.M.C. Review* on "The University of the Armed Forces," in which he declared that, because RMC had as its task the preparation of potential wartime leaders in times of peace, "the logical means to attain the ultimate object of military training is to concentrate on the mental and moral spheres."[75] He had his chance to put that view into practice when he was posted to RMC as GSO 1 in 1934, a position he held for the next five years. Other GSO 1s tended to devote most of their time to instructing the Staff College Preparatory Course; Stuart did this, too, but he found the time to take his RMC duties seriously as well. In his view as one genuinely interested in military education, cadets no longer received sufficient specialization in engineering to enable them to be adequately prepared for the courses in anything other than civil engineering at Canadian universities. Stuart was also concerned that cadets learned little about modern history, military history, imperial and international affairs, and economics. He and others at the college began to push for change, and by 1939 the curriculum had been reorganized so that the first three years became a basic science course with some history, political science, and economics, while the fourth year offered specialization in the various engineering courses or in the non-scientific subjects.[76]

Stuart's success was less marked when he attempted to tackle RMC's "recruiting," the process of moulding new entry cadets into efficient automata able to take orders, imposed by seniors each year. In Stuart's view, this "Prussian" objective had crept in after the Great War and had been influenced by the beginnings of sporting links with the United States Military Academy at West Point. The "cadet code" had come to include lying to the college officers, cribbing on examinations, and open disobedience of orders. "Truth, Duty, Valour," in other words, had been perverted. The Commandant, Brigadier H.H. Matthews, fully supported Stuart's efforts at reform, so much so that he managed to keep his professor of tactics (Stuart's title having changed from GSO 1 in 1937) at the college for an extra year.[77] But some things could not be changed, and the recruiting went on, only slightly modified.[78]

In the fall of 1938, promoted to colonel, Stuart returned to NDHQ to become Director of Military Operations and Intelligence. Harry Crerar, his predecessor in the job and the new Commandant of RMC, had pushed him forward, telling the CGS that he was "the *only* officer who, in my opinion, would suitably fill the appointment . . . at the present time." As far as Crerar was concerned, Stuart had experience, "he is intelligent, widely read, and possesses the right sort of mentality for the job." It was true that his appointment could interfere with his chances of going to the Imperial Defence College, "but, under the circumstances, this risk should be accepted."[79] Stuart was in his critical post for a year, finding the units to go into the division dispatched overseas in December 1939 and handling the myriad details of mobilization.[80]

His career seemed to be sidetracked when he was named Commandant of RMC in October 1939, replacing Crerar who was to go to London as Brigadier General Staff charged with establishing CMHQ. Much as he loved RMC, Stuart was frustrated at being shelved in what had to be seen as a wartime backwater, and his efforts to escape were almost frantic. They were also successful, for in July 1940 Crerar, now back in Canada as Chief of the General Staff, had Stuart made Director of Engineering Services at NDHQ and, almost at once, Deputy CGS and the army member on the Permanent Joint Board on Defence. The next March his title was changed to Vice Chief of the General Staff, and in November 1941, when Crerar left Ottawa to become a corps commander in Britain, Stuart (from 24 December 1941 a lieutenant-general) succeeded to the top post.[81] He had Crerar's blessings and, in light of subsequent events, it is important to note that he had his old friend McNaughton's, too: "Kenneth Stuart, in whom I have every confidence, will follow Crerar as C.G.S., Canada," he said.[82] Old Mrs Stuart would have been pleased both at the success of her boys and at their confidence in each other. Stuart's rise had been meteoric: a lieutenant-colonel in mid 1938, Stuart, just over three years later, was the man in charge of the army in Canada.

Concerns about his ability to withstand the strain of his job began to surface. He had had varicose veins removed from his legs in 1912 and, although he was quite athletic, he had weakness in the legs ever after. In 1939 he suffered from phlebitis in both legs,[83] and in March 1941 Crerar remarked that he was in the hospital again with his ailment. "He has been doing a grand job of work and I have great confidence in him," Crerar added, "but he is not fit and if things get too strenuous he is liable to crack up."[84] The Minister, Colonel Ralston, agreed. In conversation with Grant Dexter of the *Winnipeg Free Press*, Ralston indicated his regard for Stuart, but added that "his health is badly broken."[85]

Ill or not, he was the CGS with responsibilities over a vast budget — $880 million in 1941-2 and climbing — and for the raising, training, and equipping of the army as well as for the defence of Canada.[86]That was a full plate for anyone, but his first task once he took over his new job was to get approval for the "big army" plan that he, Crerar, and McNaughton all wanted and had had in the works since the late spring of 1941.[87] This plan for a huge First Canadian Army of two corps, or five divisions of which two would be armoured, as well as two armoured brigades and ancillary units, had been in preparation at NDHQ for some time. The issue was most sensitive politically. A formation of this size, with the casualties it might suffer in action requiring replacement, had in it the seeds of another conscription crisis — and that worried the Prime Minister and the Cabinet War Committee. It was also sensitive because the Conservative party, led again by Arthur Meighen, the former Prime Minister, had begun to call for "Total War" and the imposition of conscription for overseas service.

The debate in cabinet from the beginning of December 1941 was sharp. Although Ralston had his doubts about the generals at NDHQ and their grandiose plans, he supported them in the discussion. His ultimate view, one friend wrote, was "that his job is to act as counsel for the General Staff — faithfully to represent their views to the government and parliament."[88] Ralston had used the wrong phrase: he was no longer the *counsel* for the General Staff but their *advocate*, for his blinkered position virtually guaranteed that he tried his damnedest to get Stuart everything he wanted, regardless of the competing demands on the nation's resources and the political implications of the army plan.

The key to determining whether the Defence Minister and the CGS succeeded or failed was Mackenzie King, who viewed himself as the nation's main bulwark against conscription. The whole scheme, the Prime Minister wrote after reading the army's proposals, "is based on the assumption that recruiting as of a certain period can be maintained up till March 1943, this notwithstanding that it is known that there has been already increasing difficulty in keeping recruiting up to earlier standards and that it is bound to become more difficult as time goes on." He was

right. Moreover, the shrewd leader wrote in his diary, "Quite clearly matters have been worked up to the point where McNaughton would be the
commander of the army, Crerar of one Army Corps, and Pearkes, of
another Army Corps."[89] The Prime Minister understood politics, including the army variety.

On 3 December 1941, with the discussion largely deadlocked, the War
Committee called Stuart into the meeting. "Could the Army staff give any
assurance that their proposed programme could be carried out by the volunteer method?" King carefully asked. "Further, was this programme
being presented as an effective maximum Army contribution on Canada's
part, or would it be subject to increase later on?" The CGS replied that "in
his opinion, the programme proposed could be carried out on the voluntary system and it had been prepared solely on that basis. It did not represent any large addition to present commitments in manpower."* The program, he added, was the "visible ceiling."[90] As King wrote in his diary,
"these statements . . . impressed me very much."[91] From that moment,
King's support for the army program was all but guaranteed.

When approval finally was granted, Stuart was exultant, telling journalist Grant Dexter (who was everywhere and knew everyone) that this
was "absolutely all" the army wanted. "This is the kind of army a soldier
dreams of commanding, hard hitting, beautifully balanced, incredibly
powerful. It was, for example, an army which could beat Rommel in
Libya." Dexter, sceptical about the General Staff's abilities, pointed unerringly to the weak spot in Stuart's argument when he added that the problem "will be one of reinforcements — not new units."[92] Stuart knew that,
too, and on one of his trips overseas in August 1942 he said it would be
"most undesirable" to try to force conscription on the government "at the
present time." NDHQ and the army overseas had to "cut our coat accord-

---

*Certainly, Stuart was no conscriptionist at this point. He told King in February
1942 that "not a general had asked for conscription," and he expressed great bitterness at the way the Great War experience had caused disunity. It was all the
fault of the Minister of Militia and Defence, Sam Hughes, and years later Canada
was still paying the price of his folly in driving away francophones who wanted to
set up regiments. King, Diary, 9 February 1942, f. 138; Harvard University,
Pierrepont Moffat Papers, vol. 47, Memorandum of Conversation with Gen.
Stuart, 20 January 1942.

ing to the cloth." CMHQ and McNaughton had to say what they wanted and NDHQ would see if it could be provided. "If the demand exceeded the supply," Stuart went on, "it would become a matter for decision after consultation with the GOC-in-C [McNaughton] as to what course to take." Later in the conversation, the officer writing the memorandum of the meeting observed, Stuart "hinted that conscription would be brought in if no other method was possible."[93] That "hint" accorded fully with King's statement in Parliament in mid 1942 that his government's policy was "not necessarily conscription, but conscription if necessary." The home defence conscripts now could be dispatched overseas — if neces- sary. What "necessary" meant, however, remained undefined. Stuart's def- inition was to prove different from Mackenzie King's.

Stuart, meanwhile, had to deal with the new difficulties posed by the Japanese attacks of 7 December 1941 that changed the shape of the war dramatically. There was understandable fear and near-panic on the West Coast as the Japanese army, navy, and air force ran roughshod over the Allies in the Pacific. There was the disaster of Hong Kong, where the men of two Canadian battalions and a brigade headquarters were killed or cap- tured en masse — and about which Stuart would have to testify before a royal commission headed by the Chief Justice.[94] But Stuart was no alarmist. His assessment of the probable course of events was that any serious attack on North America was extremely unlikely, though there was the possibility of hit-and-run raids,[95] and he was reluctant to divert men and equipment destined for Britain to the West Coast. Ralston was a minister who considered officers like Stuart "as specialists": he "would as soon interrupt and advise a brain surgeon in the middle of an operation as to question" his CGS's competence on military matters.[96] The political reality of the fear on the West Coast was too strong for that doctrine, however, and at a Cabinet War Committee meeting on 20 February, the ministers made their decision. Canada would devote its efforts to the defeat of Germany first, but greater attention had to be paid to the defence of Canada.[97]

As a result, Stuart soon recommended the completion of a 6th Division and the mobilization of brigades for a 7th and an 8th, all for home defence.[98] By June there were nineteen infantry battalions in British Columbia, and the air and naval presence had also been greatly strengthened. When General R.O. Alexander, the General Officer Commanding-in-Chief on the West

Coast, failed to exercise command with sufficient energy, Stuart unceremoniously sacked him. While remaining CGS, Stuart himself took charge in British Columbia during the summer of 1942 to galvanize the defenders.[99] "You will remember," Ralston wrote to Mrs Stuart in 1945, "and I shall never forget, the difficulties regarding Pacific command and his striking proposal to me that he take it on personally and straighten it out on the ground. He did it."[100] This did not change his view that, as he told the Cabinet War Committee in September 1942, he saw "no reason to fear any invasion from the Pacific Coast at the present time."[101]

Stuart's work as CGS over the next year and a half involved him in the manifold details of running the army in Canada and of liaison with the First Canadian Army overseas. "Immensely intelligent," one of the NCOs who served him remembered, Stuart "worked like a bugger."[102] His job was to provide the trained men and the equipment General McNaughton wanted,[103] and he wore himself out in the process. McNaughton, too, was being ground down by the continuing burdens of command. When the decisions were made to send the 1st Canadian Infantry Division to Sicily and, more serious still, the 5th Canadian Armoured Division and the I Canadian Corps headquarters to join it in Italy, relations between Stuart and McNaughton, hitherto close and confidential, began to unravel rapidly.[104] The unhappy dénouement culminated, as we have seen, in McNaughton's relief and his temporary replacement by Stuart, freed after two years of his responsibilities as CGS, as acting commander of the First Canadian army.[105] What has usually not been said is that Stuart unquestionably acted in the best interests of the army throughout and that he behaved in exemplary fashion.[106]

His health again troubled, this time by serious respiratory infections that hospitalized him early in 1944, Stuart served in the newly created post of Chief of Staff at CMHQ,[107] in effect the key linchpin between the army and NDHQ. In this capacity he was instrumental in getting Harry Crerar named as the successor to McNaughton, an accomplishment of note given the less than enthusiastic response to Crerar from General Sir Bernard Montgomery. He also saved Tommy Burns's job as GOC of the I Canadian Corps in Italy in July 1944, demonstrating both his fidelity to old friends and his willingness to support Canadian military interests against the British generals. His main task, however, was to ensure that the field commanders received the reinforcements they needed; in the months after the D-Day invasion, casualties increased beyond expectation. The crisis over reinforcements that Stuart's words in the Cabinet War Committee had helped to put off in December 1941 was now to reach its culmination.

MAURICE POPE and Ken Stuart, longtime colleagues if not close friends, found themselves on opposite sides in the conscription crisis of 1944. The men of the First Canadian Army, fighting in France and on the Scheldt since June, and the I Canadian Corps, struggling in Italy since July 1943, had sustained heavy casualties. The infantry, their role obliging them to close with the superbly trained and well-equipped German soldiers, had suffered grievously, and the issue that tore the cabinet and country apart was the shortage of infantry reinforcements and the absolute necessity to keep the fighting battalions up to strength. Under-strength regiments suffered higher casualties than full-strength ones, fewer men being available to cover the ground, to mount attacks, and to defend against the enemy's counter-strokes. The reinforcement pipeline was long and slow, extending from the Scheldt and Ravenna through Britain and back to training camps in Canada; the process of taking a civilian off the street and making him into a trained infantryman took months. A Service Corps cook or an Ordnance clerk, their physical category permitting, could be turned into infantry, but that, too, took time. Time was something the under-strength infantry in the line did not have.*

How could such a situation have arisen? The ultimate cause lay in something called "wastage rates," the calculations that every army makes in attempting to calculate the number of reinforcements it will need in the months and years ahead. Calculated in the African desert in 1941 and 1942, the British army's wastage rates had been structured at a time when the Nazis were dominant and powerful, their Luftwaffe roaming over the

---

*There had also been much wishful thinking at NDHQ. General Maurice Pope wrote to his son, "I always told you that the reinforcements situation was O.K. This was based on N.D.H.Q. periodical statements etc setting out of which, however, left something to be desired. For instance, they included all sorts of people who were not immediately available. Actually at the moment our infantry position leaves a great deal to be desired." Pope Family Archives, Maurice Pope to Joseph Pope, 21 November 1944.

battlefield and rear areas, their artillery striking the Allies almost at will. Provision had to be made for infantry, armour, artillery, and engineer reinforcements in large numbers, but also for the various rear area and supply units to be reinforced as well. The British had calculated that 48 percent of reinforcements should be infantry, the rest being apportioned among the other arms and services. Canada had adopted the British rates in the summer of 1942, and the reinforcement pipeline was duly pushing forward forty-eight infantrymen out of every hundred reinforcements. But in the fighting in France and in Italy, infantrymen were being killed, wounded, or otherwise incapacitated at a much higher rate — seventy-seven of every one hundred casualties were foot soldiers. The British wastage rates, moreover, had been based on the assumption that half the wounded infantry would return to their units; in fact, most could only cope with less strenuous service. No reinforcement system, British, Canadian, or American, could have coped with such discrepancies. Thus, although there were more than 390,000 volunteers for overseas in the Canadian army and although the infantry establishments in Northwest Europe and Italy amounted to only 37,817 men, NDHQ could not provide sufficient reinforcements to keep the battalions at the front up to strength.[108]

The vagaries of domestic politics had led the government to create three armies in Canada. The Canadian Active Service Force was made up of volunteers for service anywhere, and its members served overseas in large numbers or trained in Canada prior to posting to the front. The Reserve Army, made up of older men and striplings trained in Canada, acted as a home defence force. Finally, the soldiers conscripted under the National Resources Mobilization Act of 1940, the Zombies as they were derisively known, were liable only for duty in Canada (with some extensions such as Alaska, Newfoundland, and the Caribbean). Some 60,000 in number in 1944, the NRMA soldiers included 16,000 trained infantry. These men could only be employed overseas, however, if the King government used the power it had given itself and specifically ordered them sent abroad.

With the casualties in Europe draining the infantry battalions of their strength, conscription was now surely necessary, said Colonel Ralston and General Stuart. Not so, said Mackenzie King and, by implication, General Pope. By "conscription if necessary" King had meant necessary to win the war. In November 1944, with the Russians pressing towards Berlin from the east and with the Allies nearing the German borders from the west, who could doubt that the war was all but won? Conscription, however, was more than a military issue. Inevitably, the question of the NRMA was emotionally charged. With approximately 26,000 francophones among the home defence conscripts, Quebec was opposed to conscription for overseas service, exactly as in 1917, and would view any decision to use the NRMA men overseas as a violation of sacred pledges made by King. On the other side, again as in 1917, the men at the front and their families at home viewed the government's temporizing and the unwillingness of Zombies to "Go Active" as political and personal cowardice and pandering to Quebec. The fate of the government, the army overseas, and possibly of the country seemed to hinge on the way this issue was played out.[109]

Stuart's role in the conscription crisis was critical. As Chief of Staff at Canadian Military Headquarters in London, as Colonel Ralston's man on the scene intent, as official historian Charles Stacey put it, on "his business to re-assert the control of Ottawa over the Canadian Army Overseas," he had to watch over the casualty figures from France and Italy and ensure that demands for reinforcements in the necessary numbers got to Canada in time enough for the system to produce them. A period of heavy casualties, as in the vicious, sustained fighting at Ortona, in Normandy, or along the Scheldt, could upset his calculations. NDHQ also kept close watch on the reinforcement situation — indeed Stacey asserts that NDHQ's views on reinforcements largely prevailed — and there were constant telegrams between London and Ottawa fretting over the numbers of infantry.[110] Some critics have accused Stuart of "camouflaging the facts" or "soft-pedalling on this question" by refusing to allow "alarmist" cables to be sent to Ottawa. Why he would have withheld information, if he did, remains a mystery, unless, as Stacey observed, he was acting "in part at least with Ralston's knowledge."[111]

What is clear, however, is that after the successful conclusion of the campaign in Normandy in August there was widespread euphoria among British, American, and Canadian military leaders that the war might well be over by Christmas 1944 and that the worries about replacements for the infantry would be swept aside by events.[112] Stuart shared these feelings. On 2 August, he had written to the Chief of the General Staff to say that "after over twelve months fighting" in Italy and France, "we have a reinforcement pool overseas with a strength in excess of three months reinforcement requirements at intense rates. This is a most satisfactory situation." He added that estimated casualties for the rest of 1944 "are about equal to our reinforcement holdings at 31 Jul. . . . Up to date our casualties have been less than the number anticipated and although our estimates may be exceeded for short periods I do not anticipate an increase of casualties over our estimates in any period of six months or over."[113] Stuart gave precisely this opinion to the Cabinet War Committee the next day, and King recorded that "he was most emphatic about there being no doubt of ultimate success and the possibility of the war being over sooner than we expected. He made clear that we had plenty of reserves. . . . that the war would likely be over before any further numbers would be required beyond those already available."[114] Optimism reigned around the council table.

The fickle fortunes of war changed the mood very quickly. Casualties increased, infantry reinforcements ran short, and Stuart scrambled with increasing desperation to find the necessary numbers to maintain the fighting units. In late August he wrote to Harry Crerar, the army commander, who had been complaining for some time about the problem, that the reinforcement situation was going to be tight for the next three or four weeks, "or until remustered personnel became available." Remustering was the conversion of non-infantry soldiers into infantry through retraining, sometimes for ludicrously brief periods.[115] CMHQ had sent 5000 infantry reinforcements to the Continent in the intervening month, Stuart went on, but "unfortunately in this period your casualties were heavy and the reinforcement situation does not appear to have improved." The situation was also difficult in Italy, he said, but his main priority was the First Canadian Army "in the decisive theatre and it is vitally important that it be kept as strong as possible for the final stages of the war."[116] At the same time, he passed on the information to Ralston. What finally put paid to Stuart's planning was the gruelling battle to clear the mouth of the Scheldt River and open Antwerp to shipping. The First Canadian Army's assault began in early October; the 355 officers and 6012 other ranks who were killed, wounded, or captured there in the next five weeks would require almost all the men who remained in Stuart's reinforcement pool to replace. Worse still, the continuing German resistance made it obvious that the war was not going to be finished until well into 1945 and the demands for infantry would continue.

This was the context in which Colonel Ralston made his final overseas visit as Minister of National Defence in September and October 1944. He talked to commanders and soldiers in Italy and Northwest Europe, and he talked to Stuart as well. Stuart was now clear in his own mind that adequate infantry reinforcements to meet the First Canadian Army's needs into 1945 could not be found from the General Service volunteers available. The only source of trained infantry left, he told the Minister, was in the NRMA in Canada.[117] As Ralston wrote later, "when he made the recommendation to me in London, he didn't consider his responsibility ended by passing it on to his Minister but he offered to come to Canada to meet face to face the questioning which he realized would be inevitable."[118] Stuart returned to Canada with Ralston ready to demand that conscription for overseas service be imposed.

In the course of the next two weeks, Stuart and the staff at NDHQ produced reams of memoranda and analyses of the manpower situation.[119] The fundamental fact, the inescapable fact, was that every projection demonstrated that General Crerar's army and the corps in Italy would be short of infantry reinforcements in 1945. As Stuart put it in a memorandum that Ralston took to the Cabinet War Committee on 19 October: "The only solution that I can see is to find an additional 15,000 infantry to add to our reinforcement pool on or before 31 Dec 44. . . . I recommend, therefore, if the numbers required cannot be found from General Service personnel in Canada, that the terms of service of N.R.M.A. personnel be extended to include overseas service in any theatre."[120] Stuart himself appeared before the Cabinet War Committee and reiterated his views. Ralston made it crystal clear that, if the Prime Minister and cabinet would not accept his recommendation that conscription now was necessary, he was prepared to resign. Maurice Pope, watching this meeting from his position as Military Secretary to the Prime Minister, wrote some years later that "poor Ken Stuart's attitude was, I must say it, cocky. He gave me the impression that he judged himself . . . 'stronger than the Government!' I so well remember Mr King, leaning forward in his chair and asking with honeyed sweetness, if he, Stuart, did not agree that the Government had a right to expect its permanent advisers to give them all possible aid in a time of crisis." Stuart's position, to Pope, seemed to be "in effect, 'There is my memorandum, take it or leave it.'"[121] Pope had no sympathy with the conscriptionist politicians or soldiers, and he had already told the Prime Minister that "it should be possible to meet the situation without resort to conscription."[122]

The crisis brought Pope, whose 1917 views on the value of conscription and "the French" had been completely altered by time, back to the centre of events. He asked to see Ralston and called on him in the morning of 21 October. He understood Ralston's responsibility to the army in the field, Pope said:

I asked him, however, to ask himself if there were not a higher duty devolving upon him, namely, a duty to his country. It came down to a question of proportion. I would, and of course, could say nothing to belittle the importance of the army fighting our battles in the field, but the army was but a part, important enough as in all conscience I well knew, but still but a part of that bigger community that is Canada. One's first duty, therefore, lay towards the country and the people who comprised it. . . . I asked him to remember that [conscription], if persisted in, would wreck the very basis of our life at home. In the last analysis, our army was fighting for peace, and with that the well-being of our people. It followed in consequence that no wise Canadian could reasonably embark on a course of action, the result of which would be to bring to naught that for which our men were fighting and dying.

This extraordinary conversation, extraordinary because Pope had two sons in the army overseas and because army officers did not talk to their Minister in this fashion, lasted for some three-quarters of an hour. It concluded, Pope wrote to his son overseas, with Ralston saying "he knew that I had been moved to come and see him simply because I felt so deeply on the matters we had discussed." That comment gratified Pope, whose "overriding loyalty" was to the country as a whole.[123] Ralston, however, told his friend Angus L. Macdonald, the Minister of National Defence (Naval Services), that he thought Pope "was sent by P.M."[124] An atmosphere of suspicion was beginning to grip the Cabinet War Committee, and Ralston, deeply honourable man that he was, feared Mackenzie King's wiles.

Well he might have, for King was engaged in secret discussions with General McNaughton, keeping him in the wings to replace Ralston if the Minister persisted in his determination to send the Zombies overseas. On 1 November, with the crisis at its peak, King saw McNaughton and ensured that he was willing to replace Ralston. McNaughton's notes of his discussion with the Prime Minister record that after reading Stuart's memorandum of 19 October, he told King that the General, the man instrumental in removing him from command of the First Canadian Army almost a year earlier, "had passed from a factual statement of army requirements to the advocacy of a political method of raising forces. Surely this was outside his province." After further discussion, McNaughton returned to Stuart "in whom I had no confidence[;] he would have to go. So would [the CGS, Lieutenant-General J.C.] Murchie who was a satellite of Stuart's. Mr King said he thought he had been helpful but I did not agree that he could stay."[125] The Prime Minister defended Murchie, who kept his post when McNaughton became Minister; significantly, he offered not a word in defence of Stuart. McNaughton thus had the great satisfaction of replacing Ralston and getting rid of Stuart, the two men who had done him in. The task of finding the necessary reinforcements, however, would now be his.

The day after McNaughton became Defence Minister, Stuart's daughter Marguerite remembered, her relieved father left the house "looking like a million dollars." He had spent two harrowing weeks since his return to Canada poring over the figures at NDHQ, as the staff and politicians struggled to find more men than they had.[126] Now the game was up. He knew McNaughton intended to replace him; he meant to resign first. Yet the result of this race was for all practical purposes a tie. Stuart was out, and ultimately his heart was broken by the crisis which "finished him," his daughter remembered. He had come to detest King, that "wretched little man," and he was angry with the treatment Ralston, a great man, had received.[127]

Stuart's army career was finished. He drafted memoranda for Ralston's use in the House of Commons,[128] and there were meetings of ministers supporting Ralston in Stuart's home. "Half the Cabinet," his daughter said, sneaked into the house through the backyard "past the garbage cans." The Stuart house was used because no one would have expected to find the ministers there.[129]

General Pope, meanwhile, continued to serve King, a man he greatly admired for his efforts to keep the country together. He prepared memoranda on the reinforcement situation for the Cabinet War Committee and attended its sessions,[130] and he asked questions of memoranda prepared in NDHQ.[131] Most extraordinarily, Pope called on the head of the British Army Staff in Washington and on President Franklin Roosevelt in Washington on King's behalf. There to attend the funeral of Field Marshal Sir John Dill, Pope met with General Sir Gordon Macready on 7 November and told him the details of the crisis. Macready said he thought this information should be passed to the Chief of the Imperial General Staff, Field

Marshal Sir Alan Brooke, in London and Pope agreed, delivering a handwritten note the next morning. In it, Pope described the reinforcement problem and pointed out that the Canadian government faced its most serious crisis since Confederation, one that might destroy the basis of Confederation itself. Macready had some second thoughts about sending the message and saw Pope again that afternoon. Again, the Canadian said, there was no reason the CIGS should not know the details. Macready's telegram, as Pope duly reported to the Prime Minister, included a paragraph "of his own the essential part of which was that you [King] would never make any request of any kind of the United Kingdom for special treatment for the Canadian Army and that in the circumstances the Field Marshal could judge for himself what to do with the information he was sending him."

Pope's account is clear that he had acted on his own in talking with Macready. Brooke, however, believed that Pope had spoken directly at King's request and that he sought to have some or all of the Canadian divisions pulled out of the battle line. His reply to Macready declared the issue a "political" one, and said flatly that if Mackenzie King wanted "any action . . . it would have to be taken up through the political channel."[132]

Pope's meeting with Roosevelt was similarly unsuccessful — if the object was to secure American help in easing the crisis. Acquainting the President with the details of the situation on 15 November, Pope told him of "the grave view" Mackenzie King took of the crisis. He added that the Prime Minister "had several times observed that should events in Canada develop in such a way as to bring about an attempt to enforce overseas conscription at this stage of the war, then there could be little or no hope of carrying the assent of our people to the proposition of the use of force contained in the Dumbarton Oaks scheme for international security." Canada, King believed, or so he said, might refuse to play its part in post-war collective security. The President, Pope's note of the conversation to the Prime Minister said, "would be glad to be of any possible help to you in the psychological field."[133] Years later, Pope added a critical detail: Roosevelt had said something inaudible when Pope finished his message from King, but then "visibly drew back . . . and said aloud, 'But no, that's operational.'"[134] Roosevelt's desire to help his neighbour could not lead him to intervene in strictly military matters.

The psychological field where Roosevelt was willing to assist was not the critical one now. McNaughton's overconfident belief that he could find the men needed overseas had foundered on the combination of the refusal of Zombies to volunteer for overseas service and the intractability of the numbers of suitable General Service men who could be quickly converted into infantry. The CGS, General Murchie, declared the game at an end in a memorandum on 22 November: "I must now advise you that in my considered opinion the Voluntary system of recruiting through Army channels cannot meet the immediate problem. The Military Members [of the Army Council] concur in this advice."[135] Although some of the generals expected to be fired at once,[136] the CGS' memorandum instead became the face-saving if secret excuse for the Prime Minister to avert an imagined "revolt of the generals"[137] by reversing course and agreeing to a limited measure of conscription for overseas service. The Cabinet War Committee duly approved an order-in-council approving the dispatch of 16,000 NRMA infantry overseas, and the conscription crisis of 1944 was effectively over. Overseas, as it turned out, the First Canadian Army's operations slowed for the winter and, though there was hard fighting ahead, the reinforcement pipeline had the respite it needed to fill the ranks. The Zombies, only 2463 of whom made it into action, turned out to be scarcely necessary.[138]

Stuart's time in retirement was brief. The illnesses he had suffered from for years came to a head, and he died on 3 November 1945 at the age of fifty-four. His estate was tiny, his widow's pension after his thirty-five years of military service an almost derisory $180 a month.[139] Colonel Ralston, whose political career had ended at the same time and for the same reason as Stuart's, telegraphed the General's widow that he had been "a great soldier, true as steel to his duty and a rare friend." T.A. Crerar, retired from the cabinet, noted in his message of sympathy that Stuart "gave fine service to his country and at the end received some shabby treatment which his many friends resented." Less cherished by Mrs Stuart and her children was Mackenzie King's telegram, which declared that Stuart had been "a deeply valued personal friend."[140] Ralston acted as an honorary pallbearer. Crerar, according to Brigadier Richard Malone, was also asked to be a pallbearer but did not accept, giving as his excuse some previous engagement. "Ralston was bitter about this refusal of Crerar's. As he put it, Crerar owed more to Gen. Stuart than would ever be known. He felt, regardless of any other commitment and despite the fact that Stuart was in bad odor after the war, Crerar should have made every effort to stand by at the funeral."[141]

Pope, promoted to lieutenant-general, successfully made the transition to the Department of External Affairs, where he was, John Holmes remembered, as much of an outsider as he had been in the army.[142] He served at the San Francisco conference that created the United Nations, and in Berlin, Bonn, the Low Countries, and Spain. He wrote many frank and perceptive dispatches on postwar policy, and also a fine memoir, *Soldiers and Politicians*, notable for its good prose and evidence of wide learning. Pope remained active right to the end of his life. He wrote to his son Harry in 1977: "I love politics. Not the back room stuff which I suppose is unavoidable but the rest of government and, in these days, political survival."[143] An avid gardener, his last letter said that he had put off going into hospital, "which was probably a mistake. I'd like to see my tomatoes come in first for I would have no one to look after my little potager. The celery looks promising."[144] He died in September 1978 at the age of eighty-nine.

Curiously, although Colonel Ralston almost always receives better treatment from historians than does Mackenzie King, General Stuart is invariably treated much more sharply than General Pope. Probably this is unfair. Both Stuart and Pope served their political masters and their country to the best of their ability — though, in the ultimate crisis of Canada's war, in very different ways. Stuart was prepared to declare conscription unnecessary so long as it was, but when it became clear to him that the needed infantry reinforcements could not be found other than in the ranks of the NRMA, he believed it was necessary to act. The country's commitment to its fighting men in Europe was at stake. Stuart believed that soldiers put their life at risk for their nation and, in return, the nation pledged to back them with the reinforcements and materiel they needed. In late 1944 the implicit contract between soldier and state was on the verge of being broken for want of reinforcements and, he believed, it had to be honoured. Pope, in contrast, took a longer and more political view than his colleague, looking beyond the battlefield to the survival of Canada as a bicultural nation. He believed that conscription might split French and English Canada irretrievably and, if it did, the country for which the soldiers were fighting and dying would be lost. The Canadian tragedy of 1944 was that both were right in their assessments. Even a half century later, it is impossible to say whose judgment was sounder.

CHAPTER 9

THE ABSENCE OF
FRANCOPHONE
GENERALS

A T THE END OF FEBRUARY 1944, Lorenzo Paré, the Ottawa columnist of the Quebec City newspaper, *L'Action Catholique*, published a bitterly sarcastic attack on the absence of French-Canadian senior officers in the army. In Paré's view, there was a virtual conspiracy among the "brass hats" in Ottawa to keep francophone officers down. The officers at National Defence Headquarters would never permit a French Canadian serving overseas to progress "higher than lieutenant colonel." He was right. There was not a single French-Canadian officer of high rank with operational troops overseas or in the headquarters in London or Ottawa. Of five lieutenant-generals, none was French-speaking; of forty major-generals, five were *Canadiens*: Panet who was on retirement leave; Vanier who was in the diplomatic service; Renaud who was commanding the Montreal military district; Tremblay, the Inspector-General for Quebec and the Maritimes; and Leclerc, commanding troops in Newfoundland, and who, Paré sneered, "had difficulty speaking French which was doubtless a great advantage in his career." The situation was little better among the brigadiers, where only seven of 144 were French Canadian, a list that included the military attaché in the Soviet Union, the district commander in Regina, and the deputy Adjutant-General, who ought not to count in any case because he was a Belgian by birth. "Sept sur 144," Paré wrote. "Pas un seul Canadien français aux postes supérieurs d'outre-mer; pas un seul au quartier général de Londres, ni même au quartier général d'Ottawa."

All this was true. But why? To Paré, the reason was simple: the brass hats were deliberately blocking the promotion of French Canadians. It had to be so. "Many French-Canadian professional soldiers," he wrote, "were fully qualified by experience and in the field. Their qualifications were recognized by the authorities."[1] But the authorities were paralyzed by fear of these brass hats, a coterie of Anglo-Canadian Colonel Blimps. And behind it all was the memory of the Conquest, something that Paré's readers implicitly understood. French Canadians would always suffer maltreatment.

There was only one problem with Paré's article. His analysis was partly correct, to be sure, but none of his conclusions was true. There were not "many" French-Canadian officers qualified "by experience and in the field." There were pitifully few. An anti-military culture, a suspicion of English Canadians, and historic memories of conscription in the Great War had seen to that. The brass hats, instead of blocking the promotion of francophone officers, in fact were desperately combing through the officer ranks to find any who could be entrusted with higher commands. The politicians in Ottawa spurred on the search, reminding the generals that this war, unlike the last, was being fought for victory *and* national unity. If that dual purpose was to be accomplished, French Canadians had to get their share of the command positions.

But French-Canadian generals could not be found. There were brave and competent French-speaking officers, but there were not enough of them. There had never been enough in either the Non-Permanent Active Militia or the Permanent Force before the war. Those the government and the army could promote it did.

THERE IS A LONG HISTORY to the francophone senior officer shortage in the Second World War that can be carried back, if not to the Conquest, then certainly to the end of the French Revolutionary wars. Later events such as the South African War (when francophones made up only 5.4 percent of the first contingent and only 2.9 percent of the next three contingents)[2] and the debate over Sir Wilfrid Laurier's naval bills added fuel to the fires of French-Canadian indifference.[3] More directly, however, the problem began in the Great War, when Québécois enthusiasm for the struggle in France and Flanders was markedly less than that of English Canadians. Recruiting in French Quebec was much more difficult than in Ontario or the West, for example. This was attributable, Québécois maintained, to the unilingualism and imperial style of the army, to the fact that Canada, unlike Britain, was not in danger, and to a long physical and psychic separation from Europe. Moreover, Quebec's French Canadians had lower literacy rates, higher mortality rates, earlier marriages, higher proportions of farmers and rural dwellers, and a generally lower average standard of education and health than English Canadians.[4] Those contributing factors were all present, of course, but the real reason that French Canada produced at best 50,000 recruits and conscripts for the Canadian Expeditionary Force (or less than 8 percent of total enlistment) was that Quebec public opinion, if it did not overtly oppose the war, certainly never supported it with anything like the fervour evident in English Canada. The Minister of Militia and Defence, Sir Sam Hughes, had slighted French Canada's military ardour with his anti-Catholic and anti-French attitudes before and during the war, and the sense that French-speaking officers in the Permanent Force (only thirty of whom in 1914 were francophones!)[5] and the militia had not received their fair share of appointments in the first and subsequent contingents was very sharp. Then, too, domestic politics immediately preceding and during the war compounded the military difficulties and exacerbated the public's grievances. Finally, the Borden government's imposition of conscription in 1917 and the overtly racist way in which it fought and won the general election of that year guaranteed that Quebec's bitterness and frustration would smoulder for years.[6]

Against those serious negative factors, there had to be set the valour of Quebec soldiers during the war. The 22e Régiment's heroism was greatly admired throughout Quebec and Canada. Battles like Courcelette, Passchendaele, and Vimy were commemorated, and Van Doos who had distinguished themselves in action, officers and men such as Kaeble, Brillant, Tremblay, and Vanier, were honoured, indeed venerated.[7] There was a lively public interest in the Van Doos' part in the war in the province, but there was simultaneously a certain self-consciousness, not to say shamefacedness, in the way Quebec's military effort in the conflict was analysed and defended.[8]

These factors mattered because they helped to shape the climate for and attitude to military service in Quebec in the interwar years. In English Canada, the postwar reaction against the causes, events, and implications of the Great War was sharp, and the military was not held in high esteem. Yet the Permanent Force, tiny and ill-equipped as it was, remained a "British" force and still attracted some English-speaking officers of quality. The Royal Military College, functioning entirely in English, continued to give a good military education to the sons of members of the upper echelons of Anglo-Canadian society. The Non-Permanent Active Militia, its real numbers always much smaller than its nominal strength, also continued to play an important social and political role in countless communities across the country. The Seaforths in Vancouver, the Hasty Pees in Belleville, the 48th in Toronto, the Carleton and Yorks in New Brunswick — such regiments remained as centres of community life and as prestigious institutions that continued to attract the local business and professional elites.

With the possible exception of a militia regiment or two in Montreal, this esteem for military life was completely absent in francophone Quebec. There the political climate continued to be dominated by grievances arising out of the Great War; there suspicions of English Canada and its institutions were fostered by nationalist writers and thinkers such as the Abbé Groulx. The numbers of francophone army officers made the low status of the military abundantly clear. The Royal 22e Régiment, the one French-speaking unit of the Permanent Force, never had more than twenty-one officers on strength between 1920 and 1939, or approximately 5 percent of PF officer strength.[9] There were a few additional officers of French-Canadian origin in other corps of the army, but only a handful. Operating as they did in a wholly English-speaking environment, they had to be fluent in English; unilingual francophones, for all practical purposes, could serve only in the Royal 22e. In all, in 1939, just before the outbreak of war, just over 10 percent — or forty-seven — of the PF's commissioned officers were francophone: two acting brigadiers, four lieutenant-colonels, ten majors, ten captains, and the rest lieutenants or second lieutenants.[10] As with the anglophone officers in the PF, that number included the aged, the infirm, and the incompetent, along with the best and brightest.

Similarly, the Royal Military College, which produced almost a third of Canada's wartime general officers, attracted only a small number of francophones between the wars. In 1937, for example, only fourteen of the forty-two vacancies designated for French Canadians on a pro rata basis were filled. Jean Pariseau and Serge Bernier, authors of the best study of French Canadians in the army, estimate that only 6 percent of RMC cadets between 1927 and 1939 were francophones.[11] If there was a powerful RMC ex-cadets' "old-boy net" in the army, as popular mythology had it during the Second World War, francophones were largely excluded because so few RMC graduates were French-speaking. Canadian Officer Training Corps contingents were also relatively unpopular at the Université de Montréal and Université Laval. Data collected by Pariseau and Bernier show that the average annual number of francophone cadets between 1921 and 1935 was only 205; the average from the much smaller anglophone Quebec community over the same period was 268.[12]

The militia was equally neglected by francophones. In 1925–6, Military Districts Nos. 4 and 5, covering the province of Quebec, managed to send only 1084 officers and men in total for training to summer camp; that number included only 353 French-speaking officers and men. Thirteen years later, matters were marginally better, 5562 going to camp in Quebec, but again more were English-speaking. Only 2589 francophone militia officers and men trained that summer, just 8.9 percent of all the NPAM soldiers at camp across Canada; yet as a percentage of the total population, francophones amounted to approximately 30 percent.[13] Collectively, these numbers ensured that when war came few francophones would rise to senior ranks. Generals, in other words, could not be created simply by putting rank badges on epaulets.

There was one crucial additional area where French-Canadian representation was almost wholly lacking, one that guaranteed the wartime shortage of senior officers. Canada had no army staff college of its own until the Second World War forcibly drew attention to the shortage of staff-trained officers; in the circumstances, between the wars, the key to advancement in the Permanent Force was attendance at the British Army Staff College at either Camberley or Quetta. Entrance was by competitive examination, and places were avidly sought. Between 1919 and 1939, sixty-three Canadian army officers attended Staff College, but only two were francophones, Major Georges Vanier and Captain R. Girard.[14] One huge step above the Staff College was the Imperial Defence College, which admitted at most one Canadian a year and which trained officers for the highest positions in the British and dominion forces. Among the Canadians who attended the IDC, for example, were Generals McNaughton, Crerar, and Burns. But no francophones were among the ten Canadian army officers who attended before the outbreak of war in 1939.[15] The lack of francophone PF officers trained at the Staff College and the IDC meant that access to high command at the beginning of the war and, to a great extent, throughout its six year duration was choked off.

Examinations for Camberley were written in English only, and this fact added to their undoubted difficulty for francophone officers. Of course, instruction at Camberley and Quetta, both British army institutions, was also in English, and only a fluently bilingual francophone could have handled the course. It could not have been otherwise, and those officers who did not meet this standard simply did not apply. Attendance at the equally unilingual IDC was by selection, and an anglophone military establishment might well have chosen its own to attend. The route to high command, in other words, much like the whole English-speaking cast of the Canadian military, tended to throw almost impassable roadblocks in the way of French-speaking Canadians.

Against these problems must be set the undoubted — if undocumentable — desire of the Van Doos to keep its officer cadre intact and in Quebec City. The Régiment's officers, linguistically isolated in the Permanent Force, naturally enough clung together. No data appear to exist on the numbers of Van Doos who tried the Staff College entrance examinations, and certainly Lt.-Col. Georges Vanier, who became the Régiment's Commanding Officer after his return from Camberley in 1925, must have encouraged his captains and majors to write them. But if others wrote, none passed. The message conveyed by these bleak figures is unambiguous. The simple truth was that aside from a relatively few PF and militia officers and men, French-speaking Canadians demonstrated scant interest in the army in the interwar years.

Unfortunately, it was also true that the army demonstrated little interest in French Canadians. Certainly there is evidence to sustain that contention. Military manuals were almost never translated into French, the effort stalled by lack of interest and a shortage of funds and translators.[16] Not until the war was this problem rectified. The politicians who headed the Department of National Defence, all anglophones between the wars, for the most part had scant interest in addressing the

French fact in the PF or the militia. For example, Colonel J.L. Ralston, the minister in the late 1920s, wrote to the incoming Chief of the General Staff of his efforts to persuade the Adjutant-General (General Panet) to retire: "The A.G. has more than once mentioned the lack of French Canadian representation on the Defence Council if he goes but I am not expecting any real difficulty on that score as I have always found my French Canadian friends most reasonable when matters were explained to them."[17] Reasonableness, in truth, seemed to require that French Canadians should know their place. The incoming CGS, General McNaughton, did not demur. The Deputy Minister, a French Canadian and vice-president of the Defence Council, he wrote, "is in a position to and can be amply trusted by our French Canadian fellow citizens to see, if it were necessary, that no discrimination is shown by the military members."[18]

If the Anglo-Canadian military establishment kept the reins of control in hand, there can be little doubt that francophone officers used the claim of linguistic representation as a crutch and as a device to secure preferment. Québécois in the forces, and not least in the Van Doos, seemed willing and able to call on politicians from their province for assistance in military matters.[19] Whether they were more or less guilty of this sin than English-Canadian officers is impossible to determine.

Politics, however, was very much part of the prewar military forces, and no French-speaking individual was more important here than the deputy minister of the Department of National Defence from 1932 to 1939, Colonel, then Major General, Léo Richer LaFlèche. Indeed, he was without question the most influential French-Canadian military figure of the period, including the Second World War. No one overcame greater opposition from the senior officers at Defence headquarters; no one rose higher in the teeth of it.

Léo LaFlèche was born at Sorel, Quebec, in 1888 and worked for the Molson Bank. He joined the army in 1914 and served overseas with great distinction in the 22e Régiment, suffering a serious wound in June 1916 at Mount Sorrel. He won the DSO, and by the end of the war was a lieutenant-colonel commanding District Depot No. 4 in Montreal. LaFlèche worked for federal agencies after the war and also played an important part in veterans' associations, ultimately becoming dominion president of the Canadian Legion in November 1929. As Chubby Power, then a Liberal

MP and a decorated veteran, said at the time, "I know of no person amongst the ex-soldiers who is better qualified through his tact, firmness, and personality to place the projects of his comrades before the highest authorities and to bring them to a more successful conclusion."[20] Perhaps as a measure of that devotion, LaFlèche was chosen by veterans to be a member of the Federal Appeal Board that decided disputed pension claims.[21] In 1932, as a result of what McNaughton described as a "very strong lobby,"[22] the Bennett government appointed him Deputy Minister of the Department of National Defence, rejecting complaints from the Toronto Orange press that he ought to have been disqualified as a French Canadian and an alleged Liberal.[23]

LaFlèche soon became unpopular with the military. He had enough military experience to think himself a soldier and enough political sense to recognize that his post as Deputy Minister and Vice-Chairman of the Defence Council gave him substantial power. That did not sit well with McNaughton, who believed that no deputy should, as he put it, "obtrude between the heads of the Fighting Services and the Minister."[24] Thus, the CGS simply ignored LaFlèche whenever he could and, with his power and prestige in the ascendancy in Bennett's Ottawa, made his case directly to his Minister. This led inevitably to (inspired) press complaints that the brass hats were seeking to bypass the deputy in "disturbing, if not entirely unconstitutional" ways.[25] But McNaughton left the scene in the spring of 1935, and the Bennett government soon followed.

LaFlèche remained, and under the new King government he began to play the policy-making role he had sought. Even the usually judicious General Maurice Pope recalled in his memoirs that LaFlèche made himself "more or less . . . a civilian chief of staff, and strove to constitute himself the channel of communication between the military staffs and the minister."[26] In his private correspondence with his wife, Pope was blunter: "notre departement est dans un état de désorganization incroyable. LaFlèche vs les chefs d'armée. . . . rien ne marche."[27] One sign that Ian Mackenzie, the Minister, sided with LaFlèche was the deputy's promotion to Major-General in 1938.[28] Another was that, in July 1938, LaFlèche reported to Mackenzie that he had talked to one of the prospective candidates for CGS, Gen. T. Victor Anderson,

and pointed out to him that there have been too many instances of thoughtless talk or action, as well as of lack of loyalty to their seniors on the part of Departmental personnel particularly on the part of Permanent Force Officers. That any further instances of this nature would have to be dealt with immediately and that it was the duty of the senior Officers of the three Services to give good example to their juniors and to see that the progress of the Department was not impeded by thoughtless or malicious talk or action. As a matter of duty and obligation, all must willingly observe instructions received from higher authority.

He was always ready to help all, LaFlèche went on, but he had told the General that he expected loyalty in return. "I was quite satisfied with General Anderson's ready acceptance of the principles I mentioned. . . . I am convinced that, if he succeeds General Ashton, he will do his utmost to assist me."[29] The "higher authority," it was clear, was LaFlèche himself.

Perhaps Anderson might have continued his alleged willingness to assist LaFlèche, but events intervened and the unhealthy situation in National Defence was corrected when the Czechoslovak crisis of 1938 finally persuaded Mackenzie that he could not wait for military advice to reach him through the Deputy Minister.[30]

That was one check to LaFlèche's upward ascent. More serious was the great political storm that developed over the Liberal government's decision to see Bren light machine guns built in Canada, a decision in which LaFlèche was deeply and directly involved. A royal commission in late 1938 investigating the letting of the contract did not point its finger directly at LaFlèche, but he was tarred by its brush — his role "had not been exemplary," said the historian of the affair.[31] He and Mackenzie were shunted aside when the war began, the politician to the Pensions portfolio, the deputy to sick leave.

In December 1939 the cabinet discussed what to do with General LaFlèche. After groping for a suitable post for him, the ministers concluded that he should be appointed Military Attaché to France "at his present salary. . . . All agreed," Mackenzie King wrote in his diary, "that it would not be wise to have him return to the Department of Defence though absolutely nothing in the way of suspicion of his integrity suggested." Later the same day the Prime Minister asked the Governor General if he thought LaFlèche might make a good High Commissioner to South Africa: "He said he was too dour. Did not think he would go down well with the people there."[32] Soon ensconced at the Canadian legation in Paris, LaFlèche was quickly up to his old tricks. In April, Colonel Georges

Vanier, the Minister to France and a Great War comrade of LaFlèche's in the 22e, talked to the Minister of National Defence about LaFlèche's position when the Canadian Division, as was then still anticipated, took its place in the Allied line. The view of Vanier and LaFlèche was that the Attaché "would be the link" between the division and the French military authorities, with the right to "correspond direct with the Canadian Military Headquarters, London and the National Defence Department, Ottawa."[33] This extraordinary attempt to recreate LaFlèche's role in his heyday as Deputy Minister would not have withstood McNaughton's awesome wrath if the Minister had gone along with it, but the potential problem disappeared along with France's armies in the debacle of May–June 1940. LaFlèche followed the French army's general headquarters in the retreat and reached England only on 21 June.[34]

LaFlèche found his next post as Associate Deputy Minister of the new Department of National War Services, where his duties included substantial responsibility for raising the home defence conscripts under the National Resources Mobilization Act of 1940. Ernest Lapointe, the Justice Minister, remained one of the General's supporters, telling the Cabinet War Committee of the "deep impression" LaFlèche had made on French Canadians and urging that his services be employed in recruiting.[35] The military had neither forgiven nor forgotten him, however. In a private conversation in the summer of 1941 with Ken Wilson of the *Financial Post*, the Chief of the General Staff, General H.D.G. Crerar, exploded when LaFlèche's name came up: "He said 'I know him very well. I worked with him closely in the Department. The man is entirely unmoral. He is very dangerous. He does not think in terms of getting a job done but rather in terms of personalities — who can be benefited, etc. He is an utter egomaniac.' . . . Someone suggested to Crerar that L. might some day come back into the Department. Crerar replied immediately: 'You may be sure I will not be there if he does.'"[36]

Soon, however, LaFlèche was being boomed for a cabinet post. Colonel J.L. Ralston, the Minister of National Defence, talked with the Prime Minister about the lobbying campaign for LaFlèche — who seemed to be in direct competition with Vanier for the post — and made clear his view: "He told me he would be always wondering what LaFlèche was scheming at, and if he was reliable." Yet, King said, the Cardinal of Quebec was in favour and Air Minister Chubby Power was convinced he could be elected in Outremont.[37] The Canadian Legion was also pushing its former president,[38] and Louis St Laurent, Lapointe's replacement as Justice Minister, and Power argued later that LaFlèche would "be very helpful in having the clergy assist in overcoming the antagonism to any phase of the war effort and that if conscription became necessary would be helpful in having it successfully met."[39] Powerful people wanted LaFlèche in the government and, after a long talk with the Prime Minister, LaFlèche entered the cabinet as Minister of National War Services on 6 October 1942.[40] The Quebec press was enthusiastic, the English-Canadian media generally favourable. Only the *Winnipeg Free Press* noted drily that LaFlèche's "elevation to Cabinet rank is . . . an event which will be regarded as something only to be justified by events." General Price Montague at CMHQ sent the editorial to Andy McNaughton without comment.[41] Still, LaFlèche's direct military involvement was all but over, though during the conscription crisis of 1944 his memoranda and advice on how to get out of the mess were solicited if not followed.[42]

LaFlèche's extraordinary career was one indication that French Canadians could get ahead in Ottawa. He was outside the usual military line of command and promotion, but his success in mobilizing political and religious supporters to help him overcome the antipathy of the military chiefs was extraordinary. In truth, only an Ottawa desperately concerned to keep Quebec on side could have permitted a Léo LaFlèche to rise as he did.

INDEED, THERE WERE many signs of the government's concern with Quebec opinion in 1939. For its part, the General Staff was fully aware of the importance of ensuring that Quebec was well represented in the war that many could see fast approaching. No one wanted to repeat the unhappy experience of the 1914–18 war. In June 1939, for example, the Chief of the General Staff wrote to the Minister of National Defence about the army's mobilization plans. General Anderson very much hoped that in the event of war a corps of two divisions would be mobilized at the outset. That was, he said, the only way to give full geographic representation to militia units from across the country and simultaneously to allow Permanent Force units to take their place in the Order of Battle. There was one additional reason for a corps to be called to the colours, Anderson argued: "We are particularly anxious, for example, that one of the infantry brigades initially mobilized should be predominantly French speaking, with a French speaking commander and staff. This would be quite impossible if only one division were mobilized."[43]

There is no reason to doubt the CGS' goodwill, despite his hope that by offering a beau geste to Quebec that would win the government plaudits in the province, he would get a larger force authorized at the outset than might otherwise be the case. The unfortunate truth, given the numbers of PF and NPAM officers who were French-speaking, was that it would have been impossible to fill the command and staff billets in that French-speaking brigade.

Neither the corps nor the brigade took form at the beginning of the war. The government authorized the formation of one division for service overseas in mid September 1939, and the Royal 22e Régiment was included in its 3rd Brigade, the sole French-speaking unit in the division. The General Officer Commanding, Major-General McNaughton, the three brigade commanders, and, with the exception of the division's Chief Signal Officer, all the principal staff officers were English-speaking. When the 2nd Canadian Infantry Division was in formation in May 1940, its 5th Brigade had two French-speaking battalions, and DND intended to see that it soon had a third. The brigade commander and as many of the staff as possible were to be French-speaking, but again there were problems, most especially in finding a brigade commander.

One name put up to the Minister of National Defence, a clear indication that the politicians wanted a francophone officer for the job, was Brigadier-General Thomas L. Tremblay. Born in Chicoutimi in 1886 and raised in Quebec City, Tremblay was an RMC graduate of 1907 who had worked as an engineer. He had joined the 22e in 1914 and then served overseas with great distinction, commanding his regiment and, in the closing months of the war, a brigade.[44] Asked if wanted the post, Tremblay stated definitely that he did not, and his name was eliminated.[45]

The second choice was Brigadier-General E. de B. Panet, born in 1881 in Ottawa. Panet was also an RMC graduate (1902) who had been in the Permanent Force artillery before 1914 and had served during the Great War as a senior staff officer in the 1st and 4th Divisions and at corps HQ.[45] He, too, showed reluctance when approached about commanding the 5th Brigade, and the Chief of the General Staff told the Minister that, while Panet might accept out of duty, "he would prefer not being asked to accept it." Moreover, as General Anderson admitted, Panet was a member of a well-known military family and had the prestige that came from that lineage, but the truth was "that he is out of date as regards modern warfare, he has never been an infantry man [and] he is getting on in years."[47]

Both Tremblay and Panet showed good sense in declining the post, more than many English-speaking officers of similar advanced age and equivalent outdated experience who took brigades and divisions overseas. Both, however, continued to serve in Canada. Tremblay was frequently consulted about the appointments of French-speaking officers,[48] became a Major-General, and was named Inspector-General for Eastern Canada, a post he held until 1946. Panet set up Canada's internment camps and later took command of Military District No. 4, based in Montreal. He retired in 1943 as a Major-General.

In the circumstances, the choice for commander of the 5th Brigade fell on Colonel P.-E. Leclerc. Born in Montreal in 1893 to Protestant francophone parents, Leclerc enlisted in January 1915 and served overseas during the Great War with the engineers and the infantry. He fell victim to battlefield stress, but he also won a Military Medal and a commission in the field. After the war, while working as a commercial traveller in the milling business, he joined the militia and rose to command the Régiment de Joliette and then a militia brigade. His record as a regimental commander was excellent ("This unit is in a very good state indeed for a rural unit," the inspection report for 1935–6 said), he had successfully completed the Militia Staff Course, and his District Officer Commanding had judged him to be "a very loyal, hardworking and good officer. A very good Brigade Commander."[49]

Leclerc took the 5th Canadian Infantry Brigade overseas, and he impressed his GOC, Major-General Victor Odlum. In his notebook, Odlum gave his first impression: "Excellent. A winning smile. Has restraint and poise."[50] Perhaps that comment on his restraint was entered in Odlum's book because Leclerc had suggested that it would not be a good idea to form a wholly French-speaking brigade. He argued that there were too few qualified staff officers to fill all the headquarters slots; moreover, the impression might arise that the 5th Brigade was the only position open to a francophone officer.[51] Odlum agreed, but he was reluctantly forced to follow the line urged by McNaughton and Price Montague of CMHQ that less strenuous standards be applied to French- than to

English-speaking officers. The two generals argued in the fall of 1940 that "the great shortage of good French speaking commanders and staff officers and . . . the importance to Cdn. national life of maintaining a high French Can. morale" made this a requirement.[52]

Leclerc, for his part, continued to impress his division commander, but his tenure in command was limited. On 24 March 1941 Odlum learned that a medical board had discovered that his Brigadier suffered from a serious case of angina. Considering Leclerc's considerable corpulence, this was scarcely surprising. "When I went to see him," Odlum wrote in his diary, "he said he was 'finished,' and wept. . . . I am very sorry. He was Div. Command calibre."[53]

McNaughton notified Ottawa of Leclerc's illness and of his relief from command on 1 April. The GOC added bluntly that the "possibility of replacement by French speaking Canadian officer has been thoroughly canvassed but there are none in Canadian Army Overseas who have the required qualifications."[54] The Minister, Colonel J.L. Ralston, was unhappy with this opinion and, in a telegram which he drafted personally, laid out the situation in Canada "which makes it so extremely desirable from point of view of national unity to give extra study to these situations." Recruiting in Quebec was generally good, his telegram went on, but "certain individuals and newspapers persist in emphasizing alleged discrimination against French Canadians in matters of appointments to senior positions." The Leclerc relief, the message went on, "will of course be used by those who allege that French Canadians being 'supplanted' by English speaking officers."

Neither the Minister nor the Chief of the General Staff, by this time Major-General Harry Crerar, doubted that there was a real problem in finding francophone senior officers, but solutions had to be found, including the drawing up of lists of promising officers and ensuring that they received proper training and employment "where they would get experience which would be useful in fitting them for eventual appointment to senior posts when vacancies occur which on the ground of fair representation could properly be filled by a suitably qualified French Canadian."[55] McNaughton promptly replied that he was "entirely in sympathy with the need of taking very special action in these circumstances."[56] Crerar shared that attitude, but he told Ralston in July that the problem could not be solved quickly "because the civil educational system of Quebec does not tend to produce, in equivalent numbers to English-speaking Canada, the 'officer-type' so essential to the purpose."[57] The comments on the educational system in Quebec had some truth in them, but how much of Crerar's judgment was based on a fixed, indeed biased, perception of "officer-types" is not clear. Certainly the shortage of francophone senior officers was and remained a continuing concern.

As for Leclerc, he returned to Canada. Colonel Ralston had intended to make him District Officer Commanding in Quebec City, but Ernest Lapointe, then still the Justice Minister and a Quebec City MP, objected strenuously, probably because Leclerc was not a Roman Catholic.[58] Instead, after a period of recuperation, he took over a brigade in training. In May 1942 NDHQ promoted him to major-general and gave him the 7th Canadian Division, a home defence formation headquartered at Debert, NS. The next year, the division having disbanded, Leclerc took command of Canadian forces in Newfoundland. He retired in 1945 on medical grounds, the first and only French-speaking officer to have commanded a division, albeit a home defence formation, in the Second World War.

The two remaining French Canadian general officers of the war were both Permanent Force. One, Georges Vanier, became very well known and ended his long, distinguished career as a much-loved Governor General. The other, Ernest Renaud, was almost completely unknown.

Renaud was born in Ottawa to well-off parents in 1890, attended Ashbury College, and went to the Royal Military College in 1909. Those attributes and credentials suggest strongly that he was or became anglicized. He graduated from RMC in 1912 and joined the Canadian Ordnance Corps, quickly establishing a good name for himself. His wartime service was primarily in England, but he ended the Great War as a twenty-eight-year-old lieutenant-colonel and was quickly on his way to Siberia with the Canadian contingent. He continued in the PF after the war and, at the outbreak of the Second World War, was a brigadier, having held important posts at headquarters, including Deputy Quartermaster-General, and in the military districts. In 1941 he took command of the Montreal military district and his promotion to Major-General was confirmed in 1943. Unknown, unsung, Renaud may well have been the most competent of the francophone generals, if the confidential reports made of him are to be believed. As an officer in the Ordnance Corps, however, he received none of the plaudits and could receive none of the field commands awarded to combatant commanders.[59]

Vanier's career was entirely different. He was born in Montreal in 1888, and he attended the English-language Loyola College (where Chubby Power was a classmate)[60] and Université Laval, where he took a law degree. Enlisting in 1914, he joined the 22e Régiment in October and proceeded overseas. Vanier became a stress casualty in 1916, recovered, and then was grievously wounded in August 1918, losing his right leg and suffering serious wounds in his left, as well as a chest wound. His heroism in action was recognized with two Military Crosses and a DSO, however, and he ended the war as a major. Despite his artificial leg, Vanier persuaded the army to accept him for the Permanent Force in this rank and, after service with the 22e, he became ADC to the Governor General, General Lord Byng. The relationship he and his bride Pauline (introduced to him by T.L. Tremblay, his former Commanding Officer in the Van Doos) formed with the Byngs was critical to his career, and the encouragement and advice Vanier received led him to take and pass the examinations for Camberley in February and March 1922.[61] Byng told Vanier not to be "too keen to write your opinions for others to read" but to "read all you can of other people's opinions before giving yours to the world."[62] Although the Staff College provided each officer with a servant and a horse, no provision was made for a cook. Believing that it was impossible for a young officer to function without a cook, Byng promptly wrote to his nephew, General Lord Cavan, the Chief of the Imperial General Staff, and "Fatty" Cavan duly found one for the Vaniers.[63] The Vaniers went to England with the most influential of friends at their service.

At the Staff College, Vanier had as his classmate, Harry Crerar, and as his syndicate Directing Staff, Colonel J.F.C. Fuller, one of the best (if strangest) minds in the British army. Vanier studied subjects as disparate as the principles of empire defence, morale, mountain warfare, and the drafting of operation orders, and he wrote an assessment of Sir John Moore in the Napoleonic Wars that was later published in the *Canadian Defence Quarterly*.[64] His confidential report declared him "a very hard-working officer of high mettle and courage" with "an attractive personality and a deep sense of loyalty and good comradeship." His "grit and determination" was complimented, and he was recommended for staff or command posts.[65]

After completing a senior officer's course in England, Vanier took command of his beloved Van Doos at Quebec City in 1925, a post he held for three years. In 1928 he went to the League of Nations as an adviser on disarmament questions, and his career diverted into diplomacy when, in 1931, he became secretary at the High Commission in London, a post he held until 1938. Then the King government named him Minister to France in 1939. Mackenzie King had had a good deal to do with the Vaniers in Geneva and in London, leading him to the conclusion, expressed in his diary, that Vanier was "an exceptionally fine character." This approbation did him no harm in his career, the Prime Minister confiding to Vanier that he was hoping to get a chance to recognize his services in "appointments soon to be made."[66] The appointment to France was that recognition.

When France fell, Vanier escaped to England on 25 June 1940.[67] Back in Canada, he quickly wrote to Colonel Ralston that he was still on the active list of Permanent Force and, moreover, "I am one of the fortunate ones who went through the Staff College at Camberley. There might be some army appointment for which you might consider me fitted." Vanier added that he thought his future lay in External Affairs, adding that he hoped his pay and allowances, if the army took him back, would be similar to those in the diplomatic service.[68] (Even a saint, it seems, had a family to feed!) Although Ralston tried to secure Vanier for the post of District Officer Commanding in Quebec City, the government left him as Minister to France, basing him in London, for the time being, a post that discouraged him as he brooded over the corruption and decadence that had brought France to its knees.[69] In May 1941 he resigned as Minister, and in August he was promoted to brigadier and named DOC of Military District No. 5.[70]

There he tried his best to turn the mood of Quebec around. His notes showed that he placed "Ré-éducation du peuple au sujet recrutement" at the top of his list. In his speeches he urged the province to do more, adding in a cautionary vein to audiences that feared conscription that voluntary service was good — providing that there were volunteers.[71] He also cultivated the church hierarchy and went so far as to warn General Elkins, GOC of Atlantic Command, against a French-Canadian officer who "does not go to Mass on Sundays very regularly." Vanier admitted that this was no military offence, but "the effect produced on civilians is bad."[72] So pronounced was Vanier's own religiosity that jokes were made about "Cardinal" Vanier, especially when he was compared with "General"

Villeneuve, the Cardinal of Quebec who actively supported the war and the federal government's efforts to prosecute it.

Vanier also had to get on with the small anglophone community, vastly more powerful then than now, and with the press and provincial politicians.[73] Soon there were suggestions, indeed as early as the fall of 1941, that Vanier might be taken into the cabinet to strengthen its Quebec representation.[74] The mood in Quebec, however, was such that Liberal party insiders feared he could not be elected, a concern that led to proposals from St Laurent that he be made a senator.[75] The effort to transform Vanier into a politician ended when Léo LaFlèche instead won the nod and joined the cabinet in October 1942. Likely somewhat perturbed at being passed over, Vanier asked King to make him Minister to the exile governments in London, and the Prime Minister agreed. Mackenzie King added in his diary that "the truth is the Department of Defence and others feel Vanier has been ineffective in his work in Quebec. I was careful, however, not to say anything of this to him."[76] That was almost the only critical word ever uttered of Georges Vanier.

His military career, though not formally ended, was in effect completed. Promoted major-general and sent to London as a diplomat,[77] Vanier also performed odd jobs for General McNaughton in Britain and followed the fortunes of his Royal 22e Régiment very closely.[78] Primarily, however, Vanier established close relations with Charles de Gaulle and became Minister and then Ambassador to France in 1944. He held that post until 1953, when he left External Affairs at the age of sixty-five. Appointed Governor General by John Diefenbaker's government in 1959, Vanier died in office in Centennial year, much admired and greatly honoured — so much so that no one seemed surprised in 1990 when the process of considering him for canonization began in Canada.[79] He had already been virtually elevated to sainthood by his old regiment, of which he had said, "It and my family fill the larger part of my heart."[80]

MUCH LIKE THE English-speaking senior officers with which Canada began the war, none of the francophone generals treated here was suitable because of age, military experience, or physical disability to command troops in the field. Where could such officers have been found, given the scant prewar numbers of qualified French-speaking officers? Certainly General McNaughton continued to be under pressure to seek them out, though he bluntly told Cardinal Villeneuve in March 1942 "that it would not be in the interests of the army generally, or of French-speaking Canada, to give promotion to French speaking personnel who had not the necessary qualifications and experience, because any unfortunate results which might follow would not redound to the credit of French speaking Canada."[81] Nonetheless, the army was moving towards a system that verged on linguistic quotas. The Deputy Minister of National Defence told a reporter in late June 1942 that "the policy was laid down some months ago that French-Canadians should have about 30% of staff positions in the Army." Yet, he admitted, it was hard to find bilingual officers, and scarcely a branch of the headquarters, let alone units overseas, had reached anything like that percentage.[82]

The problems were even greater in finding field commanders. A substantially smaller percentage of French-speaking militia units, in contrast to Quebec anglophone units, were mobilized during the war.[83] That fact alone lowered the pool of officers on which to draw. Furthermore, only four infantry battalions served overseas — the 22e in the 1st Division, Le Régiment de Maisonneuve and Les Fusiliers Mont-Royal in the 2nd, and Le Régiment de la Chaudière in the 3rd — which meant that there were only four French-Canadian unit commanders, the officers most readily promoted to command brigades. That, too, limited the pool of qualified candidates. The other likely source of brigade commanders, the artillery, was also graced with only one regiment of medium (5.5") guns and two 25-pounder batteries of French-speaking soldiers.[84] Again the potential for upward mobility was small.*

*One francophone "might-have-been" was J.-A. Leclaire, born in Montreal in 1899. Leclaire served overseas in the ranks in the Great War, then joined the Fusiliers Mont-Royal in the NPAM. By 1939, after taking the Militia Staff Course, he was a major and he proceeded overseas in 1940. By May 1942, now a brigadier, he commanded a brigade in the 7th Division at Debert, NS. But then his career collapsed, according to rumour because he became drunk on a train and insulted Cardinal Villeneuve to his face. In April 1943 Leclaire turned up as a private in the Seaforth Highlanders, by December he had been commissioned in the field and was a lieutenant in Italy, and within a year he had risen to the rank of major. Had the war lasted long enough, Leclaire, evidently a good soldier, might have received his old rank back. I am indebted to Ben Greenhous for this sad story.

In all, the army estimated, 14 percent of its officers were French-speaking, but most were very junior and, of 4090 francophone officers in February 1944, only 1339 were overseas.[85] That data, scarcely amenable to quick fixes, ought to have ended charges of discrimination, but press attacks such as Paré's demonstrated clearly how much resentment still existed.

Despite the difficulties in their path, able francophone officers had begun to emerge by 1944. The fighting in Italy and the fine part played by the Van Doos saw that regiment produce two brigadiers before the end of the war, both of whom had to command their brigades in English. J.-P.-E. Bernatchez, an RMC graduate who had been a PF lieutenant in 1939, commanded the 22e in the Italian fighting and in early 1944 took over a brigade. His successor, J.-V. Allard, commanded the Van Doos in action for more than a year before he took command of a brigade in Northwest Europe in early 1945. Yet a third francophone, J.-G. Gauvreau, led a brigade in France until he was wounded in action in the Scheldt battles. And a fourth, Brigadier G. Francoeur, commanded the vital reinforcement group in Northwest Europe.

Even here there were problems. When Ralston received complaints of discrimination against Québécois — with the delays in promoting Bernatchez to brigadier being singled out — from an officer overseas, he investigated the matter. General Ken Stuart, the Chief of Staff at Canadian Military Headquarters, replied that everyone was "bending over backwards"[86] to find suitable francophones, but, he added:

> I am afraid that Bernatchez has found his ceiling but Allard is a possibility. I may say that we put Bernatchez up even though Montgomery and Dempsey did not consider he was up to the required standard. I put Francoeur in his present job in France to get a F.C. brigadier in France. He has not been as good as I expected and Montague and I have had to withstand considerable pressure to keep him there. He is being carried at the moment by a very good brigade major. I cite this case because he would have been removed some time ago if he had been an Anglo-Saxon.[87]

Stuart was no bigot. He had been born in Trois-Rivières and he understood French, even if he was not completely bilingual.[88] His post, however, made him responsible for the lives of Canadian fighting men, French- and English-speaking, and that weighed heavily upon him. By the fall of 1944, Stuart knew, only those officers who had proven themselves in action could be placed in command of troops. All too few were francophones.

This fundamentally doleful story had no happy ending. In substantial part because of the experiences of the Great War, francophones avoided the army (and the other services, too) between the wars. The numbers guaranteed that, despite French Canada's substantially greater share in the war effort in the Second World War, Quebec received far less than its proper proportion of generals' billets and, although Ottawa and the commanders in the field apparently tried their best to rectify matters, they could not overcome the hard realities. As General LaFlèche wrote during the conscription crisis of 1944, "The French-Canadian does not believe that he has . . . a Marshal's baton in his cartridge case."[89] He didn't, and he had almost no chance for one during the war.

Why? The "system," the Canadian army's imperial cast of mind, the built-in biases of military service in an English-speaking British-style army, all conspired to deny French Canadians their due share of the most important army posts. English Canadians, in other words, deserved much of the blame for their utter insensitivity to French Canada's needs and its *amour-propre.* That is not the whole story, however, for French Canadians, ever conscious of the wrongs done to them, hung back and forbore from trying to change the system. There was never a flood of eager, able young men in the interwar years seeking to go to RMC, to join the Permanent Force, or to sign up in the militia regiments in Montreal, Joliette, or Trois-Rivières. So long as Québécois avoided the army, the system would continue as it always had.

Lorenzo Paré's complaints, loud as they were in 1944, were therefore only half right in their analysis of the problem. The needs of the war predisposed NDHQ and the cabinet to try to deal with the shortage of francophone senior officers, but the problem simply was not amenable to a speedy resolution. After the war the impetus for change sputtered, and it was not until the Quiet Revolution made English Canadians aware of the deep discontents in Quebec that efforts to alter matters definitively took place. Even then it took herculean, and ultimately successful, efforts from the 1960s on to ensure that francophone officers were given a fair chance to rise to the most senior positions in the Canadian Armed Forces.

CHAPTER 10

CONCLUSION

NATIONS GET THE POLITICIANS they deserve. That tru-
ism might also apply to generals and, if it does, for the first few
years of the Second World War, Canadians almost certainly received the
military leadership they merited. By disbanding the hard-won expertise
of the Canadian Corps so thoroughly after 1919, by starving the tiny
Permanent Force and the larger but weaker Non Permanent Active
Militia during the 1920s and 1930s, Canada's governments ensured that
when war came in September 1939 there was nothing in place to meet
its demands but good wishes. By 1945, however, everything had changed,
and the First Canadian Army with its five infantry and armoured divisions and its two armoured brigades was a well-led, splendidly equipped,
and powerful force at least equal to any Allied formation of comparable
size. Still, it was a long time between 1939 and 1945, and no one should
attempt to hide the brutal fact that Canadian soldiers probably died
from the effects of interwar neglect on their commanders and staffs.

Canadians were not alone in suffering this fate. The Chief of the
Imperial General Staff, Field Marshal Sir Alan Brooke, wrote privately
about his army's "lack of good military commanders. Half our Corps
and Divisional Commanders are totally unfit for their appointments;
and yet if I were to sack them I could find no better. They lack character,
imagination, drive and power of leadership."[1] It was all a result of the
casualties of the Great War, he said — the best men of a whole generation had died in the trenches. Those harsh, despairing remarks must be

borne in mind in assessing Brooke's comments on the sad qualities of Canadian general officers.

Still, the CIGS' judgment was correct, and the result showed at every level of the British army in the Second World War. "With certain significant exceptions," the distinguished military historian Sir Michael Howard wrote, "the British Army in the Second World War was not very good, and those of us who were fighting it knew where its weaknesses lay. Staff work was rigid, there was little encouragement of initiative, or devolution of responsibility." Instead, Howard added, there was only "an increasing reluctance to run risks and greater reliance upon massive firepower."[2] The Germans realized this, too, one assessment of British and Canadian troops in 1944 commenting that "the morale of the enemy infantry is not very high. It depends largely on artillery and air support."[3] The British had had an army before the war, relatively small, to be sure, but one that fought colonial wars, that had infantry and armoured divisions to manoeuvre in training, and that had enough officers in its ranks to allow for a proper system of promotion. That had not saved it from the doctrinal flaws noted by Howard and exploited by the Germans.

Canada's wartime army suffered from the same faults in action, and no one should be surprised by this similarity: it, too, was a British army in almost every respect. In the interwar years, its regular officers went to Britain for artillery, ordnance, and engineering courses, its best and brightest attended the staff colleges and the Imperial Defence College, and its few thinkers looked to Britain for their models. Canadian military professionalism, in other words, tried to replicate the British models. In the interwar years, however, the PF and NPAM had none of the presumed advantages given the British army by its size.

That mattered. A Permanent Force of only 450 regular officers and 4000 men could neither train itself for war nor properly train the militia. Officers spent much of their time travelling to give classes in armouries scattered across the provinces, while others worked hard on largely futile tasks in the midst of politicians and the military's bureaucratic politicking in Ottawa's National Defence Headquarters. Neither activity was conducive to mastering the military arts. Despite the obvious drawbacks under which they laboured, however, a substantial number of first-rate PF officers remained in the service, studied hard, and prepared themselves to assume great responsibilities when war came. Yet they receive scant credit in the work of historians.

Writing almost thirty years ago in the first serious assessment of the interwar Canadian military, James Eayrs observed that the prewar Canadian army "produced no soldier-strategists. There are no Canadian Douhets or Slessors, no Fullers or Liddell Harts, much less any Canadian Clausewitzes or Mahans."[4] More recently, in his able study of the Canadian army's failings in Normandy, Lieutenant-Colonel John English lamented that "a temporary major in 1939," Guy Simonds, "proved the best that the Canadian military system, despite all its expenditures in the interwar years, could put forth" during the Second World War.[5] English's overall theme was that the interwar PF devoted its time to everything except preparing for war, the task of every army. And Stephen Harris, whose *Canadian Brass* is the best study of the pre-1939 army, wrote that "it took more than a keen mind, a scientific education, and attendance at British army staff courses to make good generals out of majors and colonels who might have commanded a platoon or a company in the Great War, but who had not been in the field since." To Harris, it seemed to come as a surprise that eight of twenty-two general officers who commanded divisions, corps, and the army overseas had to be fired before they saw action, that two more were replaced after their first battles, and that another lasted only nine months in action.[6]

These harsh criticisms merit a brief examination. The distinguished American military historian, Theodore Ropp, reviewed Eayrs's book and praised it highly. But he was properly astonished that Eayrs could fret that Canada produced no great soldier-strategists "in a professional officer corps of less than four hundred [sic]. . . . One might just as well try to sort out the real intellectuals among Canada's barbers or dentists."[7] Ropp was right in finding it absurd to expect a Clausewitz to emerge from the tiny Permanent Force; the wonder was that the *Canadian Defence Quarterly* was as good as it was, and when it published the Simonds–Burns discussion on organization for armoured warfare just before the outbreak of war in 1939, it was very good indeed. Similarly, English's complaint that Simonds was the best that Canada's PF could produce despite all the interwar expenditures on defence cannot stand. What interwar expenditures? The military in Canada was deliberately kept on starvation rations by Liberal and Conservative governments for two decades. There were derisory budgets, low pay, poor equipment, and totally inadequate training in a PF commanded a good part of the time by the aged and infirm.

The real question is why someone as competent as temporary Major Guy Simonds remained in the Canadian army when, given the numbers of men and the available dollars, no training for anything that approximated modern war was possible. Even Harris's criticisms, the soundest of those advanced by the three scholars, suffer by isolating Canada's military from comparison with the experience of other armies. Did no British or American senior officers fail in the first years of the Second World War? To ask the question is to answer it, of course, and the host of Anglo-American generals who were sacked for their failings in 1940, 1941, and 1942 makes the Canadian lists look small.

The questions this book has tried to examine are quite different from those raised by other historians. The interesting point is not why so many Canadian generals failed, but why so many succeeded Not why there were no Clausewitzes, but how a force of 450 officers, many of them aged and even more never budging from their chair in the mess, could have produced a high-quality, professionally stimulating debate like that between Simonds and Burns in 1938–9. Not how much money was wasted by the army in the interwar years, but how, despite the almost total lack of funds, the army's officer corps attracted and retained any men of competence.

Very simply, for all the problems in the years after 1939, the Canadian people were remarkably well served by their army in the interwar years. Popularly regarded as freeloading parasites by good tax-paying citizens everywhere, scorned as strikebreakers by labour, and denounced by isolationist politicians, bureaucrats, and academics as imperial pawns, Canada's professional soldiers formed an armed force in microcosm. Always intended as a cadre that could be expanded on mobilization, the PF proved to be precisely that. The 450 regular officers of 1939, with the 5000 or so NPAM officers, became the basis for a wartime army of 50,000 officers and some 450,000 other ranks at its wartime peak in June 1944.[8] This was a process of remarkable growth, and it was scarcely surprising that difficulties arose as a result. Virtually every one of the sixty-eight general officers examined in this collective biography came from either the PF or the militia;[9] that was to be expected. If three-quarters had proved to be disastrous failures under the stress of war, that, too, might have been expected, given the drawbacks under which they had laboured for two decades. In fact, while some failed, most performed adequately, some did well, and a few excelled. In other words, the generals, much like any group in business or academe or athletics, had a normal distribution pattern of successes and failures. It took a number of years for the shake-out to occur and, when it did, it was often because senior British officers expressed concern about the competence of Canadian senior officers.

Most of the generals who failed were older veterans of the Great War. The Odlums, Prices, and others were not military thinkers. They had not kept up with the changes in warfare since 1919, and they con-tinued to think in terms of the trench raids and timed barrages they had perfected with the Canadian Corps; they were simply unable to adjust to the type of war that had to be fought after 1940. That is no criticism of them; these officers had served the militia well before the war, it was politically impossible for NDHQ to prevent the NPAM from securing a prominent place in the formation of the first Canadian divi-sions, and they did their best at a time when there was no one else to take their place. Literally, there was no one else. What is significant is that by the time Canadian troops went into sustained action, the for-tunes of war having ensured that this would not be until July 1943, the Great War generation of officers was almost completely gone. Of this group, only Tommy Burns and Harry Crerar commanded troops in operations, and at the end of the war only Crerar, the army's great sur-vivor, remained. All the other senior field commanders came from the postwar generation. If they, too, had their professional and personal failings and their failures, as they did aplenty, it was not from being stuck in the mud of remembrance of wars past.

A surprising number were very good indeed, proof that the army over-seas was, in many ways, a genuine meritocracy. Hoffmeister and Matthews were undoubted militia successes, young men in their thirties who rose to high rank thanks to their own abilities and courage in action. It would surely have been surprising had some of the non-professional officers, drawn from the militia's broader population base, not demon-strated great talent for war. All they needed was time for their profession-alism and their military skills to develop — and, fortunately, the army overseas had that breathing space before it saw action. PF officers such as Simonds, Foster, Vokes, and Spry, as junior in rank at the beginning of the war as Hoffmeister and Matthews, similarly rose on merit. It helped that the first three had attended Staff College and that all had time to learn and rise during the long wait in Britain.

The senior officers at the onset of war also had time to wait and to learn. McNaughton was the former Chief of the General Staff who was almost certainly the natural choice to be GOC of the first Canadian division. But time demonstrated irrefutably that McNaughton's flaws as a commander, trainer, and national commander were serious indeed and, before the end of 1943, the combined efforts of Ottawa, the British, and Harry Crerar ensured his sacking. His replacement, Crerar, was by 1943 his only natural successor. Crerar had learned much about command and politics during the first three years of war, and he was temperamentally much better fitted than McNaughton to lead a national contingent in a huge Allied army. Crerar was no Montgomery, no Patton, but despite his overweening ambition and his cravings for rank and personal power, he was a competent soldier in a good, middle-ground Canadian way. It was remarkable that the Permanent Force could produce the charismatic McNaughton and the competent Crerar, men who could play the politics of high command, and that it could produce able battlefield commanders.

Staff officers, too, mastered their craft during the war. In the interwar years, the military bureaucrats at NDHQ had laboured in obscurity, their judgments hostage to the whim of politicians and deputy ministers. But the war changed everything, and military bureaucrats like Stuart and Pope came to the fore, learned how to play the political game, and essentially demonstrated that the cabinet could be led to give them everything they wanted for the army. The army budget at its peak in 1944–5 was $2.962 billion, some six times the entire 1939 federal government budget, and those dollars supported a huge army.[10] Suspicious as he was of the General Staff, Colonel Ralston became the staff officers' willing tool, their advocate in the Cabinet War Committee. Ralston's ouster came with the conscription crisis of 1944; so, too, did General Stuart's. It was significant that General Pope stayed loyal to the Prime Minister and, fanciful stories of military revolts notwithstanding, the senior officers at NDHQ adjusted themselves to their new situation like the good professionals they were. It was also important that, by November 1944, there were both PF and NPAM officers of undoubted competence working in Ottawa, a factor that guaranteed that Prime Minister Mackenzie King would not seek revenge on the PF for the bad military advice on reinforcements given the politicians.

The Second World War put the army onto centre stage and, although for a time the first postwar years seemed set to replicate the total military demobilization and deliberate neglect that had characterized the years after 1919, the Cold War, the establishment of the North Atlantic Treaty Organization, the Korean War, and Canadian rearmament soon had the generals, and most notably Charles Foulkes, in the catbird seat once more.

The PF and NPAM story, then, is one of undoubted success, not failure. The Canadian people got a good return on their paltry investment in defence in the interwar years, far more than they deserved. Competent, if not brilliant, field commanders came to the fore, senior commanders able to represent Canada with credit in Allied discussions emerged, and the NDHQ staff demonstrated that it could play and win the political game in the army's interest.

We should not carry this praise too far, however, and certainly not when we consider Canadian operations in the field. The Canadian way of war was characterized by staff-driven and top-down control, much like Canadian business. Concerned with preventing a repetition of the horrific casualties of the Great War, Canadian operations invariably featured heavy artillery preparation and small-scale objectives. Sometimes, as historian Bill McAndrew has put it so graphically, slow and ponderous attacks went forward with nothing so much as a "Slinky toy" in mind — the infantry and armour were unable to move any further than the range of the 25-pounder gun and, if a breakthrough was achieved, the attackers tended to wait until the artillery caught up before pressing on.[11] McAndrew is correct, but perhaps this caution was necessary. The enemy's leadership, training, and equipment were better, and the massed artillery at the service of Canadian and other Allied troops was the trump card in the circumstances. Military historian John Ellis stated it simply: "All the Allied generals relied in the last analysis on firepower and sheer material superiority to win their battles rather than on any concept of unbalancing the enemy or forcing him to give up ground by threatened moves into his flanks or rear."[12] Canadian commanders, their attacks always seeming to be directed at enemy strongpoints rather than weaknesses, fit that description perfectly. Even Simonds's innovative tactics in Operation Totalize, for example, aimed to achieve only relatively limited goals, and his divisions pressed forward with caution. That he was a gunner, like McNaughton, Crerar, Matthews, and Keefler, was no accident. Even so, Simonds stands head and shoulders above every other Canadian commander as a skilled tactician, as a general unafraid to try new approaches to the horrific battlefields of the Second World War. With McNaughton and Crerar, he completes the trio of dominant military men who organized, led, and fought Canada's war.

Canadian tactical shortcomings could be blamed on the generals' British models, but what can account for the Canadians' utter lack of charisma? Brigadier J.A. Roberts's memoirs tell of the impact of his encounter with Lieutenant-General Brian Horrocks during Operation Veritable:

> Here was one of the finest officers in the British army, with a magnificent record of service and personal gallantry. Here was a man who really led, a general who talked to everyone, down to the simplest private soldier. He called his officers 'Joe,' 'Peter,' 'Reggie,' 'Mike,' or whatever. I was 'Jim' before we crawled back to the Queen's Own patrol. By his personal quali-ties of leadership he brought out a respect and an affection which made better soldiers of his officers and men. Why, I wondered, rather guiltily, were our senior officers not of the same personality; and we were supposed to be Canadians, less stiff and formal than the British. Our own army com-mander was a good soldier, a very nice man personally, and, I am sure, a man loyal to his troops as a whole. But his personality was not that of a leader of men. He addressed his officers as 'Smith,' 'Jones,' and 'Roberts.' So did Guy Simonds.[13]

McNaughton, Worthington, Hoffmeister, and possibly Vokes were the only Canadian generals who fit the Horrocks mould at all. McNaughton had the common touch in 1939 and 1940, but as he became more absorbed in developing equipment and playing politics with Ottawa and the War Office, he grew increasingly distant from his men, and especially those, unlike the 1st Canadian Division, who had not come to Britain with him in December 1939. "Fighting Frank" Worthington was a com-pelling personality, a man who could convey his enthusiasm for tanks to his troopers, but he received no chance to lead his 4th Canadian Armoured Division into action. Vokes was a rough-talking, hard-drinking womaniz-er; soldiers who admired those traits thought highly of him. A battalion, brigade, and division commander who led from the front, Hoffmeister also had something of McNaughton's early populist style, but even Hoffmeister had a certain innate reserve in his makeup. Crerar, Simonds, Burns, and Foulkes had only reserve and no charisma at all; the best among them commanded respect but never affection from their soldiers. The reasons for this grey state of affairs are probably imponderable, but may have something to do with the Canadian character, with being uptight and lacking confidence, especially when confronted with Field Marshal Lord So-and-So and General Sir Whozit. The Canadians' psychological colonial status condemned the generals to practise deference to their betters and control in the presence of subordinates. When this code was violated, as Andy McNaughton was wont to do, officers could be seen as difficult or even unstable by the British *and* the Canadians.[14]

The only place that Canadian generals let down their hair was in their internecine struggles over great issues of policy and for place and power. Harry Crerar was the undoubted master here, the skilled backroom operative who could manoeuvre his way around the politicians, undercut his military superiors, and control those junior in rank to him. Generals such as McNaughton or Burns simply lacked this talent, and they fell in substantial part because of it. Guy Simonds notably lacked political skills, but his military talents were so powerful that even Crerar, who might cheerfully have slit his throat at the end of 1943, dared not do so. Crerar, however, metaphorically did the deed when he opted for Charles Foulkes as his candidate for CGS in mid 1945. Foulkes, a Harry Crerar writ small, had risen on the basis of his knowledge of men's weaknesses and strengths as much as on his talents as a commander. This war among the generals might shock the naïve, those who assume that war obliges everyone to work for a common cause without complaint. The cause was there, and it was shared by all, but just as politicians continue their struggles for office and power during wartime, so, too, do soldiers frequently fight for more than victory over the enemy. Human nature cannot be easily controlled.

That Canada won its share of victory undoubtedly owed more to the common soldiers than to the generals. It always does. Close to 700,000 Canadian men and women served in the army during the Second World War; 17,682 were killed in action or died of wounds and 58,094 were wounded or taken prisoner; another 5235 died of disease or injury.[15] The great majority of those killed and wounded fell in the last two years of the war. This was a terrible price for a small country to pay, and it is no less terrible because the cause was just and victory so important for the democracies.

Still, that victory could not have been achieved without the generals. The first chapter of this book included reference to miracles, and it is not inappropriate that the conclusion should end the same way. The biblical story of the loaves and fishes tells how a small quantity of food miraculously doubled, redoubled, and doubled again to feed a great multitude. In September 1939, its professional military talent very thin, Canada seemed unlikely to produce the leaders necessary to command its army. Despite travails and turmoil, by 1945 the First Canadian Army had capable soldiers in command of a vaster array than anyone six years earlier could have expected. Sometimes these leaders emerged from unlikely pre-war occupations. In his splendid memoir, Brigadier Roberts told of escorting a Nazi general back to his quarters after the surrender of his command to General Simonds:

> Very little was said during the return trip. Both the Germans, as well as I, had a lot on our minds. But, somewhere during our rapid jeep ride, the German staff officer tapped me on the shoulder and indicated that the general was interested to know what was my occupation in life, was I a professional soldier? . . . I suddenly realized, with something of a shock, that my last personal and civilian employment had ended with Snow Cream in 1939. I replied then, simply, that I was never a professional soldier but that, like most Canadian soldiers, I was a civilian volunteer and that, in my former pre-war life, I had been an ice-cream manufacturer.

The German general, as might have been expected, was taken aback that he had been obliged to surrender to "a common civilian."[16] The Wehrmacht professional soldier, the product of the greatest military system the world has ever known, had been obliged to turn over his sword to the ice-cream maker and prewar militiaman, and no miracle of biblical record could match that.

There is something very Canadian in that story. Roberts, who rose from lieutenant to become a very competent brigade commander in six years of war, might even be seen as the embodiment of the militia myth, the idea that every Canadian was a natural soldier who needed no tutelage from the professionals. This book has tried to suggest as strongly as possible that the Permanent Force's professionals were needed, desperately so, but so, too, were the one-night-a-week militiamen. That the PF and the NPAM rose so magnificently to the occasion was astonishing, but, like most miraculous events, it was (to quote Wellington after the battle of Waterloo) "a damned nice thing — the nearest run thing you ever saw in your life."

As we enter the post-Cold War era, many well-meaning Canadians and many of those concerned with the growing federal deficit look to the armed forces as a place for ready savings and a peace dividend. Before Canadians press their government to hack and slash at what still remains of Canada's hard-won professional military expertise, however, they should remember just how lucky the country and the army were to find able commanders for the forces in the Second World War. The army had time, and there can be no guarantee that any future crisis would give Canada a similar breathing space. The age of miracles looks to have ended, and sensible precautions to deal with a turbulent world seem a better shield on which to rely than good wishes.

GENERAL OFFICERS IN THE SECOND WORLD WAR

This listing includes only officers who held the rank of major-general or higher, and the rank listed is the highest held at death, on retirement during the war, or at the end of the war. Francophones are in bold face. RMC ex-cadets are noted with an asterisk (*), and Permanent Force officers with a sword (†). Those who attended the British Army Staff College at Camberley or Quetta before 1939 are indicated with a number sign (#), and those who graduated from the Imperial Defence College with a circumflex (^). Only the most senior wartime posts are noted in brackets.

†#MGen Alexander, R.O. (GOC-in-C Pacific Command)
*†#MGen Anderson, T.V. (CGS)
†LGen Ashton, E.C. (Inspector-General Central Canada)
†MGen Browne, B.W. (Adjutant-General)
*†#^MGen Burns, E.L.M. (GOC I Cdn Corps)
MGen Chisholm, Brock (Director-General Medical Services)
*†#MGen Constantine, C.F. (DOC Military District No. 2)
*†#^Gen Crerar, H.D.G. (CGS, GOC I Cdn Corps, GOC-in-C First Cdn Army)
†MGen D.B. Dewar (Director-General, Dept of Munitions and Supply)
*†MGen Elkins, W.H.P (GOC-in-C Atlantic Command)

MGen Fenwick, C.P. (Director-General Medical Services)

*†#MGen Foster, Harry (GOC 4th Cdn Armd Div, 1st Cdn Div)

MGen Foster, W.W. (Special Commissioner Defence Projects in Northwest Canada)

†#LGen Foulkes, Charles (GOC I Cdn Corps, CGS)

MGen Ganong, H.N. (GOC 8th Cdn Div)

MGen Gibson, R.B. (Vice CGS)

MGen Griesbach, W.A. (Inspector-General Western Canada)

MGen Hertzberg, C.S.L. (Chief Engineer, First Cdn Army)

†#MGen Hertzberg, H.F.H. (Commandant, RMC)

MGen Hoffmeister, B.M. (GOC 5th Cdn Armd Div)

*†MGen Howard, G.B. (Deputy Chairman, Inspection Board of UK and Canada)

MGen Keefler, R.H. (GOC 3rd Cdn Div)

*†#MGen Keller, R.F.L. (GOC 3rd Cdn Div)

MGen Kennedy, H. (Quartermaster-General)

Brig Kitching, George (GOC 4th Cdn Armd Div)

MGen **LaFlèche, L.R.** (Military Attaché in France)

MGen Letson, H.F.G. (Adjutant-General)

MGen **Leclerc, P.E.** (GOC 7th Cdn Div)

†MGen Luton, R.M. (Director Medical Services, CMHQ)

*†MGen Macdonald, D.J. (Inspector-General Central Canada)

MGen Mackenzie, J.P. (Quartermaster-General)

*†MGen MacQueen, J.V. (Master-General of the Ordnance)

MGen Matthews, A.B. (GOC 2nd Cdn Div)

†MGen Matthews, H.H. (Adjutant-General)

MGen McCuaig, G.E. (Commandant, Camp Borden)

†#^Gen McNaughton, A.G.L. (GOC 1st Cdn Div, GOC Cdn Corps, GOC-in-C First Cdn Army, Minister of National Defence)

LGen Montague, P.J. (Chief of Staff, CMHQ)

*†#LGen Murchie, J.C. (CGS)

MGen Nash, A.E. (Inspector-General Central Canada)

MGen Odlum, V.W. (GOC 2nd Cdn Div)

†MGen Page, L.F. (GOC 4th Cdn Armd Div)

*MGen **Panet, E. de B.** (DOC Military District No. 4)

†#^MGen Pearkes, George (GOC 1st Cdn Div, GOC-in-C, Pacific Command)

MGen Phelan, F.R. (Commander Newfoundland)

†#^LGen Pope, M.A. (Military Assistant to Prime Minister)

MGen Potts, A.E. (GOC 6th Cdn Div)

MGen Price, C.B. (GOC 3rd Cdn Div)

*†MGen **Renaud, E.J.** (DOC Military District No. 4)

MGen Riley, H.J. (Joint Associate Director, National Selective Service)

*†MGen Roberts, J.H. (GOC 2nd Cdn Div)

†#MGen Salmon, H.L.N. (GOC 1st Cdn Div)

†#LGen Sansom, E.W. (GOC II Cdn Corps)

*†MGen Schmidlin, E.J.C. (Quartermaster-General)

*†#LGen Simonds, G.G. (GOC II Cdn Corps)

MGen Spencer, A.C. (Commandant, Camp Borden)

†MGen Spry, D.C. (GOC 3rd Cdn Div)

*†#MGen Stein, C.R.S. (GOC 5th Cdn Armd Div)

*†^LGen Stuart, Kenneth (CGS, Acting GOC-in-C First Cdn Army, Chief of Staff CMHQ)

*MGen **Tremblay, T.L.** (Inspector-General Eastern Canada)

†#^MGen Turner, G.R. (DA&QMG, First Cdn Army)

†#MGen **Vanier, G.P.** (DOC Military District No. 5)

*†#MGen **Vokes, C.** (GOC 1st Cdn Div, 4th Cdn Armd Div)

MGen Walford, A.E. (DA&QMG, First Canadian Army, Adjutant-General)

†#MGen Weeks, E.G. (MGen i/c Administration, CMHQ)

MGen White, J.B. (Commander, Canadian Forestry Corps)

†MGen Worthington, F.F. (GOC 4th Cdn Armd Div)

†#MGen Young, H.A. (Quartermaster-General)

*MGen Young, J.V. (Master-General of the Ordnance)

KEY ARMY POSITIONS IN CANADA AND OVERSEAS

CANADA
National Defence Headquarters
Chief of the General Staff
Vice Chief of the General Staff
Adjutant-General
Quartermaster-General
Master-General of the Ordnance
Operational Commanders
GOC-in-C Atlantic Command
GOC-in-C Pacific Command
GOC 6th Division
GOC 7th Division
GOC 8th Division
Commander, Combined Newfoundland and Canadian Military Forces
  Newfoundland

OVERSEAS
Canadian Military Headquarters, London
Senior Combatant Officer (to Dec 1943)

Chief of Staff
Field Commanders
GOC-in-C, First Canadian Army
GOC, I Canadian Corps
GOC, 1st Canadian Infantry Division
GOC, 5th Canadian Armoured Division
Commander, 1st Canadian Armoured Brigade
GOC, II Canadian Corps
GOC, 2nd Canadian Infantry Division
GOC, 3rd Canadian Infantry Division
GOC, 4th Canadian Armoured Division
Commander, 2nd Canadian Armoured Brigade

ARMY OFFICER RANKS

Field Marshal
General
Lieutenant-General
Major-General
Brigadier
Colonel
Lieutenant-Colonel
Major
Captain
Lieutenant
Second Lieutenant

NOTES

ABBREVIATIONS USED IN NOTES

CWC	National Archives of Canada, Privy Council Office, Cabinet War Committee Records
DCER	*Documents on Canadian External Relations* (Ottawa: Department of External Affairs)
DHist	Directorate of History, Department of National Defence
DND	National Archives of Canada, Department of National Defence Records
IWM	Imperial War Museum, London
LHC	University of London, King's College, Liddell Hart Centre for Military Archives
NA	National Archives of Canada, Ottawa
NPRC	National Archives of Canada, National Personnel Records Centre
Prem	Public Record Office, Prime Minister's Office Records
PRO	Public Record Office, London
QUA	Queen's University Archives, Kingston
RMC	Royal Military College Archives and/or Library, Kingston
USAMHI	United States Army Military History Institute, Carlisle, Pa
USNA	United States National Archives, Washington
WO	Public Record Office, War Office Records

Prewar and wartime rank abbreviations are given in the traditional form (Lieut-Col., Maj.-Gen., etc.) while postwar ranks appear in the style now used by the Canadian Forces (LCol, MGen, etc.).

CHAPTER 1 INTRODUCTION: THE OLD ARMY

1 Michael Howard, "Haig-bashing," *London Review of Books*, 25 April 1991, 5.

2 John Colville, *The Fringes of Power: 10 Downing Street Diaries 1939–1955* (New York 1985), 275.

3 Edward Meade, *Remember Me* (Toronto 1965), 133.

4 Farley Mowat, *My Father's Son* (Toronto 1992), 201, 209. Smith left the army in 1962 and became a major corporate executive in Britain. The only stockbroker to command a division was Major-General Bruce Matthews, who did rise on merit.

5 Noel Annan, "Hello to All That," *New York Review of Books*, 26 March 1992, 15.

6 (London 1988), 22.

7 A.M.J. Hyatt, "Canadian Generals of the First World War and the Popular View of Military Leadership," *Social History* 12 (November 1979), 418ff. Hyatt's overall group, which included seventy-seven brigadier-generals, had five lieutenant-generals and forty-three major-generals.

8 The birthplace of one general could not be determined.

9 For General Page's "free-thinker" status I am indebted to his daughter, P.K. Page [Mrs Arthur Irwin], telephone interview, 30 July 1992. The religion of ten generals could not be determined from the available sources, including personnel files in the NPRC, which are often surprisingly incomplete.

10 The rural/urban origins of sixteen generals could not be uncovered from the available evidence.

11 The pre-Second World War corps of nine generals could not definitively be determined.

12 These data are derived from *Who's Who* entries, army public-relations biographies, records in the NPRC, and other sources. Edward Coffman and P.F. Herrly, "The American Regular Army Officer Corps between the World Wars," *Armed Forces and Security* 4 (November 1977), 55ff, demonstrate that American regular officers were much more likely to be rural in origin and to have attended military academy (in this case West Point) than their Canadian peers. For an analysis of the most senior British officers of the Second World War, see John Keegan, ed., *Churchill's Generals* (London 1991), 7ff. The British were mainly born in the 1880s, educated in public schools, service academies, and staff schools, and did not have university degrees; most were infantrymen and had been decorated for Great War service. They sound much like their Canadian counterparts. A study of Canadian general officers between the wars, not surprisingly, replicates my conclusions for the wartime generals. See R.H. Gimblett,

"Social Background as a Factor in Defence Policy Formulation: The General Officer Corps of the Canadian Militia 1923–1939" (MA paper, Trent University 1980).

13 It is also worth noting that the sons of older generals served during the war. Gens McNaughton, Price, H.F.H. Hertzberg, R.O. Alexander, and J.V. Young had sons killed in action; General Vokes's brother was killed in action in Italy.

14 *Report of the Department of National Defence . . . 1939* (Ottawa 1939), 70. In November 1938 PF authorized strength was 10,000, peacetime establishment was 6928, and actual strength was 4178. NA, Ian Mackenzie Papers, vol. 39, file D-72, CGS to Minister, 16 November 1938.

15 *Report of the Department of National Defence . . . 1939*, 73.

16 Stephen E. Ambrose, "The Man Who Gave Us West Germany," *New York Times Book Review*, 29 July 1990, 13.

17 "Note on 'The Canadian Army 1939–45,'" *R.M.C. Review* 29 (1948), 66.

18 "R.M.C. War Record," ibid., 28 (1947), 132–3.

19 Strength on 31 March 1939 was, by year, 43, 44, 57, and 56 for a total of 200. DHist 171.013(D3). The history of the college is R.A. Preston, *Canada's RMC: A History of the Royal Military College* (Toronto 1969).

20 "Terms from the Opening of the College," *R.M.C. Review* 29 (1948), 65–6.

21 The author, a graduate of RMC in 1961, has College No. 5105. Between 1948, when RMC reopened after the war, and his graduation, as many cadets were admitted to RMC and its sister colleges, Royal Roads and Le Collège Militaire Royal de St-Jean, as in the entire history of the college to its 1942 closing.

22 NA, E.L.M. Burns Papers, vol. 6, "Is the Royal Military College Worth What It Costs?" (unpublished paper). Geoffrey Hayes, "The Development of the Canadian Army Officer Corps, 1939–1945" (PhD dissertation, University of Western Ontario 1992), 26, shows 118 RMC graduates joining the PF between 1928 and 1939, some 43 percent of all officer appointments.

23 "Ex-Cadets of the Royal Military College of Canada," *R.M.C. Review* 3 (May 1921), 86–7; "Ex-Cadets . . . Who Have Attained the Rank of Major-General or Above," ibid., 7 (1925), 59.

24 "War Analysis," ibid., 27 (1947), 133.

25 "Ex-Cadets of the Royal Military College of Canada," ibid., 3 (May 1921), 86–7.

26 There is a good account of these and other RMC scandals in Guy Simonds Papers (North Gower, Ont.), Memoirs box, Draft Memoirs chap. 3; letter to author from MGen M.P. Bogert, 8 Jan. 1993.

27 DHist 113.1009(D7), "Lecture to Senior Class R.M.C.," September 1936.

28 For example, ex-cadets in the Canadian Army Occupation Force purchased tulip bulbs in the college colours for RMC. Fred Vokes Papers (Ottawa), Brig. J.D.B. Smith to Gen. Chris Vokes, 29 October 1945, and reply, 6 November 1945.

29 R.G.C. Smith, ed., *As You Were! Ex-Cadets Remember*, vol. 1: *1876–1918* (np, 1984), 281. In 1943 Lieut.-Gen. Harry Crerar felt constrained to tell all senior officers in I Canadian Corps that the idea that officers came from "moneyed families" and the "upper classes" was dead. "There is now no reason or excuse for the inclusion of 'family,' or 'money,' as factors in respect to appointment to Commissioned rank." DND, vol. 10771, file D283, Crerar to Commanders, 18 June 1943.

30 Mackenzie Papers, vol. 38, DND Estimates 1939–40; John Bassett, Jr, "Truth, Duty, Valour," *Maclean's*, 1 February 1940, 13ff.

31 "Introduction to Book II," in Smith, ed., *As You Were!* 279.

32 BGen R.T. Bennett interview, 22 May 1991; Preston, *Canada's RMC*, 238ff, 270ff.

33 Tony Foster, *Meeting of Generals* (Toronto 1986), 53.

34 Christopher Vokes, *Vokes: My Story* (Ottawa 1985), 161.

35 The PF made sporadic and largely unsuccessful efforts to seek out candidates for commissions from the universities. See QUA, J. Sutherland Brown Papers, box 1, file 8, Brown to Brig. T.V. Anderson, 4 December 1930.

36 House of Commons, *Debates*, 15 February 1944, 514. Maj.-Gen. Harry Letson remembered the CGS seeking his support for an appointment to the Army Council during the Second World War: "He is a RMC graduate, you see, and I don't know whether this will be against him." DHist, Letson biographical file, Letson interview, 27 May 1981.

37 Colin McDougall, *Execution* (New York 1958), 17–18, 188.

38 Brig. Frank Lace interview, 17 May 1991. Most of those interviewed for this book, PF or NPAM, ex-cadet or not, tended not to believe in the power of the old-boy network.

39 LGen W.A.B. Anderson interview, 21 May 1991.

40 For a sensible account of the planning, see Stephen Harris, *Canadian Brass: The Making of a Professional Army 1860-1939* (Toronto 1988), 170ff.

41 The best account of the interwar Permanent Force is ibid., 141ff.

42 The officers' routine was September to April: study and provisional schools; May: regimental training; June–August: NPAM training; September: leave. MGen H.A. Sparling interview, 18 April 1991. On officer training generally, see Harris, *Canadian Brass*, chap. 10. The best Canadian account of interwar Staff

College training is John A. Macdonald, "In Search of Veritable: Training the Canadian Army Staff Officer, 1899 to 1945" (MA thesis, Royal Military College 1992), 76ff. See also John A. English, *The Canadian Army and the Normandy Campaign: A Study of Failure in High Command* (New York 1991), 94–95.

43 MGen C.B. Ware interview, 24 February 1992; Foster, *Meeting of Generals*, 77–8.

44 Docs on DND, vol. 6502, file HQ313-1-2-18; NA, Georges Vanier Papers, vol. 4, file 4-17, Staff College Entrance Examinations 1922. On Staff College, see C.P. Stacey, "The Staff Officer," *Canadian Defence Quarterly 3* (winter 1973–4), 43ff; H.F. Pullen, "Staff Training and Staff Colleges in the Canadian Army, 1867–1967," *Snowy Owl* (1966–7), 9ff; and Martin Creveld, *The Training of Officers* (London 1990), 47ff.

45 Data in Burns Papers, vol. 6, "Is the Royal Military College Worth What It Costs?"; Macdonald, "In Search of Veritable," 272ff, shows four cavalry graduates between the wars, eighteen artillery, eleven engineers, eleven signallers, and sixteen infantrymen. Col. English charges McNaughton with studiedly ignoring infantry and cavalry officers — but he could scarcely have written their Staff College examinations for them. English, *Canadian Army*, 47.

46 Sutherland Brown Papers, box 9, file 195, "Memorandum on the Examination for Admission to the Staff Colleges . . . February–March, 1929," 16 September 1929.

47 That British examinations, examiners, and standards were the determinants for advancement in the Canadian army sounds more odd today than it did sixty or seventy years ago. See James Eayrs, *In Defence of Canada: From the Great War to the Great Depression* (Toronto 1964), 89–90.

48 DND, vol. 6502, file HQ313-1-2-18, "Provisional Instructions Relating to the Staff College."

49 Keegan, ed., *Churchill's Generals*, 9.

50 Simonds Papers, Memoirs box, Draft Memoirs, chap. 4; Harry Foster Papers (Halifax), Diary, 7 August 1941.

51 See "Four Generations of Staff College Students — 1896 to 1952," *Army Quarterly* 65 (October 1952), 49ff.

52 Macdonald, "In Search of Veritable," 271–2, gives a list and year of attendance. Stacey, "The Staff Officer," 48, says forty-four had passed Staff College between the wars.

53 See, for example, NA, H.D.G. Crerar Papers, vol. 10, 958C.009(D211), M.A. Pope to Crerar, 14 May, 27 July 1936; docs on Sutherland Brown Papers, box 10, file

219–37; Roy, *For Most Conspicuous Bravery: A Biography of Major-General George R.H. Pearkes...*, (Vancouver 1977), 126ff.

54 A list of army IDC graduates is in R.H. Gimblett, "'Buster' Brown: The Man and His Clash with 'Andy' McNaughton" (BA thesis, Royal Military College 1979), appx. D.

55 DHist, 113.302009(D138), "Vote Permanent Force."

56 See Vokes, *Vokes: My Story*, 36.

57 *Pay and Allowance Regulations . . . 1937* (Ottawa 1942), 16. University of Victoria Archives, Brig. S.E.E. Morres interview, 12–19 June 1979; Brig. J.S. Ross interview, 22–29 August 1978; Simonds Papers, Memoirs box, Draft Memoirs, chap. 5. Privates' pay was $1.70 a day in 1923; in 1924 it was reduced to $1.20 and remained at that level.

58 These comments are based on a number of interviews. More generally, on drink during the war see Paul Fussell, *Wartime: Understanding and Behavior in the Second World War* (New York 1989), chap. 8.

59 Foster, *Meeting of Generals*, 60.

60 Tony Foster Papers (Halifax), Gen. Harry Foster recollections, taped, nd.

61 Sutherland Brown Papers, box 3, file 42, Brown to Col. H.H. Matthews, 19 April 1932.

62 It is worth noting that PF other ranks (ORs) and NCOs proved a fruitful source of wartime officers. A nominal roll of PF officers overseas, October 1945, found 305 in all, of whom only ninety had been officers in 1939. The remaining 215 were either NCOs, ORs, or officers receiving commissions during the war. Five of that group overseas, all NCOs or ORs, reached the rank of lieutenant-colonel during the war. Simonds Papers, Canadian Forces in Netherlands box, "Nominal Roll of Permanent Force Officers Cdn Army Overseas . . . " nd.

63 D.C. Spry Papers (Ottawa), "Roger Sunray," draft memoir; Simonds Papers, Memoirs box, Draft Memoirs, chap. 5.

64 "I was only Militia you know," Maj.-Gen. Harry Letson recollected, "and they are lower than the dirt with some people." DHist, Letson Biography file, transcript of interview with Letson, 27 May 1981. See also Archives of Ontario, Maclean-Hunter Records, box 51, file B-1-2-a, George Drew to Col. J.B. Maclean, 22 February 1938: "the old attitude . . . that the Permanent Force constitute a group of Junior Gods before whom every Non-Permanent officer should bow in awed respect." The PF phrase in rebuttal was "bloody militia."

65 Considering that in 1935 Canada held in all only enough ammunition for ninety minutes fire at Great War rates, five rounds per gun may have been exces-

sive. See Mackenzie Papers, vol. 29, file X-4, "The Defence of Canada," 28 May 1935, and "The Requirements of Canadian Defence," 12 November 1935.

66 *Report of the Department of National Defence for . . . 1940* (Ottawa 1940), 15.

67 Harris, *Canadian Brass*, 196; USNA, RG 165, Military Intelligence Division Correspondence 1917–41, box 1770, item 2694-58, despatch #35559, from Military Attaché, London, 16 April 1934; B. Greenhous, *Dragoon: The Centennial History of the Royal Canadian Dragoons, 1883–1983* (np, 1983), 289. MGen C.B. Ware, a PPCLI officer, remembered that he had never seen half his regiment when war broke out. Interview, 24 February 1992.

68 Harris, *Canadian Brass*, 198; *Report of the Department of National Defence . . . 1939*, 31–2.

69 Spry Papers, "Record of Service."

70 Burns Papers, vol. 6, "Promotion in the Permanent Force," unpublished mss, nd. Compare Sutherland Brown Papers, box 1, file 9, Brown to Brig. T.V. Anderson, 12 October 1929.

71 See generally on the problems this created, H. L'Etang, "Ill Health in Senior Officers," *The Practitioner* 86 (April 1961), 503ff.

72 Information derived from Department of National Defence, *Defence Forces List, November 1939* (Ottawa 1939).

73 See, for example, Mackenzie Papers, vol. 30, file X-40, CGS to Minister, 7 October 1937, 4 June 1938.

74 DND, vol. 6574, file HQ 1230-21, Col. J.S. Brown to Chief of Staff, 7 December 1925.

75 Simonds Papers, CGS box, "M" file, Simonds to MGen R.E.A. Morton, 15 June 1955. For an example of musical chairs, see Mackenzie Papers, vol. 30, file X-40, CGS to Minister, 6 October 1938.

76 Simonds Papers, II Cdn Corps box, Vokes to Simonds, 8 May 1945.

77 Maclean-Hunter Records, box 72, series B-2-2, file Reports, Special Interviews 1942, Ken Wilson interview with Currie, 8 October 1942.

78 D.C. Watt, *How War Came* (London 1989), 450–1.

79 USNA, RG 165, Military Intelligence Division Correspondence 1917–41, box 1769, item 2694-36, "Canadian Trip (June 1926)."

80 The "war has left Canada very indifferent to the cause of Empire . . . the most indifferent men are those who went overseas." House of Lords, London, Lord Beaverbrook Papers, Bennett Scrapbook 10, R.B. Bennett to Beaverbrook, 16 November 1922. See also NA, W.L.M. King Papers, Diary, 16 and 18 December 1936, f. 599, f. 1060; Churchill College, Cambridge, Burgen Bickersteth Papers, 1937 letter, nd [April].

81 But not always. The Elgin Regiment in St Thomas, Ontario, had linotype operators in the mid-1930s as its CO, senior company commander, and adjutant, while junior officers included shopclerks, a farmer, and a hotel manager. See Strome Galloway, *The General Who Never Was* (Belleville, Ont., 1981), 25–6.

82 J.M. Savage, "Some Recollections of the NPAM in the Depression," in Smith, *As You Were!* 1: 382–4.

83 Burns Papers, vol. 6, "Is the Royal Military College Worth What It Costs?"

84 Col. John Page interview, 11 February 1992. This interview was done by Jock Vance, and I am most grateful to him for sharing it with me.

85 Sutherland Brown Papers, box 1, file 10, Lieut.-Col. Harry Coghill to Brown, nd [1930].

86 Senate, *Debates*, 8 June 1936, 428.

87 J.L. Rutledge, "This Soldier Business," *Maclean's*, 15 August 1939, 22.

88 Sutherland Brown Papers, box 1, file 11, Brown to Col. W.W. Foster, 31 December 1932.

89 See on the NPAM generally, T.C. Willett, *A Heritage at Risk: The Canadian Militia as a Social Institution* (Boulder, Col., 1987), 70–2.

90 Brig. H.P. Bell-Irving interview, 4 March 1992.

91 NA, G.W.L. Nicholson Papers, vol. 3, Gunners II drafts file, Simonds' notes on chap. 2.

92 DND, vol. 6506, file HQ 313-33-18, LCol G.R. Pearkes to Col. W.G. Beeman, 23 September 1932; R.H. Roy, *The Seaforth Highlanders of Canada 1919–1965* (Vancouver 1969), 49.

93 Sutherland Brown Papers, box 9, file 195, Militia Orders No. 465-467, 2 October 1929. See on the MSC, Macdonald, "In Search of Veritable," 83ff.

94 DND, vol. 6506, file HQ 313-33-18, "Report of 11th Militia Staff Course, Practical Portion, Lennoxville, PQ, 1932"; ibid., Brig. W.B. Anderson to secretary, DND, 4 September 1929.

95 Ibid., "Militia Staff Course, 1931–32," nd; Roy, *For Most Conspicuous Bravery*, 93–4, 106ff; MGen Bruce Matthews interview, 25 April 1991.

96 C.B. Ware Papers (Victoria), Col. F.B. Ware Scrapbooks, extract from letter from LCol Hugh Niven, June 1936.

97 DND, Mf C5137, file HQS 8151, Brig. C.V. Stockwell to secretary, DND, 26 January 1940. In the planning in 1939 for staff positions for the expeditionary force and for the overseas headquarters, almost no NPAM officers were slotted in. See DHist, 114.1(D3), DMO&I to CGS, 21 September 1939,

and Brig. E.J. Schmidlin to QMG, 12 June 1939. Macdonald, "In Search of Veritable," 87, says 400 NPAM officers had qualified on the Militia Staff Course by 1939.

98 M.B. Watson, "The Advanced Militia Staff Course," *Canadian Defence Quarterly* 16 (October 1938), 68–9; Howard Graham, *Citizen and Soldier: The Memoirs of Lieutenant-General Howard Graham* (Toronto 1987), 103–5. Macdonald, "In Search of Veritable," 87, says twenty-nine NPAM officers qualified on the Advanced Militia Staff Course by 1939.

99 National Defence College, Kingston, A.E. Walford Papers, "Examination for Qualification for the Rank of Colonel N.P.A.M.," nd.

100 Mackenzie Papers, vol. 37, file D-2, Announcement, nd [1936]; ibid., vol. 37, file D13, CGS to Minister, 9 July 1936.

101 See, for example, Sutherland Brown Papers, box 8, file 190, Brown to G.M. Endacott, 6 January 1933; W.A. Morrison, "Major-General A.G.L. McNaughton, the Conference of Defence Associations, and the 1936 N.P.A.M. Re-organization," Canadian Historical Association paper, 1982.

102 *Report of the Department of National Defence for . . . 1940*, 15; *Toronto Star*, 30 June 1939.

103 *Report of the Department . . . 1940*, 27ff, gives details of the last peacetime summer training. The Essex Scottish took 29 officers and 166 men to camp; the Algonquin Regiment, 32 and 221; the Governor General's Foot Guards, 26 and 244; Les Fusiliers Mont-Royal, 25 and 199; the West Nova Scotia Regiment, 32 and 243. With an infantry battalion's establishment at approximately one thousand, the disparities are all too obvious.

104 DND, vol. 2468, file HQS 3498, CGS to Minister, 28 September 1938; ibid., vol. 2646, HQS 3498, Maj.-Gen. E.C. Ashton to CGS, 23 November 1938; Roy, *For Most Conspicuous Bravery*, 49.

105 USNA, Department of State Records, 842.20 MID Reports/5/6, "Canada Combat Estimates," 1 July 1939.

106 C.P. Stacey, *Six Years of War* (Toronto 1955), 35.

CHAPTER 2   THE OLD BRIGADE

1 Eric Larrabee, *Commander in Chief: Franklin Delano Roosevelt, His Lieutenants, and Their War* (New York 1987), 101.

2 E.M. Coffman and P.F. Herrly, "The American Regular Army Officer Corps between the World Wars," *Armed Forces and Society* 4 (fall 1977), 55.

3 D. Clayton James, *A Time for Giants: Politics of the American High Command in World War II* (New York 1987), 52.

4 Guy Simonds Papers (North Gower, Ont.), II Canadian Corps box, unmarked file, Vokes to Simonds, 8 May 1945. There were attempts to change the Canadian system. See DND, vol. 6574, file HQ1230-21, Col. J. Sutherland Brown to Chief of Staff, 7 December 1925. "The primary function of the professional military body between wars is to produce wartime leaders," the American military historian Martin Blumenson wrote. The officer system "is supposed not only to turn up and push ahead the qualified but also to weed out the incapable." "America's World War II Leaders in Europe: Some Thoughts," *Parameters* 4 (December 1989), 4. It is worth noting that in Germany the average age of colonels in 1932 was fifty-six; four years later, after Hitler's coming to power, it was thirty-nine. John Keegan, *The Mask of Command* (New York 1987), 269.

5 Simonds Papers, CGS box, "M" file, Simonds to Gen. R.E.A. Morton, 15 June 1955. On the musical chairs, see, for example, NA, Ian Mackenzie Papers, vol. 30, file X-40, Ashton to Minister, 4 June and 6 October 1938.

6 NA, H.D.G. Crerar Papers, vol. 1, 958C.009 (D13), "Observations on Canadian Requirements in Respect to the Army," nd [June 1940].

7 C.P. Stacey, *Six Years of War* (Ottawa 1955), 415.

8 NA, L.B. Pearson Papers, N8, vol. 1, Diary, 28 October 1939.

9 C.J.V. Murphy, "The First Canadian Army," *Fortune*, January 1944, 164.

10 Trumball Warren interview, 27 May 1991. See also John A. English, *The Canadian Army and the Normandy Campaign: A Study of Failure in High Command* (New York 1991), 135-6.

11 IWM, Trumball Warren Papers, Montgomery to Warren, 25 April 1942.

12 Ibid., 1 June 1942. Montgomery's critique of Price is in NA, A.G.L. McNaughton Papers, vol. 200, file PA 6-9-M4, "Notes on the Command Element in Canadian Corps," 6 March 1942. Terry Copp is critical of Montgomery's approach and judgments. See *The Brigade: The Fifth Canadian Infantry Brigade, 1939–1945* (Stoney Creek, Ont., 1992), 28ff.

13 Crerar Papers, vol. 8, 958C.009(D182), Montgomery's Notes on Beaver IV, 13 May 1942.

14 Warren Papers, Montgomery to Warren, 27 June 1942.

15 Ibid., 27 July 1942.

16 Ibid., 10 August 1942; docs on DHist, H.D.G. Crerar Papers, Price file. "It's probably understandable that some of the British professional soldiers tended to look down on the Canadians," Brig. Stanley Todd, a very able militia artilleryman,

remembered. "They thought we were toy soldiers. They thought we had amazing men with amazing courage, no discipline and stupid officers." Quoted in D. and S. Whitaker, *Dieppe: Tragedy to Triumph* (Toronto 1992), 95. All these officers had their defenders, however, not least George Pearkes, whose biography is R.H. Roy, *For Most Conspicuous Bravery* (Vancouver 1977). Gen. Price's was an especially sad case: on an exercise in 1942 designed in substantial part to test his command capacities, he learned that his son had been killed on RCAF service. Price carried on but scant mercy was shown him. Brig. George Pangman interview, 23 April 1991; Giles Perodeau interview, 24 March 1992. Price himself continued to speak highly of Montgomery. University of Victoria Archives, George Pearkes Papers, Acc. 74-1, box 9, file 2, R.H. Roy interview with Price, 12 June 1966.

17 Crerar Papers, vol. 8, 958C.009 (D182), Montgomery's Notes on Beaver IV, 13 May 1942.

18 Harry Foster Papers (Halifax), Diary, 28 August 1942: "After months of persistent rumours Gen Pearkes today was put on 24 hrs notice to return to Canada. . . . The division was broken hearted. He's too good to do that to — how the big shots hate him — just jealousy." For Gen. Crerar's comments, quite different from Foster's, see Pearson Papers, vol. 3, Crerar file, Crerar to Pearson, 25 April 1942.

19 York University Archives, J.L. Granatstein Papers, Father Mike Dalton Diary, 8 July 1942.

20 Crerar Papers, vol. 8, 958C.009(D182), Montgomery's "Beaver III, Notes on Commanders," 25 April 1942; Copp, *The Brigade*, 31.

21 On Dieppe, see inter alia, Whitaker, *Dieppe*; B. Villa, *Unauthorized Action: Mountbatten and the Dieppe Raid* (Toronto 1989); WO219/1867, "German Report on the Dieppe Raid"; docs on WO106/4197; and Goronwy Rees, *A Bundle of Sensations* (London 1960), 139ff.

22 WO106/4197, Capt. Hughes-Hallett covering letter to his report, 30 August 1942.

23 Crerar Papers, vol. 1, 958C.009 (D23), Crerar to McNaughton, 5 March 1943.

24 Goronwy Rees, "Operation Jubilee," in *Sunday Times*, 28 July 1963.

25 RMC, Christopher Vokes Papers, looseleaf binder, "The Adriatic Front — Winter 1944," 12. See also QUA, C.G. Power Papers, box 77, Trips file, Diary of Mission to U.K. 1942, 16 August 1942. Gen. Crerar told Power that the average age of battalion commanding officers was thirty-nine in 1941 and thirty-two a year later, and that this elimination of the older men had raised morale.

26 J.A. Roberts, *The Canadian Summer: The Memoirs of James Alan Roberts* (Toronto 1981), 72.

27 QUA, J. Sutherland Brown Papers, box 11, file X-246, Anderson to Brown, 30 June 1938. This assessment of the older officers was expressed by many of those interviewed and forcibly by LGen Geoffrey Walsh, 24 May 1991, and Brig. William Ziegler, 23 October 1991.

28 C.L. Shaw, "Canada Calls General Odlum," *Toronto Star Weekly*, 27 April 1940; C.L. Shaw, "Odlum: O.C. 2nd Division," *Maclean's*, 15 May 1940, 10, 65–6. On Odlum's brigade at Vimy, see Michael Boire, "Battle for Hill 145 Vimy Ridge 1917: A Near Run Thing," paper presented at Wilfrid Laurier University Centre for Military and Strategic History Conference, December 1992.

29 Maurice A. Pope, *Letters from the Front 1914–1919* (ed. Joseph Pope, (Toronto 1992), 71.

30 QUA, Norman Rogers Papers, box 2, file 1a 1939, Odlum to Rogers, 1 November 1939.

31 Robert J. Sharpe, *The Last Day, the Last Hour: The Currie Libel Trial* (Toronto 1988), 91.

32 Docs on NPRC, Odlum file.

33 P.W. Luce, "Odlum of the 2nd Division," *Saturday Night*, 13 April 1940, 4.

34 See, for example, NA, Escott Reid Papers, vol. 1, file 1, "Canadian Politics: Notes on Interviews 1930–2," interview with Odlum, 31 August 1931.

35 NA, V.W. Odlum Papers, vol. 26, Odlum to T.V. Scudamore, 11 October 1939.

36 Ibid., Odlum to Col. F.R. Phelan, 10 October 1939.

37 NA, W.L.M. King Papers, Odlum to King, 26 October 1939, f. 233123.

38 Odlum Papers, vol. 1, Odlum–Rogers correspondence, November 1939–March 1940.

39 Ibid., vol. 1, C.W. Peck to King, 18 December 1939. The strength of the "citizen-soldier" myth can be gained from *Winnipeg Free Press* editor John W. Dafoe's dedication to his *Over the Canadian Battlefields* (Toronto 1919): "To General Sir Arthur Currie . . . the civilian commander of the conquering Canadian civilian army."

40 King Diary, 2 April 1940. See also King's account of his conversation with Odlum, ibid., 8 April 1940, ff. 364ff.

41 NA, E.W. Sansom Papers, Sansom to his wife, 6, 7 April 1940.

42 Brig. H.P. Bell-Irving interview, 4 March 1992.

43 See on discussions in the United Kingdom, RMC, W.F.P. Elkins Papers,

MGO file, "Notes on Conference . . . 20 April 1940," and "Notes on Discussion . . . 26 April 1940." See also University of Toronto Archives, Vincent Massey Papers, vol. 310, Diary, 25 April 1940.

44 QUA, Grant Dexter Papers, Memorandum, 31 May 1940.

45 Odlum Papers, vol. 26, Correspondence files, Brig. C.B. Topp to Odlum, 3 July 1940.

46 Stacey, *Six Years of War*, 83ff.

47 CWC, Minutes, 4 July 1940.

48 King Diary, 20 July 1940, f. 723.

49 Odlum Papers, vol. 26, Officers of 2nd Div. file, notebook pages.

50 Ibid., McNaughton correspondence file, Odlum to McNaughton, 7 August 1940; ibid., War Diary file, 7 September 1940.

51 Ibid., docs on Musical bands file.

52 Ibid., McNaughton correspondence file, Odlum to McNaughton, 3 May 1941.

53 Ibid., McNaughton to Odlum, 10 September 1941.

54 Harry Foster Papers, Diary, 13 November 1941.

55 Dr W.J. McAndrew Papers (Ottawa), MGen M.P. Bogert to McAndrew, nd; LCol Don Mingay interview, 6 June 1991; MGen H.A. Sparling interview, 18 April 1991.

56 LHC, Viscount Alanbrooke Papers, file 3/A/IV, "Notes on My Life," 266, 279; NA, A.G.L. McNaughton Papers, vol. 193, file PA 6-1-10, Brooke to McNaughton, 11 September 1941. A senior British officer later told B.H. Liddell Hart that "the older Canadian commanders were rather poor. Odlum had been a joke." LHC, Liddell Hart Papers, 11/1943/36, "Notes for History," 9–10 June 1943.

57 DND, mf C5437, file HQS 20-5-2-2, McNaughton to CGS, 25 September 1941.

58 King Diary, 2 October 1941, f. 884.

59 NA, J.L. Ralston Papers, vol. 64, English Trip — Diary file, entry 14 October 1941. King's letter is in King Papers, ff. 264544–5.

60 King Papers, Odlum to King, 7 December 1941, ff. 264549–52. Compare, ibid., telegram, High Commission to Secretary of State for External Affairs, 26 November 1941, f. 263720.

61 Ibid., Odlum to Mackenzie, 28 May 1942, ff. 282449ff.

62 For example, McNaughton Papers, vol. 229, file CC7/Odlum/18, Odlum to McNaughton, 23 July 1942.

63 King Papers, Odlum to Ottawa, 10, 12 January, and reply, 12 January 1942, ff. 28306ff; CWC Minutes, 14 January 1942. See J.F. Hilliker, "Distant Ally:

Canadian Relations with Australia during the Second World War," *Journal of Imperial and Commonwealth History* 13 (October 1984), 52ff.

64 *New York Times*, 15 January 1942.

65 King Papers, telegrams, Odlum to Ottawa, passim, ff. 282316ff.

66 Ibid., Odlum to King, 21 February 1942, ff. 282360–1, 4 February 1942, ff. 282332–7.

67 CWC, 18 March 1942.

68 Department of External Affairs, Department of External Affairs Records, file 4851-40, Memo to Minister, 22 February 1957. On Odlum's ambassadorship in China, see John W. Holmes, *The Shaping of Peace*, vol. 2: *1943-57* (Toronto 1982), 134–5.

69 NA, J.H. MacBrien Papers, vol. 8, Imperial Conference file, MacBrien to Minister, 23 April 1926.

70 Mrs D.C. Spry interview, 18 March 1992; MGen T.V. Anderson, "The Late Major-General H.F.H. Hertzberg," *The Canadian Sapper*, 28 January 1960.

71 Sutherland Brown Papers, box 8, file 190, Brown to Hertzberg, 5 January 1933, and reply, 20 January 1933.

72 McNaughton Papers, vol. 103, Crerar file, Crerar to McNaughton, 29 July 1928.

73 As DOC in 1937–8, Hertzberg's pay was $5110. DHist, 113.302009(D138), "Vote — Permanent Force."

74 NA, Mackenzie Papers, vol. 30, file X-40, CGS to Minister, 7 October 1937.

75 Thea Hertzberg Gray interview, 12 February 1992; Dagmar Hertzberg Nation interview, 27 February 1992.

76 King Diary, 2 April 1940.

77 Sansom Papers, Sansom to his wife, 7 March 1940.

78 DND, Mf C5252, file HQS 8670, Crerar to Ralston, 4 October 1940.

79 McNaughton Papers, vol. 248, War Diary 1940, McNaughton to Crerar, 3 October 1940. This critical comment was curious indeed, since Hertzberg's daughters remember McNaughton as a close friend of their father's. Gray and Nation interviews.

80 McNaughton Papers, vol. 248, War Diary 1940, McNaughton to Skelton for Ralston, 29 June 1940.

81 *R.M.C. Review* 26 (1945), 16. Compare R.A. Preston, *Canada's RMC: A History of the Royal Military College* (Toronto 1969), 295–6.

82 H.F.H. Hertzberg Papers (Victoria), "Commandant's Address, Graduation," 20 June 1942.

83 Ibid., Hertzberg to his wife, 27 September 1943.

84 Docs on NPRC, Hertzberg file.

85 C.S.L. Hertzberg Papers (Toronto), "Major-General Charles Sumner Lund Hertzberg," nd [a biographical sketch].

86 Ibid., Diary, 28 August 1939.

87 *Toronto Star*, 2 November 1939.

88 C.S.L. Hertzberg Papers, Diary, 22 December 1939.

89 Gen Walsh interview, 24 May 1991.

90 H.F.H. Hertzberg Papers, Hertzberg to his wife, 8 August 1943.

91 Ralston Papers, vol. 37, Age Limits file, Crerar to Minister, 7 October 1941. On age limits, see Stacey, *Six Years of War*, 417–19.

92 McNaughton Papers, vol. 248, War Diary, Memo, 6 January 1942.

93 CWC Documents, Adjutant-General to Minister, 4 May 1943.

94 C.S.L. Hertzberg Diary, 12 June 1943.

95 Crerar Papers, vol. 2, Memo, "Senior Appointments," 11 June 1943.

96 C.S.L. Hertzberg Diary, 1943, passim; R.F. Legget, "The Engineer in War," *Queen's Quarterly* 58 (1951).

97 H.F.H. Hertzberg Papers, Hertzberg to his wife, 4 September 1943.

98 On Sansom's early life and war service, see T.G. Roberts, "A Man from the Nashwak," *Canadian Military Gazette* 56(May 1941), 6–7, and Scott Young, "Sansom Moves Fast," *Maclean's*, 1 June 1943, 16, 53.

99 Brereton Greenhous, *Dragoon: The Centennial History of the Royal Canadian Dragoons, 1883–1983* (Belleville, Ont. 1983), 275–6.

100 Mrs F.F. Worthington interview, 23 May 1991.

101 Sansom Papers, letters to his wife.

102 Ibid., 5 February 1940.

103 Certainly that was the view held by another of McNaughton's key staff officers, Guy Turner. Col. Malcolm Turner interview, 10 October 1990.

104 Sansom Papers, 18 January 1940.

105 Ibid., 26 April 1940.

106 Ibid., 20 February 1940. See Gen Guy Simonds's comments on Pearkes's style and manner in University of Victoria Archives, George Pearkes Papers, Acc. 74-1, vol. 25, file 26, Simonds to R.H. Roy, 29 December 1972.

107 Sansom Papers, 29 February 1940.

108 Ibid., 18 March, 7 April 1940. In fact, Sansom received no pay increase and had to get an advance on his pay to cover his expenses. Ibid., 5 May 1940.

109 Ibid., 11 April 1940.

110 *Toronto Star*, 13 April 1940.

111 See Stacey, *Six Years of War*, 258ff.

112 DND, Mf C5252, file HQS 8670, Crerar to Minister, 4 October 1940.

113 Stacey, *Six Years of War*, 84ff. A GOC's salary overseas in 1942 was $8760 yearly plus allowances that could bring the pay to a maximum of $10,863. By contrast, a private's pay on enlistment was $1.30 a day, rising after six months service to $1.50 a day or $547.50 a year. Ralston Papers, vol. 71, Pay Rates file, chart; vol. 75, Memo, Paymaster-General to ADM, 6 May 1943.

114 Fred Cederberg, *The Long Road Home* (Toronto 1989), 27.

115 Pearson Papers, vol. 3, Crerar file, Crerar to Pearson, 25 April 1942.

116 DND, Mf C5438, file HQS 20-5-26-2, McNaughton to Stuart, 17 November 1942.

117 L.S.B. Shapiro, "Canada's Fourth Soldier," *Saturday Night*, 27 March 1943, 8.

118 WO106/4226, "Comments by Commander-in-Chief Home Forces," March 1943.

119 Liddell Hart Papers, 11/1943/9, "Main Impressions of the 'Spartan' Exercise, March 1–12, 1943."

120 Docs on DHist, H.D.G. Crerar Papers, Sansom file; McNaughton Papers, vol. 132, file PA 1-3-2, Memorandum of McNaughton-Brooke conversation, 8 April 1943. See also John Swettenham, *McNaughton*, vol. 2: *1939–1942* (Toronto 1969), 283–4.

121 McNaughton Papers, vol. 202, file PA 6-9-5-2, pen note, 29 July 1943. After further exercises, McNaughton discussed Sansom with the CIGS, Gen. Brooke, and was told that Paget thought he was not up to commanding a corps. McNaughton's reply was that he "was not prepared to accept General Paget's views." Ibid., vol. 198, file PA 6-9-C-9, McNaughton memo of conference with Brooke, 14 September 1943. In November, McNaughton told Col. Ralston that Sansom had "done better," but Ralston added that "Paget felt this was not the case." Public Archives of Nova Scotia, A.L. Macdonald Papers, file F386/12, Ralston's diary notes, 8 November 1943.

122 Ralston Papers, vol. 54, undated [spring 1943] comments on senior officers.

123 LGen Robert Moncel interview, 6 October 1991.

124 MGen M.P. Bogert interview, 8 September 1991.

125 Confidential source.

126 DND, vol. 10033, file 9/Sr Appts/1/2, Montague to Warren, 5 January

1944. A memo,"Changes in Senior Appointments since December 27, 1943," in the Ralston Papers, vol. 37, Appointments Overseas file, notes that the Chief of Staff, CMHQ, the army commander, two corps commanders, and three division commanders had all recently been changed. Sansom was in good company.

127 DND, vol. 10033, file 9/Sr Appts/1/2, Stuart to Ralston and Murchie, 7 January 1944.

128 Ibid., Montague to Minister, 5 January, and Stuart to Ralston, 7 January 1944. The public relations officer at CMHQ noted that any explanation for Sansom's replacement "based on ill-health is likely to be received with considerable scepticism in view of the fact that this was the reason advanced so recently to explain the change of command at First Canadian Army." Ibid., Abel to BGS, 10 January 1944.

129 Massey Papers, box 312, Diary, 31 January 1944. Montgomery had told McNaughton in Sicily on 24 August 1943. McNaughton Papers, vol. 134, file PA 1-3-14-2, McNaughton memo "Visit to General Sir Bernard Montgomery," 1 September 1943.

130 DND, vol. 10033, file 9/Sr Appts/1/2, telegram, Stuart to Ralston, 7 January 1944.

131 Crerar Papers, vol. 8, 958C.009(D168), McNaughton-Crerar telegrams, 4 and 19 November 1944.

132 See C.P. Stacey, *Arms, Men and Governments: The War Policies of Canada 1939–1945* (Ottawa 1970), 468ff.

133 Pearkes Papers, Acc. 74-1, vol. 25, file 17, Sansom to R.H. Roy, 9 December 1971. See also Roy, *For Most Conspicuous Bravery*, 227ff.

134 Macdonald Papers, vol. 1500, file 292/15, Sansom to McNaughton, 20 March 1945; Crerar Papers, vol. 29, "Report on Survey of Reinforcement Situation — Canadian Army Overseas," 29 March 1945; Stacey, *Arms, Men and Governments*, 480. The account in Swettenham, *McNaughton*, vol. 3: *1944–1966*, 66, 69, is incorrect.

135 CWC Minutes, 22 March, 11 April 1945.

136 Pearkes Papers, vol. 25, file 17, Sansom to Roy, 15 January 1970.

CHAPTER 3 McNAUGHTON: THE GOD THAT FAILED

1 MGen J.D.B. Smith interview, 14 September 1991.

2 NA, E.W. Sansom Papers, Sansom to his wife, 29 January 1940.

3 "I wish that our commanders had the terrific energy of McNaughton." R. Macleod and D. Kelly, eds., *The Ironside Diaries 1937–1940* (London 1962), 242.

4 USAMHI, Gen. R.E. Lee Papers, London Journal, 13 October 1940. Lee's diary has been published, heavily edited: J. Leutze, ed., *The London Journal of General Raymond E. Lee 1940–1941* (Boston 1971).

5 Lee Papers, 16 May 1941.

6 Ibid., 1 September 1941.

7 NA, W.L.M. King Papers, Diary, 21 June 1941; LHC, Viscount Alanbrooke Papers, file 3/A/VI, Notes on My Life, 9, 25 July 1943 and file 3/A/VII, Notes on My Life, 23, 24 September 1942. See also J. Barnes and D. Nicholson, eds., *The Empire at Bay: The Leo Amery Diaries 1929–45* (London 1988), 812.

8 Alanbrooke Papers, file 3/A/VII, Notes on My Life, 24 September 1942.

9 McGill University Archives, A.G.L. McNaughton Papers, RSC lecture 1913, CSCE lecture 1912.

10 John Swettenham, *McNaughton,* vol. 1: *1887–1939* (Toronto 1968), chap. 1.

11 Docs on NPRC, McNaughton file.

12 McGill, McNaughton Papers, COTC lecture 1913.

13 A.G.L. McNaughton, "The Capture of Valenciennes," *Canadian Defence Quarterly* 10 (April 1933), 279. On McNaughton's artillery role, see Bill Rawling, *Surviving Trench Warfare: Technology and the Canadian Corps, 1914–1918* (Toronto 1992), 93ff, 111–12, 190.

14 John A. English, *The Canadian Army and the Normandy Campaign: A Study of Failure in High Command* (New York 1991), 18.

15 NPRC, McNaughton file, Confidential Report, nd [1919?].

16 NA, Sir Arthur Currie Papers, vol. 11, file 34, Currie to MacBrien, 13 December 1919, 15 March 1920.

17 NPRC, McNaughton file, Confidential Report, 21 December 1921.

18 Ibid., Confidential Report, January 1924.

19 NA, J.H. MacBrien Papers, vol. 8, Imperial Conference 1926 file, MacBrien to Minister, 23 April 1926.

20 NPRC, McNaughton file, Confidential Report, 12 December 1927. The Canadian government had also noticed his reliability on imperial questions. See King Papers, memo to King, 19 May 1927, f. 122882.

21 G/C V.C.H. Stuart interview, 31 January 1991.

22 See NA, A.G.L. McNaughton Papers, vol. 111, Ralston file, Ralston to McNaughton, 18 November 1928, and reply, 25 November 1928. (Unless otherwise stated, all references to the McNaughton Papers are to those in NA.)

23 Ibid., vol. 109, McNaughton to MacBrien, 13 March 1923.

24 Ibid., vol. 103, Crerar file, McNaughton to Crerar, 27 August 1928; NA,

H.D.G. Crerar Papers, vol. 22, file 958C.009 (D380), Crerar to McNaughton, nd, and reply, 13 July 1931.

25 McNaughton Papers, vol. 347, Address to Canadian Military Institute, Toronto, 2 May 1929.

26 Confidential source.

27 Stephen Harris, *Canadian Brass: The Making of a Professional Army 1860–1939* (Toronto 1988), 156.

28 See W. Alex Morrison, "Major-General A.G.L. McNaughton, the Conference of Defence Associations and the 1936 N.P.A.M. Reorganization," Canadian Historical Association paper, 1982.

29 QUA, J. Sutherland Brown Papers, box 1, file 9, Brown to W.G. Beeman, 24 April 1930. On Sutherland Brown see Charles Taylor, *Six Journeys* (Toronto 1977), 1ff, and R.C. Gimblett, "'Buster' Brown: The Man and His Clash with 'Andy' McNaughton" (BA thesis, Royal Military College 1979), 45ff. Before these incidents, the McNaughtons and Browns had been very friendly. Malcolm and Athol Sutherland-Brown interviews, 27 February 1992.

30 Sutherland Brown Papers, box 2, file 31, Brown to MacBrien, 29 August 1930. Brown's views, much less colourfully phrased, were frequently offered by many of those interviewed for this book as descriptive of McNaughton's wartime career.

31 Ibid., box 1, file 11, Brown to W.W. Foster, 31 December 1932.

32 C.J. Frowde, "Chief of Staff: The Personality of Major-General McNaughton," *Saturday Night*, 26 December 1931. See McNaughton's "Modern Machines and Weapons of Land-Warfare with an Historical Introduction," *Royal Canadian Military Institute Selected Papers 1931–32* (Toronto, nd), 54ff. For a critique of McNaughton's approach, see English, *Canadian Army*, 45ff.

33 See on the camps, Pierre Berton, *The Great Depression 1929–39* (Toronto 1990), 156ff, 266–7, 299ff.

34 PRO, Cabinet Records, Cab 63/81, Hankey to Sir G. Pearce, 2 January 1935; ibid., Hankey's "Impressions of Canadian Defence Policy — December 1934."

35 Archives of Ontario, Maclean-Hunter Records, box 51, file B-1-2-a, George Drew to Maclean, 22 February 1938: "Bennett kicked him upstairs . . . because he was fearful of the criticism by radical elements of the work done under McNaughton . . . under the unemployment relief scheme."

36 McNaughton Papers, vol. 100, Bennett file, Memoranda, 27, 28 May 1935.

37 Ibid., vol. 107, Transfer of CGS file, PC 1481, 1 June 1935. The salary and pension arrangements drew criticism in Parliament: House of Commons, *Debates*, 4 March 1936, 759; 22 February 1937, 946. See also English, *Canadian Army*, 39-40.

38 Crerar Papers, vol. 10, 958C.009 (D211), Crerar to R.H. Haining, 5 June 1935.

39 Swettenham, *McNaughton*, 220ff.

40 McGill, McNaughton Papers, "Aeroplane Location . . ." 1926–30.

41 "Trajectory Chart," supplement to *Canadian Artillery Summary* 1937; "Auto Sights," June 1939, with R.H. Field. On use of the "McNaughton Graph for Air Burst Ranging," see RMC, W.H.P. Elkins Papers, Semi-Official Correspondence file, LCol Ellis to Elkins, 28 August 1941. On complaints about complexity, see NA, G.W.L. Nicholson Papers, vol. 3, Gunners II draft chapter 3 file, C. Harrington to Nicholson, 7 June 1968; W. Simcock to Nicholson, 18 April 1968.

42 King Papers, "Report from Canadian Manufacturers Assn Delegation to United Kingdom," 5 September 1939, ff. C154961ff.

43 Confidential interview.

44 McNaughton Papers, vol. 116, Drew file, McNaughton to Chalmers, 17 March 1938; to Drew, 8 April 1938. See also Harris, *Canadian Brass*, 158.

45 King Papers, McNaughton to King, 3 September 1939, f. 231052.

46 King Diary, 22 September 1939, f. 1077.

47 McNaughton Papers, vol. 241, Offer of service file, Memo, 5 October 1939; QUA, Norman Rogers Papers, "Conversations with Major-General McNaughton regarding his acceptance of Command. . ." 4 October 1939; King Diary, 5 October 1939, f. 1120.

48 King Diary, 6 October 1939, f. 1123ff. See Douglas LePan, *Bright Glass of Memory* (Toronto 1979), 18.

49 King Diary, 7 December 1939, ff. 1294–5.

50 *Winnipeg Free Press*, 9 October 1939.

51 LePan, *Bright Glass of Memory*, 16.

52 Col. J.A. Calder interview, 4 May 1992.

53 Sansom Papers, Sansom to his wife, 11 February 1940.

54 Ibid., 18 January 1940.

55 CWC Minutes, 12 February 1940; *DCER*, VII, 740ff.

56 Sansom Papers, Sansom to his wife, 29 February, 3 March 1940. This was a constant concern. See, for example, Crerar Papers, vol. 19, 958C.009(D338), Crerar to Burns, 24 May 1941; ibid., 958C.009 (D333), Burns to Crerar, 16 July 1941; NA, L.B. Pearson Papers, N1, vol. 3., Crerar file, Pearson to Crerar, 13 August 1940.

57 LHC, Gen. Richard Dewing Diaries, 16 April 1940.

58 *DCER*, VII, 754; Rogers Papers, box 8, file III Department Papers, "Record of Visit to United Kingdom . . . " 18–20 April 1940.

59 Sansom Papers, Sansom to his wife, 26 April 1940.

60 Harry Foster Papers (Halifax), Diary, 23 May 1940.

61 University of Toronto Archives, Vincent Massey Papers, box 310, Diary, 24 May 1940. On the strain, see Gen. Nye's comments to Col. Ralston in Public Archives of Nova Scotia, Angus L. Macdonald Papers, vol. 1503, F386/115, Ralston Diary notes, 18 December 1943.

62 *DCER*, VII, 774–5.

63 University of Victoria Archives, George Pearkes Papers, Acc. 74-1, vol. 11, file 3, Minutes of Conference held at HQ 1 Cdn Div, 9 June 1940.

64 McNaughton's account of some of these events is in McNaughton Papers, vol. 197, file PA6-9-C-4, Memo, 6 August 1940.

65 Ibid. vol. 226, file CC7/1, Notes by Senior Officer, 26–27 June 1940; Cabinet War Committee Minutes, 11 July 1940. His pay at this point was $14,000 a year inclusive of all allowances. NPRC, McNaughton file, PC 34/5923, 23 October 1940.

66 A sense of the coverage on McNaughton can be gleaned at the Toronto Reference Library, where the file of clippings on his wartime career is extensive and includes articles such as Greg Clark, "McNaughton a Miracle Man," *Star Weekly*, 9 May 1942.

67 Brig. E.W. Haldenby, "A Battalion Commander's Experience in the First Year of the War," *The Empire Club of Canada, Addresses . . . 1940–1* (Toronto 1941), 126.

68 McNaughton Papers, vol. 248, War Diary 1940, telegram, McNaughton to Ralston, 29 June 1940; ibid., vol. 227, file CC7/Crerar/6, Crerar to McNaughton, 16 July 1940.

69 This naturally enough upset Vincent Massey, the High Commissioner, who was as vain as McNaughton and as concerned about status. See, for example, Massey's diary entry of a conversation with Toronto publisher George McCullagh: Massey Papers, box 311, 16 April 1943, and LePan, *Bright Glass of Memory*, 24–5.

70 DND, vol. 10431, file 210.051 (D1), "Memorandum on 'Victor' Exercise, January 1941," 24 May 1941; C.P. Stacey, *A Date with History* (Toronto 1983), 74–6.

71 McNaughton Papers, vol. 252, War Orders file, McNaughton to Brooke, 1 February 1941, and reply, 5 February 1941.

72 Alanbrooke Papers, file 3/A/IV, Notes on My Life, 252. See on McNaughton's constitution-mindedness, Peter Kasurak, "Pawn in the Game of National Politics," *Canadian Defence Quarterly* 5 (winter 1975), 43. On Brooke, see David Fraser, *Alanbrooke* (New York 1982).

73 Alanbrooke Papers, file 3/A/IV, Notes on My Life, 266, 279. Brooke told the same thing to Col. Ralston on 12 November 1943. Macdonald Papers, vol. 1503, F386/15, Ralston Diary notes. The best critique of McNaughton as a trainer is English, *Canadian Army*, 79–80 and 107ff.

74 Crerar Papers, vol. 19, 958.C009 (D333), Burns to Crerar, 7 May, 16 July 1941. For comment on one exercise, "Fox," in 1941, see R.H. Roy, *For Most Conspicuous Bravery: A Biography of Major-General George R. Pearkes* (Vancouver 1977), 162–3.

75 Guy Simonds Papers (North Gower, Ont.), 1945–9 box, loose files, Memo, BGS to Army Commander, 12 December 1941.

76 McNaughton Papers, vol. 193, file PA 6-1-9, Medical report, 31 October 1941; Crerar Papers, vol. 19, file 958C.009 (D333), Crerar to Col. D. White, 21 November 1943; CWC Minutes, 6 November 1941. For a novelist's look at McNaughton, see Earle Birney, *Turvey* (Toronto 1976), 79.

77 Col. G.S. Currie Papers (Ottawa), Diary, 6 April 1944, conversation with Crerar. There is a typed version of this diary, with some important alterations, in NA, J.L. Ralston Papers, vol. 43, Currie Overseas Trip 1944 file. A contemporary if guarded comment on Crerar's view of the state of training is in Pearson Papers, vol. 3, Crerar file, Crerar to Pearson, 25 April 1942.

78 Nigel Hamilton, *Monty*, vol. 1: *The Making of a General 1887–1942* (London 1987), 480.

79 For example, McNaughton Papers, vol. 200, Montgomery's "Notes on Beaver IV," 13 May 1942; "Notes on the Command Element in the Canadian Corps," 6 March 1942. See also Montgomery's blunt comments on the Canadian commanders in his letters in IWM, Trumball Warren Papers, and Hamilton, *Monty*, 474ff.

80 McNaughton Papers, vol. 200, McNaughton to Montgomery, 26 May 1942.

81 Warren Papers, Montgomery to Warren, 27 June 1942.

82 LHC, Liddell Hart Papers, file 11/1942/101, "Notes for History," 25 November 1942.

83 This is C.S.A. Ritchie's phrase (interview, 9 June 1971). Ritchie served at the Canadian High Commission in London during the war.

84 Ralston Papers, vol. 54, Notes on Senior Officers, nd. This is confirmed by interviews: for example, MGen Elliot Rodger, 21 May 1991; MGen M.P. Bogert, 8 September 1991.

85 Pearkes Papers, Acc. 74-1, vol. 25, file 66, Simonds to R.H. Roy, 9 December 1972.

86 This is a constant refrain in the interviews done for this book. See also Massey Papers, vol. 311, Diary, 27 August 1943.

87 Pearkes Papers, vol. 25, file 66, Simonds to Roy, 9 December 1972; Roy, *For Most Conspicuous Bravery*, 165. Again, this is confirmed by many interviews: for example, MGen Elliot Rodger; LGen Geoffrey Walsh, 24 May 1991.

88 Terry Copp interview with LGen W.A.B. Anderson, May 1987.

89 Bogert interview; BGen R.T. Bennett interview, 22 May 1991; MGen Bruce Matthews interviews, 25 April, 10 June 1991.

90 "Canada's McNaughton," *Observer*, 20 September 1942. See Wallace Reyburn, "General in Battle Dress," *Maclean's*, 15 February 1943, 38. McNaughton's gadgets included flamethrowers mounted on Bren Gun carriers. See "Flame Warfare," *Canadian Military Gazette* 60 (August 1945), 24ff.

91 Massey Papers, vol. 311, Diary, 17 September 1942. McNaughton's papers (file PA9-M-1) contain his voluminous correspondence with Dr C.J. Mackenzie, head of the National Research Council, on scientific questions.

92 Brig. G.E. Beament interview, 24 May 1991.

93 McNaughton Papers, vol. 182, file PA 5-3-2, Brooke to McNaughton, 7 January 1942.

94 Macdonald Papers, vol. 1503, file F386/4, Ralston diary notes, 30 July 1943. This squares exactly with Gen. Harry Letson's view. DHist, Letson Biography file, Interview transcript, 27 May 1981.

95 Prem 3/406, Cherwell to Churchill, 21 April 1943; Simonds Papers, Prewar box, *The Advance Post*, 1–13 March 1943.

96 Alanbrooke Papers, file 3/A/VIII, Notes on My Life, 653; Macdonald Papers, vol. 1503, F386/6, Ralston Diary, 3 August 1943; Massey Papers, box 311, Diary, 14 July 1943. The best defence of McNaughton's performance on Spartan is in Swettenham, *McNaughton*, vol. 2 (Toronto 1969), chap. 10.

97 WO 106/4226, "Comments by C-in-C Home Forces," March 1943. Liddell Hart was equally critical. Liddell Hart Papers, file 11/1943/9, "Main Impressions of the 'Spartan' Exercise, March 1–12, 1943"; he changed his mind later. Ibid., LH2/M, McNaughton obituary, 16 August 1966. McNaughton's corps commanders, or at least LGen E.W. Sansom of II Canadian Corps, took much of the blame for the Spartan errors, but, as Gen. Pearkes commented later with some bitterness, "these were McNaughton's appointments." Pearkes Papers, Acc. 74-1, vol. 13, f. 28, Comments on Swettenham's *McNaughton* by Gen. Pearkes, nd. Word of the harsh critique of McNaughton reached both diplomats and the Combined Chiefs of Staff in Washington (see NA, Maurice

Pope Papers, War Diary, 16 June 1943) and Ottawa (see King Diary, 10 July 1943, f. 533).

98 McNaughton Papers, vol. 160, file PA 4-2-1Q, Simonds to GOC-in-C, 29 April 1943.

99 The War Office had been concerned to find employment for the Canadian divisions at least since November 1940. See WO 106/4872, "Possible Employment for Canadian Forces," 25 November 1940.

100 Alanbrooke Papers, file 3/A/VII, Notes on My Life, 15 October 1942.

101 McNaughton Papers, vol. 132, file PA 1-3-2, McNaughton to Stuart, 31 March 1942. The month before, Stuart had pressed Clement Attlee, the UK Deputy Prime Minister, with the necessity to get Canadians into action. Prem 3/83/1, Attlee to Churchill, 8 February, and reply, 12 February 1943.

102 McNaughton Papers, vol. 227, file CC7/Crerar/6, Crerar to McNaughton, 19 May 1941.

103 King Diary, 20 May 1941, f. 410.

104 IWM, F.M. Harding Papers, Montgomery to Harding, 2 December 1943.

105 C.P. Stacey, "Canadian Leaders of the Second World War," *Canadian Historical Review* 66 (1985), 67.

106 C.P. Stacey, *Arms, Men and Governments: The War Policies of Canada 1939–1945* (Ottawa 1970), chap. 5; Swettenham, *McNaughton*, 2: *1939–1943*, chaps. 9–10.

107 This caused some substantial inconvenience to the War Office. See docs on WO 216/163, Alanbrooke Papers, file 3/A/VIII, Notes on My Life, 23 April 1943, and McNaughton Papers, vol. 132, file PA 1-3-2, Memorandum of Discussion, McNaughton–Brooke, 23 April 1943.

108 See PRO, Cabinet Records, Cab 65/39, WM(43), 117th Conclusion, Minute 2, Confidential Annex, 19 August 1943; docs on Prem 3/83/3; and docs on WO 214/55.

109 King Diary, 10 August 1943, f. 625.

110 On the final decision to send the corps to Italy: King Diary, 8 October 1943, ff. 890a ff. McNaughton had not always been consistent in his opposition to sending the corps. If it were returned to Britain in time to take part in "major operations based on U.K." that would be satisfactory. Macdonald Papers, vol. 1503, F386/8, Ralston Diary, 5 August 1943. The GOC-in-C's memos of his meetings with Ralston in August 1943 are in McNaughton Papers, vol. 182, file PA 5-3-1.

111 Prem 3/83/6, Athlone to Churchill, 4 September 1943.

112 Macdonald Papers, vol. 1503, F386/45, "Substance of Conversations between ... Brooke ... and ... Stuart ..." 13 November 1943. In Ralston Papers, vol. 66, "Overseas Trips — Record of Diary Excerpts file," "Draft," nd, Ralston says Brooke spoke to him in Washington about McNaughton.

113 Stuart proposed this to Col. Ralston on 29 July 1943 in the United Kingdom. NA, Kenneth Stuart Papers, vol. 1, CMHQ War Reinforcements file, "Employment of Canadian Army in the Mediterranean," nd.

114 Alanbrooke Papers, file 3/A/IX, Notes on My Life; Macdonald Papers, vol. 1503, F386/6, Ralston diary, 3 August 1943. Even the Governor General, Athlone, got into the act telegraphing Churchill about "a job in research in England" for McNaughton (Prem 3/83/6, 29 August 1943). That suggested how widespread the governmental concern about McNaughton was in Canada.

115 Massey Papers, box 311, Diary, 14 July 1943.

116 King Diary, 10 July 1943, f. 533.

117 Ibid., f. 626. Copies of Ralston's diary notes of his conversations in Britain in July–August 1943 are in Macdonald Papers, vol. 1503, F386/3-9. See for the "die is cast" reference, F386/8, 5 August 1943.

118 King Diary, 14 August 1943, f. 645.

119 Ibid., f. 647.

120 McNaughton Papers, vol. 134, file PA 1-3-14-7, "Report of Visit to North Africa 6–20 July 1943," 22 July 1943.

121 WO 214/55, Viscount Alexander Papers, Alexander to Montgomery, 16 July 1943.

122 Montgomery of Alamein, *The Memoirs of Field Marshal Montgomery* (London 1958), 184. See on this incident Carlo D'Este, *Bitter Victory* (London 1988), app. L, 614ff.

123 Alexander Papers, Alexander–Brooke telegrams, 18, 19, 22 July 1943; Alanbrooke Papers, file 3/A/IX, Notes on My Life, 21 July 1943.

124 Ibid. McNaughton's account of his interview with Brooke is in McNaughton Papers, vol. 134, file PA 1-3-14.

125 Eisenhower Library, D.D. Eisenhower Pre-Presidential Papers, box 167, Butcher Diary, 18 July 1943. See also ibid., W. Bedell Smith Papers, box 7, Chief of Staff Personal Papers, 1942–4, Smith to Gen Sir K. Anderson, 23 August 1943. McNaughton blamed Montgomery for the rebuff, and his relations with him, after one further meeting, ceased. See his sarcastic memo of their meeting in Sicily, 24–25 August 1943, in McNaughton Papers, vol. 134, file PA 1-3-14. Montgomery noted that "he never spoke to me again." Warren Papers, Montgomery to Warren, 1 January 1969.

126 IWM, Viscount Montgomery Papers, file BLM 1/101, Brooke to Montgomery, 29 September 1943.

127 Ralston Papers, vol. 45, Employment of Canadian Army file, "Substance of Conversation . . . November 5, 1943"; "Substance of Conversation . . . November 6th, 1943." Brooke's diary (Alanbrooke Papers, file 3/A/X, Notes on My Life) has the meeting with the Canadians on 8 November 1943.

128 Ralston Papers, vol. 45, Employment of Canadian Troops file, "Substance of Conversation . . . Nov. 8, 1943."

129 Ibid., "The Minister, General McNaughton and General Stuart . . . Nov. 8, 1943." McNaughton's memoranda of his talks with Ralston and Stuart are in McNaughton Papers, vol. 167, file PA 5-0-3-2.

130 Massey Papers box 312, Diary, 9 November 1943.

131 Alanbrooke Papers, file 3/A/X, Notes on My Life, 12 November 1943. The Governor General's chief aide, Sir Shuldham Redfern, after reading all the correspondence, noted: "It appears to me that almost all the blame for this unfortunate matter rests with the English Generals" who ought to have acted sooner about their doubts of McNaughton. NA, Governor General's Records, Acc. 1988-89/081, box 23, file 195-C-1, Note, 16 February 1944.

132 King Diary, 28 October 1943, ff. 949–50.

133 These brief statements are based on a mass of documentation: docs on Ralston Papers, vol. 52, McNaughton resignation file; Massey Papers, vol. 311, Diary, 10 November 1943 ff; DHist, 312.009 (D60), High Level Correspondence of Stuart re McNaughton, 10 November 1943 ff; QUA, C.G. Power Papers, "Memorandum re Ralston–McNaughton Incident," 16 November 1943; docs on McNaughton Papers, vol. 167, file PA 5-0-3-2; Macdonald Papers, vol. 1503, F386/10-118; King Diary, November–December 1943. The defence of McNaughton is presented in Swettenham, *McNaughton*, vol. 2, chap 10. A medical report is in DHist, H.D.G. Crerar Papers. McNaughton file, 26 November 1943. McNaughton's retirement statement to the troops and Mackenzie King's announcement, both dated 27 December 1943, are in DHist, McNaughton biographical file.

134 Macdonald Papers, vol. 1503, F386/12, telegram, CIGS to Vice CIGS, 16 December 1943; Ralston Papers, vol. 52, McNaughton resignation file, telegram, Ralston to Prime Minister, 18 December 1943, and ibid., "Alternative Courses . . ." 12 December 1943.

135 McNaughton Papers, vol. 167, file PA5-0-3-2, Memorandum of Discussion with . . .Stuart . . . 25 November 1943"; NA, Georges Vanier Papers, vol. 13, file 13-14, Memo, "Spearhead in Europe," 16 December 1943.

136 Rodger interview.

137 Massey Papers, box 312, Diary, 20 January 1944; Alanbrooke Papers, file 3/B/XI, Notes on My Life, 20 January 1944.

138 King Diary, 7 February 1944, f. 130.

139 King Papers, ff. C212127ff; Power Papers, vol. 1, Black Binder, Ralston Statement, nd.

140 Confidential source; Massey Papers, vol. 312, Diary, 8 March 1944; *Time*, 28 February 1944, 24. In DHist, McNaughton biographical file, there is a collection of press clippings and editorials on McNaughton's return to Canada in February 1944.

141 DHist, 312.009(D52), Ralston to Stuart, 25 June 1944.

142 Docs on McNaughton Papers, vol. 267, Progressive Conservative Party file.

143 Ibid., Memorandum, 13 October 1944.

144 J.L. Granatstein, *The Politics of Survival: The Conservative Party of Canada 1939–1945* (Toronto 1967), 176ff.

145 McNaughton Papers, vol. 266, Drew file, Note, nd [received 17 November 1944]; Hon. R.A. Bell interview, 17 August 1973.

146 Gen. A.G.L. McNaughton interview, 23 March 1966; King Papers, J17, vol. 6, file 8, R. MacGregor Dawson interview with Gen. Murchie, 21 January 1953. See also Swettenham, *McNaughton*, vol. 3 (Toronto 1969), chap. 2.

147 Gen. J.C. Murchie, the former CGS, expressed his view of this period in a letter to Angus L. Macdonald in Macdonald Papers, F379/43A, 15 March 1950.

148 Pearson Papers, vol. 10, Montague file, Pearson to Gen. Montague, 15 December 1944. See also Swettenham, *McNaughton*, vol. 3, chap. 3.

149 LHC, Gen. Lord Ismay Papers, file V/B17/1a, Burgen Bickersteth to Ismay, 1 June 1945; King Papers, J17, vol. 6, file 8, R. MacGregror Dawson interview with Gen. A.E. Walford, 2 February 1953; Harvie Walford interview, 4 May 1992.

150 Massey Papers, box 312, Diary, 6 November 1944.

151 Pope Papers, vol. 1, Diary, 18 November 1944.

152 Prem 3/83/6, Churchill to King, 7 February, and reply, 10 February 1945; Alanbrooke Papers, file 3/B/XV, Notes on My Life, 19 March 1945.

153 Granatstein, *Politics of Survival*, 183ff.

154 For example, Hon. D.C. Abbott interview, 29 October 1971; Farley Mowat, *The Regiment* (Toronto 1955), 246–7; LePan, *Bright Glass of Memory*, 49–50.

155 McNaughton Papers, vol. 267, King file, handwritten memo, 17 June 1945.

CHAPTER 4 CRERAR: AMBITION REALIZED

1 A PhD dissertation covering Crerar's prewar and wartime role by Paul Dickson was completed in January 1993 at the University of Guelph.

2 Stephen Leacock, "Generals I Have Trained," *R.M.C. Review* 40 (1959), 156 (reprinted from *Last Leaves*, 1945).

3 *R.M.C. Review* 2 (November 1921), 59.

4 RMC, Registrar's Records, Crerar entry; RMC, Central Registry Records, Crerar file; NA, H.D.G. Crerar Papers, vol. 19, 958C.009(D338), Crerar to O'Leary, 1 August 1940.

5 RMC, Royal Military College Club of Canada, Crerar Record Sheets; Crerar Papers, vol. 19, 958C.009 (D338), Crerar to O'Leary, 1 August 1940.

6 RMC, Royal Military College Club of Canada, Crerar Record Sheets; Crerar Papers, vol. 20, 958C.009 (D313), Crerar to LGen Sir Otto Lund, 17 October 1952; LHC, Viscount Alanbrooke Papers, file 3/A/I, Notes on My Life, 62.

7 NPRC, Crerar file, Confidential report, nd.

8 A.J. Crerar obituary in *R.M.C. Review* 32 (1951).

9 For example, NA, A.G.L. McNaughton Papers, vol. 103, Crerar file, Crerar to McNaughton, 29 July 1928, and reply, 27 August 1928.

10 Crerar earned the enmity of the Royal Canadian Horse Artillery for proposing that its name be dropped. See G.W.L. Nicholson, *The Gunners of Canada*, vol. 2 (Toronto 1972), 9–10.

11 Crerar's Staff College notes and papers are in RMC, H.D.G. Crerar Papers, Vertical File.

12 Ibid., Scrapbook, Jack Mosher, "General Crerar Says," clipping, nd [1942].

13 NPRC, Crerar file, Annual Confidential Report, 30 November 1926; Crerar Papers, vol. 19, 958C.009(D338), Crerar to O'Leary, 1 August 1940.

14 *Canadian Defence Quarterly* 3 (October 1925), 71ff. Crerar also passed tests as an interpreter in French, something necessary both in Canada and overseas in an Allied force. His skill, however, was never better than "Diefenbaker French," or so one of his ADCs recalled. LGen Henri Tellier interview, 22 May 1991.

15 *The Journal of the Royal United Services Institute* 71 (August 1926), 441ff, and *Canadian Defence Quarterly* 3 (July 1926), 423ff; NA, W.L.M. King Papers, Memorandum, 19 May 1927, f. 122882.

16 Crerar's confidential reports for his regimental and RMC duties are in his NPRC file. See also MGen H.A. Sparling interview, 18 April 1991.

17 Crerar Papers, vol. 19, 958C.009(D338), Crerar to O'Leary, 1 August 1940.

18 QUA, J. Sutherland Brown Papers, box 2, file 19, T.V. Anderson to Brown, 10 April 1929.

19 Mrs Margaret Crerar Palmer interview, 9 April 1991.

20 Sutherland Brown Papers, box 1, file 11, Brown to W.W. Foster, 31 December 1932, pronounced Crerar "a very nice fellow . . . very susceptible to gunner influence." See Stephen Harris, "Or There Would Be Chaos: The Legacy of Sam Hughes and Military Planning in Canada, 1919–1939," *Military Affairs* 46 (October 1982), 123.

21 Docs on Crerar Papers, vol. 9, 958C.009(D215).

22 DND, vol. 2693, file HQS 5195-A, "Appreciation of Canada's Obligations with Respect to the Maintenance of Neutrality, in Event of a War between the United States of America and Japan," 14 October 1936.

23 McNaughton Papers, vol. 103, Crerar file, Crerar to McNaughton, nd, encl. "An Attempt to Appreciate the Present Policy of the United Kingdom Government in the Italo-Ethiopian Dispute," 20 September 1935.

24 Ibid., Crerar to Escott Reid, 7, 14 January 1936; NA, L.B. Pearson Papers, N1, Crerar file, Crerar to Edgar Tarr, 25 November 1937.

25 USNA, RG 165, Military Intelligence Division Correspondence 1917–41, box 1770, file 2694-67, Secretary of State to Secretary of War, 8 April 1938 and attached memo; Crerar Papers, vol. 9, 958C.009(D215), Crerar to CGS, 13 December 1937, and Crerar to minister, 31 December 1937.

26 WO 32/4124, CIGS Minute to file, 23 June 1937; PRO, Dominions Office Records, DO35/547/D185/3, S. Holmes to R. Sedgwick, 15 July 1937. Crerar also served on an interdepartmental committee working on the implications of the Statute of Westminster. See Paul Dickson, "The Education of a Canadian General. . ." Canadian Historical Association paper, 1990, 20–1.

27 Brig. George Pangman interview, 23 April 1991; RMC, Crerar Diaries. The diaries contain RMC entertainment expenses, notebooks of Great War establishments, lecture notes, aide-memoires for writing orders, and notes on courses. Characteristically, Crerar sought a special grant of $500 to cover the costs of decorating his quarters and entertaining at RMC. To support his request, he itemized his entertaining in his first year as Commandant: 26 guests to lunch, 346 to tea, 94 to dinner, 133 to supper, 467 for refreshments, and 54 for overnight, a grand total of 1120 entertained at personal expense. NPRC, Crerar file, Crerar to Secretary, DND, 16 June 1939.

28 Crerar Papers, vol. 20, 958C.009(D313), Crerar to Lund, 17 October 1952. See on the IDC, David Fraser, *Alanbrooke* (New York 1982), 103ff.

29 Crerar Papers, vol. 1, 958C.009(D3), Confidential Report, 13 December 1934. Crerar in his interwar higher military training was following the same pattern as almost all officers who reached high rank in Allied armies. See, for example, E.F. Puryear, Jr, *19 Stars: A Study in Military Character and Leadership* (Novato, CA, 1992), 377–8.

30 For example, Pearson Papers, N1, vol. 3, Crerar file, Crerar to Pearson, 10 February 1937.

31 See Crerar's "Disarmament," in *Royal Canadian Military Institute Selected Papers 1931–2* (nd), 74ff. The date of this talk was 22 February 1933.

32 Crerar Papers, vol. 22, 958C.009(380), Crerar to McNaughton, nd [10 July 1931].

33 DHist, 77/490, Transcript of interview with BGen Orde, 1974, 120–1; LGen Geoffrey Walsh interview, 24 May 1991.

34 Crerar Papers, vol. 1, 958C.009(D3), Crerar to CGS, 30 September 1937, and reply, 3 December 1937.

35 NA, Ian Mackenzie Papers, vol. 30, file X-40, CGS to Minister, 7 October 1937.

36 See, for example, ibid., 6 October 1938.

37 Harris, "Or There Would Be Chaos," 125.

38 Crerar Papers, vol. 1, 958C.009(D3), Crerar to Ken Greene, 5 September 1939.

39 QUA, Norman Rogers Papers, vol. 2, file 1a, Crerar to Rogers, 20 September 1939.

40 Crerar Papers, vol. 1, 958C.009(D3), Anderson to Crerar, 25 September 1939.

41 DHist, 114.1(D3), "The Formation of an Overseas Headquarters," 21 September 1939.

42 Crerar Papers, vol. 1, 958C.009(D3), Crerar to CGS, nd [22 September 1939]. Crerar's stock and bond holdings in October 1939 were $17,916.40, and he allotted $335 a month from his pay to his wife and children and provided for his son's school fees. Docs on ibid., vol. 22, 958C.009(D336).

43 RMC, Crerar Papers, Scrapbook, *Sunday Graphic,* 7 January 1940; *Montreal Standard,* 3 February 1940; Mrs Palmer interview.

44 McNaughton Papers, vol. 252, War Orders file, "Higher Organization for War," 19 October 1939.

45 Pearson Papers, N8, vol. 1, Diary, 29 October 1939.

46 Ibid.

47 University of Toronto Archives, Vincent Massey Papers, vol. 310, Diary, 23 November 1939; vol. 366, Mrs Crerar–Mrs Massey correspondence.

48 LHC, Gen. Richard Dewing Diary, 6 November 1939.

49 PRO, Cabinet Office Records, War Cabinet 75(39), 8 November 1939, and 78(39), 10 November 1939. For Crerar's account, see his "Some Reminiscences of 1939–45," *The Empire Club of Canada Addresses . . . 1949–50* (Toronto 1950), 108–9.

50 Pearson Papers, N8, vol. 1, Diary, 4–9, 12 December 1939; RMC, W.H.P. Elkins Papers, Col. G.P.O. Loggie file, Loggie to Elkins, 28 November 1939, and MGO Papers, "Notes on Discussion . . . 26 Apr 40"; Rogers Papers, box 2, file 1a 1939, Crerar to Rogers, 2 December 1939; Queen's University Archives, T.A. Crerar Papers, box 155, 1942 file, Diary, 7 December 1939.

51 DND, Mf C5137, file HQS 8151, telegrams, 23 December, and reply, 29 December 1939.

52 DHist, H.D.G. Crerar Papers, box 13, telegram, 27 January 1940. (Unless otherwise stated, all references to the H.D.G. Crerar Papers are to those in NA.)

53 Crerar Papers, vol. 22, 958C.009 (D335), Crerar to McNaughton, 29 January 1940.

54 Rogers Papers, box 3, file 1a 1940, Crerar to Rogers, 15 February 1940.

55 Ibid., Crerar to Rogers, pen note, nd; RMC, W.H.P. Elkins Papers, MGO Papers file, Crerar to Minister, 7 May 1940. Rogers did not take this lobbying amiss. See his comment on Crerar, House of Commons, *Debates*, 21 May 1940, 97.

56 Puryear, *19 Stars*, 71.

57 McNaughton Papers, vol. 241, file CD/P-5, Crerar to McNaughton, 15 February 1940.

58 Crerar Papers, vol. 1, 958C.009 (D9), Crerar to Rogers, 10 June 1940; Crerar to Ralston, 17 June 1940.

59 DHist 77/490, Orde transcript, 143–5.

60 McNaughton Papers, vol. 248, War Diary 1940, McNaughton to Skelton, 29 June 1940; DHist, Crerar Papers, box 13, telegram, Ottawa to Canmilitry, 5 July 1940. Crerar's promotion to major-general was duly made substantive on 6 July 1940. Compare DND, Mf C8336, file HQS 7434, CGS to Minister, 10 July 1940.

61 Dewing Diary, 8 July 1940.

62 McNaughton Papers, vol. 227, file CC7/Crerar/6, Crerar to McNaughton, 16 July 1940. McNaughton's reply is in Crerar Papers, vol. 1, 958C.009(D1), 7 August 1940.

63 Crerar Papers, vol. 1, 958C.009(D13),"Observations on Canadian Requirements . . ." nd; vol. 1, 958C.009(D7), Crerar to Montague, 3 October

1940. Crerar wanted every good PF officer to be given the opportunity to serve overseas "for sake his own future." NA, M.H.S. Penhale Papers, vol. 5, file CMHQ — development of CEF, telegram Crerar to Montague, 29 August 1940. Still, he believed that militia officers who were equal in ability to PF officers deserved preferment. "My reason is simple. If the nonpermanent man has been able, by sheer ability, to attain equality with the permanent soldier who has had the advantage of a lifetime of training, it is logical to assume that the nonpermanent man will, three months hence, be a better soldier." L.S.B. Shapiro, "These Are Our Generals," *Maclean's,* 1 July 1944, 12.

64 Pearson Papers, N1, vol. 3, Crerar file, Crerar to Pearson, 27 July 1940. On Crerar's reorganization of NDHQ, see Geoffrey Hayes, "The Development of the Canadian Army Officer Corps, 1939–1945" (PhD dissertation, University of Western Ontario 1992), 67ff.

65 *Newsweek,* 21 August 1944, 30; Tellier interview.

66 Pearson Papers, N1, vol. 3, Crerar file, Crerar to Pearson, 4 September 1940.

67 USNA, RG 165, Military Intelligence Division, box 1770, 2694-70, Military Attaché Report 128, 27 July 1940.

68 Crerar Papers, vol. 1, 958C.009(D12), Crerar to McNaughton, 8 August, 9 September 1940.

69 Ibid.

70 NA, J.L. Ralston Papers, vol. 38, "The Canadian Army," 3 September 1940.

71 NA, C.D. Howe Papers, vol. 48, S14 ND(1), CGS to Minister, 24 September 1940.

72 See J.L. Granatstein and J.M. Hitsman, *Broken Promises: A History of Conscription in Canada* (Toronto 1985), 150–1.

73 McNaughton Papers, vol. 227, file CC7/Crerar/6, Crerar to McNaughton, 16 April 1941, and Crerar to Minister, 27 June 1941, with attached *Globe and Mail* article, 27 June 1941; Crerar Papers, vol. 1, 958C.009(D12), Crerar to McNaughton, 19 May, 26 June 1941; vol. 19, 958C.009 (D338), Crerar to Burns, 24 May 1941; vol. 1, 958C.009 (D7), Crerar to Montague, 9 June 1941; Archives of Ontario, Maclean-Hunter Records, box 405, F-3-2-a & b, Crerar to Napier Moore, 27 July 1941.

74 QUA, Grant Dexter Papers, Memorandum, 13 September 1940. Crerar believed this was "a war of industry, not of men." See USNA, Department of State Records, 842.20-Defense/42, Moffat memo of conversation with Crerar, 12 October 1940. He also spoke very critically of the role of deputy ministers to the U.S. minister. Harvard University Archives, Pierrepont Moffat Papers, Memo of Conversation, 12 February 1941.

75 Dexter Papers, Memo, 10 October 1941.

76 Ibid., 25 March 1941.

77 Ibid., 12 June 1941.

78 Crerar Papers, vol. 22, 958C.009(336), Crerar to Ralston, 31 March 1941. Compare ibid., 17 October 1940, 29 January 1941.

79 WO 106/4872, Note of Meeting in War Office, 17 December 1940.

80 CWC Minutes, 28 January 1941, and Documents, telegram, Ralston to Prime Minister, 5 January 1941; King Diary, 27–28 January 1941; McNaughton Papers, vol. 227, file CC7/Crerar/6, Crerar to McNaughton, 4 March 1941.

81 Dexter Papers, Memo, 12 June 1941.

82 McNaughton Papers, vol. 227, file CC7/Crerar/6, Crerar to McNaughton, 11 August 1941; Floyd Chalmers Papers (Toronto), Conversations 1941 file, Memo of Conversation with Crerar, 25 September 1941.

83 Crerar's submission for this force structure is in Public Archives of Nova Scotia, Angus L. Macdonald Papers, vol. 1501, F304/10, "Army Programme 1942–43," 18 November 1941.

84 Cabinet Office Records, Cab 53/8, CID, COS Subcommittee 217th Meeting, 1 October 1937; 240th Meeting, 13 June 1938.

85 USAMHI, OCMH WWII SHAEF Records, Forrest Pogue interviews, Grasett interview, 23–24 February 1947.

86 *Report on the Canadian Expeditionary Force to the Crown Colony of Hong Kong* (Ottawa 1942), 14; docs on WO106/2412. This file (especially COS(41), 403rd Meeting, 1 December 1941) makes clear that on 6 December 1941, Britain was on the verge of asking Canada for more troops for Hong Kong. Compare Carl Vincent, *No Reason Why: The Canadian Hong Kong Tragedy* (Stittsville, Ont., 1981), 24ff.

87 Ralston Papers, vol. 52, "Hong Kong Enquiry — Mr Ralston's notes . . ."; vol. 70, Memorandum re Hong Kong, 28 February 1942; MGen H.A. Sparling interview, 18 April 1991.

88 See NA, R.B. Hanson Papers, file W-560S, Drew to King, 11 July 1942, for Drew's assessment of the Royal Commission report, setting out as well his attitude to NDHQ's role in preparing the expedition.

89 For Crerar's reaction to the request he return to testify, see Pearson Papers, N1, vol. 3, Crerar file, Crerar to Pearson, 25 April 1942.

90 *Report*, 34, 44, 46.

91 G.S. Currie Papers (Ottawa), Diary of Lieut. Colonel George S. Currie's Trip Overseas . . . October 12th to November 3rd, 1941.

92 Massey Papers, vol. 310, Diary, 22 October 1941.

93 John Swettenham, *McNaughton*, vol. 2: *1939–1943* (Toronto 1969), 184.

94 McNaughton Papers, vol. 193, PA6-1-10, McNaughton pencil note, 14 October 1941; Pearson Papers, N8, Diary, 28 April 1941. Crerar's brief account of his posting overseas is in DHist, 82/983, Official Comments on Vol. I of Official History of Canadian Army [1951], 153, and in Crerar Papers, vol. 8, 958C.009(D182), Notes on Enclosed Correspondence, Dec 46.

95 Ibid., vol. 19, 958C.009(D333), Crerar to D.A. White, 21 November 1941; Ralston Papers, vol. 64, English Trip — Diary file, Diary, 27 October 1941.

96 CWC Minutes, 6 November 1941.

97 McNaughton Papers, vol. 197, PA6-9-C-4, McNaughton to Brooke, nd. Pearkes, not unnaturally, was very unhappy. See Pearson Papers, N1, vol. 3, Crerar file, Crerar to Pearson, 25 April 1942; Crerar Papers, vol. 1, Memorandum, 9 May 1942.

98 DHist, Crerar Papers, Crerar file, Crerar to McNaughton, 10 December 1941[?].

99 There were attempts to build up his public relations by photographing him as the "Hamilton tiger" holding a Sten gun, but these simply did not wash. Tellier interview.

100 DHist, Crerar Papers, Crerar file, Crerar to McNaughton, 10 December 1941[?]. For Pearkes's response to Crerar's supplanting him, see R.H. Roy, *For Most Conspicuous Bravery: A Biography of Major-General George R. Pearkes . . .* (Vancouver 1977), 168–9.

101 Crerar Papers, vol. 22, 958C.009(D335), Brooke to Crerar, 31 December 1941.

102 Ibid. vol. 1, Crerar to BGS, Cdn Corps, 11 January 1942; vol. 8, 958C.009(182), Notes on Enclosed Correspondence . . . Dec 46. The best account of Montgomery's impact on Canadian training and commanders is John A. English, *The Canadian Army and the Normandy Campaign: A Study of Failure in High Command* (New York 1991), chap. 6. See, for an account of a Monty visit to one unit, R.H. Roy, *Sherwood Lett: His Life and Times* (Vancouver 1991), 105–6, and, on this period, Kim Beattie, *Dileas: History of the 48th Highlanders of Canada, 1929–1956* (Toronto 1957), 158ff.

103 IWM, Viscount Montgomery Papers, BLM 20/5, Brooke to Montgomery, 8 January 1942. Crerar learned, for example, that Montgomery had "an aversion both to Gunner Officers commanding Infantry Brigades and to fat officers in any capacity." McNaughton Papers, file PA6-9-6-3, Crerar to McNaughton, 6 September 1943.

104 Nigel Hamilton, *Monty*, vol. 1: *The Making of a General 1887–1942*

(London 1981), 474ff. This otherwise competent biography unfortunately reads backwards from Crerar's 1944 difficulties with Montgomery to assume — in the face of the evidence in Crerar's Papers, never consulted by Hamilton — that relations were bad from the outset.

105 Crerar Papers, vol. 8, 958C.009(D182), Montgomery to Crerar, 30 May 1942; IWM, Trumball Warren Papers, Montgomery to Warren, 1 June 1942. See also George Kitching, *Mud and Green Fields: The Memoirs of General George Kitching* (Langley, BC, 1985), 122–3.

106 McNaughton Papers, vol. 133, PA1-3-1, Crerar to McNaughton, 27 September 1942; Crerar Papers, vol. 4, 958C.009(D142), Montgomery to Crerar, 9 January 1943. Crerar went to North Africa in January 1943.

107 Massey Papers, vol. 311, Diary, 12 March 1943.

108 Crerar Papers, vol. 2, "Memorandum of Conversation with . . . Montgomery . . ." 4 July 1942.

109 See, for example, RMC, Crerar Papers, Scrapbook, undated [1943?] clipping by L.S.B. Shapiro, "Crerar of the Canadian Corps." For a contradictory view, see W. Denis and S. Whitaker, *Dieppe: Tragedy to Triumph* (Toronto 1992).

110 This is largely based on Guy Simonds Papers (North Gower, Ont.), Memoirs box, "Dieppe," nd; on a similar letter to C.P. Stacey, 10 February 1969; and Simonds to Lord Mountbatten, 22 January 1969, in NA, Adm. John Hughes-Hallett Papers, Correspondence 1969 file. Crerar's account, in an interview for television done much later, is quite different. NA, George Ronald Papers, Crerar interview, nd. On the operation generally, the best book is Brian Villa, *Unauthorized Action: Mountbatten and the Dieppe Raid* (Toronto 1989).

111 Simonds Papers, Memoirs box, "Dieppe." Compare *Globe and Mail*, 7 November 1945. The Whitakers, *Dieppe*, agree. After the war Crerar claimed, moreover, that post-Dieppe he developed the techniques of assault landing subsequently used. "Some Reminiscences," *Empire Club Addresses*, 110–11.

112 Massey Papers, vol. 311, Diary, 20 August 1942.

113 This mightily offended Guy Simonds. See Simonds Papers, Memoirs box, "Dieppe," nd.

114 Massey Papers, vol. 311, Diary, 10 June 1942.

115 Alanbrooke Papers, file 3/A/VIII, Notes on My Life, 10 February 1943.

116 Ibid., file 3/A/IX, 18 June 1943.

117 Ralston Papers, vol. 66, Overseas Trips 1943 file, Diary, 30 July 1943. By this time Ralston had reached the conclusion that Crerar should replace McNaughton. King Diary, 10 July 1943, f. 533.

118 Crerar Papers, vol. 2, 958C.009(D21), Crerar to McNaughton, 19 October, and reply, 21 October 1942; McNaughton Papers, vol. 240, Miscellaneous Correspondence, Crerar to McNaughton, 21 October 1942.

119 Alanbrooke Papers, file 3/A/VIII, Notes on My Life, 6 March 1943. See also Ralston Papers, vol. 54, notes on Canadian senior officers: Crerar "has made a high reputation in recent 'Spartan' exercises and has been referred to as the outstanding leader shown up by that test."

120 Alanbrooke Papers, Notes on My Life, file 3 A VIII, 31 March 1943.

121 Massey Papers, vol. 311, Diary, 12 May 1943.

122 Ibid., 14 July 1943.

123 McNaughton Papers, vol. 167, file PA5-0-3-2, Memorandum of Discussions, 15 November 1943; Ralston Papers, vol. 51, McNaughton — Diary and Documents file, Diary, 14 November 1943. McNaughton said the same thing a year later. McNaughton Papers, vol. 268, file Time Magazine, McNaughton to D.W. Bishop, 25 September 1944.

124 Ralston Papers, vol. 53, Montgomery file, Ralston Diary, 23 November 1943.

125 Crerar Papers, vol. 4, 958C.009(D172), Montgomery to Crerar, 9 January 1943.

126 G.W.L. Nicholson, *The Canadians in Italy* (Ottawa 1957), 355.

127 Ralston Papers, vol. 64, Diaries and Notes file, Diary, 29 November 1943.

128 DND, vol. 10663, 215C1.049(D1), Crerar to Minister, 29 November 1943.

129 QUA, C.G. Power Papers, box 1, binder, Ralston to Prime Minister, 19 December 1943; Ralston Papers, vol. 52, McNaughton Resignation file, "Alternative Courses . . . ," 12 December 1943.

130 Ralston Papers, vol. 53, Mediterranean trip file, Diary, 30 November 1943.

131 Ibid.

132 WO 214/55, Viscount Alexander Papers, CIGS to Alexander, 4 January 1944.

133 IWM, Sir Oliver Leese Papers, box 2, Leese to his wife, 17 January 1944. One Canadian officer noticed amusedly that Crerar had "a much swankier" staff car than Leese. NA, H.H. Usher Papers, vol. 1, Usher to his wife, 24 February 1944.

134 Daniel Dancocks, *The D-Day Dodgers* (Toronto 1991), 214–17.

135 RMC, Christopher Vokes Papers, Looseleaf book, "The Adriatic Front — Winter 1944"; Strome Galloway, *The General That Never Was* (Belleville, Ont., 1981), 184. Crerar actually sent out a memo giving his daily routine. Crerar

Papers, vol. 1, 958C.009(D18), 24 January 1944. For his views on "stress casualties" or shell shock, see W.J. McAndrew, "Stress Casualties: Canadians in Italy 1943–45," *Canadian Defence Quarterly* 17 (winter 1987–8), 50.

136 Alanbrooke Papers, file 3/B/XII, Notes on My Life, 29 March 1944. Col. Ralston had wanted a report on Crerar's performance in Italy, but Gen. Stuart persuaded him that there was de facto concurrence from Brooke and Montgomery: "It can be safely assumed therefore that both are satisfied that Crerar has proved himself." DND, Mf C5438, file HQS 20-5-26-2, Stuart to Ralston, 27 February 1944.

137 DND, vol. 10798, "Personal Diary of Brigadier N.E. Rodger, C. of S. 2 Cdn Corps," entries 24, 31 March, 4 May 1944.

138 Massey Papers, vol. 312, Diary, 19 March 1944. He said the same to Mackenzie King. King Diary, 17 May 1944, f. 498.

139 Currie Papers, pocket diary, 4 April 1944.

140 Montgomery Papers, BLM 73/1, Diary, 26 May 1944.

141 Crerar Papers, vol. 3, 958C.009(D67), Crerar's notations on Stuart to Crerar, 26 May 1944.

142 DHist, 312.009(D59), Crerar to Stuart, 10 June 1944.

143 Cabinet Office Records, Cab 106/1064, GOC-in-C First Canadian Army War Diary, 19 June 1944.

144 Quoted in Richard Lamb, *Montgomery in Europe 1943–1945* (London 1983), 253.

145 Montgomery Papers, BLM 126/9, Montgomery to Brooke, 7 July 1944. A Canadian journalist described Crerar as "austere as a bishop, grave as a judge." *Toronto Star*, 21 November 1944.

146 Montgomery Papers, BLM 1/97, Brooke to Montgomery, 11 July 1944.

147 Ibid., BLM 126/12, Montgomery to Brooke, 14 July 1944.

148 See Crerar's comments in Kitching, *Mud and Green Fields*, 228.

149 Crerar Papers, vol. 3, 958C.009(D178), Crerar memo to C of S CMHQ, 2 July 1944.

150 Alanbrooke Papers, 14/1, Montgomery to Brooke, 26 July 1944.

151 Crerar Papers, vol. 8, Crerar to Stuart, 10 July 1944.

152 C.P. Stacey, *The Victory Campaign* (Ottawa 1960), 196–8.

153 Alanbrooke Papers, 14/1, Montgomery to Crerar, 26 July 1944; Gen Bruce Matthews interview, 25 April 1991. See the account in English, *Canadian Army*, 191-5.

154 Alanbrooke Papers, 14/29, Montgomery to Brooke, 9 August 1944. Crerar's orders and addresses do not convey the anxiety Montgomery detected. See, for

example, NA, Churchill Mann Papers, Totalize file, Crerar's Notes on Telephone Conversation . . . 7 August 1944, and his address prior to Totalize, nd. Montgomery's reluctance to reinforce the Canadians has been the subject of criticism, notably Carlo d'Este, *Decision in Normandy* (London 1983), 437ff. See also Russell Weigley's snide comment on Crerar in *Eisenhower's Lieutenants* (Bloomington 1981), 284, and his letter to the author, 8 May 1991: "Perhaps I should not have made the statement."

155 Vancouver City Archives, Sherwood Lett Papers, vol. 3, file 6, Crerar to Lett, 24 August 1944.

156 See Terry Copp and Robert Vogel, "'No Lack of Rational Speed': 1st Canadian Army Operations, September 1944," *Journal of Canadian Studies*, 16 (Fall-Winter 1981), 145ff.

157 DHist, 86/544, "Notes re Situation which Developed. . ." 4 September 1944; ibid., Montgomery to Crerar, 7 September 1944; Nigel Hamilton, *Monty* vol. 3: *The Field Marshal 1944-1976* (London 1986), 34ff; Lamb, *Montgomery*, 254-6. Compare Francis de Guingand, *Operation Victory* (London 1947), 467-8. After the war Montgomery was much less charitable about Crerar: "What I suffered from that man." Warren Papers, Montgomery to Warren, 1 January 1969.

158 DHist, 86/544, Mann to Gen. Foulkes, 2 April 1963.

159 DHist, Crerar Papers, Crerar file, Stuart to Weeks, 28 September 1944.

160 MGen Elliot Rodger interview, 21 May 1991; MGen R.P. Rothschild interview, 24 May 1991; Lamb, *Montgomery*, 253.

161 Crerar's son believes that there was a Montgomery–Simonds plot to displace Crerar permanently and that his father, warned by a telephone conversation from Brig. Churchill Mann, his Chief of Staff, returned from sick leave early. Peter Crerar interview, 14 April 1991.

162 Crerar Papers, vol. 7, 958C.009(D172), Montgomery to Crerar, 27 October 1944; Montgomery Papers, BLM 119/35, Montgomery to CIGS, 17 November 1944; DND, Mf C5438, file HQS 20-5-26-2, press release, 21 November 1944. Crerar's pay was retroactively raised from $14,000 to $16,000 a year in 1945. NPRC, Crerar file, PC 5437, 3 August 1945.

163 Massey Papers, box 312, Diary, 6 November 1944. Ottawa did not press to reunite the army, but early in the New Year, I Canadian Corps left Italy. By March it was in action as part of First Canadian Army.

164 Giles Perodeau telephone interview, 24 March 1992; Finlay Morrison interview, 2 March 1992 (these were two of Crerar's ADCs); Eisenhower Library, BGen J.W. Bishop oral history interview, 20 January 1973, 96–7.

165 LGen W.A.B. Anderson interview, 21 May 1991.

166 Brig. G.E. Beament interview, 24 May 1991.

167 Letter to author, 28 September 1992. More facetiously, McAndrew attributed this military doctrine to "deep societal roots — Canada Post goes to war"!

168 Brian Horrocks, *A Full Life* (London 1960), 253; Morrison interview. On Veritable, see W. Denis and S. Whitaker, *Rhineland: The Battle to End the War* (Toronto 1989); H. Essame, *The Battle for Germany* (London 1969), 144ff.

169 Stacey recalled seeing Crerar tearing a strip off his pilot "who had been unfortunate enough to be missing when the army commander wanted to fly somewhere." There was, he said, "some element of terror in his manner of command." C.P. Stacey, "Canadian Leaders of the Second World War," *Canadian Historical Review* 66 (March 1985), 68.

170 Peter Crerar interview. The V-E Day message is quoted in R.G.C. Smith, ed., *As You Were! Ex-Cadets Remember*, vol. 2 (1984), 212.

171 McNaughton Papers, vol. 267, King correspondence file, McNaughton pen memo, 17 June 1945; G.R. Stevens, *The Royal Canadian Regiment*, vol. 2: *1933-66* (London 1967), 193. Crerar also had to interpret British honours for Gen. W.H. Simpson of United States 9th Army, who had been told by Monty he would be made "K.B." Simpson "cornered General Crerar . . . in the hall afterwards and asked him what in hell this KB was. It was the 'KBE' of course . . . a good citation, he said." USAMHI, W.H. Simpson Papers, Diary — Personal Calendar, 4 February 1945.

172 Docs on King Papers, ff. C166425ff.

173 Ibid., King memo, 6 November 1946, f. C166489.

174 Mrs Palmer interview.

CHAPTER 5   TOMMY BURNS: PROBLEMS OF PERSONALITY

1 RMC, Gen. Christopher Vokes file, SPC MS FC582.37.18.V6, "The Adriatic Front — Winter 1944," 21–2.

2 Dr Mary Burns interview, 22 May 1991.

3 RMC, Registrar's Office, Ledgers; R.A. Preston, *Canada's RMC: A History of the Royal Military College* (Toronto 1969), 213.

4 Arlington B. Conway [E.L.M. Burns], "In Praise of War," *American Mercury* 11 (August 1927), 387. For RMC policy on the commissioning of cadets during the war, see Preston, *Canada's RMC*, 214ff.

5 RMC, Central Registry, Burns file, Report, 23 June 1915; ibid., Record Sheet.

6 Dr Mary Burns interview.

7 LGen E.L.M. Burns, *General Mud: Memoirs of Two World Wars* (Toronto 1970), 83.

8 RMC, Central Registry, Burns file, Louise Burns to Col. [sic, Brig.-Gen.] Perreau, 10 June 1919.

9 Conway, "In Praise of War," 387ff. The account in *General Mud*, 43ff, closely parallels this article.

10 Arlington B. Conway, "The Training of the Soldier," *American Mercury* 8 (June 1924), 212.

11 See Burns's unpublished piece, "Promotion in the Permanent Force" (1937?) in NA, E.L.M. Burns Papers, vol. 6, Articles, papers, speeches file.

12 MGen Elliot Rodger interview, 21 May 1991.

13 E.L.M. Burns and R.H. Field, "A Plotter for High Oblique Photographs," *Canadian Journal of Research* 13 (1935); Burns and Field, "The Radial Stereotyper," ibid., 15 (1937). He was also sent to attend the International Congress of Photogrammetry in Paris and the Dominion and Colonial Surveyors Conference in London in the summer of 1935; NA, A.G.L. McNaughton Papers, vol. 112, McNaughton to Vanier, 4 June 1935.

14 NPRC, E.L.M. Burns file, confidential reports. I am most grateful to Dr Mary Burns for permission to make use of this file.

15 RMC, Central Registry, Burns file, Mrs Burns to Perreau, 10 June 1919.

16 Dr Mary Burns interview.

17 NA, Macbeth Papers, Burns to Macbeth, 26 October 1928, ff. 1599–1600; 19 August 1929, ff. 1689–90.

18 Burns, *General Mud*, 88.

19 9 (July 1925), 291ff.

20 Macbeth Papers, Burns to Macbeth, 20 December 1925, f. 1301.

21 13 (December 1929), 457ff.

22 16 (February 1932), 167ff. Burns published additional articles in *American Mercury* in February 1926, February 1928, October 1930, September 1932, August 1935, and March 1937.

23 He published short stories in *Ace High*, *War Stories*, and other magazines and had a play — really a skit — produced on stage by the Canadian company, The Originals. Macbeth Papers, vol. 5, A.B. Conway file, Burns biography; ibid., Burns to Macbeth, 27 October 1925, f. 1242.

24 Ibid., Burns to Macbeth, 15 June 1924, ff. 1036–37a. On *The Land of*

Afternoon and its impact, see Sandra Gwyn, *The Tapestry of War* (Toronto 1992), 185–6.

25 Macbeth Papers, vol. 5, Burns to Macbeth, 27 October 1925, ff. 1242–4.

26 Ibid., vol. 5, A.B. Conway file, Burns biography.

27 Ibid., Burns to Macbeth, 19 August 1929, ff. 1689–93. Eleanor Burns, who as a good Catholic might have been expected to be offended by the references to the church in the book, was not perturbed, but Burns added she was "habituated to agnosticism." Ibid., 28 August 1929, f. 1692.

28 A good example is Burns's review of Hoffman Nickerson, *Can We Limit War?* in *Canadian Defence Quarterly* 11 (July 1934), 476–7.

29 Ibid., 2 (October 1924), 22ff, and 3 (April 1926), 319ff.

30 Brereton Greenhous, *Dragoon: The Centennial History of the Royal Canadian Dragoons* (Belleville, Ont., 1983), 277.

31 Burns, *General Mud*, 89.

32 *Canadian Defence Quarterly* 4 (January 1927), 168ff, and 9 (October 1931), 88ff.

33 For example, QUA, J. Sutherland Brown Papers, box 1, file 11, Brown to Col. W.W. Foster, 31 December 1932.

34 LHC, Liddell Hart Papers, 2/B, Burns to Liddell Hart, 10 December 1931. For a good wartime comment on Burns's articles, see A.E. Prince, "The Military Ideas of Canada's Commander in Italy, Gen. Burns," *Saturday Night*, 3 June, 1944, 2.

35 The initial articles were in *Canadian Defence Quarterly* 15 (April 1938), 282ff, and (July 1938), 413ff. The ripostes were Burns's "Where Do the Tanks Belong?" 16 (October 1938), 28ff, and Simonds's "What Price Assault without Support?" 16 (January 1939), 142ff. See also LCol H.F. Wood, "The Old Defence Quarterly," *Canadian Army Journal* 14 (Spring 1960), 35ff, and James Lutz, "Canadian Military Thought, 1923–1939: A Profile Drawn from the Pages of the Old Canadian Defence Quarterly," *Canadian Defence Quarterly* 9 (Autumn 1979), 45-7. As late as 1951, Burns was still thinking on this subject and corresponding with Liddell Hart about it. Liddell Hart Papers, file 2/B, Burns to Liddell Hart, 8 March 1951.

36 NA, Peter Stursberg Papers, vol. 28, Burns interview, 16 May 1978.

37 University of Toronto Archives, Vincent Massey Papers, Diary, 28 September, 12, 16 October 1939; NPRC, Burns file, Massey to Ian Mackenzie, 14 September 1939.

38 LHC, Gen. Richard Dewing Diary, 10 October 1939.

39 Burns, *General Mud*, 99.

40 Ibid., pp. 99–100.

41 For example, Burns Papers, vol. 7, Articles, papers, speeches file, "The Strength of the Canadian Army," 1 May 1940; RMC, Gen. W.H.P. Elkins Papers, "Notes on Discussion between the Minister of National Defence, and Maj-Gen. Crerar . . . 26 Apr 40."

42 McNaughton Papers, vol. 241, file CD/P-5, Crerar to McNaughton, 5 April 1940; DHist, H.D.G. Crerar Papers, Burns file, Rogers to Acting Minister, 3 May 40.

43 NPRC, Burns file, Crerar to Minister, 5 July 1940; Crerar to McNaughton, 24 July 1940.

44 NA, L.B. Pearson Papers, N1, vol. 3, Crerar file, Gen. Crerar to Pearson, 27 July 1940; NA, H.D.G. Crerar Papers, vol. 1, 958.C009 (D12), Crerar to McNaughton, 8 August 1940. (Unless otherwise stated, all references to the Crerar Papers are to those in NA.)

45 G.S. Currie Papers (Ottawa), Diary Notebook Fall 1940, 5 November 1940.

46 QUA, Grant Dexter Papers, Memo, 25 March 1941.

47 *Globe and Mail*, 21 June 1943.

48 NA, Gen. Victor Odlum Papers, vol. 26, Diary, 10 December 1940.

49 Crerar Papers, vol. 1, 958.C009 (D7), Crerar to Montague, 8 February 1941; Crerar to McNaughton, 4 March 1941.

50 DHist, Crerar Papers, Murchie file, Crerar to McNaughton, 5 February 1941. For an example of Burns's planning on the armoured formations, see DND, mf. reel C5437, file HQ 20-5-7-2, Burns to CGS, 11 February 1941.

51 Harold Morrison telephone conversation, 27 June 1991.

52 NPRC, Burns file, Pownall to McNaughton, 5 August 1941, and reply, 6 August 1941. There is no indication of any kind that Burns was targeted or set up by British or Canadian "enemies." The opening of his letter seems to have been merely a routine action by the postal censors.

53 QUA, C.G. Power Papers, box 77, Trips file, Diary, 3 July 1941, refers to one meeting Burns attended with the Minister.

54 Dr Mary Burns interview.

55 Docs on NPRC, Burns file. Burns abjectly apologized to McNaughton for the incident, but denied that his attitude was defeatist, presumably McNaughton's overall reaction to the thrust of his comments. DHist, Crerar Papers, Burns file, Burns to McNaughton, 6 August 1941. The account of this incident in Richard Malone's *A Portrait of War 1939–1943* (Toronto 1983), 72, is wrong.

56 NPRC, Burns file, McNaughton to Crerar, telegram no. 1408, nd.

57 Ibid., Crerar to Minister, 25 August 1941.

58 Ibid., Ralston Memo, 27 August 1941.

59 Docs on DHist, Crerar Papers, Burns file.

60 Burns's diary of this period is in Burns Papers, vol. 7.

61 See ibid., vol. 1, "Conversion WWII 4 Canadian Armoured Division" file.

62 Ibid., vol. 12, Scrapbook, telegram, McNaughton to Stuart, 17 January 1942.

63 DND Records, vol. 10033, file 9/Sr Appts/1, Memorandum, 2 May 1943.

64 NA, J.L. Ralston Papers, vol. 54, officer assessments, nd [mid 1943]. Gen. Kenneth Stuart is usually thought to be the author, but as Burns's command is given as the 1st Division, instead of the 2nd, this seems unlikely.

65 Liddell Hart Papers, file 11/1943/36, Notes for History, 9–10 June 1943.

66 DND Records, vol. 10033, file 9/Sr Appts/1/2, Montague to Warren, 5 January 1944. Ralston queried Burns's appointment because he had been training his division to fight in Northwest Europe: "Is it logical . . . to put him in a completely different job and terrain?" How much, if anything, of the earlier opinions Ralston had formed of Burns was in this comment is unclear. Ibid., Ralston to Stuart, 6 January 1944.

67 DHist, 86/544, Crerar to Stuart, 25 January 1944.

68 Burns Papers, vol. 1, Burns' War Diary, 23 January 1944. G.W.L. Nicholson, *The Canadians in Italy* (Ottawa 1957), 691, gives the changeover as 29–30 January 1944.

69 Burns, *General Mud*, 133.

70 For an example of Montgomery's belief, see his handwritten letter to Crerar, 9 January 1943, in DND, vol. 10651, file 215C1.019. Burns's views on the issue are found in a letter he sent W.J. McAndrew on 26 August 1983. I am grateful to Dr McAndrew for this letter.

71 IWM, Sir Oliver Leese Papers, box 2, Leese to his wife, 2, 16 February 1944.

72 York University Archives, J.L. Granatstein Papers, Brig. William Murphy Letters, Murphy to family, 5 February 1944. MGen H.A. Sparling, who was CRA of 5th Canadian Armoured Division, remembered a sharp disagreement with Burns over the use of Very signals for artillery defensive fire. Burns lit into Sparling in the mess and later apologized to him, ensuring that another officer was there to hear. Sparling, no admirer of Burns as a commander, said he took his hat off to him for his conduct in this situation. Interview, 18 April 1991.

73 Crerar Papers, vol. 8, file 958C.009 (D167), Crerar to Stuart, 12 February 1944.

74 Ralston Papers, vol. 37, Appointments Overseas file, Stuart to Ralston, 24 February 1944; DND, Mf. C5438, file HQS 20-5-26-2, vol. 4, Stuart to Ralston, 29 February 1944, and other correspondence in this file. Burns's surprise is noted in Stursberg Papers, Burns interview.

75 Crerar Papers, vol. 7, file 958C.009 (D183), Burns to Crerar, 15 March 1944.

76 Currie Papers, pocket diary, March–April 1944, 6–7 April 1944; Ralston Papers, vol. 43, Currie Overseas Trip 1944 file, typed diary. There are significant discrepancies between the handwritten and typed diaries, but the thrust of this comment is absolutely clear.

77 Crerar Papers, vol. 3, file 958C.009 (D178), Crerar to Stuart, 16 May 1944. According to Mackenzie King's diary, Crerar told him on 17 May 1944 in the United Kingdom that he thought Simonds, "a very good soldier, though he might not be the best man for post-war planning," should be his successor. NA, W.L.M. King Diary, f. 498.

78 WO 216/168, Leese to Kennedy, 16 April 1944.

79 Terry Copp and Bill McAndrew, *Battle Exhaustion: Soldiers and Psychiatrists in the Canadian Army, 1939–1945* (Montreal 1990), 79ff.

80 WO 216/168, Leese to Kennedy, 19, 26 May 1944; Leese Papers, box 2, Leese to his wife, 23 May 1944.

81 See the diary entries of Brig. McCarter in DND, vol. 17507, McCarter to Col. Nicholson, 3 April 1951.

82 The corps headquarters fought the battle, but the army headquarters was responsible for allocating traffic routes. The best account of this campaign, John Ellis, *Cassino: The Hollow Victory* (London 1984), 444–5, puts the blame for the mishandling of the campaign squarely on Alexander. See also W.G.F. Jackson, *The Battle for Rome* (London 1969), chap. 9; Gregory Blaxland, *Alexander's Generals* (London 1979), 106ff; D. Graham and S. Bidwell, *Tug of War* (London 1986), 260ff; and G.W.L. Nicholson, *The Canadians in Italy 1943–1945* (Ottawa 1957), chaps. 13–14.

83 Leese Papers, box 2, Leese to wife, 4 June 1944. At least one Canadian officer, MGen. Desmond Smith, believed the traffic mixups were Eighth Army's fault. Interview, 14 September 1991.

84 IWM, Field Marshal Viscount Montgomery Papers, BLM 97/22, Leese to Montgomery, 11 June 1944.

85 WO 216/168, Leese to Kennedy, 8 June 1944.

86 W.J. McAndrew, "Eighth Army at the Gothic Line: Commanders and Plans," *RUSI Journal* 131 (June 1986), 54, suggests that the change in Leese's atti-

tude might have been sparked by Burns's frank after-action report that acknowledged Canadian errors, but also pointed to Eighth Army mistakes. Rowland
Ryder, *Oliver Leese* (London 1987), offers a defence of its subject.

87 Burns found the sacking of "some of my good friends . . . a difficult thing
to do" and recollected that he did this on Leese's order. Stursberg Papers, Burns
interview. The account in Malone, *A Portrait of War*, 233–4, is again quite wrong
in its account.

88 J. Douglas Crashley telephone conversation, 14 May 1991. Another ADC,
Major Harry Pope, lamented that Burns could give junior officers hell but
couldn't do this to major-generals. "Probably he lacked the battle experience to
give him confidence in his own ability." Interview, 3 April 1991.

89 MGen George Kitching interview, 25 February 1992; MGen. M.P. Bogert
interview, 8 September 1991; confidential interview. Burns did write, however, to
the father of one of his officers taken prisoner in the fighting in Italy. Harry Pope
Papers (Uxbridge, Ont.), Burns to Gen. M.A. Pope, 5 June 1944. When the officer
escaped, Burns duly wrote to his mother. Ibid., Burns to Simonne Pope, 8
October 1944.

90 Chris Vokes's view, as offered in his memoir *Vokes: My Story* (Ottawa
1985), 153–5, was, "As far I was concerned, my soldiers could go into battle in
their BVDs or bare-assed if they wanted to. All I was concerned about was that
they take the objective."

91 Crerar Papers, vol. 7, file 958C.009 (D183), Burns to Crerar, 7 June 1944.
Burns drafted a memo for his new BGS, Brig. J.D.B. Smith, on "Lessons from Recent
Fighting" that stressed movement factors; this was expanded on in another paper,
"The Pursuit from the Melfa to Anagni." Burns Papers, vol. 1, 12 June, 5 July 1944.

92 WO 214/55, Alexander to CIGS, 29 June 1944; copy in DND, vol. 11005,
file 215C1.069 (D1), vol. 1. There is some support for Alexander's view of
Canadian attitudes to the breakup of the corps in Dr W.J. McAndrew Papers
(Ottawa), MGen M.P. Bogert to Dr W.J. McAndrew, 27 November 1983.

93 W.J. McAndrew concludes that Leese's deliberate policy was to mix
Commonwealth troops indiscriminately — this "tended to break down selfish
nationalistic points of view." McAndrew, "Commanders and Plans," 52.

94 Vokes, *Vokes: My Story*, 158.

95 Crerar Papers, vol. 3, file 958C.009 (D178), Memorandum to C of S
CMHQ, 2 July 1944.

96 Ralston Papers, vol. 39, Burns file, Stuart to Murchie, 2 July 1944, and
reply, 3 July 1944.

97 Not unnaturally, Burns was angry that Leese had recommended his replacement after telling him that he could stay on. Burns described Leese as "two-faced," adding, "I was never able to have a very frank and free association with him afterwards." Stursberg Papers, Burns interview.

98 Maj.-Gen. Bert Hoffmeister's recollection of his interview with Stuart was that he had refused to say anything, repeatedly avoiding answers to Stuart's questions. "Why didn't Stuart have the guts to interview me in Burns' presence?" Interview, 2 March 1992. See also Vokes's account in *Vokes: My Story*, 183–4.

99 Crerar Papers, vol. 3, file 958C.009(D178), "Notes by Lt-Gen K. Stuart Regarding His Trip to Italy," 21 July 1944. (There are copies of this memo and other related correspondence in DHist, 86/544.) In a letter to the CIGS, however, Alexander said he had urged Stuart to seek a new corps commander after more Canadians had battle experience. LHC, Viscount Alanbrooke Papers, file 14/10, Alexander to Brooke, 18 July 1944.

100 Leese Papers, box 2, Leese to wife, 14 July, 14, 15 September 1944.

101 Alanbrooke Papers, file 14/10, Leese to Alexander, 15 July 1944, encl. Leese to Stuart, 14 July 1944; Stuart's quite contradictory account in his last letter to Leese is in WO 214/55, 21 July 1944; Leese Papers, vol. 4, Leese to Maj.-Gen. Kennedy, 25 July 1944. In this letter, Leese complained that Stuart knew nothing of modern battle "and appeared to me only to be interested in Canadian politics. He seemed to take little interest in the main war effort."

102 Crerar Papers, vol. 3, file 958C.009 (D178), Crerar to Stuart, 15 July 1944. So too was the Cabinet War Committee. See CWC Minutes, 3 August 1944; King Papers, Diary, 3 August 1944, f. 719; Public Archives of Nova Scotia, Angus L. Macdonald Papers, vol. 1503, f. 392, War Cabinet, 3 August 1944.

103 Crerar Papers, vol. 3, file 958C.009 (D178), "Notes on Meeting with CIGS ... 19 Jul 44."

104 See correspondence on DND, vol. 11005, file 215C1.069 (D1), vol. 1.

105 WO 214/55, Brooke to Alexander, 22 July 1944; Alanbrooke Papers, file 14/10, Brooke to Gen. Wilson, 2 August 1944.

106 On this point, see the conversation between P.J. Grigg, UK Secretary for War, and Vincent Massey, Massey Papers, box 312, Diary, 22 November 1944.

107 Crerar Papers, vol. 7, file 958C.009 (D183), Burns to Crerar, 12 August 1944.

108 Burns "stated that he had been ordered by Stuart to continue to command the Corps. He added that he felt he was capable of doing so and that he considered the Canadian Corps would fight better as a Corps than if the divisions

were placed under other corps." Leese Papers, vol. 4, Leese to Kennedy, 25 July 1944.

109 Certainly this was Burns's view in his memo to Crerar commenting on the reasons offered for his firing by his superiors in Italy. Crerar Papers, vol. 4, file 958C.009 (D178), Burns to Crerar, 12 November 1944.

110 The best account of the battle is W.J. McAndrew, "Eighth Army at the Gothic Line: The Dog-Fight," *RUSI Journal* 131 (June 1986), 55ff. There were some later suggestions from Burns that his plans for this battle were shaped by reinforcement shortages. See John Gardam, *Forty Years After* (Burnstown, Ont., 1990), 87–8.

111 Burns Papers, vol. 1, Leese to Burns, 9 September 1944.

112 NA, Ken Stuart Papers, vol. 1, Personal file, Leese to Stuart, 15 September 1944.

113 Ibid., Alexander to Stuart, 17 September 1944.

114 Burns, *General Mud*, 188–9.

115 McAndrew places the blame for the failure of exploitation on Leese, acknowledging, however, that his reservations about Burns's competence skewed his grouping of forces. "The Dog-Fight," 62. This view of Leese's "criminal inertia" is shared by Graham and Bidwell, *Tug of War*, 350, 357ff.

116 WO 214/55, McCreery to Alexander, 24 October 1944. The only instance of humour any of my interviewees could recall of Burns was his comment at one staff meeting to a medical officer who announced the availability of penicillin for treating venereal disease: "penicillin for putrid pricks." LCol E.T. Winslow interview, 2 March 1992. But see also George Kitching, *Mud and Green Fields* (Langley, BC, 1986), 192.

117 NA, M.H.S. Penhale Papers, vol. 1, file Correspondence: Preparations for Departure, Vokes to Penhale, 2 November 1944. Gen Hoffmeister denied flatly that he was prepared to resign if Burns remained. Interview, 2 March 1992. Burns's BGS, Desmond Smith, later said that relations between Burns and the divisions' GOCs were so bad that "when I visited either Vokes or Hoffmeister I usually carried an olive branch as a token of peace." McAndrew Papers, MGen Smith to McAndrew, 29 August 1980. MGen Bogert also said: "I heard Vokes speak to Burns on the telephone in an almost insubordinate way that should never have been permitted; it was as if Burns deferred to Vokes instead of asserting his authority." Ibid., Bogert to McAndrew, nd. And MGen Hoffmeister remembered that he demanded to be paraded before the army commander when he found Burns going over an operation with one of his brigadiers. That was his

job, Hoffmeister said, and only with difficulty did Burns get him to withdraw his demand. There was at least one other similar instance of Burns doing "stupid things." Interview.

118 Kitching, *Mud and Green Fields*, 238; confidential interview.

119 Crerar Papers, vol. 4, file 958C.009 (D178), Montague to Murchie and Stuart, 4 November 1944, quoting cable W125, Weeks to Montague. There is an interview with Alexander, done while he was governor-general in Canada, that treats the Burns affair. See USAMHI, OCMH, World War II Mediterranean, Sidney Mathews Collection, Alexander interview [1949?], pt. II, 16. MGen Desmond Smith, Burns's BGS, and MGen Bert Hoffmeister confirmed the tenor of Weeks's comments. Interviews. Vokes's final comment on Burns was: "I always liked Tommy, the man. I never liked Burns, the general." Vokes, *Vokes: My Story*, 181.

120 Burns later believed that if Col. Ralston had not left the cabinet in early November 1944, "perhaps I might have received a stronger support." Burns Papers, vol. 1, UNTSO/UNEF Reappointment file, Burns to I.N. Smith, 28 September 1956.

121 WO 214/55, Burns to Alexander, 7 November 1944.

122 Crerar Papers, vol. 4, file 958C.009 (D178), Crerar to MGA, [date obscured].

123 Ibid., Burns to Crerar, 12 November 1944. His daughter remembered that Burns did not want to be a disaffected general. Her mother had told her not to ask about the war, and Burns volunteered nothing. Dr Mary Burns interview.

124 Bogert to McAndrew, 27 November 1983.

125 See Crerar Papers, vol. 4, file 958C.009 (D178), Montague to Crerar, 20 November 1944; Burns Papers, vol. 1, Montague to Gen. M.W.A.P. Graham, 4 December 1944.

126 Dr Mary Burns interview.

127 John Bassett interview, 5 June 1991.

CHAPTER 6   SIMONDS: MASTER OF THE BATTLEFIELD

1 IWM, Trumball Warren Papers, Montgomery to Warren, 1 January 1969.

2 Omar Bradley, *A General's Life* (New York 1983), 293.

3 Quoted in Ronald Lewin, *Montgomery as Military Commander* (London 1971), 227.

4 Brian Horrocks, *A Full Life* (London 1960), 254.

5 Max Hastings, *Overlord: D-Day and the Battle for Normandy* (London 1984), 56.

6 Based on a conversation with Col. Charles Simonds, 23 August 1992, on Guy Simonds Papers (North Gower, Ont.), Memoirs box, draft memoirs, chap. 1, and on W.E.J. Hutchison, "Test of a Corps Commander: Lieutenant-General Guy Granville Simonds Normandy — 1944" (MA thesis, University of Victoria 1982), chap. 2.

7 Simonds Papers, Memoirs box, Draft Memoirs, chaps. 2–3; ibid., Prewar box, *The Ashburian* 4 (June 1920), 8, 9, 26; 5 (December 1920), 4, 23; 5 (March 1921), 12, 17.

8 Conversation with Col. Simonds.

9 RMC, Registrar's Ledgers, Simonds entry.

10 Simonds Papers, Draft Memoirs, chap. 3.

11 Ibid.; J.S. McMahon, *Professional Soldier: General Guy Simonds — A Memoir* (Winnipeg 1985), chap. 2; R.A. Preston, *Canada's RMC: A History of the Royal Military College* (Toronto 1969), chap. 10.

12 *R.M.C. Review* 2–6 (1921–5), passim.

13 RMC, Central Registry, Simonds file, Reports, especially for term ending December 1922.

14 *R.M.C. Review* 7 (November 1925), 23ff; 6 (May 1925), 24.

15 McMahon, *Professional Soldier*, 11.

16 This was not unusual. Christopher Vokes's father, a major on the RMC staff, sold his son's greatcoat to another cadet for $37. RMC, Central Registry, Major F. Vokes file, undated memorandum.

17 Docs on ibid., Simonds file.

18 Significantly, there is no mention of the financial difficulties that plagued him in Simonds Papers, Draft Memoirs, chap. 3.

19 RMC, Central Registry, Simonds file, Macdonnell to Leonard, 26 June 1922.

20 NA, G.W.L. Nicholson Papers, vol. 3, Gunners II drafts file, Simonds's notes on chaps 1 and 2, nd.

21 Simonds Papers, Memoirs box, Draft Memoirs, chaps. 4, 5.

22 Ibid.; *Winnipeg Tribune,* 21 October 1929; G.D. Mitchell, *RCHA — Right of the Line* (Ottawa 1986), 59.

23 Mrs F.F. Worthington interview, 23 May 1991. Brig. P.A.S. Todd agreed; interview, 8 May 1991.

24 Confidential source; *Saturday Night,* 10 September 1932; clippings, nd, in Simonds Papers, Prewar box.

25 On Mrs Simonds, Mrs E.C. Plow interview, 19 December 1991.

26 Simonds Papers, Prewar box, Income Tax Assessment Notice, 10 April 1935.

27 Ibid., Draft Memoirs, chap. 6.

28 Ibid., Prewar box, Miscellaneous Artillery Papers file, Staff College 1937 list; ibid., papers.

29 Confidential source; Simonds Papers, Prewar box, Vanier to Simonds, 24 March 1938.

30 LGen W.A.B. Anderson interview, 21 May 1991.

31 *Canadian Defence Quarterly* 15 (July 1938); 16 (January, July 1939).

32 Simonds Papers, Draft Memoirs, chap. 3.

33 Malcolm Sutherland-Brown interview, 27 February 1992.

34 NA, E.W. Sansom Papers, Sansom to his wife, 3 April 1940.

35 Simonds Papers, Prewar box, Major Simonds Personal File, "Memo of CIGS Conference . . . 16 May 1940."

36 MGen R.P. Rothschild interview, 24 May 1991; Mitchell, *RCHA*, 84ff.

37 DND, vol. 11004, file CC7/28, Memorandum, 17 September 1940.

38 Ibid., vol. 9874, file 2/Staff/4, Simonds's "Report on the First Canadian Junior War Staff Course," 20 April 1941. See also John A. Macdonald, "In Search of Veritable: Training the Canadian Army Staff Officer, 1899 to 1945" (MA thesis, RMC 1992), 123–6.

39 Simonds Papers, Prewar box, CJSWC syllabus.

40 D.D. Eisenhower Library, BGen J.W. Bishop Oral History interview, 20 January 1973.

41 Col. John Page interview, 11 February 1992 (done by Jock Vance of York University).

42 Macdonald, "In Search of Veritable," 293. Some of the passes were conditional.

43 DHist, CMHQ Historical Officers Report #22, 24 April 1941.

44 NA, V.W. Odlum Papers, vol. 26, Copies of Letters to McNaughton, Odlum to McNaughton, 12 August 1941.

45 DHist 86/544, Simonds to Crerar, 15 December 1943. Crerar's rebuttal of these perceptions is in ibid., "Memorandum . . . on Contents of Letter dated 15 Dec 43," 21 December 1943.

46 NA, H.D.G. Crerar Papers, vol. 1, 958C.009 (D23), Crerar to C.S.L. Hertzberg, 11 September 1942.

47 NA, A.G.L. McNaughton Papers, vol. 248, War Diary 1942, 5 August 1942; docs on ibid., vol. 135, file PA 1-7-1; LHC, Viscount Alanbrooke Papers, file 3/A/VI, Notes on My Life, 9, 25 July 1942.

48 McNaughton Papers, vol. 248, War Diary 1942, McNaughton to Simonds et al., 13 September 1942. Simonds was becoming noticed elsewhere for "promise." LHC, Liddell Hart Papers, file 11/1943/36, "Talks at 1st [British] Corps Headquarters," 9–10 June 1943.

49 NA, J.L. Ralston Papers, vol. 54, appraisals of senior officers, nd.

50 WO 214/55, Viscount Alexander Papers, telegram, CIGS to Eisenhower, 24 April 1943.

51 Crerar Papers, vol. 8, 958C.009 (D182), Montgomery to Crerar, 30 May 1942.

52 McNaughton Papers, vol. 132, file PA 1-3-3, Simonds to GOC-in-C, 22 April 1943, and Report on Visit to Eighth Army, 29 April 1943. See also L.S.B. Shapiro, "These Are Our Generals," *Maclean's*, 1 July 1944, 12, which suggests that Simonds made a substantial impression on UK officers on this visit.

53 Simonds Papers, Memoirs box, Draft Typing file, "Sicilian Campaign." See also George Kitching's memoir, *Mud and Green Fields* (Langley, BC, 1986).

54 Simonds Papers, 1945–9 box, Sicily Diary, D-Day and D+1.

55 C.B. Ware Papers (Victoria), Scrapbooks, Ware to his mother, 25 July 1943.

56 Dr W.J. McAndrew Papers (Ottawa), Major A.T. Sesia Diary, 16 July 1943. The Canadian people likely would have said that Simonds was earning his pay, just as the private soldiers under fire were earning their $1.30.

57 For a critique of Simonds's tactics in Sicily, see W.J. McAndrew, "Fire or Movement? Canadian Tactical Doctrine, Sicily — 1943," *Military Affairs* 51 (July 1987), 140ff, and Kitching, *Mud and Green Fields*, 167–8.

58 IWM, Oliver Leese Papers, vol. 4, Leese to friends and family, July 1943, and vol. 2, Leese to C. Leicester-Warren, 7 August 1943.

59 McNaughton Papers, file PA 6-9-M-4, Montgomery to McNaughton, 26 July 1943.

60 Stephen Brooks, ed., *Montgomery and the Eighth Army* (London 1991), 247.

61 McAndrew Papers, Sesia Diary, 17 July 1943; Trumball Warren interview, 27 May 1991. Compare Howard Graham, *Citizen and Soldier: The Memoirs of Lieutenant-General Howard Graham* (Toronto 1987), 158ff.; Kitching, *Mud and Green Fields*, 169–70; D.G. Dancocks, *The D-Day Dodgers: The Canadians in Italy, 1943–1945* (Toronto 1991), 54ff.

62 McNaughton Papers, vol. 202, file PA 6-9-S-7, McNaughton Memo of Conversation with Simonds, 25 August 1943; Memo of Conversation Brig. Wyman and Simonds, 24 August 1943. McNaughton, visiting the Canadians in Sicily, noted that he had decided Simonds had enough to do with his division and

Wyman was not under his operational command. Simonds did not take this "very graciously though nothing was said directly at the time."

63 Simonds Papers, 1945–9 box, clipping, nd.

64 McNaughton Papers, vol. 202, file PA 6-9-S-7, Simonds to McNaughton, August and 30 July 1943; see also ibid., "Memo of Discussion Lieutenant-General McNaughton–Major-General Richardson . . . 26 August 1943."

65 MGen Bert Hoffmeister interview, 2 March 1992. On Valguarnera, see G.W.L. Nicholson, *The Canadians in Italy* (Ottawa 1957), 96ff.

66 Tony Foster Papers (Halifax), Interview with General Vokes, 5 April 1984.

67 McNaughton Papers, vol. 134, file PA 1-3-14-2, McNaughton's "Visit to General Sir Bernard Montgomery . . . 24–25 Aug, 43."

68 Simonds Papers, Prewar box, 1 Canadian Division file, Simonds to Dempsey, 22 September 1943; Nicholson, *The Canadians in Italy*, 229ff.

69 DHist 86/544, "Memorandum by GOC 1 Cdn Corps on contents of letter," 21 December 1943.

70 DND, vol. 10033, file 9/Sr Appts/1, McNaughton-Montgomery telegrams, 14, 16 October 1943; Fred Vokes Papers (Ottawa), clipping, 6 November 1943.

71 Brig. Jack Christian interview, 31 May 1991.

72 York University Archives, J.L. Granatstein Papers, Maj. G.D. Johnston letters, Johnston to Fav., 19 November 1943.

73 Crerar Papers, vol. 7, 958C.009 (D180), Simonds to Crerar, 8 December 1943.

74 Peter Suedfeld of the Department of Psychology at the University of British Columbia has pioneered the study of the quantitative measure of differentiation and integration in information processing. See his "The Role of Integrative Complexity in Military Leadership: Robert E. Lee and His Opponents," *Journal of Applied Social Psychology* 16 (1986), 498ff, and "Deciphering of Hidden Messages: Archival Measurement of Psychological Processes" (paper presented to the International Congress of Psychology, Sydney, Australia, August 1988). At my request, he applied his technique to the Simonds–Crerar exchange. His judgment, based solely on the letters, concluded that Simonds "devoted more intellectual effort (and perhaps time, emotion, ego) to minor matters than necessary" and that "in his confrontation with Crerar, he may have been showing the signs of serious stress." His analysis shows Crerar as very cool throughout, a dogged man with a straight ahead approach. I am most grateful to Professor Suedfeld.

75 John A. English, *The Canadian Army and the Normandy Campaign: A Study of Failure in High Command* (New York 1991), 186ff; Crerar Papers, correspon-

dence, vol. 7, file 958C.009 (D180); DHist, 86/544; DND, vol. 10663, file 215C1.049 (D1), Crerar to Stuart, 17 January 1944; Simonds Papers, 1945-9 box, Crerar to Simonds, 6 January 1944; LGen S.F. Clark interview, 24 February 1992; MGen George Kitching interview, 25 February 1992, and Kitching, *Mud and Green Fields*, 178–80; R.S. Malone, *Portrait of War 1939–43* (Toronto 1983), 199–200.

76 NA, W.L.M. King Diary, 17 May 1944, f. 498.

77 Nigel Hamilton, *Monty*, vol. 2: *Master of the Battlefield 1942–1944* (London 1983), 465. Crerar's letter to Montgomery was written on 17 December. The letter quoted here was dated 23 December 1943.

78 University of Toronto Archives, Vincent Massey Papers, box 312, Diary, 31 January 1944.

79 Shapiro, "These Are Our Generals," 44.

80 The gossip was that Simonds refused to have officers older or who had once been senior to him under his command. Gen. Worthington was said to have begun to pack as soon as he heard Simonds had the corps. Mrs Plow interview.

81 Clark interview, 24 February 1992; DND, vol. 10798, Brig. Elliot Rodger Personal Diary, 14 February 1944.

82 Nicholson Papers, vol. 4, Drafts IX file, Simonds to Nicholson, 25 February 1970.

83 DND, Rodger Diary, 22 February 1944; Clark interview.

84 DHist, Charles Foulkes Papers, Black binder, "Operational Policy," 17 February 1944; NA, Kenneth Stuart Papers, vol. 1, "Efficiency of Command," 19 February 1944; D.C. Spry Papers (Ottawa), "Honours and Awards," 26 February 1944.

85 "Operational Policy." Dr W.J. McAndrew has suggested that this "palaver" was lifted from Simonds's prewar articles in *Canadian Defence Quarterly*: "did he learn from practical experience?" Letter to author, 28 September 1992.

86 Terry Copp, *The Brigade: The Fifth Canadian Infantry Brigade, 1939–1945* (Stoney Creek, Ont., 1992), 46.

87 IWM, Viscount Montgomery Papers, BLM 120/1, Simonds to Trumball Warren, 19 February 1944, with attached memo, "2 Cdn Corps Study Period 13–18 March," 16 February 1944.

88 "Efficiency of Command."

89 *DCER*, X, 182.

90 Montgomery Papers, file BLM 1197-8, Gen. Crocker to Dempsey, 5 July 1944; Dempsey to Montgomery, 6 July 1944; Montgomery to Crerar, 8 July 1944. Montgomery passed his doubts about Keller on to the CIGS: ibid., file BLM 126/9, 7 July 1944); Brooke's "very worried" reply is in BLM 1/97, 11 July 1944.

91 Based on LCol Don Mingay interview, 6 June 1991; LCol Peter Bennett interview, 6 September 1991; and three confidential interviews. Mingay was the GSO 1 of the 3rd Canadian Infantry Division.

92 Crerar Papers, vol. 1, Memorandum, 3 May 1943. Crerar in May 1944 thought Keller would be a good "two-fisted" corps commander, but noted that interest in high policy was outside his ken. DND, vol. 11005, 215C1.061 (D1), Crerar to Stuart, 16 May 1944.

93 Ibid., vol. 11005, 215C1.061 (D1), Memorandum, 14 July 1944.

94 Ibid., Simonds to Dempsey, 27 July 1944.

95 After the war, Simonds said that Keller was "a blusterer with a very bold front. . . . I was saved from a very very embarrassing situation by Keller being wounded and invalided home before I had to act which I had become convinced was necessary." University of Victoria Archives, George Pearkes Papers, Acc. 74-1, vol. 25, file 26, Simonds to R.H. Roy, 29 December 1972.

96 See on this point Terry Copp's "Brief to the Veterans Affairs Committee of the Senate of Canada Concerning the CBC Series 'The Valour and the Horror,'" June 1992. It is worth noting that Crerar supported Simonds's decision to let Keller stay in command. Crerar Papers, vol. 3, 958C.009 (D178), Crerar to Stuart, 15 July 1944.

97 Even before Simonds had had a chance to make his mark in Normandy, Montgomery was singing his praises. He was "far and away the best general [the Canadians] have; he is the equal of any British Corps Commander, and is far better than Crerar." Alanbrooke Papers, file 14/28, Montgomery to Brooke, 14 July 1944.

98 The casualties suffered by the Black Watch (Royal Highland Regiment) in Operation Spring on 25 July 1944 were a subject of controversy immediately after the war. See docs on DND, vol 12745, file 24/AH1/1/6. Simonds's 1946 view is in ibid., Simonds to Chief of Staff, CMHQ, 31 January 1946. For Gen. Foulkes's view, see DHist, 83/269, comments of 24 April 1959 on Official History, vol. 3. The controversy was revived — in ways most unfavourable to Simonds — in the CBC-TV series, "The Valour and the Horror," in 1992.

99 Terry Copp and Robert Vogel, *Maple Leaf Route: Falaise* (Alma, Ont., 1983), 46. See also English, *The Canadian Army*, chap. 10.

100 John A. English, *On Infantry* (New York 1981), 38, notes that Liddell Hart had suggested artificial moonlight as early as 1933.

101 See on Totalize, C.P. Stacey, *The Victory Campaign* (Ottawa 1960), chap. 9; J.A. Roberts, *The Canadian Summer: The Memoirs of James Alan Roberts* (Toronto 1981), 66–8; LHC, Chester Wilmot Papers, file LH 15/15/130, "Queries for General

Simonds," nd [Wilmot's notes of an interview with Simonds]; University of Victoria Archives, R.H. Roy Papers, Acc. 82-5, box 1, file 1, Gen. G. Kitching's "The Background to Totalize," October 1980; Foulkes Papers, Black binder, "Notes on Corps Comd's Conference 31 Jul 44"; ibid., Simonds to Foulkes, 2 August 1944, and attached outline plan; and DND, vol. 10797, "GOC's Activities"; Crerar Papers, vol. 2, Simonds to Crerar, 6 August 1944. On conversion of Priests to armoured personnel carriers, see University of Victoria Archives, Col. C.R. Boehm interview, 8 June 1978. MGen Elliot Rodger remembered that the night armoured attack was greeted with some scepticism. "But it's never been done before," one officer said. "That's why I'm doing it," Simonds rejoined. Rodger interview, 21 May 1991.

102 John Ellis, *Brute Force: Allied Strategy and Tactics in the Second World War* (New York 1990), 379.

103 Foster Papers, Meyer's Dorchester file, Command Chaplain's visit report, 31 December 1948.

104 See, on the August 1944 battles, Carlo d'Este, *Decision in Normandy* (London 1983), passim, and especially chap. 26. MGen George Kitching has a narrative on these actions in Roy Papers, Acc. 82-5, box 1, file 1.

105 MGen M.P. Bogert in a letter to LCol J.A. English, 1 February 1992. See also Kitching, *Mud and Green Fields*, 227–8; Stacey, *Victory Campaign*, 275–7; Tony Foster, *Meeting of Generals* (Toronto 1986), 381ff.

106 Simonds Papers, Memoirs box, Draft Typing file, "Operations of 2 Canadian Corps in the Pursuit Across the Seine."

107 David Belchem, *All in the Day's March* (London 1978), 222; "How Canada Smashed the Germans," *The Canadian*, 5 October 1968, 19. On Simonds's assessment of the strategic possibilities missed on the way to Belgium, see E.K.G. Sexsmith, *Eisenhower as Military Commander* (New York 1972), 170.

108 USAMHI, OCMH Personal Papers, D.D. Eisenhower Diary, bk. XIII, p. 1734a, Eisenhower to Gen. Marshall, 21 September 1944.

109 The best account of the Scheldt campaign is J.L. Moulton, *Battle for Antwerp* (London 1978). See also Denis and Shelagh Whitaker, *Tug of War: The Canadian Victory That Opened Antwerp* (Toronto 1984).

110 Simonds Papers, 2 Cdn Corps box, file 2, Simonds to GOC-in-C, First Cdn Army, 21 September 1944; Stacey, *Victory Campaign*, 369ff; Moulton, *Battle for Antwerp*, chap. 6.

111 Wilmot Papers, LH 15/15/130, Simonds interview, nd; DND, Rodger Diary, 29 September 1944; Brig. G.E. Beament interview, 24 May 1991. Later studies showed that bursting the dykes put about half the enemy batteries out of

action. WO 106/4473, Army Operational Research Group Report No. 299, 10 October 1945, "The West Kapelle Assault on Walcheren." Serious controversy between the services continued after the successful conclusion of the operation. See Simonds Papers, 2 Cdn Corps box, envelope, Simonds to GOC-in-C First Cdn Army, 1 January 1945.

112 Montgomery Papers, BLM 115/69, VCIGS to Montgomery, 21 October 1944. Montgomery had also made it clear to Col. Ralston that he preferred Simonds. King Diary, 18 October 1944, f. 988.

113 This was Montgomery's view. Massey Diary, 31 January 1944. It was widely shared. BGen Denis Whitaker interview, 19 March 1991; Rothschild interview; Christian interview; Todd interview.

114 Roberts, *The Canadian Summer*, 80.

115 C.P. Stacey, "Canadian Leaders of the Second World War," *Canadian Historical Review* 66 (March 1986), 68.

116 Simonds Papers, 2 Canadian Corps box, file 2, Dempsey to Simonds, 2 April 1945; IWM, LCol H.M. Baker Diary, file 87/44/1, entry, 4 April 1945; Simonds Papers, 2 Canadian Corps box, Col. and Mrs Mathers to Simonds, 6 October 1943.

117 Crerar Papers, vol. 4, 958C.009 (D179), Crerar to Murchie, 5 July 1945.

118 NPRC, Foulkes file, Staff College Final Report, 15 December 1938. Foulkes's other assessments in the PF are also found here.

119 Todd interview.

120 Crerar Papers, vol. 5, 958C.009 (D924), Recommendations for Promotion, 5 June 1942.

121 Ibid., vol. 2, 958C.009 (D21), Crerar to McNaughton, 11 August 1943.

122 McNaughton Papers, file PA 6-9-C-3, Crerar to McNaughton, 9 October 1943. This was also MGen M.P. Bogert's view. Interview, 8 September 1991.

123 Public Archives of Nova Scotia, Angus L. Macdonald Papers, vol. 1503, F386/50, Ralston diary, 17 November 1943.

124 Stacey, "Canadian Leaders," 69. "We all detested Foulkes," Gen Harry Foster said. Foster, *Meeting of Generals*, 340.

125 Ibid., 84.

126 Simonds Papers, Prewar box, 1 Cdn Div files, Simonds's "Report on Incident Resulting in Change of Command . . . WNS Regt, nd [12 June 1943]; Christopher Vokes, *Vokes: My Story* (Ottawa 1985), 140–1; MGen W.J. Megill interview, 18 January 1992; Brig. George Pangman interview, 23 April 1991.

127 Conversation with Mr Bull, Royal Canadian Military Institute, 1 April 1992.

128 George Kitching Diary [Victoria], entry, 2 August 1944; Kitching, *Mud and Green Fields*, 206; Moncel interview.

129 See Kitching, *Mud and Green Fields*, 232; Jeffery Williams, *The Long Left Flank* (Toronto 1988), 26.

130 DND, Rodger Diary, 27 January 1945; Kitching interview.

131 Confirmed in Rothschild interview.

132 Col. Robert Raymont interview, 23 May 1991. James Eayrs, *In Defence of Canada*, vol. 3: *Peacemaking and Deterrence* (Toronto 1972), 62, offers a different though quite similar account of this incident.

133 See Graham, *Citizen and Soldier*, 214–15. One political slip Foulkes, as the new CGS, did make was to attempt to argue for peacetime conscription, an impossibility in Mackenzie King's Canada. Bryan Brulotte, "Visions of Grandeur: Planning for the Canadian Post-War Army 1944–1947" (MA thesis, Carleton University 1991), chaps. 2–3.

134 DHist, 86/544, Foulkes to Murchie, 2 November 1945. Simonds's fate was a subject of army gossip. For example, NA, M.H.S. Penhale Papers, vol. 1, Correspondence: Preparations for Departure from CMHQ file, W.C. Hyde to Penhale, 20 March 1946.

135 DHist 86/544, Foulkes to Minister, 21 August 1946. Montgomery discussed this possibility with Mackenzie King. King Papers, "Notes re Conversation at Laurier House," 9 September 1946, ff. C166968ff.

136 DHist 86/544, Foulkes to Simonds, 31 October 1947. There were press suggestions of rivalry between Foulkes and Simonds. See, for example, Powell Smily, "Is Foulkes the Man for the Job?" *New Liberty*, March 1949, 9ff.

137 DHist, 86/544, Simonds to Foulkes, 24 January, and reply, 27 January 1950.

138 Foulkes told diplomat Escott Reid: "I always leave my office at four. If I can't organize my office well enough that I can leave at four you'd better get yourself another chairman of the chiefs of staff." Escott Reid, *Radical Mandarin* (Toronto 1989), 244. Also Rothschild interview; Raymont interview; and Graham, *Citizen and Soldier*, 224.

139 MGen H.A. Sparling interview, 18 April 1991; MGen George Kitching, "Guy Simonds — in Appreciation," *Canadian Defence Quarterly* 4 (Autumn 1974), 10.

140 See, for example, Toronto *Globe and Mail*, 17, 18 June 1955; *Toronto Star*, 13 June 1955.

141 DHist 86/544, Foulkes to Gen. A.M. Gruenther, 18 February, and reply, 5 March 1955; Eisenhower Library, Alfred M. Gruenther Papers, NATO Series, vol.

4, Simonds file, Gruenther to Simonds, 7 April 1955. Kitching ("Guy Simonds — in Appreciation," 10) and others have suggested that Montgomery wanted Simonds as commander-in-chief of land forces in Central Europe and that this appointment was blocked by Ottawa. Gruenther's letter of 5 March 1955 makes clear, however, that "Monty's reaction was that we have no spot for him, nor can we create one."

142 Gruenther Papers, NATO Series, vol. 4, Canada Farewell Trip file, Briefing Book 1955.

143 Dr Donald Schurman Papers (Kingston), Schurman's letter to his father, April 1956, regarding a meeting at which Simonds spoke; G.G. Simonds, "Canada's Survival," *The Legionary*, May 1956; G.G. Simonds, "Where We've Gone Wrong on Defence," *Maclean's*, 23 June 1956, 66ff; *Globe and Mail*, 22 February, 13 March, 13 June, 1 July 1956.

CHAPTER 7   MATTHEWS AND HOFFMEISTER: MILITIA SUCCESSES

1 DHist, Charles Foulkes Papers, Discussions between Commander 1 Canadian Corps . . . file, "Last Battle of the British in Holland," nd.

2 For example, NA, Victor Odlum Papers, vol. 26, C.W. Peck to W.L.M. King, 18 December 1939.

3 York University Archives, J.L. Granatstein Papers, Brig. William Murphy letters, Murphy to his family, 20 February 1944.

4 Based on Gen. Bruce Matthews interviews, 25 April and 10 June 1991, and on NPRC, Matthews file. I am greatly indebted to the late Gen. Matthews for permission to use his personnel file.

5 Ibid., Confidential Report, 7 May 1935.

6 NA, G.W.L. Nicholson Papers, vol. 3, Gunners II drafts file, Simonds's comments on chap. 2, nd.

7 Comments based on Bruce Matthews Papers (Toronto), photo albums, 1928–39.

8 Matthews interviews.

9 NPRC, Matthews file, Alec [?] to Gen. Harold Matthews, 7 December 1939.

10 Matthews interviews.

11 LCol Peter Bennett interview, 6 September 1991.

12 Matthews interviews; Matthews Papers, scrapbooks, photographs.

13 DND, vol. 10033, file 9/Selection/1, LCol W. McNeill to senior officer, CMHQ, 3 November 1942; ibid., Mf. C5438, file HQS 20-5-26-2, vol. 3,

Canmilitry to Defensor, 14 January 1943; Matthews Papers, scrapbook, Particulars of Officer, RCA.

14 Nicholson Papers, vol. 4, Gunners II drafts file, Matthews to Nicholson, 15 March 1969.

15 Matthews interviews.

16 G.W.L. Nicholson, *The Gunners of Canada*, vol. 2 (Toronto 1972), 151n. Col. Ralston wrote to Matthews's wife to say he had seen him in Italy "characteristically, 'up the line' where he was most needed that morning." Matthews Papers, Scrapbook, Ralston to Mrs V. Matthews, 24 January 1944.

17 Daniel Dancocks, *The D-Day Dodgers: The Canadians in Italy, 1943–1945* (Toronto 1991), 171–2.

18 DND, vol. 10033, file 9/Sr Appts/1/2, Canmilitry to I Cdn Corps, 31 January 1944; Dancocks, *The D-Day Dodgers*, 221.

19 IWM, Gen. Sir Oliver Leese Papers, box 2, Leese to his wife, 29 February 1944.

20 DND, vol. 10798, "Personal Diary of Brig. N.E. Rodger," 26 May 1944.

21 Matthews interviews. On these operations, see C.P. Stacey, *The Victory Campaign* (Ottawa 1960), chaps. 7–10.

22 DHist, 958C.009 (D178), vol. 4, telegram, GOC-in-C to Canmilitry, 8 November 1944. On Crerar's concerns about artillery officers in high command posts, see docs on NA, H.D.G. Crerar Papers, vol. 3.

23 DND, vol. 10798, Rodger Diary, 17 November 1944.

24 For a critical appraisal of Foulkes, see Terry Copp, *The Brigade: The Fifth Canadian Infantry Brigade, 1939–1945* (Stoney Creek, Ont., 1992), 36 and chap. 3 ff.

25 Ibid., 170.

26 Matthews interviews; Terry Copp interview with Gen Matthews, 10 June 1987; Brig. Frank Lace interview, 17 May 1991; Gen W.J. Megill interview, 18 January 1992.

27 Matthews interviews.

28 G.G. Simonds Papers (North Gower, Ont.), II Canadian Corps box, unmarked file, "Future Service — General Officers and Brigadiers," nd [May 1945].

29 Ibid., Matthews to Simonds, 10 May 1945.

30 Matthews Papers, scrapbook, Simonds to Matthews, 18 October 1945.

31 Matthews interviews.

32 Fred Vokes Papers (Ottawa), Matthews to Gen. Vokes, 5 November 1945.

33 Matthews Papers, scrapbook, Walford to Matthews, 4 January 1946.

34 Matthews interviews.

35 Dr W.J. McAndrew Papers, Transcript of interview conducted by McAndrew and B. Greenhous with Gen. Hoffmeister, nd (referred to subsequently as McAndrew–Hoffmeister interview).

36 J.L. Rutledge, "This Soldier Business," *Maclean's*, 15 August 1939, 22.

37 Gen. M.B. Hoffmeister interview, 2 March 1992.

38 McAndrew–Hoffmeister interview; Brig. H.P. Bell-Irving interview, 4 March 1992.

39 McAndrew–Hoffmeister interview.

40 Ibid.; Hoffmeister interview.

41 Ibid.; Terry Copp and Bill McAndrew, *Battle Exhaustion: Soldiers and Psychiatrists in the Canadian Army, 1939–1945* (Montreal 1990), 16ff.

42 Hoffmeister interview.

43 Ibid. See DHist 530.03 (D1), "Canadian War Staff Course 'A' Wing" for his grade.

44 Christopher Vokes, *Vokes: My Story* (Ottawa 1985), 76.

45 Dr W.J. McAndrew interview with MGen Chris Vokes, June 1980. Vokes thought problems were widespread in his brigade. For a frank assessment of the Seaforths at this period, see R.H. Roy, *The Seaforth Highlanders of Canada* (Vancouver 1969), chap. 5.

46 DND, Access Box 34, file 221C1 (D284), Salmon to GOC 1 Cdn Corps, 20 March 1943. Harry Crerar agreed. Ibid., Crerar to McNaughton, 2 April 1943. Compare docs on DHist, H.D.G. Crerar Papers, Hoffmeister file.

47 Dancocks, *The D-Day Dodgers*, 68, 83.

48 G.W.L. Nicholson, *The Canadians in Italy* (Ottawa 1957), 160; Roy, *The Seaforth Highlanders*, chap. 4; Vokes, *Vokes: My Story*, 119. This was also said to be Montgomery's view. Gen. A.E. Potts Papers (Toronto), Capt. J.J. Conway to Potts, 2 November 1943. Hoffmeister's combined arms assault drew notice in *Maclean's*: L.S.B. Shapiro, "These Are Our Generals," 1 July 1944, 44.

49 Hoffmeister interview. Hoffmeister's approach is documented in Dr W.J. McAndrew's interview with LCol S.W. Thompson, 6 April 1980.

50 Hoffmeister interview.

51 Crerar Papers, vol. 1, 958C.009 (D23), McNaughton to Stuart, nd; ibid., Minutes of Special Meeting . . . 26 September 1943; ibid., Crerar to McNaughton, 28 September 1943; DND, vol. 10033, file 9/Sr Appts/1, McNaughton to Tow, 16 October 1943.

52 McAndrew–Hoffmeister interview; Vokes, *Vokes: My Story*, 134, wrote that Hoffmeister was his "most capable" battalion commander.

53 McAndrew–Hoffmeister interview; McAndrew Papers, letter to

McAndrew, 2 April 1982.

54 RMC, Christopher Vokes Papers, Vertical File, notebook. The casualties covered all December 1943 and left a deficiency of 59 officers and 992 men after reinforcements had been factored in.

55 McAndrew–Hoffmeister interview.

56 Brereton Greenhous, "Would It Not Have Been Better to Bypass Ortona Completely . . . ? A Canadian Christmas, 1943," *Canadian Defence Quarterly* 19 (April 1989), 51ff. See also Nicholson, *The Canadians in Italy*, chaps. 10–11.

57 NA, J.L. Ralston Papers, vol. 37, Appointments Overseas file, Ralston to Stuart, 2 February 1944.

58 DND, Mf. C5438, file HQS 20-5-26-2, Stuart to Murchie, 3 March 1944.

59 Leese Papers, box 2, Leese to his wife, 4 March, 8 May 1944, and box 1, Mss Autobiography, XII, 1; WO 216/168, Leese to Gen. Kennedy, 16 April 1944.

60 Hoffmeister interview.

61 MGen J.D.B. Smith interview, 14 September 1991; McAndrew Papers, Smith to McAndrew, 29 August 1980. See also Dancocks, *The D-Day Dodgers*, 233–4.

62 Hoffmeister interview; Dr W.J. McAndrew interview with MGen A.E. Wrinch, June 1980.

63 McAndrew-Hoffmeister interview. McAndrew's interview with Brig. Ian Johnston, June 1980, suggests that the 11th Brigade still needed delicate handling when Johnston took command in June 1944. For another comment, see LCol J.A. English, "Reflections on the Breaking of the Gothic Line," unpublished paper, nd, 2–3.

64 McAndrew-Hoffmeister interview; Hoffmeister interview; McAndrew to author, 28 September 1992.

65 Brig. Jack Christian interview, 31 May 1991; Col. Clement Dick interview, 7 May 1991.

66 DND, vol. 10779, McCarter to Col. Nicholson, 3 April 1951 and attached diary, entries 24–25 May 1944. See also WO 216/168, Leese to Kennedy, 8 June 1944. McCarter himself was sacked after the battle at Leese's insistence. The McAndrew–Wrinch interview attests to communications problems.

67 Hoffmeister interview; DND, vol. 10982, "Report on Brig. T.E. Snow," nd. [June 1944]; ibid., vol. 10774, Snow's "Report on the Battle of the Liri Valley," nd. For the corps commander's view of Snow, see Crerar Papers, vol. 7, file 958C.009 (D183), Burns to Crerar, 7 June 1944.

68 With some qualifications largely relating to staff work, the British thought so too: WO 214/55, Alexander to CIGS, 29 June 1944.

69 Crerar Papers, vol. 7, file 958C.009 (D183), Burns to Crerar, 7 June 1944.

70 W.J. McAndrew, "Eighth Army at the Gothic Line: The Dog-Fight," *RUSI Journal* 131 (June 1986), 57. An account of Hoffmeister's training of one of his new battalions, a unit transformed into infantry from anti-aircraft artillery, is in Fred Cederberg, *The Long Road Home* (Toronto 1989), 147.

71 Christian interview; McAndrew–Johnston interview; McAndrew interview with C.H. Drury, June 1980. "You did a better job for Hoffmeister than for Simonds," Christian said, because "you could talk to him; you couldn't with Simonds who knew so much more than everyone else."

72 Leese Papers, vol. 4, Leese to Montgomery, 2 September 1944. See also WO 216/168, Leese to Kennedy, 8 September 1944.

73 Rowland Ryder, *Oliver Leese* (London 1987), 290–1.

74 English, "Reflections," 15.

75 Hoffmeister interview; Crerar Papers, vol. 4, 958C.009 (D178). Weeks to Montague incorporated in Montague to Murchie and Stuart, 4 November 1944.

76 Crerar Papers, vol. 7, 958C.009 (D183), Burns to Crerar, 17 November 1944. One officer who served under Leese and Gen. McCreery, his successor at Eighth Army, suggests they did not believe Hoffmeister was corps commander material. McAndrew Papers, letter to McAndrew, 23 October 1980.

77 Hoffmeister interview. There is a Hoffmeister-like character in the novel *Execution* by Colin McDougall (New York 1958). See especially 17–18 and the comments on Brig. Kildare's attitude to regular officers.

78 Farley Mowat, *My Father's Son* (Toronto 1992), 232–3, refers to the differences.

79 Hoffmeister interview; Peter Hertzberg interview, 19 December 1991; Stacey, *The Victory Campaign*, 578–9.

80 Hoffmeister interview.

81 Bell-Irving interview and others.

82 DND, vol. 10624, 215C.009C240, Gibson to Murchie, 25 May 1945; ibid., Lister to Montague, 27 May 1945.

83 Ibid., Mf. C5439, file HQC 20-5-26-2, "Record of Discussion Between Gen. Murchie and Gen. Gibson," 28 May 1945.

84 McAndrew-Hoffmeister interview; MGen H.A. Sparling interview, 18 April 1991.

85 NA, A.G.L. McNaughton Papers, vol. 267, King file, Notes of meeting with King, 17 June 1945.

86 House of Commons, *Debates*, 15 December 1945, 3557.

87 Hoffmeister interview.

88 MGen Elliot Rodger interview, 21 May 1991.

CHAPTER 8 POPE AND STUART: SOLDIERS AND POLITICIANS

1 Quoted in Tim Travers, *How the War Was Won* (London 1992), 106. See also Travers's *The Killing Ground* (London 1987), 108–9.

2 Charles Yale Harrison, *Generals Die in Bed* (1930; Hamilton 1975), 138–42. Harrison, an American who had been a reporter with the *Montreal Star*, served with the Royal Montreal Regiment.

3 Maurice A. Pope, *Letters from the Front 1914–1919*, edited by Joseph Pope (Toronto 1992), 31-2. On Generals Mercer and Williams, see Desmond Morton, *Silent Battle: Canadian Prisoners of War in Germany 1914–1919* (Toronto 1992), 29ff.

4 Hon. J.W. Pickersgill interview, 21 May 1991.

5 LGen M.A. Pope, *Soldiers and Politicians* (Toronto 1962), 5.

6 Ibid.

7 DHist, Worthington biographical file, "Notes of Interviews with . . . Pope," 5, 27 July, 23 August 1977.

8 Pope, *Letters*, 23–4, 39–41, 43–7, 53.

9 Pope Family Archives (Toronto), Maurice Pope Scrapbook, Odlum to Sir Joseph Pope, 9 January 1918; Odlum to M. Pope, 6 June 1918.

10 Pope, *Letters*, 48–9, 55, 57–8.

11 Pope, *Soldiers*, 45ff.

12 Harry Pope interview, 3 April 1991; Joseph Pope interview, 15 March 1991.

13 Harry Pope interview.

14 Pope Family Archives, Pope Scrapbook, Department of National Defence, Staff College Examinations, 28 May 1923; Hertzberg to Pope, 30 May 1923.

15 Ibid., Pope's paper on "The Art of Command," 11 February 1924; lecture, November 1924; Confidential Report, 1 December 1925.

16 Ibid., Pope to Sir Joseph Pope, 5 March 1925.

17 Harry Pope Papers (Uxbridge, Ont.), Pope to Harry, 9 August 1926.

18 Pope Family Archives, Pope to wife, 29 June 1928.

19 *Victoria Times*, 21 December 1927.

20 For example, reviews of *The Army and Sea Power*, *Canadian Defence Quarterly* 5 (April 1928); *America Comes of Age*, ibid., 6 (January 1929); articles: "The March of the 104th Foot from Fredericton to Quebec, 1813," ibid., 7 (July 1930); "The European Crisis — 1904–1918," ibid., 12 (October 1934); and the prize essay, ibid., 8 (January 1931).

21 Ibid. 8 (January 1931), 165; Pope Family Papers, Scrapbook, Ken Stuart to Pope, 15 December 1930.

22 Ibid., Scrapbook, pen note, "From Confidential Report — War Office 1932"; ibid., McNaughton to Lady Pope, 29 November 1932.

23 R.G.C. Smith, ed., *As You Were! Ex-Cadets Remember*, vol. 2: *1919–1984* (1984), 356.

24 MGen Elliot Rodger interview, 21 May 1991.

25 Pope Family Archives, Pope to wife, 24 July 1934; Pope, *Soldiers*, 82ff.

26 DHist, Pope interview.

27 Pope Family Archives, Pope to wife, 4 November 1935.

28 DHist, Pope interview.

29 QUA, J. Sutherland Brown Papers, box 1, file 7, Brown to Lt.-Col. W.G. Beeman, 9 December 1929.

30 NA, H.D.G. Crerar Papers, vol. 10, 958C.009 (D211), Pope to Crerar, 14 May 1936.

31 Ibid., 27 July 1936.

32 Ibid., vol. 9, 958C.009 (D125), Crerar to CGS, 29 March 1938.

33 Docs on DND, vol. 2768, file HQS 6615-6, vol. 1 and vol. 2759, file HQS 6615; Pope, *Soldiers*, chap. 7; Stephen Harris, "The Canadian General Staff and the Higher Organization of Defence, 1919–1939," *War and Society* 3 (May 1985), 93–4.

34 Pope's view of the evacuation decision is in *Soldiers*, 177-8. On his prewar attitudes, see Daniel Robinson, "Planning for the 'Most Serious Contingency': Alien Internment, Arbitrary Detention and the Canadian State 1938–39," *Journal of Canadian Studies*, forthcoming.

35 DND, vol. 2648, file HQS 3498, vol. 20, Pope to CGS, 27 October 1939.

36 Pope Family Archives, Pope to his wife, 1 June 1940.

37 Ibid., Pope to Lt.-Gen. Sir Robert Haining, 4 April 1941.

38 USNA, RG 165, Military Intelligence Division Correspondence 1917-41, box 1770, Hem 2694-70/18, Maj. J.S. Gullet Report 434, 22 April 1941.

39 For example, PRO, Cabinet Records, Cab 122/626, "Canadian Representation in Washington — Record of Meeting Held in Ottawa," 20 June 1941.

40 NA, Maurice Pope Papers, vol. 1, Diary, 18 March 1942; CWC Minutes, 11 March 1942.

41 NA, Pope Papers, vol. 1, Diary, 15–16, 27–28 March, 3 April 1942.

42 NA, L.B. Pearson Papers, N1, vol. 3, Crerar file, Pearson to Crerar, 24 March 1944. For one sign, see USNA, RG 165, ABC Decimal File 336 Canada, JCS 82, 14 August 1942, "Coordination of U.S. and Canadian War Effort."

43 WO 106/4896, "Canadian Military Delegation in Washington, Major-General M.A. Pope," nd [July 1944].

80 See on Stuart's role, Stephen Harris, "Or There Would Be Chaos: The Legacy of Sam Hughes and Military Planning in Canada, 1919–1939," *Military Affairs* 46 (October 1982), 124.

81 Stacey, *Six Years of War* (Ottawa 1955), 540, gives the date of Stuart's taking over as CGS as 24 December 1941. That was the official handover date, though Crerar had already left for Britain long before; moreover, Stuart was attending War Committee meetings and signing memoranda as CGS in November.

82 McNaughton Papers, vol. 197, file PA6-9-C-4, McNaughton to Gen. Brooke, 21 November 1941.

83 NPRC, Stuart file, Case History Sheet, 6 May 1945.

84 Crerar Papers, vol. 1, Crerar to McNaughton, 4 March 1941.

85 QUA, Grant Dexter Papers, Memo, 25 March 1941. Ralston repeated this comment in May 1942. Ibid., Memo, 16 May 1942.

86 Grant Dexter, "The Army's Keyman," *Maclean's*, 15 June 1942, 11.

87 Dexter Papers, Memorandum, 12 June 1941.

88 NA, J.W. Dafoe Papers, Dexter to Dafoe, 14 April 1942. Dexter was close to Sifton, and he added that Ralston was surrounded by "permanent force incompetents" with his only source of advice being Stuart, "which makes Ralston the willing eager tool of incompetence." Stuart, he went on, was "not equipped for his job," but "shows a surprising agility in self protection." See also on Ralston and the General Staff, J.E. Rae, "A View from the Lectern," *Journal of the Canadian Historical Association*, No. 2 (1991), 12ff.

89 King Diary, 2 December 1941, ff. 1069–70.

90 CWC, Minutes, 3 December 1941. See also CWC, Documents, Manpower Memorandum No. 3, 27 November 1941, Stuart to Minister, 26 November 1941, and Crerar to Minister, 18 November 1941. These documents lay out the army program and the manpower assumptions behind it. See also NA, J.L. Ralston Papers, vol. 148, Stuart's memo "The Influence of Compulsory Service on the Size of the Canadian Army and its Reinforcing Organization," 25 January 1942. In May 1942 Stuart told King that "the only thing that might necessitate conscription would be some terrible fighting where large numbers of lives would be lost." King Diary, 13 May 1942, f. 418.

91 Ibid., 3 December 1941, ff. 1075–7.

92 Dexter Papers, Memorandum, 12 January 1942.

93 NA, M.H.S. Penhale Papers, vol. 5, CMHQ file, "Memorandum of Conference CGS and AG Held in Office of BGS, CMHQ, Thursday, 6 Aug 42."

94 Crerar Papers, vol. 1, 958C.009 (D55), Stuart to Crerar, 18 March 1942, enclosing his twenty-eight-page paper "Hong Kong Inquiry," 1 March 1942.

95 DHist 193.009 (D3), Monthly Appreciation, 15 January 1942; King Diary, 7 December 1941, f. 1105; Patricia Roy et al., *Mutual Hostages: Canadians and Japanese during the Second World War* (Toronto 1990), 82.

96 Dafoe Papers, Dexter to Dafoe, 14 April 1942.

97 King Diary, 20 February 1942, ff. 168–9. Certainly Stuart's view was that Germany had to be beaten first. See Dexter, "The Army's Keyman," *Maclean's*, 15 June 1942, 37.

98 Stacey, *Six Years of War*, 171. Stuart realized that the 8th Division at least was unnecessary, but he recognized, as Maurice Pope recalled later, that he would have been "out of a job" if he had not recommended it. "So I put it in." DHist 82/983, Official Comments on Vol. I of Official History of Canadian Army, Pope comments, 287.

99 Docs on DHist 322.009 (D363) refer to Alexander's removal. See C.P. Stacey, *Six Years of War*, 173; C.P. Stacey, *Arms, Men and Governments* (Ottawa 1970), 116.

100 G/C Stuart Papers, Ralston to Mrs Stuart, 24 December 1945. Stuart and Ralston had a sharp set-to over Canadian participation in the Aleutians in 1943. See Galen Perras, "Eyes on the Northern Route to Japan: Plans for Canadian Participation in an Invasion of the Kurile Islands," *War and Society* 8 (May 1990), 104.

101 Roy et al., *Mutual Hostages*, 98.

102 Harold Morrison telephone conversation, 27 June 1991.

103 See, for example, King Diary, 4 March 1943, ff. 161ff.

104 There can be no doubt that Stuart was the motive force in the decisions to send troops to Italy. See, for example, University of Toronto Archives, Vincent Massey Papers, vol. 311, Diary, 28 July 1943; Ralston Papers, vol. 66, Overseas Trips file, Diary memos, 29 July 1943 and ff.

105 McNaughton bitterly opposed Stuart's succeeding him, even temporarily. Ralston Papers, vol. 52, McNaughton resignation file, McNaughton to Ralston, 24 December 1943.

106 Certainly that was Vincent Massey's view. See, for example, Massey Papers, vol. 312, Diary, 13 November 1944. Sir Shuldham Redfern at Rideau Hall agreed, asserting that "everyone, in my opinion, with the exception of Stuart, made mistakes. I dislike Stuart personally, but I think he played his difficult part with considerable skill and good judgment." NA, Governor-General's Records, Acc. 1988-89/081, box 23, file 195-C-1, Redfern to Sir A.F. Lascelles, 17 February 1944. McNaughton, naturally enough, did not agree and would not forgive

Stuart. McNaughton Papers, vol. 167, PA5-0-3-2, vol. 1, "Memorandum of Discussion with Lt-Gen K. Stuart . . . 25 November 1943."

107 On the reasons for his appointment as C of S, CMHQ, see Public Archives of Nova Scotia, Angus L. Macdonald Papers, vol. 1503, file 386/82, telegram, Ralston to Prime Minister, 1 December 1943; QUA, C.G. Power Papers, vol. 1, binder, telegram, Ralston to Prime Minister, 19 December 1943.

108 E.L.M. Burns, *Manpower in the Canadian Army* (Toronto 1956), 5–6.

109 Based on J.L. Granatstein and J.M. Hitsman, *Broken Promises: A History of Conscription in Canada* (Toronto 1985), chap. 6.

110 Stacey, *Arms*, 426, 433; John Swettenham, *McNaughton*, vol. 3: *1944–1966* (Toronto 1969), 24-5. See also, for example, DHist, Letson Biography file, transcript of interview with MGen Harry Letson, 27 May 1981. Compare DHist 77/490, Transcript of interview with BGen Orde.

111 W. Denis and Shelagh Whitaker, *Tug of War: The Canadian Victory That Opened Antwerp* (Toronto 1984), 214; Stacey, *Arms*, 426–7. McNaughton's biographer, as might be expected, is also critical of Stuart. Swettenham, *McNaughton*, 29.

112 See Stacey, *Arms*, 432ff.

113 Ralston Papers, vol. 88, Stuart to CGS, 2 August 1944.

114 King Diary, 3 August 1944, ff. 719–20; Confidential source; CWC, Minutes, 3 August 1944.

115 See Whitaker, *Tug of War*, 217ff.

116 Crerar Papers, vol. 8, 958C.009 (D176), Stuart to Crerar, 25 September 1944.

117 Stuart Papers, vol. 1, CMHQ War Reinforcements file, memos of 14, 15 October 1944.

118 G/C Stuart Papers, Ralston to Mrs Stuart, 24 December 1945.

119 See, for example, Ralston Papers, vol. 43, Stuart to Minister, 30 October 1944; Stuart Papers, vol. 1, CMHQ War Reinforcements file, memos of 23, 24, 29, 31 October 1944.

120 Macdonald Papers, file F288/43, Stuart to Minister, 19 October 1944; CWC, Minutes, 19 October 1944.

121 Pope Family Archives, Pope to S.F. Wise, 28 September 1968. See also King Diary, 19 October 1944, f. 1000. Some years later, Pope remarked that "I was a couple of years older than Ken Stuart and had to be most careful how I played him." DHist 82/983, Official Comments on Vol. III of Official History of Canadian Army, Pope comments, 539.

122 King Diary, 19 October 1944, f. 995.

123 NA, Pope Papers, Diary, 21 October 1944; Pope Family Archives, Maurice Pope to Joseph Pope, 30 October 1944.

124 Confidential source. A very useful source on the atmosphere of crisis in this period is a memo by Col. G.S. Currie, recently retired as deputy minister of National Defence (Army), who was called for advice by Ralston. A copy is in Macdonald Papers, file 385/6, 4 November 1944.

125 McNaughton Papers, vol. 267, Appointment to Cabinet file, pen notes; King Diary, 1 November 1944, ff. 1092ff.

126 For example, Power Papers, box 3, Power's "Notes of Discussions on the Conscription Crisis," 26 October 1944.

127 Mrs Shortreed interview; King Diary, 3 November 1944, f. 1121.

128 Ralston Papers, vol. 85, "Reinforcements–I" and "Reinforcements–II," 17 November 1944.

129 Shortreed interview.

130 Macdonald Papers, vol. 1500, file 288/55, Memorandum, 26 October 1944.

131 Stuart Papers, vol. 1, CMHQ War Reinforcements file, "Answers to Questions Submitted by Major-General Pope," 31 October 1944.

132 Pope Family Archives, Pope to Prime Minister, 22 November 1944. Pope's strong assertion that he acted on his own is contained in ibid., Scrapbook, Pope to C.P. Stacey and James Eayrs, 29 October 1963, and Pope to S.F. Wise, 28 September 1968. See King Diary, 6 November 1944, f. 1139–40; Stacey, *Arms*, 468. Vincent Massey's diary records a conversation with the British Secretary of War, P.J. Grigg, who said that Pope had asked for Canadian troops to be pulled out of the line to ease the reinforcement shortage. Grigg told Brooke "that this was a very unfair proposal to make to a soldier and that if the Government of Canada really intended that this course should be followed . . . then the request should be made by the Canadian Prime Minister to Churchill direct." Massey Papers, Diary, 22 November 1944.

133 *DCER*, X, 336–7; Pope, *Soldiers*, 253.

134 Pope Family Archives, Scrapbook, Pope to C.P. Stacey and James Eayrs, 29 October 1963.

135 Granatstein and Hitsman, *Broken Promises*, 228n. See Macdonald Papers, vol. 1503, file 379/43a, Gen. Murchie to Macdonald, 15 March 1950. Pope also seemed to agree: It might be possible to rectify the situation by voluntary means, he told his son on 21 November, "but as to this I don't really know nor does anyone else." What was clear to him was "the conviction that we at least must not bust up our country." Pope Family Archives, Maurice Pope to Joseph Pope, 21 November 1944.

136 Or so Gen. Stuart later told Angus L. Macdonald. Macdonald Papers, Diary, 7 February 1945. See also King Papers, J17, vol. 6, file 8, R. MacG. Dawson interview with Gen. A.E. Walford, 2 February 1953.

137 On the "revolt," see Pope Family Archives, Pope to Dr W.I. Smith, May 1977; Swettenham, *McNaughton*, 59–60; and King Papers, J17, vol. 6, file 8, Dawson's interview notes from 1952–3. Dawson talked to a number of generals (Walford, Murchie, Gibson, McNaughton, Hugh Young) and found no revolt. His book, *The Conscription Crisis of 1944* (Toronto 1961), 93, declared the NDHQ generals "perverse, unco-operative, and disposed to throw in their resignations if they did not get their own way." The evidence of his interviews, however, does not sustain the statement that the generals were ready to resign, Murchie and Gibson flatly stating the opposite, and Walford making it clear that the senior officers knew resignations might bring down the government and thus "they were very conscious of their responsibility." Only Young indicated that resignation was a possibility. I am most grateful to Dr Greg Johnson, who discovered Dawson's interviews in an obscure section of the King Papers and drew them to my attention.

138 Granatstein and Hitsman, *Broken Promises*, 224ff.

139 Stuart Papers, vol. 1, docs on Last Will and Testament file.

140 Ibid., vol. 1, telegrams, 3, 6, 9 November 1945.

141 Dexter Papers, Malone memorandum, 19 January 1950. Crerar was in Toronto. See DHist, Stuart biographical file, DND (Army) Public Relations, press release, 6 November 1945, detailing funeral arrangements.

142 John W. Holmes interview, 29 July 1979; Hon. C.M. Drury interview, 20 June 1977.

143 Harry Pope Papers, Pope to Harry, 28 January 1977.

144 Ibid., Pope to Harry, 24 July 1978.

CHAPTER 9   THE ABSENCE OF FRANCOPHONE GENERALS

1 *L'Action Catholique*, 29 février 1944.

2 Jean Pariseau et Serge Bernier, *Les Canadiens français et le bilinguisme dans les Forces armées canadiennes*, tome 1: *1763-1969, le spectre d'une armée bicephale* (Ottawa 1987), annexe G, tableau 2, 282–5.

3 See on the pre-Confederation background, chap. 4 in Fernand Ouellet's *Economy, Class and Nation in Quebec* (Toronto 1991); on the post-Confederation

background, D.P. Morton, "French Canada and War, 1868–1917: The Military Background to the Conscription Crisis of 1917," in J.L. Granatstein and R.D. Cuff, *War and Society in North America* (Toronto 1971), 84ff.

4 See, for example, the pamphlet "Our Volunteer Army" published by Montreal's *La Presse* in 1916. In the Second World War, partial data again suggest a lower health standard in Quebec. A House of Commons return published in April 1944 found more unfit call-ups for military service in Quebec than fit, and more unfit from Quebec than Ontario, despite the latter's higher population. *Ottawa Journal,* 28 April 1944. I have benefited greatly from a discussion with my colleague Fernand Ouellet on this subject.

5 Pariseau et Bernier, *Les Canadiens français,* 70. Many francophone PF officers were older than their anglophone compatriots and probably more demonstrably inefficient.

6 See, for example, the account in J.L. Granatstein and J.M. Hitsman, *Broken Promises: A History of Conscription in Canada* (Toronto 1985), chaps. 2–4.

7 The list of decorations won by members of the 22e runs to eight-and-a-half single-spaced pages in Jean-Pierre Gagnon, *Le 22e Bataillon* (Ottawa and Québec 1986), 413ff. For a popular anglophone view of the Van Doos, see Alice Sharples, "Soldiers of French Canada," *Maclean's,* 15 February 1940, 13ff.

8 See, especially, Jacques Michel, *La Participation des Canadiens français à la Grand Guerre* (Montréal 1938), and Desmond Morton, "The Limits of Loyalty: French Canadian Officers and the First World War," in E. Denton, ed., *The Limits of Loyalty* (Waterloo 1979).

9 Pariseau et Bernier, *Les Canadiens français,* annexe M, tableau 1, 301. Additional sources of data are the annual Reports of the Department of National Defence.

10 A name check, admittedly not the most reliable method, of the *Defence Forces List 1939* shows one francophone officer in the Royal Canadian Dragoons, five in the artillery, none in the engineers, four in the signal corps, three in the service corps, two in the medical corps, two in the ordnance corps, and so on. See also Pariseau et Bernier, *Les Canadiens français,* 106 (which gives the number for September 1939 as 52 francophones of 514 PF officers), and annexe O, 319. It is an interesting speculation if the disproportionate representation of francophones was paralleled in other areas of Canadian society. Certainly it was the same in the upper ranks of the federal public service in this period. See J.L. Granatstein, *The Ottawa Men: The Civil Service Mandarins 1935–57* (Toronto 1982), 4–6, 21–2.

11 R.A. Preston, *Canada's RMC: A History of the Royal Military College* (Toronto 1969), 263; Pariseau et Bernier, *Les Canadiens français,* 102 and annexe M, tableau 4, 304.

12 Pariseau et Bernier, *Les Canadiens français,* 305. Ouellet has demonstrated that francophones were underrepresented in the social classes most likely to produce officers. See Ouellet, *Economy,* especially 242, 244. This mattered: Gagnon, *Le 22e,* 369, demonstrates that officers in the R22eR during the Great War were drawn heavily from those underrepresented classes.

13 Pariseau et Bernier, *Les Canadiens français,* 302–3.

14 A list of Canadian attendees is in DHist 530.03 (D1).

15 A list of IDC attendees is in Richard H. Gimblett, "'Buster' Brown: The Man and His Clash with 'Andy' McNaughton" (BA thesis, Royal Military College 1979), appx. D.

16 Pope Family Papers (Toronto), Ernest [Légaré] to Maurice Pope, 10 June 1929.

17 NA, A.G.L. McNaughton Papers, vol. 111, Ralston file, Ralston to McNaughton, 18 November 1928.

18 Ibid., McNaughton to Ralston, 25 November 1928.

19 That was the view of Gen. Henri Panet in 1926. See NA, Georges Vanier Papers, vol. 5, file 5-20, Panet to Vanier, 20 August 1926: "We have been very much upset at Headquarters by various political interference on behalf of some of the officers of the Royal 22nd Regiment."

20 QUA, C.G. Power Papers, box 6, LaFlèche file, Power to LaFlèche, 30 November 1929.

21 Desmond Morton and Glenn Wright, *Winning the Second Battle: Canadian Veterans and the Return to Civilian Life 1915–1930* (Toronto 1987), 210.

22 NA, Gen. Sir Arthur Currie Papers, vol. 11, file Correspondence General 1933, McNaughton to Currie, 4 October 1932.

23 James Eayrs, *In Defence of Canada,* vol. 1: *From the Great War to the Great Depression* (Toronto 1964), 259n. LaFlèche later told Mackenzie King he had been appointed on the direct recommendation of Sir Arthur Currie. There is no evidence of this. NA, W.L.M. King Papers, Diary, 5 October 1942, f. 829.

24 Currie Papers, vol. 11, file Correspondence General 1933, McNaughton to Currie, 4 October 1932.

25 Quoted in Stephen Harris, *Canadian Brass: The Making of a Professional Army 1860–1939* (Toronto 1988), 157–8.

26 Maurice Pope, *Soldiers and Politicians: The Memoirs of Lt.-Gen. Maurice A. Pope* (Toronto 1962), 77. For a defence of LaFlèche, see R.H. Roy, *For Most*

Conspicuous Bravery: A Biography of Major-General George R. Pearkes . . . (Vancouver 1977), 117.

27 Pope Family Papers, Pope to his wife, 8 avril 1937. Pope later called LaFlèche "a boss intriguer of the very first water." NA, Maurice Pope Papers, Washington diaries, 13 March 1943. McNaughton put it that LaFlèche's "seizure of autocratic powers" and his attempt to be "a sort of super Chief of Staff" had meant that "only partial and garbled advice" had got through to the cabinet. RMC, W.H.P. Elkins Papers, untitled file, McNaughton memo, 9 September 1939.

28 See Montreal *Gazette*, 11 August 1938.

29 NA, Ian Mackenzie Papers, vol. 30, file X-40, LaFlèche to Minister, 6 July 1938.

30 Harris, *Canadian Brass*, 159. See Elkins Papers, McNaughton memo, 9 September 1939, and M.A. Hooker, "Serving Two Masters: Ian Mackenzie and Civil-Military Relations in Canada, 1935–1939," *Journal of Canadian Studies* 21 (spring 1986), 38ff.

31 David MacKenzie, "The Bren Gun Scandal and the Maclean Publishing Company's Investigation of Canadian Defence Contracts, 1938–1940," *Journal of Canadian Studies* 26 ll 1991), 147; Patrick Brennan, "'A Responsible, Civilized Relationship': Reporting the Nation's Business, 1937–57," (PhD dissertation, York University 1989), 64ff. See especially Archives of Ontario, Maclean-Hunter Records, box 63, file Bren Gun Inquiry #2, Moore to Colonel Maclean, 4 August 1939 and attached memo.

32 King Diary, 5–6 December 1939, ff. 1282, 1291. *Report of the Royal Commission on the Bren Machine Gun Contract* (Ottawa 1939), 51: "I think it right to say that there is no evidence (nor is there in the evidence any ground for suspicion) that the . . . Deputy Minister . . . was guilty of any act of corruption or anything in the nature of corruption."

33 QUA, Norman Rogers Papers, box 3, file 1a 1940, Vanier to Rogers, 11 May 1940. Vanier added in a separate note that he had "thought it best not to put it on record" in the official minute of conversation.

34 For an account of his adventures, see Vanier Papers, vol. 11, file 11-16, and USAMHI, Gen. Raymond E. Lee Papers, London Journal, 21 June 1940. Lee noted sceptically, "his name is LaFlèche and he claims to be deputy minister of national defence for Canada."

35 CWC, Minutes, 30 May 1941.

36 Maclean-Hunter Records, box 73, file Bren Gun investigation, Memo, 27 August 1941. See also Vanier Papers, vol. 11, file 11-24, Willis O'Connor to Vanier, 18 November 1941, quoting Crerar's views of LaFlèche.

37 King Diary, 24 September 1942, f. 788; Vanier Papers, vol. 11, file 11-24, Willis O'Connor to Vanier, 16 October 1941. Power later told R. MacGregor Dawson that "LaFlèche was a nitwit and a damned nuisance." King Papers, J17, vol. 6, file 8, Dawson interview with Power, 16 February 1953.

38 Vanier Papers, vol. 11, file 11-24, Willis O'Connor to Vanier, 18 November 1941.

39 King Diary, 1 October 1942, f. 814.

40 Ibid., 5–6 October 1942, ff. 826ff. Compare Maclean-Hunter Records, vol. 72, file Reports Special Interviews 1942 book 2, Memo [Ken Wilson?], 8 October 1942, that offers an assessment of King's, Power's, Ralston's and St Laurent's negative views of LaFlèche. LaFlèche won election to Parliament in a by-election on 30 November in Outremont. For an account of the campaign, hotly contested by anti-conscriptionist *nationalistes*, see Donald Horton, *André Laurendeau: French-Canadian Nationalist 1912–1968* (Toronto 1992), 119–21.

41 McNaughton Papers, file PA6-9-M-2, received 11 December 1942. See also *Canadian Business*, December 1942, 53–4; *Saturday Night*, 12 September 1942, 7, and 17 October 1942, 8.

42 For a very critical view of LaFlèche's role in Quebec recruiting see "Backstage at Ottawa," *Maclean's*, 15 December 1944, 12–13, 53.

43 DND, vol. 2648, HQS 3498, vol. 22, Anderson to Minister, 12 June 1939. See also C.P. Stacey, *Six Years of War* (Ottawa 1955), 44.

44 Obituary in *R.M.C. Review* 33 (1952), 144–5; NPRC, Tremblay personal file. Tremblay had a stern approach to discipline. See especially Gagnon, *Le 22e*, 301–2.

45 DND, Mf. C5437, file HQ 20-5-2-2, CGS to Minister, 19 May 40. Earlier there had been rumours in Montreal military circles that Tremblay might be named GOC of the 2nd Division. See NA, Victor Odlum Papers, vol. 26, Peck to Odlum, 13 February 1940.

46 RMC, Central Registry, Panet file; Jacques Gouin and Lucien Brault, *Legacy of Honour: The Panets, Canada's Foremost Military Family* (Toronto 1985), 131ff.

47 DND, Mf. C5437, file HQ 20-5-2-2, CGS to Minister, 19 May 40.

48 For example, see DND, Mf C8336, file HQS 7434, Crerar to Tremblay, 4 July 1941.

49 DND, Mf. C5131, file HQS 8151, Report on Officers, nd; ibid., Mf. C5437, file HQS 20-5-2-2, Lawson to CGS, 21 May 1940.

50 Odlum Papers, vol. 26, Officers file, notebook.

51 Stacey, *Six Years of War*, 45; MGen W.J. Megill interview, 18 January 1992; DHist 82/983, vol. 3, Senior Officer Comments on drafts of Official History, Vol.

I, 71, Odlum comments. The idea of a French-speaking brigade continued to linger at Headquarters in Ottawa. See ibid., 112.3S2009 (D36), "The Recruiting Problem in the Province of Quebec," 9 June 1941.

52 Odlum Papers, vol. 26, War Diary, 20 September 1940. McNaughton was unable in August 1940 to recommend a francophone for brigadier in the 3rd Division. The only name the CGS could produce was of one officer who "is not bright but no one can decry his record as a combatant officer." DND Records, Mf. C5252, file HQS 8670, CGS to Minister, 23 August 1940. The officer in question did not get the post. Montague later was said to be prejudiced against French Canadians, or so Ernest Lapointe told Ralston. NA, J.L. Ralston Papers, vol. 45, file 499-75, Lapointe to Ralston, 7 August 1941.

53 Odlum Papers, vol. 26, War Diary, 24 March 1941. Later Odlum declared Leclerc "one of the best I have come across." Ibid., vol. 26, Odlum to Gen. Basil Price, 3 July 1942. But compare DHist, H.D.G. Crerar Papers, Leclerc file, Gen. Montague's Memo for file, 6 June 1941. Curiously, Leclerc's tenure in command of the 5th Brigade gets no mention at all in Terry Copp, *The Brigade: The Fifth Canadian Infantry Brigade, 1939–1945* (Stoney Creek, Ont., 1992).

54 DND, Mf. C5437, file HQ 20-5-2-2, McNaughton to Defensor, 1 April 1941. More than a year later, Gen. Odlum, now High Commissioner in Australia, wrote to Gen. Basil Price, GOC of the 3rd Canadian Division, that he saw he was without a francophone Brigade commander. "You evidently have had the same problem which faced the rest of us." Odlum Papers, vol. 26, Odlum to Price, 3 July 1942.

55 DND, Mf. C5437, file HQ 20-5-2-2, telegram, Defensor to Canmilitry, 14 April 1941, and pen note, Crerar to Minister, 14 April 1941. The procedure followed by the army in England for choosing officers for staff and command positions is laid down in ibid., vol. 10033, file 9/Selection, "Notes on Submitting Recommendations for Command and Staff," nd [1940–1?]. How much Ralston believed these things is unclear. See QUA, Grant Dexter Papers, Memorandum, 9 December 1941. Commanding officers like J.-P.-E. Bernatchez made some attempts to keep the ablest officers with the Van Doos, rather than sending them on staff courses (see chap. 7). LGen Henri Tellier interview, 22 May 1991.

56 King Papers, Canmilitry to Defensor, 19 April 1941, f. 262447. An earlier telegram from Gen. Montague at CMHQ made the point: "In view of conditions which go back many generations a long view is necessary and we must be careful not to ask officers to assume responsibilities until they have been adequately trained." DND, Mf. C5137, file HQS 8151, Montague to Defensor, 19 March 1941.

57 DHist, 112.3S2009 (D36), Crerar to Minister, July 1941.

58 NA, Ernest Lapointe Papers, vol. 18, file 46, Ralston to Lapointe, 24 May 1941, and reply, 30 May 1941. Leclerc himself was aware of the disability posed by his religion in Quebec. See DND, Mf C8336, file HQS 7434, Crerar to Tremblay, 4 July 1941.

59 Based on RMC Club records; RMC Central Registry, Renaud file; NPRC, Renaud file.

60 See Power's obituary address, 6 March 1967, on Vanier in Power Papers, Vanier file.

61 A complete set of the Staff College admission exams is in Vanier Papers, vol. 4, file 4-17. On the relationship with Byng, see Jeffery Williams, *Byng of Vimy: General and Governor General* (London 1983), 284ff, and Robert Speaight, *Vanier: Soldier, Diplomat and Governor General* (Toronto 1970), 92ff.

62 Vanier Papers, vol. 4, file 4-15, Byng to Vanier, 18 November 1922.

63 Ibid., vol. 4, file 4-14, Gen. Fiset to secretary of Governor General, 11 July 1922; file 4-19, Byng to Vanier, 3 January 1923.

64 Ibid., vol. 4, file 4-23, Staff College Notebook. The Moore paper drew Fuller's praise. It is in *Canadian Defence Quarterly* 3 (July 1926), 420ff.

65 Vanier Papers, vol. 5, file 5-16, Maj. J. Archambault to Vanier, 27 January 1925; Speaight, *Vanier*, chap. 6.

66 King Diary, 23 November 1938, f. 915; 2 September 1937, f. 643

67 See Speaight, *Vanier*, 216.

68 Vanier Papers, vol. 11, file 11-11, Vanier to Ralston, 23 July 1940. See also Vanier's file in NPRC, "Comparative Statement — Salary and Allowances," which demonstrated that his pay as a Brigadier would be $1481 less than his diplomatic pay of $8720.

69 CWC, Minutes, 20 August 1940; House of Commons, *Debates*, 24 February 1941, 978; King Diary, 7 October 1940.

70 DND, Mf. C8336, file HQS 7434-2, Crerar to Minister, 11 August 1941.

71 Vanier Papers, vol. 11, file 11-25, Notes; vol. 12, file 12-3, *Montreal Star*, 7 January 1942. See also Speaight, *Vanier*, 232ff.

72 Elkins Papers, Semi-official Correspondence, vol. 3, Vanier to Elkins, 30 April 1942.

73 Tellier interview, 22 May 1991.

74 Vanier Papers, vol. 11, file 11-24, Willis O'Connor to Vanier, 16 October, 18 November 1941.

75 King Diary, 24 March 1942, f. 256; Maclean-Hunter Records, vol. 72, file Reports Special Interviews 1942, book 2, Memo [Ken Wilson?], 8 October 1942.

76 King Diary, 12 October 1942, ff. 860–1. Some discreet sense of the difficulties can be found in DND, vol. 13274 f. 1, War Diary, DAG(O), appendix 1, Kennedy to Adjutant-General, 7 December 1942.

77 Ibid., Adjutant-General to Minister, 26 December 1942.

78 University of Toronto Archives, Vincent Massey Papers, vol. 311, Diary, 4 May 1943; IWM, Sir Oliver Leese Papers, box 3, Leese to his wife, 27 April, 6 July 1944; Vanier Papers, vols. 13–14, correspondence in files 13–40 and 14–26.

79 See Toronto *Globe and Mail,* 11 April 1990.

80 NA, Brooke Claxton Papers, vol. 87, Vanier file, Vanier to Claxton, 10 July 1959.

81 McNaughton Papers, vol. 203, PA6-9-V-1, Vanier to McNaughton, 28 August 1942, enclosing memo, 19 March 1942.

82 Dexter Papers, H. DesRosiers to Dexter, 29 June 1942. In a letter of 14 June 1942 to Dexter, DesRosiers had said there were 2 French Canadians of 6 in the minister's office, 18 of 92 in the General Staff branch, 2 of 45 in the Quartermaster General's branch, and 4 of 175 in the Master General of the Ordnance's office.

83 Jean-Yves Gravel, "Le Québec Militaire, 1939–1945," in Gravel, ed., *Le Québec et la Guerre* (Montréal 1974), 87.

84 DHist 112.3S2009 (D36), French-Canadian Representation in the Army Progress Report, 1 March 1944. See also Pariseau et Bernier, *Les Canadiens français,* annexe T, 329ff.

85 C.P. Stacey, *Arms, Men and Governments* (Ottawa 1970), 420ff; DHist 112.3S2009 (D36), "French-speaking Officers in the Canadian Army," 1 February 1944. The total included 4 major-generals, 7 brigadiers, 12 colonels, 90 lieutenant-colonels, and 311 majors. In the fall of 1944, there were serious shortages of francophone reinforcements for the infantry battalions in Northwest Europe. See, for example, NA, Kenneth Stuart Papers, vol. 1, Reinforcements file, telegram Macklin to Stuart, 28 October 1944; MGen Bruce Matthews interview, 25 April 1991. A year later, a list of Permanent Force officers overseas at that time was prepared. Of 305 officers, no more than 15 were francophones. Guy Simonds Papers (North Gower, Ont.), Canadian Forces in Netherlands box, "Nominal Roll of Permanent Force Officers Cdn Army Overseas," nd.

86 That was also the recollection of the Adjutant-General, MGen Harry Letson. See DHist, Letson biographical file, Interview transcript, 27 May 1981.

87 Ibid., 312.009 (D52), Ralston to Stuart, 15 July 1944, and reply, 4 September 1944. A search of the Montgomery Papers (IWM) and Dempsey Papers (WO) has failed to find anything to confirm or deny Stuart's claim about

Bernatchez, who was widely admired as a fighting soldier. MGen M.P. Bogert interview, 8 September 1991.

88 G/C V.C.H. Stuart interview, 31 January 1991.

89 Public Archives of Nova Scotia, Angus L. Macdonald Papers, vol. 1500, file 289/5, Memo, 6 November 1944.

CHAPTER 10　CONCLUSION

1 LHC, Viscount Alanbrooke Papers, file 2/VI, Notes for My Memoirs, 3.

2 Quoted in Bill McAndrew, "Operational Art and the Northwest European Theatre of War, 1944," *Canadian Defence Quarterly* 21 (December 1991), 24.

3 John Ellis, *Brute Force: Allied Strategy and Tactics in the Second World War* (New York 1991), 381.

4 James Eayrs, *In Defence of Canada: From the Great War to the Great Depression* (Toronto 1964), 104.

5 John A. English, *The Canadian Army and the Normandy Campaign: A Study of Failure in High Command* (New York 1991), 308.

6 Stephen Harris, *Canadian Brass: The Making of a Professional Army 1860–1939* (Toronto 1988), 211.

7 Typescript review in author's possession, nd.

8 C.P. Stacey, *Six Years of War* (Ottawa 1955), 522.

9 The available records suggest that Maj.-Gens. McCuaig, Panet, Tremblay, and White did not serve in the NPAM after 1919 but were put into war postings after September 1939. Maj.-Gen. George Kitching, after British army service, came to Canada in the late 1930s and enlisted at the beginning of the war. The records, it must be stressed, are far from complete.

10 Stacey, *Six Years of War*, 527.

11 Dr W.J. McAndrew interview, 20 February 1991.

12 Ellis, *Brute Force*, 535.

13 J.A. Roberts, *The Canadian Summer: The Memoirs of James Alan Roberts* (Toronto 1981), 108.

14 The relative lack of contact with American senior officers during the war likely prevented a similar situation from developing; after the war, when Canada's imperial masters changed, the same deferential traits may well have been in evidence, Charles Foulkes being an example. See chap. 6.

15 Stacey, *Six Years of War*, 524.

16 Roberts, *The Canadian Summer*, 144.

SELECTED LIST OF PRIMARY SOURCES

CANADA
Archives of Ontario
Maclean-Hunter Records

Directorate of History, National Defence Headquarters
Biographical files
Gen H.D.G. Crerar Papers
Gen Charles Foulkes Papers
Kardex files

McGill University Archives
Gen A.G.L. McNaughton Papers

National Archives of Canada
Henry Borden Papers
John Bracken Papers
LGen E.L.M. Burns Papers
Cabinet War Committee Minutes and Records (Privy Council Office Records)
Loring Christie Papers
Brooke Claxton Papers
Gen H.D.G. Crerar Papers
Gen Sir Arthur Currie Papers
Department of External Affairs Records
Department of National Defence Records
Personnel Records (NPRC)
Governor General's Records
Gerald Graham Papers
MGen J. Griesbach Papers
R.B. Hanson Papers
Adm J. Hughes-Hallett Papers

W.L.M. King Papers and Diaries
Ernest Lapointe Papers
Madge Macbeth Papers
MGen James MacBrien Papers
I.A. Mackenzie Papers
MGen Churchill Mann Papers
Gen A.G.L. McNaughton Papers
Col G.W.L. Nicholson Papers
MGen Victor Odlum Papers
Office of Special Commissioner for Defence Projects in NW Canada
L.B. Pearson Papers
MGen M.H.S. Penhale Papers
LGen M.A. Pope Papers
J.L. Ralston Papers
Sir Shuldham Redfern Papers
George Ronald Papers
LGen E.W. Sansom Papers
Graham Spry Papers
LGen Kenneth Stuart Papers
Peter Stursberg Papers
H. Usher Papers
Gen Georges P. Vanier Papers
J.F. Wallace Papers

National Defence College Library, Kingston, Ont.
MGen A.E. Walford Papers

Public Archives of Nova Scotia
Angus L. Macdonald Papers

Queen's University Archives
BGen J. Sutherland Brown Papers
Grant Dexter Papers
C.G. Power Papers
Norman Rogers Papers
T.A. Crerar Papers

Royal Military College, Kingston
Central Registry Files
Gen H.D.G. Crerar Diaries and Scrapbooks

MGen W.H.P. Elkins Papers
Ex-Cadet Club Records
Kardex Files, Protocol and Information Office
Public Relations Office and Protocol Records
Transcript Ledgers, Registrar's Office
MGen C. Vokes file and notebook, RMC Library
Yearbooks

University of Toronto Archives
Vincent Massey Papers

University of Victoria Archives
MGen George Pearkes Papers
R.H. Roy Papers
Interview Transcripts

Vancouver City Archives
Brig Sherwood Lett Papers

York University Archives, North York, Ont.
J.L. Granatstein Papers
   incl. Father Mike Dalton Diary
   incl. Jack Dickinson Letters
   incl. G.D. Johnston Letters
   incl. Brig. William Murphy Letters

Private Collections
Brig Colin Campbell Papers (Queensville, Ont.)
Col George S. Currie Papers (Ottawa)
MGen H.W. Foster Papers (Halifax, NS)
Tony Foster Papers (Halifax, NS)
MGen C.S.L. Hertzberg Papers and Diaries (Toronto)
MGen H.F.H. Hertzberg Papers (Victoria)
MGen George Kitching Diary (Victoria)
MGen A. Bruce Matthews Scrapbooks (Toronto)
Pope Family Archives (Toronto)
Maj Harry Pope Papers (Uxbridge, Ont.)
MGen A.E. Potts Papers (Toronto)
LGen Guy Simonds Papers (North Gower, Ont.)
MGen D.C. Spry Papers (Ottawa)

G/C V.C.H. Stuart Papers (London)
MGen Guy R. Turner Scrapbooks (Chester, NS)
MGen Christopher Vokes Papers (Ottawa)
Col F.B. Ware Scrapbooks (Victoria)
MGen F.F. Worthington Papers (Ottawa)

UNITED STATES

Eisenhower Library, Abilene, Kans.
Gen Dwight D. Eisenhower Papers and Diaries
Gen Alfred M. Gruenther Papers
Gen Lauris Norstad Papers
Oral History Transcripts
SHAEF Selected Records
Gen W. Bedell Smith Papers

Harvard University, Boston, Mass.
J. Pierrepont Moffat Papers

George C. Marshall Library, Lexington, Va.
Gen G.C. Marshall Papers
Gen Lucian K. Truscott Papers
Marshall Verifax Collection

U.S. Army Military History Institute, Carlisle, Pa.
Gen Dwight D. Eisenhower Diaries (OCMH Personal Papers)
MGen Raymond E. Lee Papers
Sidney Mathews Collection (OCMH Papers)
Forrest Pogue Interview Transcripts (OCMH Papers)
SHAEF Papers (OCMH Papers)
Gen W.H. Simpson Papers

United States National Archives, Washington, DC
Department of State Records
Joint Chiefs of Staff Records
War Department General and Special Staffs Records
ABC Decimal Files
Military Intelligence Division Records

UNITED KINGDOM

Churchill College, Cambridge
Burgen Bickersteth Papers
P.J.G. Grigg Papers

Imperial War Museum, London
LCol H.M. Baker Diary
FM Lord Harding Papers
Gen Sir Oliver Leese Papers
FM Viscount Montgomery Papers
LCol Trumball Warren Papers

Liddell Hart Centre, King's College, University of London, London
FM Viscount Alanbrooke Papers and Diaries
Gen M.C. Dempsey Papers
LGen Richard Dewing Diaries
FM Sir John Dill Papers
Liddell Hart Papers
    incl. MGen P. Hobart Papers
    incl. Chester Wilmot Papers
Gen. Lord Ismay Papers

Public Record Office, London
Cabinet Records
Dominions Office Records
Prime Minister's Office Records
War Office Records
    incl. FM Viscount Alexander Papers
    incl. Gen M.C. Dempsey Papers

INTERVIEWS

Hon. D.C. Abbott, Ottawa, 29 October 1971
LGen W.A.B. Anderson, Ottawa, 21 May 1991
John W.H. Bassett, Toronto, 5 June 1991
Brig G.E. Beament, Old Chelsea, Que., 24 May 1991
Hon. R.A. Bell, Ottawa, 17 August 1973
Brig H.P. Bell-Irving, Vancouver, 4 March 1992
LCol Peter Bennett, London, England, 6 September 1991
BGen Robert Bennett, Stittsville, Ont., 22 May 1991
MGen M.P. Bogert, Newbury, England, 8 September 1991

Col J. Allan Calder, Montreal, 4 May 1991

Brig Jack Christian, Thornhill, Ont., 31 May 1991

LGen S.F. Clark, Victoria, 24 February 1992

Col Jack Clarry, Toronto, 16 October 1991

Col Ernest Cote, Ottawa, 19 July 1991

J.D Crashley, telephone interview, 14 May 1991

Peter Crerar, Toronto, 14 April 1991

Col Clement Dick, Toronto, 7 May 1991

Hon. C.M. Drury, Ottawa, 20 June 1977

Mrs Simonne Pope Fletcher, Ottawa, 23 May 1991

Tony Foster, Halifax, 2 October 1991

Mrs Thea Hertzberg Gray, Toronto, 12 February 1992

Peter Hertzberg, Toronto, 18 December 1991

MGen Bert Hoffmeister, Vancouver, 2 March 1992

J.W. Holmes, Toronto, 29 July 1979

MGen George Kitching, Victoria, 25 February 1992

Brig Frank Lace, Toronto, 17 May 1991

MGen H.F.G. Letson, Ottawa, 21 May 1991

Mrs Sherwood Lett, Vancouver, 2 March 1992

Brig Beverley Matthews, Toronto, 16 September 1991

MGen A. Bruce Matthews, Toronto, 25 April 1991, 10 June 1991

Dr W.J. McAndrew, Toronto, 20 February 1991

Gen A.G.L. McNaughton, Ottawa, 23 March 1966

MGen W.J. Megill, Kingston, 18 January 1992

LCol J. Donald Mingay, Creemore, Ont., 6 June 1991

LGen Robert Moncel, Mahone Bay, NS, 4 October 1991

George Montague, Toronto, telephone interview, 26 May 1992

H.O. Moran, Ottawa, telephone interview, 19 July 1992

Finlay A. Morrison, Vancouver, 2 March 1991

Harold Morrison, Toronto, telephone interview, 27 June 1991

Mrs Dagmar Hertzberg Nation, Victoria, 27 February 1992

Ms P.K. Page [Mrs Arthur Irwin], telephone interview, Victoria, 30 July 1992

Mrs Margaret Crerar Palmer, Oakville, Ont., 9 April 1991

Brig George Pangman, Cambridge, Ont., 25 April 1991

Maj Giles Perodeau, Sidney, BC, telephone interview, 23 March 1992

Mrs G. Price Perodeau, Sidney BC, telephone interview, 23 March 1992

Hon. J.W. Pickersgill, Ottawa, 21 May 1991

Mrs E.C. Plow, Brockville, Ont., 19 December 1991

Maj Harry Pope, Uxbridge, Ont., 3 April 1991

Joseph Pope, Toronto, 15, 29 March, 12 July 1991

Mr Justice J.J.H. Potts, Toronto, 1 February 1992

Col Robert Raymont, Ottawa, 23 May 1991

C.S.A. Ritchie, London, England, 9 June 1971

MGen N. Elliot Rodger, Ottawa, 21 May 1991

MGen Robert P. Rothschild, Ottawa, 24 May 1991

MGen Roger Rowley, Ottawa, 23 May 1991

Mrs Marguerite Stuart Shortreed, Toronto, 26 February 1991

Col Charles Simonds conversation, Battersea, Ont., 23 August 1992

MGen J.D.B. Smith, London, England, 17 September 1991

MGen H.A. Sparling, Oakville, Ont., 18 April 1991

Mrs D.C. Spry, Ottawa, 21 January, 18 March 1992

Toby Spry, Ottawa, 23 January 1992

W.F.R. Stein, Nanaimo, BC, 1 March 1992

G/C Victor Stuart, London, Ont., 31 January 1991

Malcolm and Athol Sutherland-Brown, Victoria, 27 February 1992

MGen J. Tedlie, Victoria, 25 February 1992

LGen Henri Tellier, Stittsville, Ont., 22 May 1991

Brig P.A.S. Todd, Ancaster, Ont., 8 May 1991

Col Malcolm Turner, Chester, NS, 10 October 1990

Maj Frederick Vokes, Ottawa, 24 May 1991

Harvie Walford, Montreal, 4 May 1992

LGen Geoffrey Walsh, Ottawa, 24 May 1991

MGen C.B. Ware, Victoria, 24 February 1992

BGen Denis Whitaker, Toronto, 19 March 1991

LCol E.T. Winslow, Vancouver, 2 March 1992

Mrs F.F. Worthington, Ottawa, 23 May 1991

Peter Worthington, Toronto, 28 March 1991

William Young, Ancaster, Ont., 17 December 1991

Brig W.S. Ziegler, Edmonton, 23 October 1991

INDEX